Lecture Notes in Computer Science   8286

Commenced Publication in 1973
Founding and Former Series Editors:
Gerhard Goos, Juris Hartmanis, and Jan van l

Editorial Board

David Hutchison
Lancaster University, UK

Takeo Kanade
Carnegie Mellon University, Pittsburgh, PA, USA

Josef Kittler
University of Surrey, Guildford, UK

Jon M. Kleinberg
Cornell University, Ithaca, NY, USA

Alfred Kobsa
University of California, Irvine, CA, USA

Friedemann Mattern
ETH Zurich, Switzerland

John C. Mitchell
Stanford University, CA, USA

Moni Naor
Weizmann Institute of Science, Rehovot, Israel

Oscar Nierstrasz
University of Bern, Switzerland

C. Pandu Rangan
Indian Institute of Technology, Madras, India

Bernhard Steffen
TU Dortmund University, Germany

Madhu Sudan
Microsoft Research, Cambridge, MA, USA

Demetri Terzopoulos
University of California, Los Angeles, CA, USA

Doug Tygar
University of California, Berkeley, CA, USA

Gerhard Weikum
Max Planck Institute for Informatics, Saarbruecken, Germany

Rocco Aversa   Joanna Kołodziej
Jun Zhang   Flora Amato   Giancarlo Fortino (Eds.)

Algorithms and Architectures for Parallel Processing

13th International Conference, ICA3PP 2013
Vietri sul Mare, Italy, December 18-20, 2013
Proceedings, Part II

 Springer

Volume Editors

Rocco Aversa
Seconda Università di Napoli, Dipartimento di Ingegneria Industriale
e dell'Informazione, Aversa, Italy
E-mail: rocco.aversa@unina2.it

Joanna Kołodziej
Cracow University of Technology, Institute of Computer Science
Cracow, Poland
E-mail: jokolodziej@pk.edu.pl

Jun Zhang
Deakin University, School of Information Technology
Waurn Ponds, VA, Australia
E-mail: jun.zhang@deakin.edu.au

Flora Amato
Università degli Studi di Napoli Federico II
Dipartimento di Ingegnerial Elettrica e Tecnologie dell' Infomazione
Naples, Italy
E-mail: flora.amato@unina.it

Giancarlo Fortino
Università della Calabria, DIMES, Rende, Italy
E-mail: g.fortino@unical.it

ISSN 0302-9743   e-ISSN 1611-3349
ISBN 978-3-319-03888-9   e-ISBN 978-3-319-03889-6
DOI 10.1007/978-3-319-03889-6
Springer Cham Heidelberg New York Dordrecht London

Library of Congress Control Number: 2013954770

CR Subject Classification (1998): F.2, D.2, D.4, C.2, C.4, H.2, D.3

LNCS Sublibrary: SL 1 – Theoretical Computer Science and General Issues

© Springer International Publishing Switzerland 2013
This work is subject to copyright. All rights are reserved by the Publisher, whether the whole or part of
the material is concerned, specifically the rights of translation, reprinting, reuse of illustrations, recitation,
broadcasting, reproduction on microfilms or in any other physical way, and transmission or information
storage and retrieval, electronic adaptation, computer software, or by similar or dissimilar methodology
now known or hereafter developed. Exempted from this legal reservation are brief excerpts in connection
with reviews or scholarly analysis or material supplied specifically for the purpose of being entered and
executed on a computer system, for exclusive use by the purchaser of the work. Duplication of this publication
or parts thereof is permitted only under the provisions of the Copyright Law of the Publisher's location,
in ist current version, and permission for use must always be obtained from Springer. Permissions for use
may be obtained through RightsLink at the Copyright Clearance Center. Violations are liable to prosecution
under the respective Copyright Law.
The use of general descriptive names, registered names, trademarks, service marks, etc. in this publication
does not imply, even in the absence of a specific statement, that such names are exempt from the relevant
protective laws and regulations and therefore free for general use.
While the advice and information in this book are believed to be true and accurate at the date of publication,
neither the authors nor the editors nor the publisher can accept any legal responsibility for any errors or
omissions that may be made. The publisher makes no warranty, express or implied, with respect to the
material contained herein.

Typesetting: Camera-ready by author, data conversion by Scientific Publishing Services, Chennai, India

Printed on acid-free paper

Springer is part of Springer Science+Business Media (www.springer.com)

Message from the General Chairs

Welcome to the proceedings of 13th International Conference on Algorithms and Architectures for Parallel Processing (ICA3PP 2013), organized by the Second University of Naples with the support of St. Francis Xavier University. It was our great pleasure to hold ICA3PP 2013 in Vietri sul Mare in Italy. In the past, the ICA3PP 2013 conference series was held in Asia and Australia. This was the second time the conference was held in Europe (the first time being in Cyprus in 2008).

Since its inception, ICA3PP 2013 has aimed to bring together people interested in the many dimensions of algorithms and architectures for parallel processing, encompassing fundamental theoretical approaches, practical experimental projects, and commercial components and systems. ICA3PP 2013 consisted of the main conference and four workshops/symposia. Around 80 paper presentations from 30 countries and keynote sessions by distinguished guest speakers were presented during the three days of the conference.

An international conference of this importance requires the support of many people and organizations as well as the general chairs, whose main responsibility is to coordinate the various tasks carried out with other willing and talented volunteers. First of all, we want to thank Professors Andrzej Gościński, Yi Pan, and Yang Xiang, the Steering Committee chairs, for giving us the opportunity to hold this conference and their guidance in organizing it. We would like to express our appreciation to Professors Laurence T. Yang, Jianhua Ma, and Sazzad Hussain for their great support in the organization.

We would like to also express our special thanks to the Program Chairs Professors Joanna Kołodziej, Kaiqi Xiong, and Domenico Talia, for their hard and excellent work in organizing a very strong Program Committee, an outstanding reviewing process to select high-quality papers from a large number of submissions, and making an excellent conference program. Our special thanks also go to the Workshop Chairs Professors Rocco Aversa and Jun Zhang for their outstanding work in managing the four workshops/symposia, and to the Publicity Chairs Professors Xiaojun Cao, Shui Yu, Al-Sakib Khan Pathan, Carlos Westphall, and Kuan-Ching Li for their valuable work in publicizing the call for papers and the event itself. We are grateful to the workshop/symposia organizers for their professionalism and excellence in organizing the attractive workshops/symposia, and the advisory members and Program Committee members for their great support. We are grateful to the local organizing team, for their extremely hard working, efficient services, and wonderful local arrangements.

Last but not least, we heartily thank all authors for submitting and presenting their high-quality papers to the ICA3PP 2013 main conference and workshops/symposia.

December 2013   Beniamino Di Martino
                                                     Albert Y. Zomaya
                                                  Christian Engelmann

Symposium and Workshop Chairs' Message

The editors are honored to introduce Vol. II of the refereed proceedings of the 13th International Conference on Algorithms and Architectures for Parallel Processing, ICA3PP 2013, held in Vietri sul Mare, Italy, during December 18-21, 2013. ICA3PP 2013 is the 13th in this series of conferences started in 1995 that, by now traditionally, provides an appreciated international forum to present and discuss a wide-range spectrum of theoretical and experimental issues covering the research activities connected with algorithms and architectures for parallel processing. This second volume consists of four sections including 35 papers from one symposium and three workshops held in conjunction with the ICA3PP 2013 main conference. These are 13 papers from the 2013 International Symposium on Advances of Distributed and Parallel Computing (ADPC 2013), which provides the title of this volume, five papers from the International Workshop on Big Data Computing (BDC 2013), ten papers from the International Workshop on Trusted Information in Big Data (TIBiDa 2013) as well as seven papers belonging to the Workshop on Cloud-Assisted Smart Cyber-Physical Systems (C-SmartCPS 2013).

The volume starts with a section reserved for the International Symposium on Advances of Distributed and Parallel Computing (ADPC 2013) that collects a selection of the papers submitted to ICA3PP 2013, so as to provide an additional forum for discussing the frontiers of conference topics . It is a fact that over the last few years parallel processing and distributed computing have occupied a well-defined place in computer science and information technology, thanks to the availability of commodity hardware components (e.g., multiprocessor chips inside a standard PC) and to the widespread use of parallel applications in research, industry, and social media. However, this success story continues demanding new ideas to improve the efficiency, performance, reliability, security, and interoperability of distributed computing systems and applications and to face the emerging challenges issued by GPU/CPU systems, high-throughput cloud/grid systems, and green computing.

In fact, this year's symposium selection covered crucial themes in cloud computing environments such as data placement, task scheduling, and trust evaluation in cloud federations. Different papers, addressed the programming and scheduling issues connected to the efficient use of multi-core architectures like GPU. Forefront topics such as software solutions for energy optimization in HPC systems, the definition of social influence model, and quality control in crowdsourcing-based applications were also discussed.

The symposium and workshops programs are the result of the difficult and meticulous work of selection that involved many people in the Organizing Committee and the Program Committee members. The editors, finally, wish to

cordially thank all the authors for preparing their contributions as well as the
reviewers who supported this effort with their constructive recommendations.

December 2013   Rocco Aversa
                                                      Joanna Kołodziej
                                                           Jun Zhang
                                                         Flora Amato
                                                    Giancarlo Fortino

Organization

ICA3PP 2013 was organized by the Second University of Naples, Italy, Department of Industrial and Information Engineering, and St. Francis Xavier University, Canada, Department of Computer Science. It was hosted by the Second University of Naples in Vietri sul Mare (Italy) during December 18–20, 2013.

Steering Committee

Andrzej Gościński	Deakin University, Australia
Yi Pan	Georgia State University, USA
Yang Xiang	Deakin University, Australia

Advisory Committee

Minyi Guo	Shanghai Jiao Tong University, China
Ivan Stojmenovic	University of Ottawa, Canada
Koji Nakano	Hiroshima University, Japan

Conference Organizers

General Chairs

Beniamino Di Martino	Second University of Naples, Italy
Albert Y. Zomaya	The University of Sydney, Australia
Christian Engelmann	Oak Ridge National Laboratory, USA

Program Chairs

Joanna Kołodziej	Cracow University of Technology, Poland
Domenico Talia	Università della Calabria, Italy
Kaiqi Xiong	Rochester Institute of Technology, USA

Workshop Chairs

Rocco Aversa	Second University of Naples, Italy
Jun Zhang	Deakin University, Australia

ADPC 2013 Symposium Chairs

Rocco Aversa	Second University of Naples, Italy
Joanna Kolodziej	Cracow University of Technology, Poland
Luca Tasquier	Second University of Naples, Italy

BDC 2013 Workshop Chairs

Jun Zhang	Deakin Univerisity, Australia
Parimala Thaulasiraman	University of Manitoba, Canada
Laurent Lefevre	INRIA, France

TIBiDa 2013 Workshop Chair

Flora Amato	University of Naples "Federico II"

C-SmartCPS 2013 Workshop Chairs

Giancarlo Fortino	University of Calabria, Italy
Giuseppe Di Fatta	University of Reading, UK
Antonio Liotta	TU/e, The Netherlands
Jun Suzuki	University of Massachusetts, Boston, USA
Athanasios Vasilakos	University of Western Macedonia, Greece

Publicity Chairs

Xiaojun (Matt) Cao	Georgia State University, USA
Shui Yu	Deakin University, Australia
Al-Sakib Khan Pathan	International Islamic University of Malaysia, Malaysia
Carlos Westphall	Federal University of Santa Catarina, Brazil
Kuan-Ching Li	Providence University, Taiwan

Web Chair

Sazzad Hussain	St. Francis Xavier University, Canada

Technical Editorial Committee

Sazzad Hussain	St. Francis Xavier University, Canada
Magdalena Szmajduch	Cracow University of Technology, Poland

Local Organization

Pasquale Cantiello	Second University of Naples, Italy
Giuseppina Cretella	Second University of Naples, Italy
Luca Tasquier	Second University of Naples, Italy
Alba Amato	Second University of Naples, Italy
Loredana Liccardo	Second University of Naples, Italy
Serafina Di Biase	Second University of Naples, Italy
Paolo Pariso	Second University of Naples, Italy
Angela Brunitto	Second University of Naples, Italy
Marco Scialdone	Second University of Naples, Italy
Antonio Esposito	Second University of Naples, Italy
Vincenzo Reccia	Second University of Naples, Italy

Program Committee

Alba Amato	Second University of Naples, Italy
Henrique Andrade	JP Morgan, USA
Cosimo Anglano	Università del Piemonte Orientale, Italy
Ladjel Bellatreche	ENSMA, France
Jorge Bernal Bernabe	University of Murcia, Spain
Ateet Bhalla	Oriental Institute of Science and Technology, Bhopal, India
George Bosilca	University of Tennessee, USA
Surendra Byna	Lawrence Berkeley National Lab, USA
Aleksander Byrski	AGH University of Science and Technology, Poland
Massimo Cafaro	University of Salento, Italy
Pasquale Cantiello	Second University of Naples, Italy
Eugenio Cesario	ICAR-CNR, Italy
Ruay-Shiung Chang	National Dong Hwa University, Taiwan
Dan Chen	University of Geosciences, Wuhan, China
Jing Chen	National Cheng Kung University, Taiwan
Zizhong (Jeffrey) Chen	University of California at Riverside, USA
Carmela Comito	University of Calabria, Italy
Raphal Couturier	University of Franche-Comté, France
Giuseppina Cretella	Second University of Naples, Italy
Gregoire Danoy	University of Luxembourg, Luxembourg
Eugen Dedu	University of Franche-Comté, France
Ciprian Dobre	University Politehnica of Bucharest, Romania
Susan Donohue	College of New Jersey, USA
Bernabe Dorronsoro	University of Lille 1, France
Todd Eavis	Concordia University, Canada
Deborah Falcone	University of Calabria, Italy
Massimo Ficco	Second University of Naples, Italy
Gianluigi Folino	ICAR-CNR, Italy
Agostino Forestiero	ICAR-CNR, Italy
Franco Frattolillo	Universitá del Sannio, Italy
Karl Fuerlinger	Ludwig Maximilians University Munich, Germany
Jose Daniel Garcia	University Carlos III of Madrid, Spain
Harald Gjermundrod	University of Nicosia, Cyprus
Michael Glass	University of Erlangen-Nuremberg, Germany
Rama Govindaraju	Google, USA
Daniel Grzonka	Cracow University of Technology, Poland
Houcine Hassan	University Politecnica de Valencia, Spain
Shi-Jinn Horng	National Taiwan University of Science & Technology, Taiwan

Yo-Ping Huang	National Taipei University of Technology, Taiwan
Mauro Iacono	Second University of Naples, Italy
Shadi Ibrahim	Inria, France
Shuichi Ichikawa	Toyohashi University of Technology, Japan
Hidetsugu Irie	University of Electro-Communications, Japan
Helen Karatza	Aristotle University of Thessaloniki, Greece
Soo-Kyun Kim	PaiChai University, Korea
Agnieszka Krok	Cracow University of Technology, Poland
Edmund Lai	Massey University, New Zealand
Changhoon Lee	Seoul National University of Science and Technology (SeoulTech), Korea
Che-Rung Lee	National Tsing Hua University, Taiwan
Laurent Lefevre	Inria, University of Lyon, France
Keqiu Li	Dalian University of Technology, China
Keqin Li	State University of New York at New Paltz, USA
Loredana Liccardo	Second University of Naples, Italy
Kai Lin	Dalian University of Technology, China
Wei Lu	Keene University, USA
Amit Majumdar	San Diego Supercomputer Center, USA
Tomas Margale	Universitat Autonoma de Barcelona, Spain
Fabrizio Marozzo	University of Calabria, Italy
Stefano Marrone	Second University of Naples, Italy
Alejandro Masrur	TU Chemnitz, Germany
Susumu Matsumae	Saga University, Japan
Francesco Moscato	Second University of Naples, Italy
Esmond Ng	Lawrence Berkeley National Lab, USA
Hirotaka Ono	Kyushu University, Japan
Francesco Palmieri	Second University of Naples, Italy
Zafeirios Papazachos	Aristotle University of Thessaloniki, Greece
Juan Manuel Marn Pérez	University of Murcia, Spain
Dana Petcu	West University of Timisoara, Romania
Ronald Petrlic	University of Paderborn, Germany
Florin Pop	University Politehnica of Bucharest, Romania
Rajeev Raje	Indiana University-Purdue University Indianapolis, USA
Rajiv Ranjan	CSIRO, Canberra, Australia
Etienne Riviere	University of Neuchatel, Switzerland
Francoise Saihan	CNAM, France
Subhash Saini	NASA, USA
Johnatan Pecero Sanchez	University of Luxembourg, Luxembourg
Rafael Santos	National Institute for Space Research, Brazil
Erich Schikuta	University of Vienna, Austria
Edwin Sha	Chongqing University, China

Sachin Shetty   Tennessee State University, USA
Katarzyna Smelcerz   Cracow University of Technology, Poland
Peter Strazdins   Australian National University, Australia
Ching-Lung Su   National Yunlin University of Science and
                                   Technology, Taiwan
Anthony Sulistio   High Performance Computing Center Stuttgart
                                   (HLRS), Germany
Magdalena Szmajduch   Cracow University of Technology, Poland
Kosuke Takano   Kanagawa Institute of Technology, Japan
Uwe Tangen   Ruhr-Universität Bochum, Germany
Jie Tao   University of Karlsruhe, Germany
Luca Tasquier   Second University of Naples, Italy
Olivier Terzo   Istituto Superiore Mario Boella, Italy
Hiroyuki Tomiyama   Ritsumeikan University, Japan
Tomoaki Tsumura   Nagoya Institute of Technology, Japan
Gennaro Della Vecchia   ICAR-CNR, Italy
Luis Javier Garca Villalba   Universidad Complutense de Madrid (UCM),
                                   Spain
Chen Wang   CSIRO ICT Centre, Australia
Gaocai Wang   Guangxi University, China
Lizhe Wang   Chinese Academy of Science, Beijing, China
Martine Wedlake   IBM, USA
Wei Xue   Tsinghua University, Beijing, China
Toshihiro Yamauchi   Okayama University, Japan
Laurence T. Yang   St. Francis Xavier University, Canada
Bo Yang   University of Electronic Science and
                                   Technology of China, China
Zhiwen Yu   Northwestern Polytechnical University, China
Justyna Zander   HumanoidWay, Poland/USA
Sherali Zeadally   University of Kentucky, USA
Sotirios G. Ziavras   NJIT, USA
Stylianos Zikos   Aristotle University of Thessaloniki, Greece

BDC 2013 Program Committee

David Allenotor   University of Nigeria, Nigeria
Tarek Abdelrahman   University of Toronto, Canada
Alecio Binotto   IBM Research, Brazil
Pavan Balaji   Argonne National Lab, USA
Jesus Carretero   Universidad Carlos III de Madrid, Spain
Massimo Cafaro   University of Salento, Italy
Silvio Cesare   Deakin University, Australia
Wei Fang   Nanjing University of Science and Technology,
                                   China
Jinguang Han   Nanjing University of Finance and Economics,
                                   China

Jun (Luke) Huan	University of Kansas, USA
Yonggang Huang	Beijing Institute of Technology, China
Ami Marowka	Bar-Ilan University, Ramat-Gan, Israel
Hitoshi Oi	The University of Aizu, Japan
Yongli Ren	Deakin University, Australia
Michela Taufer	University of Delaware, USA
Dayong Ye	University of Wollongong, Australia

TIBiDa 2013 Program Committee

Massimiliano Albanese	George Mason University, USA
Carlo Allocca	Knowledge Media Institute (KMi), UK
Valentina Casola	University of Naples "Federico II", Italy
Giusy De Lorenzo	IBM Research IBM Technology Campus of Dublin, Ireland
Massimo Esposito	Institute for High Performance Computing and Networking (ICAR), Italy
Anna Rita Fasolino	University of Naples "Federico II", Italy
Francesco Gargiulo	Centro Italiano Ricerche Aereospaziali, Italy
Natalia Kryvinska	University of Vienna, Austria
Kami Makki	Lamar University, Beaumont (Texas), USA
Emanuela Marasco	West Virginia University, USA
Antonino Mazzeo	University of Naples "Federico II", Italy
Nicola Mazzocca	University of Naples "Federico II", Italy
Vincenzo Moscato	University of Naples "Federico II", Italy
Francesco Moscato	Second University of Naples, Italy
Antonio Picariello	University of Naples "Federico II", Italy
Carlo Sansone	University of Naples "Federico II", Italy

C-SmartCPS 2013 Program Committee

Pruet Boonma	Chiang Mai University, Thailand
Toshimi Munehira	OGIS-RI, Co. Ltd., Japan
Shingo Omura	OGIS International, Inc., USA
Hiroshi Wada	NICTA, Australia
Carmelo Ragusa	SAP Ireland, Ireland
Achilleas Achilleos	University of Cyprus, Cyprus
Adetola Oredope	University of Surrey, UK
Aldo Campi	University of Bologna, Italy
Antonis Hadjiantonis	University of Cyprus, Cyprus
Dmitri Jarnikov	Irdeto, Netherlands
Stefano Galzarano	University of Calabria, Italy
Paolo Trunfio	University of Calabria, Italy
Mukaddim Pathan	Telstra, Australia
Wenfeng Li	Wuhan University of Technology

Alfredo Cuzzocrea	ICAR-CNR, Rende, Italy
Min Chen	Huazhong University, China
Xin Wu	Duke University, USA
Moustafa Youssef	Egypt-Japan University, Egypt
Xin Zhang	Google, USA
Fangming Liu	Huazhong University, China
Liang Zhou	Nanjing University, China
Bogdan Carbunar	Florida International University, USA

Message from Workshop Organizers

Message of the Big Data Computing (BDC-2013) Workshop Organizers

Jun Zhang[1], Parimala Thaulasiraman[2], and Laurent Lefevre[3]

[1] School of Information Technology, Deakin University, Australia
[2] Department of Computer Science, University of Manitoba, Canada
[3] The French Institute for Research in Computer Science, France

"Big Data", as a new ubiquitous term, is now invading in every aspect of our daily life and promise to revolutionize our life. We face the most challenging issue, i.e., safe and effective computing on a large amount of data. Many works have been carried out focusing on business, application and information processing level from big data. However, the issue of safe and effective computing has not been well addressed. This workshop offers a timely venue for researchers and industry partners to present and discuss their latest results in safe and effective big data computing, which is organized in 2013 for the first time. We have got a good number of submissions, only a very small set of the high quality papers have been selected. The main theme and topics are listed as follows.

- Computational Models for Big Data
- Parallel/Distributed Computing for Big Data
- Energy-efficient Computing for Big Data
- Software Techniques in Big Data Computing
- Big Social Data Management
- Big Data Computing for Mobile Applications
- Architecture, Storage, User Interfaces for Big Data Management
- Search and Mining in Big Data
- Semantic-based Big Data analysis
- Privacy Preserving of Big Data
- High Performance Cryptography
- Threat and Vulnerability Analysis in Big Data
- Secure Big Data Computing
- Big Data Analytics
- Experiences with Big Data Project Deployments
- Big Data Computing as a Service
- Case Study on Big Data Computing

Message of the Trusted Information in Big Data (TIBiDa) Workshop Organizer

Flora Amato

University of Naples "Federico II", Dipartimento di Ingegneria Elettrica e Tecnologie dell'Informazione, via Claudio 21, 80125, Naples, Italy

The term "Big Data" refers to the continuing massive expansion in volume and diversity of data in nowadays applications. Volume and heterogeneity result in increasing attention to complexity of procedures that manage and use data, as well as to problems in trusted information management. Anyway, analysis of Big Data is crucial in several social and scientific fields.

Effective processing of big data requires both new algorithms for data analysis, able to face dramatic data growth, and new techniques able to enact proper and safe management procedures.

The Workshop on Trusted Information in Big Data brings together scientists, engineers and students with the aim of sharing experiences, ideas, and research results about Big Data Management and Trust Computing. The workshop intends to present innovative researches, technologies, methods and techniques related to the rising research activities about Big Data and Trusted Information.

The workshop has been organized in 2013 for the first time. We have got a good number of submissions, only a very small set of the high quality papers have been selected.

The main themes and topics are listed as follows:

- Trust Models and Algorithms for Big Data Processing
- Trust Management in Big Data
- System architectures for big data analysis
- Benchmarks, metrics, and workload characterization for big data
- Debugging and performance analysis tools for analytics and data-intensive computing
- Implications of data analytics to mobile and embedded systems
- Data management and analytics for vast amounts of unstructured data
- Artificial Intelligence, Evolutionary Agents
- Data Mining, Data Fusion
- Information Extraction, Retrieval, Indexing
- Enabling Technologies (Social Networking, Web 2.0, Geographical Information Systems, Sensors, Smart Spaces, Smart Cities, Context-Aware Computing, Web Services)

Message of the Cloud-Assisted Smart Cyber-Physical Systems (C-SmartCPS-2013) Workshop Organizers

Giancarlo Fortino[1], Giuseppe Di Fatta[2], Antonio Liotta[3],
Jun Suzuki[4], and Athanasios Vasilakos[5]

[1] University of Calabria, Italy
[2] University of Reading, UK
[3] Technical University of Eindhoven, The Netherlands
[4] University of Massachussets, Boston, USA
[5] University of Western Macedonia, Greece

The advances of body area networks, mobile computing, wireless networking, multi-agent systems, data mining, and cloud computing offer tremendous opportunities in providing newer, better and smarter distributed cyber-physical systems (CPS). The main objective of this workshop is to provide a medium for researchers and practitioners to present their research findings related to the synergy among Cloud computing and cutting-edge CPS-enabling technologies such as body area networks, wireless sensor and actuator networks, multi-agent systems, machine-to-machine (M2M) communication, data mining, with the aim of developing ubiquitous, cloud-assisted smart cyber-physical distributed systems.

This workshop offers a timely venue for researchers and industry partners to present and discuss their latest results in cyber-physical systems based on smart technology (such as software agents) and cloud computing. C-SmartCPS has been organized in 2013 for the first time. We have got a good number of submissions, only a very small set of the high quality papers have been selected. The main themes and topics are listed as follows:

- Basic technology supporting CPS (e.g. Wireless Sensor Networks, RFID, etc)
- Multi-Agent Systems
- Communication, information and software architectures
- Integration techniques between clouds and CPS
- A cloud of clouds for CPS
- Massively large-scale CPS
- Cloud-assisted data management, mining and processing for CPS
- Cloud-assisted decision support systems with CPS
- Cloud-CPS infrastructures for data acquisition
- Pervasive services for mobile cloud users
- Autonomic CPS
- Smart CPS
- Intelligence and optimization between clouds and CPS
- Data Mining for data collected/produced by CPS
- Heterogeneity of in/on-body and ambient sensors/actuators
- Nanoscale smart sensors and communication in/on/around human bodies
- Applications and practical experience in Smart Cities

Table of Contents – Part II

Part I: 2013 International Symposium on Advances of Distributed and Parallel Computing (ADPC 2013)

On the Impact of Optimization on the Time-Power-Energy Balance of
Dense Linear Algebra Factorizations.............................. 3
    *Peter Benner, Pablo Ezzatti, Enrique Quintana-Ortí, and
Alfredo Remón*

Torus-Connected Cycles: An Implementation-Friendly Topology for
Interconnection Networks of Massively Parallel Systems............... 11
    Antoine Bossard and Keiichi Kaneko

Optimization of Tasks Scheduling by an Efficacy Data Placement and
Replication in Cloud Computing 22
    Esma Insaf Djebbar and Ghalem Belalem

A Normalization Scheme for the Non-symmetric s-Step Lanczos
Algorithm... 30
    Stefan Feuerriegel and H. Martin Bücker

Efficient Hybrid Breadth-First Search on GPUs 40
    Takaaki Hiragushi and Daisuke Takahashi

Adaptive Resource Allocation for Reliable Performance in
Heterogeneous Distributed Systems 51
    Masnida Hussin, Azizol Abdullah, and Shamala K. Subramaniam

Adaptive Task Size Control on High Level Programming for GPU/CPU
Work Sharing 59
    *Tetsuya Odajima, Taisuke Boku, Mitsuhisa Sato, Toshihiro Hanawa,
Yuetsu Kodama, Raymond Namyst, Samuel Thibault, and
Olivier Aumage*

Robust Scheduling of Dynamic Real-Time Tasks with Low Overhead
for Multi-Core Systems 69
    Sangsoo Park

A Routing Strategy for Inductive-Coupling Based Wireless 3-D NoCs
by Maximizing Topological Regularity 77
    *Daisuke Sasaki, Hao Zhang, Hiroki Matsutani,
Michihiro Koibuchi, and Hideharu Amano*

Semidistributed Virtual Network Mapping Algorithms Based on
Minimum Node Stress Priority.................................... 86
    Yi Tong, Zhenmin Zhao, Zhaoming Lu, Haijun Zhang,
    Gang Wang, and Xiangming Wen

Scheduling Algorithm Based on Agreement Protocol for Cloud
Systems 94
    Radu-Ioan Tutueanu, Florin Pop, Mihaela-Andreea Vasile, and
    Valentin Cristea

Parallel Social Influence Model with Levy Flight Pattern Introduced
for Large-Graph Mining on Weibo.com 102
    Benbin Wu, Jing Yang, and Liang He

Quality Control of Massive Data for Crowdsourcing in Location-Based
Services... 112
    Gang Zhang and Haopeng Chen

Part II: International Workshop on Big Data Computing (BDC 2013)

Towards Automatic Generation of Hardware Classifiers 125
    Flora Amato, Mario Barbareschi, Valentina Casola,
    Antonino Mazzeo, and Sara Romano

PSIS: Parallel Semantic Indexing System - Preliminary Experiments.... 133
    Flora Amato, Francesco Gargiulo, Vincenzo Moscato,
    Fabio Persia, and Antonio Picariello

Network Traffic Analysis Using Android on a Hybrid Computing
Architecture... 141
    Mario Barbareschi, Antonino Mazzeo, and Antonino Vespoli

Online Data Analysis of Fetal Growth Curves 149
    Mario A. Bochicchio, Antonella Longo, Lucia Vaira, and
    Sergio Ramazzina

A Practical Approach for Finding Small Independent, Distance
Dominating Sets in Large-Scale Graphs 157
    Liang Zhao, Hiroshi Kadowaki, and Dorothea Wagner

Part III: International Workshop on Trusted Information in Big Data (TIBiDa 2013)

Robust Fingerprinting Codes for Database 167
    Thach V. Bui, Binh Q. Nguyen, Thuc D. Nguyen,
    Noboru Sonehara, and Isao Echizen

Heterogeneous Computing vs. Big Data: The Case of Cryptanalytical
Applications.. 177
    Alessandro Cilardo

Trusted Information and Security in Smart Mobility Scenarios:
The Case of S^2-Move Project 185
    Pietro Marchetta, Eduard Natale, Alessandro Salvi, Antonio Tirri,
    Manuela Tufo, and Davide De Pasquale

A Linguistic-Based Method for Automatically Extracting Spatial
Relations from Large Non-Structured Data 193
    Annibale Elia, Daniela Guglielmo, Alessandro Maisto, and
    Serena Pelosi

IDES Project: A New Effective Tool for Safety and Security in the
Environment 201
    Francesco Gargiulo, G. Persechino, M. Lega, and A. Errico

Impact of Biometric Data Quality on Rank-Level Fusion Schemes 209
    Emanuela Marasco, Ayman Abaza, Luca Lugini, and Bojan Cukic

A Secure OsiriX Plug-In for Detecting Suspicious Lesions in Breast
DCE-MRI 217
    Gabriele Piantadosi, Stefano Marrone, Mario Sansone, and
    Carlo Sansone

A Patient Centric Approach for Modeling Access Control in EHR
Systems 225
    Angelo Esposito, Mario Sicuranza, and Mario Ciampi

A Privacy Preserving Matchmaking Scheme for Multiple Mobile Social
Networks 233
    Yong Wang, Hong-zong Li, Ting-Ting Zhang, and Jie Hou

Measuring Trust in Big Data 241
    Massimiliano Albanese

Part IV: Cloud-assisted Smart Cyber-Physical Systems (C-SmartCPS 2013)

Agent-Based Decision Support for Smart Market Using Big Data 251
    Alba Amato, Beniamino Di Martino, and Salvatore Venticinque

Congestion Control for Vehicular Environments by Adjusting IEEE
802.11 Contention Window Size..................................... 259
    Ali Balador, Carlos T. Calafate, Juan-Carlos Cano, and
    Pietro Manzoni

QL-MAC: A Q-Learning Based MAC for Wireless Sensor Networks   267
  Stefano Galzarano, Antonio Liotta, and Giancarlo Fortino

Predicting Battery Depletion of Neighboring Wireless Sensor Nodes   276
  Roshan Kotian, Georgios Exarchakos,
  Decebal Constantin Mocanu, and Antonio Liotta

TuCSoN on Cloud: An Event-Driven Architecture for Embodied /
Disembodied Coordination   285
  Stefano Mariani and Andrea Omicini

Integrating Cloud Services in Behaviour Programming for Autonomous
Robots   295
  Fabrizio Messina, Giuseppe Pappalardo, and Corrado Santoro

RFID Based Real-Time Manufacturing Information Perception and
Processing   303
  Wei Song, Wenfeng Li, Xiuwen Fu, Yulian Cao, and Lin Yang

Author Index   311

Table of Contents – Part I

Distinguished Papers

Clustering and Change Detection in Multiple Streaming Time Series ... 1
  Antonio Balzanella and Rosanna Verde

Lightweight Identification of Captured Memory for Software
Transactional Memory 15
  Fernando Miguel Carvalho and João Cachopo

Layer-Based Scheduling of Parallel Tasks for Heterogeneous Cluster
Platforms 30
  Jörg Dümmler and Gudula Rünger

Deadline-Constrained Workflow Scheduling in Volunteer Computing
Systems 44
  Toktam Ghafarian and Bahman Javadi

Is Sensor Deployment Using Gaussian Distribution Energy Balanced?... 58
  Subir Halder and Amrita Ghosal

Shedder: A Metadata Sharing Management Method across
Multi-clusters 72
  *Qinfen Hao, Qianqian Zhong, Li Ruan, Zhenzhong Zhang, and
  Limin Xiao*

PDB: A Reliability-Driven Data Reconstruction Strategy
Based on Popular Data Backup for RAID4 SSD Arrays 87
  Feng Liu, Wen Pan, Tao Xie, Yanyan Gao, and Yiming Ouyang

Load and Thermal-Aware VM Scheduling on the Cloud 101
  *Yousri Mhedheb, Foued Jrad, Jie Tao, Jiaqi Zhao,
  Joanna Kołodziej, and Achim Streit*

Optimistic Concurrency Control for Energy Efficiency in the Wireless
Environment 115
  Kamal Solamain, Matthew Brook, Gary Ushaw, and Graham Morgan

POIGEM: A Programming-Oriented Instruction Level GPU Energy
Model for CUDA Program 129
  Qi Zhao, Hailong Yang, Zhongzhi Luan, and Depei Qian

Regular Papers

PastryGridCP: A Decentralized Rollback-Recovery Protocol
for Desktop Grid Systems 143
  Heithem Abbes and Thouraya Louati

Improving Continuation-Powered Method-Level Speculation for JVM
Applications.. 153
  Ivo Anjo and João Cachopo

Applicability of the (m,k)-firm Approach for the QoS Enhancement
in Distributed RTDBMS 166
  *Malek Ben Salem, Fehima Achour, Emna Bouazizi,
  Rafik Bouaziz, and Claude Duvallet*

A Parallel Distributed System for Gene Expression Profiling
Based on Clustering Ensemble and Distributed Optimization 176
  Zakaria Benmounah and Mohamed Batouche

Unimodular Loop Transformations with Source-to-Source Translation
for GPUs 186
  Pasquale Cantiello, Beniamino Di Martino, and Francesco Piccolo

HMHS: Hybrid Multistage Heuristic Scheduling Algorithm
for Heterogeneous MapReduce System 196
  Heng Chen, Yao Shen, Quan Chen, and Minyi Guo

Dynamic Resource Management in a HPC and Cloud Hybrid
Environment 206
  Miao Chen, Fang Dong, and Junzhou Luo

Candidate Set Parallelization Strategies for Ant Colony Optimization
on the GPU 216
  Laurence Dawson and Iain A. Stewart

Synchronization-Reducing Variants of the Biconjugate Gradient and
the Quasi-Minimal Residual Methods 226
  Stefan Feuerriegel and H. Martin Bücker

Memory Efficient Multi-Swarm PSO Algorithm in OpenCL
on an APU... 236
  Wayne Franz, Parimala Thulasiraman, and Ruppa K. Thulasiram

Multi-objective Parallel Machines Scheduling for Fault-Tolerant Cloud
Systems 247
  Jakub Gąsior and Franciszek Seredyński

Exploring Irregular Reduction Support in Transactional Memory 257
  *Miguel A. Gonzalez-Mesa, Ricardo Quislant, Eladio Gutierrez, and
  Oscar Plata*

Coordinate Task and Memory Management for Improving Power
Efficiency   267
*Gangyong Jia, Xi Li, Jian Wan, Chao Wang, Dong Dai, and
Congfeng Jiang*

Deconvolution of Huge 3-D Images: Parallelization Strategies
on a Multi-GPU System   279
Pavel Karas, Michal Kuderjavý, and David Svoboda

Hardware-Assisted Intrusion Detection by Preserving Reference
Information Integrity   291
*Junghee Lee, Chrysostomos Nicopoulos, Gi Hwan Oh,
Sang-Won Lee, and Jongman Kim*

A DNA Computing System of Modular-Multiplication over Finite Field
$GF(2^n)$ 301
Yongnan Li, Limin Xiao, Li Ruan, Zhenzhong Zhang, and Deguo Li

A Message Logging Protocol Based on User Level Failure Mitigation . . .   312
*Xunyun Liu, Xinhai Xu, Xiaoguang Ren, Yuhua Tang, and
Ziqing Dai*

H-DB: Yet Another Big Data Hybrid System of Hadoop and DBMS   324
Tao Luo, Guoliang Chen, and Yunquan Zhang

Sequential and Parallelized FPGA Implementation of Spectrum Sensing
Detector Based on Kolmogorov-Smirnov Test   336
*Roman Marsalek, Martin Pospisil, Tomas Fryza, and
Martin Simandl*

A Reconfigurable Ray-Tracing Multi-Processor SoC with Hardware
Replication-Aware Instruction Set Extension   346
*Alexandre S. Nery, Nadia Nedjah, Felipe M.G. França,
Lech Jozwiak, and Henk Corporaal*

Demand-Based Scheduling Priorities for Performance Optimisation
of Stream Programs on Parallel Platforms   357
Vu Thien Nga Nguyen and Raimund Kirner

A Novel Architecture for Financial Investment Services on a Private
Cloud   370
*Ranjan Saha, Bhanu Sharma, Ruppa K. Thulasiram, and
Parimala Thulasiraman*

Building Platform as a Service for High Performance Computing
over an Opportunistic Cloud Computing   380
*German A. Sotelo, Cesar O. Diaz, Mario Villamizar,
Harold Castro, Johnatan E. Pecero, and Pascal Bouvry*

A Buffering Method for Parallelized Loop with Non-Uniform
Dependencies in High-Level Synthesis 390
  Akihiro Suda, Hideki Takase, Kazuyoshi Takagi, and Naofumi Takagi

Character of Graph Analysis Workloads and Recommended Solutions
on Future Parallel Systems 402
  Noboru Tanabe, Sonoko Tomimori, Masami Takata, and Kazuki Joe

HySARC^2: Hybrid Scheduling Algorithm Based on Resource Clustering
in Cloud Environments 416
  Mihaela-Andreea Vasile, Florin Pop, Radu-Ioan Tutueanu, and
  Valentin Cristea

M&C: A Software Solution to Reduce Errors Caused by Incoherent
Caches on GPUs in Unstructured Graphic Algorithm 426
  Kun Wang, Rui Wang, Zhongzhi Luan, and Depei Qian

Interference-Aware Program Scheduling for Multicore Processors 436
  Lin Wang, Rui Wang, Cuijiao Fu, Zhongzhi Luan, and Depei Qian

WABRM: A Work-Load Aware Balancing and Resource Management
Framework for Swift on Cloud 446
  Zhenhua Wang, Haopeng Chen, and Yunmeng Ban

Cache Optimizations of Distributed Storage for Software Streaming
Services.. 458
  Youhui Zhang, Peng Qu, Yanhua Li, Hongwei Wang, and
  Weimin Zheng

AzureITS: A New Cloud Computing Intelligent Transportation
System 468
  Siamak Najjar Karimi

Author Index... 479

Part I
2013 International Symposium on Advances of Distributed and Parallel Computing (ADPC 2013)

On the Impact of Optimization
on the Time-Power-Energy Balance
of Dense Linear Algebra Factorizations

Peter Benner[1], Pablo Ezzatti[2], Enrique Quintana-Ortí[3], and Alfredo Remón[1]

[1] Max Planck Institute for Dynamics of Complex Technical Systems,
Magdeburg, Germany
{benner,remon}@mpi-magdeburg.mpg.de
[2] Instituto de Computación, Universidad de la República,
11.300–Montevideo, Uruguay
pezzatti@fing.edu.uy
[3] Dept. de Ingeniería y Ciencia de los Computadores,
Universidad Jaime I, Castellón, Spain
quintana@icc.uji.es

Abstract. We investigate the effect that common optimization techniques for general-purpose multicore processors (either manual, compiler-driven, in the form of highly tuned libraries, or orchestrated by a runtime) exert on the performance-power-energy trade-off of dense linear algebra routines. The algorithm employed for this analysis is matrix inversion via Gauss-Jordan elimination, but the results from the evaluation carry beyond this particular operation and are representative for a variety of dense linear algebra computations, especially, dense matrix factorizations.

Keywords: Matrix inversion, optimization, performance, energy.

1   Introduction

Energy consumption is a major constraint for the design of future supercomputers due to the growing economic costs of electricity, the negative effect of heat on the reliability of hardware components, and the environmental impact of carbon dioxide emissions. While the advances in the performance of the systems in the Top500 list [2] show that an Exascale system may be available by 2022, a machine of that capacity would dissipate around 311 MW [1] and cost 311 million dollars per year, rendering this approach clearly impractical.

The processor (including among others all levels of on-chip cache) and the DDR RAM are responsible for a significant fraction of power usage of current HPC facilities (other factors being the interconnect, storage media, etc.) [4,7,8]. During the past decades, a vast effort has been dedicated to the performance analysis and optimization of dense linear algebra routines on almost any existing architecture, from the old vector processors and shared-memory platforms, to the recent general-purpose multicore processors. This research is well justified as *i)* many complex scientific computations can be decomposed into dense linear

J. Kołodziej et al. (Eds.): ICA3PP 2013, Part II, LNCS 8286, pp. 3–10, 2013.
© Springer International Publishing Switzerland 2013

algebra operations; and *ii)* the regularity of these algorithms eases the performance analysis and bottleneck detection of the underlying architectures. On the other hand, the studies that focus on the performance-power trade-off of dense linear algebra routines on current architectures are more limited [5,3,12].

In this paper we assess the impact that well-known optimization techniques (manually encoded, automatically applied by the compiler, or embedded into dense linear algebra kernels and task-parallel runtimes) have on the performance-power trade-off of matrix inversion via Gauss-Jordan elimination (GJE) [11], and how these two factors combine to yield a given energy efficiency. The selection of matrix inversion and GJE is not arbitrary. When blocked, this operation exhibits an algorithmic pattern and parallelization akin to those of the conventional LU, QR factorizations and Cholesky factorization [11]. Therefore, we expect that most of the conclusions of our study apply to these other operations.

The rest of the paper is structured as follows. In Section 2 we briefly review matrix inversion via GJE and describe the different implementations – optimizations of the GJE method; In Section 3 we evaluate these variants. Finally, Section 4 contains a few concluding remarks and an outline of future research.

2   Optimization of GJE on Multicore Processors

Matrix inversion via GJE exhibits a computational cost and numerical properties analogous to those of approach based on the LU factorization [11], but superior performance on a number of architectures, from clusters [13] to general-purpose multicore processors and GPUs [6]. The cost of matrix inversion via both the unblocked and blocked variants of GJE [13] is $2n^3$ flops (floating-point arithmetic operations). In both cases as well, the inversion is performed in-place so that, upon completion, the entries of A are overwritten with those of its inverse.

For our evaluation we developed several implementations of the GJE algorithm that incorporate progressive optimization levels and/or techniques. Thus, variant v introduces additional optimizations to those already present in variant $v - 1$.

The first four variants, GJE_{v0}–GJE_{v3}, simply rely on optimizations automatically applied by the compiler, processing the unblocked code with the flags -O0 to -O3, respectively. Variant GJE_{v4} replaces the loops of the unblocked code by calls to the BLAS-1 and BLAS-2. HPC implementations of these kernels employ loop unrolling, frequently combined with (software) prefetching instructions embedded into the code to help the hardware to improve memory-arithmetic overlapping.

All these initial variants present a critical flaw. Concretely, they decompose the matrix inversion into building blocks (e.g., vector scaling or rank-1 updates) that perform $O(1)$ operations per data item, resulting in a sequence of memory-bounded computations. In current architectures, with a large gap between the CPU performance and the memory latency, these variants will thus be far from attaining the peak flops/s rate. However, this drawback is not intrinsic to matrix-inversion, as this requires $2n^3$ flops but operates with $n \times n$ data, so that the flops -to-memory ratio, $2n$, is quite favorable. The memory bottleneck can be overcome by reorganizing the bulk of the computations into BLAS-3 operations, particularly matrix-matrix products (hereafter, kernel **gemm**). The next two variants, GJE_{v5} and GJE_{v6}, exploit this appealing property of blocked algorithms. In the former implementation we employ a straight-forward implementation of **gemm**, compiled with -O3. GJE_{v6} goes one step further and replaces our simple **gemm** by a highly tuned implementation of the kernel, which internally employs a variety of block sizes that target different cache levels, repacks and possibly transposes matrix blocks to ensure access to contiguous data, etc. [9]. Variant GJE_{v7} also employs the blocked algorithm linked to a tuned **gemm**, but now leverages a multithreaded implementation of the kernel to perform a seamless parallel matrix inversion using all cores of the target platform.

Now, as the number of cores increases, the time spent in the updates (**gemm**) is reduced and the factorization of the panel, a serial computation, rapidly becomes a bottleneck. One partial solution is to further accelerate the factorization of the panel. Thus, variant GJE_{v8} employs a blocked algorithm to factorize the panel, and casts part of the its computations in terms of the fast and tuned **gemm** (operating on small blocks though), while retaining the larger block size for the outer matrix multiplications, to ensure a favorable flops-to-memory ratio during most of the computations. Variant GJE_{v9} explores look-ahead [15] as a complementary technique to alleviate the panel factorization bottleneck, mimicking analogous approaches applied with success to other panelwise algorithms. Look-ahead is similar to software pipelining [10] (though at the panel level) in that it shifts operations from "next" iterations of the inversion procedure to be overlapped with computations of the current iteration. Concretely, the look-ahead of depth 1 implemented in GJE_{v9} reorganizes the order of the algorithmic "tasks" (factorization and matrix-matrix products) of the loop body, so that the factorizing of the $k + 1$-th panel is overlapped with the update of the panels during the k-th iteration. Under ideal conditions, the outcome is a perfect overlap of these operations, which removes the panel factorization from the critical path of the algorithm. The drawback of this approach is that it involves complex programming. Finally variant GJE_{v10} applies look-ahead with dynamic depth (variable at run time), that in principle removes the panel factorization bottleneck, and does not require a great programming effort. For this purpose, we leverage the SMPSs runtime [14] which, at execution time, automatically decomposes the algorithm into tasks, identifies the dependencies between these tasks, and schedules them for execution to the cores of a parallel platform in the appropriate order, balancing the workload and exploiting a significant fraction of the concurrency intrinsic to the operation.

3   Experimental Evaluation

We next evaluate the 11 implementations described previously, from the points of view of performance, power consumption, and energy efficiency. Three platforms with Intel processors were employed. The first platform, NEHALEM, contains 2 Intel Xeon quad-core E5504 processors (8 cores) and 32 GB of RAM; and features

Table 1. Run time, GFLOPS (GFS), power, energy and net energy of the GJE implementations on NEHALEM, SANDY and ATOM (top, middle and bottom, respectively)

Variant	Small problem, n=2,048					Large problem, n=8,192				
	Time	GFS	Power	Energy	Net E.	Time	GFS	Power	Energy	Net E.
GJE_{v0}	84.52	0.2	70.4	5950.1	2781.5	5381.80	0.2	71.9	387166.9	185403.1
GJE_{v1}	24.44	0.7	72.7	1777.8	861.4	1495.72	0.7	75.4	112762.4	56687.8
GJE_{v2}	18.56	0.9	74.6	1385.6	689.7	1143.36	1.0	74.5	85157.5	42292.9
GJE_{v3}	9.39	1.8	82.2	772.5	420.2	578.97	1.9	82.0	47504.5	25798.9
GJE_{v4}	7.56	2.3	81.3	614.8	331.3	645.16	1.7	78.6	50741.9	26554.8
GJE_{v5}	6.79	2.5	74.5	505.9	251.3	451.50	2.4	71.0	32056.6	15129.8
GJE_{v6}	1.72	10.0	72.5	124.6	60.2	103.30	10.6	73.0	7539.1	3666.3
GJE_{v7}	0.46	37.4	122.0	56.0	38.8	17.47	62.9	128.7	2248.2	1593.1
GJE_{v8}	0.35	48.4	117.6	41.7	28.4	15.32	71.8	124.7	1909.4	1335.2
GJE_{v9}	0.34	50.2	126.0	43.1	30.3	21.81	50.4	122.5	2671.8	1854.1
GJE_{v10}	0.36	47.7	117.1	42.1	28.7	19.01	57.8	123.6	2349.8	1637.1

Variant	Time	GFS	Power	Energy	Net E.	Time	GFS	Power	Energy	Net E.
GJE_{v0}	42.21	0.4	54.9	2317.9	1452.6	2671.76	0.4	55.9	149348.9	94577.7
GJE_{v1}	8.44	2.0	58.2	491.0	318.0	509.64	2.2	60.1	30644.5	20197.0
GJE_{v2}	6.75	2.5	57.7	389.8	251.4	400.75	2.7	60.4	24221.3	16005.9
GJE_{v3}	4.01	4.3	61.3	245.8	163.7	262.52	4.2	62.7	16448.3	11066.6
GJE_{v4}	3.92	4.4	61.2	240.0	159.6	257.51	4.3	62.5	16092.0	10813.1
GJE_{v5}	1.47	11.7	56.9	83.7	53.6	112.71	9.8	60.6	6829.0	4518.5
GJE_{v6}	0.43	40.2	63.4	27.3	18.5	23.06	47.7	64.9	1496.7	1024.0
GJE_{v7}	0.17	101.7	127.4	21.5	18.1	7.24	151.8	136.0	985.4	836.9
GJE_{v8}	0.14	125.4	128.7	17.6	14.8	5.29	207.8	144.0	762.3	653.8
GJE_{v9}	0.14	126.3	134.9	18.3	15.6	7.40	148.5	134.6	996.1	844.4
GJE_{v10}	0.13	128.2	120.9	16.2	13.5	6.69	164.4	133.3	891.4	754.3

Variant	Time	GFS	Power	Energy	Net E.	Time	GFS	Power	Energy	Net E.
GJE_{v0}	266.14	0.06	15.5	4125.2	5323	17046.36	0.06	17.8	303425.2	73299.3
GJE_{v1}	91.72	0.18	17.6	1614.3	376.1	5904.32	0.18	18.0	106277.8	26569.4
GJE_{v2}	86.47	0.19	17.8	1539.2	371.8	5531.95	0.19	18.5	102341.1	27659.7
GJE_{v3}	86.67	0.19	16.4	1421.4	251.3	5564.74	0.19	18.6	103504.2	28380.2
GJE_{v4}	34.30	0.50	20.1	689.4	226.4	2287.87	0.48	21.4	48960.4	18074.2
GJE_{v5}	75.34	0.22	17.0	1280.8	263.7	5641.16	0.19	18.3	103233.3	27077.6
GJE_{v6}	10.49	1.63	15.6	163.6	22.0	642.56	1.71	17.1	10987.8	2313.2
GJE_{v8}	10.33	1.66	14.9	153.9	14.5	635.53	1.73	17.4	11058.2	2478.6

a single precission (SP) peak performance of 128 GFLOPS and 37.5 W of idle power. The second platform, SANDY, is based on the Intel i7-3930K processor (6 cores), with a peak of 307 SP GFLOPS, and 24 Gbytes of RAM. ATOM is a laptop with a low-power Intel Atom N270 (single-core) processor, contains 1 GB of RAM and a peak of 3.2 SP GFLOPS. We use CentOs 6.2, Intel icc v12 and MKL 10.3 on NEHALEM and SANDY; and CentOs 6.4, gcc 4.4.7 and MKL

11.0 on ATOM. On NEHALEM, all power measurements were collected using an internal wattmeter, which samples the consumption of the motherboard with a rate of 30 samples/s. For SANDY we leveraged Intel's RAPL interface to query the power dissipated by the processor only. The use of this technology forced us to record power samples in the same platform running the experiment, and thus, a low sampling rate of 10 Hz was selected to reduce the overhead. On ATOM, we could only employ an external *WattsUp?Pro* wattmeter, thus measuring the power of the complete platform, collecting 1 sample/s (the maximum offered by this device). All tests were executed for a minimum of 1 minute, after a warm up period of 2 minutes. Given the variety of technologies employed to measure power consumption, a direct comparison between the power/energy efficiency of each platform is delicate. All experiments were performed using IEEE SP arithmetic, though we do not expect significant qualitative differences if double precision was employed. In the results, execution time is reported in seconds (s), power in Watts (W) and energy in Joules (J). We employed two problem sizes in the experiments, $n=2,048$ and 8,192; for the blocked algorithms, a variety of block sizes was evaluated, but we only report the results corresponding to the best case.

Table 1 (top) shows the results obtained by the 11 implementations in NE-HALEM. Let us consider their performance first. The results of variants GJE_{v0} to GJE_{v3} illustrate the convenience of the compiler optimizations, with GJE_{v3} being nearly 10× faster than GJE_{v0}. Interestingly, the results from GJE_{v4} show that, for the smaller problem size, the transparent effort performed by the compiler is preferable to the optimizations embedded into the BLAS1 and BLAS2 routines from a highly tuned library. Nevertheless, the unblocked versions are all clearly outperformed by the blocked algorithms, by a small factor in case we use a simple implementation of kernel **gemm** (GJE_{v5}), or by a much wider margin in case the MKL implementation is leveraged (variant GJE_{v6}). An additional raise in the GFLOPS rate is obtained by relying on a parallel BLAS in GJE_{v7} (multi-threaded **gemm**), especially for the large problem. From then on, we observe small improvements due to the blocked panel factorization incorporated to GJE_{v8}; and minor variations for the small problem or significant losses for the large case and the versions with look-ahead (GJE_{v9}–GJE_{v10}) on this platform.

Let us focus now on the (average) power dissipation in NEHALEM. We observe a moderate increase in power for variants GJE_{v0} to GJE_{v3} which is suddenly turned into a steady decrease for the next three variants, GJE_{v4}–GJE_{v6}, and the small problem size. For the large problem size, there is a decrease in power as well, but only for GJE_{v4} and GJE_{v5}, followed by a slight increment from GJE_{v5} to GJE_{v6}. The exploitation of concurrency in the remaining four implementations, GJE_{v7}–GJE_{v10}, yields a considerably higher power draft, about 50 W independently of the problem dimension, but only represents an increase by a factor of 1.77 whereas the number of cores is multiplied by 8. This is easily explained if we consider that, when idle, this platform already dissipates 37.5 W, but also by the power that is necessary to feed the uncore elements of the processor (LLC, core interconnect, etc.), that need to be turned on independently of the number of active cores. At this point, it is worth pointing out that, for the small problem size, most of these hardware resources are wasted (the speed-up of the 8-core parallel GJE$_{v7}$ with respect to the sequential GJE$_{v6}$ is only 2.26) and so is part of the additional power required by the parallel execution. Furthermore, we also note that the highest performance observed in our experiments with this platform is 71.8 GFLOPS (variant GJE$_{v8}$ and the largest problem size), which represents only 56.0% of the SP peak throughput for this architecture (128.0 GFLOPS), and also indicates that a significant part of hardware resources are not fully utilized with the consequent waste of power.

If we consider the (total) energy, we observe that its behavior mimics that of the execution time, as could be expected since power only experiences moderate variations for the sequential variants (GJE$_{v0}$–GJE$_{v6}$), while the significant increase for the parallel implementations (GJE$_{v7}$–GJE$_{v10}$) comes together with a proportionally higher decrease of execution time, yielding a global reduction of energy usage. We also show the net energy, which is calculated by subtracting the energy consumption due to the idle power from the total energy. This value thus offers a different, possibly more accurate, view of the energy. If we consider idle power as a wasted resource (but unavoidable in most cases), for the same problem dimension, a shorter execution time yields a more efficient use of these resources, as the percentage of net energy over the total energy is then increased. For example, for the largest problem size, the net energy for GJE$_{v0}$ represents 47.8%, while for GJE$_{v8}$ (the fastest variant) this ratio raises to 69.9%.

The performance-power-energy trade-offs for SANDY, in the middle of Table 1, are similar to those already observed for NEHALEM. Small differences between the trends of these two architectures are, in general, due to the SANDY being a more powerful and energy-efficient processor, as well as the fact that our measurements with SANDY's RAPL interface necessarily only include the power (and therefore energy) consumed by the processor, but cannot capture that of the DDR memory, which is also an important power sink for compute-intensive dense linear algebra operations. On the other hand, we note that the highest arithmetic throughput for all implementations (207.8 GFLOPS for GJE$_{v8}$ and the largest problem size) represents only 67.6% of the SP peak performance of this 6-core platform, which indicates that this problem size is likely too small to justify the exploitation of all processor cores. If we consider energy, though, we can expect that any nonnegligible reduction of execution time, easily translates into less energy being consumed, leading to the counterintuitive conclusion that an inefficient use of resources renders a more efficient energy usage. On the positive side, we observe as well that, for this same case, the net energy represents a high 85.7% of the total energy, a higher ratio than that observed for NEHALEM.

For the single-core ATOM (bottom of Table 1) we only evaluated the sequential implementations of the GJE algorithm, plus GJE$_{v8}$ (blocked panel factorization). While the GFLOPS rates for this architecture are quite low, so is its SP peak performance, of only 3.2 GFLOPS. Thus, the fastest implementation achieves 53.1% of the theoretical peak performance for the largest problem size, compared with GJE$_{v6}$ (fastest sequential version), that on XEON attained 66.2% of the peak, while on SANDY this same variant achieved an impressive 93.1%. From the point of view of power efficiency, starting with an idle power of 13.5 W, the small variations that occur are more important than in principle could seem. For the largest problem size, for example, the highest point is observed for GJE_{v4} (21.4 W if we consider total power or just 7.90 W if we subtract idle power) and the lowest for GJE_{v6} (17.1 and 3.60 W for total and net power, respectively). A second consequence of the small differences between total and idle power is the low fraction that the net energy represents over the total energy, though it must be taken into account that, on ATOM, we are measuring the power dissipation of the complete platform (including, e.g., hard disk, display, etc.). For the GJE_{v6} and the largest problem size, e.g., this is only 22.4%. A conclusion is that this type of low-power processors need to incorporate several cores, to improve their performance and net energy-to-total energy ratio, and thus be able to compete with the complex out-of-order architectures.

4   Concluding Remarks and Future Directions

We have presented a complete evaluation of the impact that different optimization techniques have on the performance, power draft and energy efficiency of a dense linear algebra computation on the two latest processor generations from Intel (Nehalem and Sandy-Bridge) and a low-power architecture (Intel Atom). In total, 11 implementations of the GJE for matrix inversion were evaluated, obtained from the application of manual (programmer-driven) and automatic (compiler-driven) optimizations, as well as the use of tuned MKL kernels and the task-parallel SMPSs runtime. We believe that our study comprises most of the optimization techniques that are in use today, covering also a wide variety of compute-bounded dense linear algebra operations on current multicore processors.

One major observation from this analysis is that, in general, optimization leads to significant reductions of execution time, but the variations of power (usually increases) that accompany those are rather small, which results in important reductions of energy. A second observation is noted by comparing the highest performance observed in the experiments with the theoretical peak of each platform. The conclusion in this case is that, at least for the problem dimensions considered in the experiments, dedicating a large number of cores to the computation of the operation results in a significant waste of hardware resources and power. For example, when using all cores, the highest fraction of SP peak performance was 67.6% for SANDY and 53.1% for ATOM; however if we consider only one core, these ratios varied to 66.2% and 93.1% for NEHALEM and SANDY. The analysis of the net versus total energy shows a remarkable improvement in the Sandy-Bridge generation of processors from Intel. This observation implicitly hints the high impact of idle power, and offers the general conclusion that, for compute-bounded operations, a power-hungry approach like *race-to-idle* is to be preferred. Combined with our previous observation, we can therefore note the counterintuitive observation that a more inefficient use of resources (as occurs when all cores of the platform are employed) results in a more efficient use of energy (as this reduces the time as much as possible).

As part of future research we plan to analyze the impact of similar optimization techniques on memory-bounded dense linear algebra operations. Additionally, we also plan to extend our study to other low-power processors with a large number of cores, from Intel and ARM.

References

1. The Green500 list (2013), http://www.green500.org
2. The top500 list (2013), http://www.top500.org
3. Alonso, P., Dolz, M.F., Igual, F.D., Mayo, R., Quintana-Ortí, E.S.: DVFS-control techniques for dense linear algebra operations on multi-core processors. Computer Science - Research and Development, 1–10
4. Ashby, S., et al.: The opportunities and challenges of Exascale computing. Summary Report of the Advanced Scientific Computing Advisory Committee (2010)
5. Bekas, C., Curioni, A.: A new energy aware performance metric. Computer Science - Research and Development 25, 187–195 (2010)
6. Benner, P., Ezzatti, P., Quintana-Ortí, E.S., Remón, A.: Matrix inversion on CPU-GPU platforms with applications in control theory. Concurrency and Computation: Practice & Experience 25(8), 1170–1182 (2013)
7. Dongarra, J., et al.: The international ExaScale software project roadmap. Int. J. of High Performance Computing & Applications 25(1), 3–60 (2011)
8. Duranton, M., et al.: The HiPEAC vision for advanced computing in horizon 2020 (2013), http://www.hipeac.net/roadmap
9. Goto, K., van de Geijn, R.A.: Anatomy of a high-performance matrix multiplication. ACM Transactions on Mathematical Software 34(3) (2008)
10. Hennessy, J.L., Patterson, D.A.: Computer Architecture: A Quantitative Approach, 5th edn. Morgan Kaufmann Pub., San Francisco (2012)
11. Higham, N.J.: Accuracy and Stability of Numerical Algorithms, 2nd edn. Society for Industrial and Applied Mathematics, Philadelphia (2002)
12. Ltaief, H., Luszczek, P., Dongarra, J.: Profiling high performance dense linear algebra algorithms on multicore architectures for power and energy efficiency. Computer Science - Research and Development 27(4), 277–287 (2012)
13. Quintana-Ortí, E.S., Quintana-Ortí, G., Sun, X., van de Geijn, R.A.: A note on parallel matrix inversion. SIAM J. Sci. Comput. 22, 1762–1771 (2001)
14. SMPSs project home page, http://www.bsc.es/plantillaG.php?cat_id=385
15. Strazdins, P.: A comparison of lookahead and algorithmic blocking techniques for parallel matrix factorization. Technical Report TR-CS-98-07, Department of Computer Science, The Australian National University, Australia (1998)

Torus-Connected Cycles:
An Implementation-Friendly Topology
for Interconnection Networks of Massively
Parallel Systems

Antoine Bossard[1] and Keiichi Kaneko[2]

[1] Advanced Institute of Industrial Technology
Tokyo Metropolitan University, Japan
[2] Graduate School of Engineering
Tokyo University of Agriculture and Technology, Japan

Abstract. The number of nodes inside supercomputers is continuously increasing. As detailed in the TOP500 list, there are now systems that include more than one million nodes; for instance China's Tianhe-2. To cope with this huge number of cores, many interconnection networks have been proposed in the literature. However, in most cases, proposed topologies have shown gaps preventing these topologies from being actually implemented and manufactured. In this paper, we propose a new, *implementation-friendly*, topology for interconnection networks of massively parallel systems: torus-connected cycles (TCC). Torus-based networks have proven very popular in the recent years: the Fujitsu K and Cray Titan are two examples of supercomputers whose interconnection networks are based on the torus topology.

1 Introduction

Modern supercomputers are including hundreds of thousands of computing nodes. As detailed in the TOP500 list of June 2013 [1], there are even massively parallel systems that embed more than one million nodes, such as China's Tianhe-2. In order to handle this huge number of cores as efficiently as possible, numerous topologies have been proposed as interconnection networks for massively parallel systems. However, in most cases, proposed topologies have shown hardware or software gaps preventing these topologies from being actually implemented and manufactured.

As of today, many network topologies that aim at connecting a large quantity of nodes while retaining a low degree and a small diameter have been described in the literature: metacubes [2, 3], hierarchical cubic networks [4–6] and hierarchical hypercubes [7–10] are some examples. Cube-connected cycles [11] are also related to our work. However, there is a gap between these theoretical propositions and actual hardware implementations.

One can thus understand that the properties aimed by these networks topologies (high order, low degree, small diameter) are, even if important, not sufficient

J. Kołodziej et al. (Eds.): ICA3PP 2013, Part II, LNCS 8286, pp. 11–21, 2013.
© Springer International Publishing Switzerland 2013

to lead to actual hardware implementation. Other critical parameters have a significant impact on hardware architecture decisions.

Network *scalability* and topology *simplicity* are two of these critical parameters. And these are two of the reasons why modern supercomputers are often based on torus interconnects. At the beginning of supercomputing, the hypercube network [12] was popular due to its simplicity. This topology is no more applicable though due to the high number of nodes involved now. This critical property (simplicity) has been mostly relegated in modern interconnection networks proposals. Also, nowadays such machines need to be easily expandable, for example to add new nodes that will increase the computing power (see computer clusters). Now, on a reversed point of view, scalability and simplicity are two of the reasons why other, more complex topologies as mentioned earlier are not found in any hardware implementation.

So, it is reasonable to compromise on the order and diameter of a network at the benefit of scalability and ease of implementation. This is what hardware manufacturers are actually doing when designing their massively parallel systems.

So, we propose to build a hierarchical network that is based on a torus for all its advantages, and that includes an additional layer so that we can increase the network order while shrinking its diameter.

On the one hand, hierarchical interconnection networks based on torus are rare; one can merely cite H3D-torus [13] and Symmetric Tori Connected Torus Network [14] as examples. One of the main reason for this is the difficulty to establish the network diameter, and thus optimal (shortest) routing algorithms. On the other hand, torus-based interconnection networks have proven very popular with modern supercomputers: the Fujitsu K and Cray Titan both use, amongst others, a torus-based interconnection network. Aiming at reasonable network size and hardware applicability, we propose in this paper a torus-connected cycles (TCC) topology.

The rest of this paper is organised as follows. We define the torus-connected cycles network topology in Section 2. General notations and definitions are also given. Then, we estimate the network diameter of a TCC in Section 3; a simple routing algorithm can be subsequently deduced. Next, we give an algorithm finding a Hamiltonian cycle in Section 4. Finally, this article is concluded in Section 5.

2 Definitions

In this section, we define the torus-connected cycles (TCC) topology and give additional notations used throughout the paper.

Definition 1. [15] *An n-dimensional mesh has k_i nodes on the i-th dimension, where $k_i \geq 2$ and $0 \leq i \leq n$, thus resulting in $k_0 \times k_1 \times \ldots \times k_{n-1}$ nodes in total. A node u is addressed with n coordinates $(u_0, u_1, \ldots, u_{n-1})$. Two nodes u, v are adjacent if and only if $u_i = v_i$ holds for all i, $0 \leq i \leq n-1$, except one, j, where either $u_j = v_j + 1$ or $u_j = v_j - 1$.*

Definition 2. [15] *An n-dimensional torus of arity k, also called (n, k)-torus, is an n-dimensional mesh with all k_i's equal to k and with wrap-around edges: two nodes u, v are adjacent if and only if $u_i = v_i$ holds for all i, $0 \leq i \leq n - 1$, except one, j, where either $u_j = v_j + 1$ (mod k) or $u_j = v_j - 1$ (mod k) holds.*

We note that an (n, k)-torus is of degree n if $k = 2$, and $2n$ otherwise.

Definition 3. *An n-dimensional TCC of arity k, denoted by TCC(n, k), connects 2n-cycles according to an (n, k)-torus. A node of a TCC is written as a pair (σ, π) with $-(n - 1) \leq \pi \leq n - 1$ an integer coded in ones' complement (i.e. +0 and -0 are distinguished), and σ an n-tuple of natural numbers ranging from 0 to $k - 1$. For a node $u = (\sigma, \pi)$, the set of the neighbours of u is $N(u) = \{(\sigma, -\pi), (\sigma, -\frac{\pi}{|\pi|}((|\pi|+1) \bmod n))), (\sigma + \frac{\pi}{|\pi|}e^{|\pi|} \bmod k, -\pi)\}$ with e^i the unit vector $[0, 0, \ldots, 0, 1, 0, \ldots, 0]$ for the dimension i, and with the conventions $-(+0) = -0$, $-1 * 0 = -0$, $-0/0 = -1$ and $+0/0 = 1$.*

One should note that $|\pi|$ indicates the dimension "covered" by a node. The $2n$-cycles connected are also called clusters; the cluster of a node u is denoted by $C(u)$. Additionally, we note that a TCC(n, k) is of degree 3. We distinguish two types of edges in a TCC: *internal* edges connect nodes of a same cluster, while *external* edges connect nodes of distinct clusters. So, each node of a TCC has two internal neighbours and one external neighbour. A TCC(2, 3) is illustrated in Figure 1.

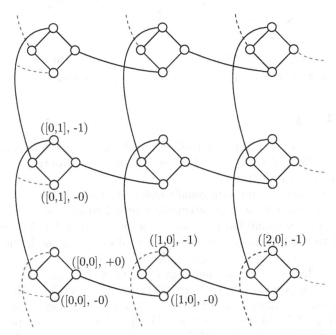

Fig. 1. A TCC(2, 3): 4-cycles are connected according to an (n, k)-torus

Finally, we recall several definitions and notations related to networks in general.

A path is an alternate sequence of distinct nodes and edges $u_0, (u_0, u_1)$, $u_1, \ldots, u_{k-1}, (u_{k-1}, u_k), u_k$, which can be simplified to $u_0 \rightarrow u_1 \rightarrow \ldots \rightarrow u_k$ and abbreviated to $u_0 \rightsquigarrow u_k$. The length of a path corresponds to its number of edges; in this example, the path length is equal to k. Two nodes of a graph are diagonally opposed if and only if the length of a shortest path connecting them is equal to the graph diameter, that is the maximum length of a shortest path between any pair of nodes.

3   Diameter and Simple Routing

We estimate in this section the diameter of a $\text{TCC}(n, k)$. The algorithm described can be subsequently used to perform simple routing (i.e. point-to-point). TCC routing is closely related to cycle traversal. Effectively, each of the n dimensions are iterated by traversing the corresponding nodes inside cycles of a TCC. So we can consider the traversal of one unique $2n$-cycle to describe routing: one external edge for a dimension corresponds to the internal edge between the two nodes on the cycle covering that dimension. See Figure 2. Two nodes u, v covering the same dimension are adjacent; we call u the counterpart of v, and vice-versa.

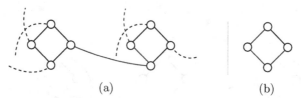

(a)   (b)

Fig. 2. TCC Routing (a) can be reduced to cycle traversal (b)

3.1   Case $k = 2$

The case $k = 2$ is a special case. Effectively, an $(n, 2)$-torus is a hypercube and so there is no effect of wrap-around edges. Shortest-path routing is described below; the diameter is deduced.

Consider two nodes s and d diagonally opposed. If $n = 2$, select the external edge $s \rightarrow s'$ incident with s, then select the internal edge $s' \rightarrow u$ such that the external edge of u is connected to $C(d)$, say $u \rightarrow v \in C(d)$. Lastly, we traverse half of $C(d)$ to reach d, thus requiring 2 internal edges. In total, the selected path $s \rightarrow s' \rightarrow u \rightarrow v \rightsquigarrow d$ is of length 5. See Figure 3.

Now, if $n \geq 3$, select the external edge incident with s; this induces a cycle traversal direction (see Figure 4). Continue traversing the cycle in this direction so as to consume 1 external edge for each of the $n - 1$ remaining dimensions, finally reaching $C(d)$; this takes $1 + 2(n - 1)$ edges. Lastly, $\delta \leq n$ internal edges in $C(d)$ are required to reach d. If $\delta = n$, then we discard the selected path and start again by traversing the cycle in the opposite direction (i.e. we first

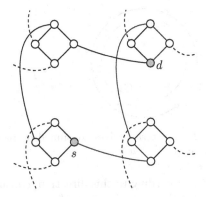

Fig. 3. Shortest-path routing in a TCC(2, 2)

select the internal edge incident with s and its counterpart). Because this time the $n-1$ dimensions are consumed in reverse order compared with the previous selection, we arrive in $C(d)$ at the diagonally opposed position as previously, and thus $\delta \leq n-2$ (actually $\delta = 0$). So, in total, the selected path is of length at most $1 + 2(n-1) + (n-1) = 3n-2$. Note that if $\delta = n$ in the first place, s and d are not diagonally opposed since they can be connected with the second path in $2n$ edges.

Fig. 4. Selecting an edge incident with s induces a cycle traversal direction. Here the external edge of s is selected; it induces the arrowed direction.

3.2   Case $k \geq 3$ and k Even

Consider an (n, k)-torus. In the case k even, two diagonally opposed nodes are separated from the same number of edges, no matter the direction in which you traverse the torus to join these two nodes. So, in a TCC(n, k), we can freely choose the rotation direction inside the cycle without impacting the number of external edges needed to join a diagonally opposed cycle. We describe below an algorithm finding a shortest path between two diagonally opposed nodes in a TCC. An illustration is given in Figure 5 and examples in Figure 6.

1. Consider two special positions on the cycle: the position of the source node s, and the position of the external neighbour d' of d.
2. Traverse the cycle in the direction where the position of d' is reached before the counterpart position for the same dimension.

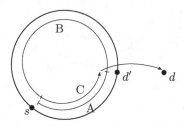

Fig. 5. Cycle traversal: $k/2 - 1$ external edges consumed on part A ($s \rightsquigarrow d'$), $k/2$ on part B ($d' \rightsquigarrow s$) and 1 on part C ($s \rightsquigarrow d'$)

3. By traversing the cycle according to this direction, consume $k/2 - 1$ external edges per dimension for the dimensions on the $s \rightsquigarrow d'$ part of the cycle, d' dimension included.
4. Then, continue the cycle traversal by consuming $k/2$ external edges per dimension for the dimensions on the $d' \rightsquigarrow s$ part of the cycle, this time d' dimension not included.
5. Finally, achieve the cycle traversal by consuming 1 external edge per dimension for the dimensions on the $s \rightsquigarrow d'$ part of the cycle.

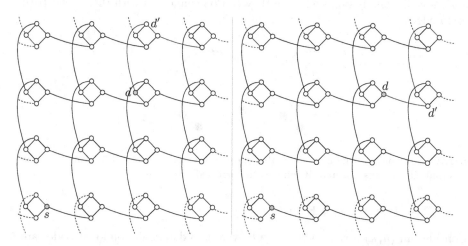

Fig. 6. Two cases of diagonally opposed nodes s, d connected with a shortest path (length 8)

This way we are ensured that no internal edge will be selected inside $C(d)$. The length of such path can be computed as follows.

Consuming one external edge on one dimension requires 1 internal edge on the cycle and 1 external edge. So, on the $s \rightsquigarrow d'$ part of the cycle, assuming δ dimensions are consumed on this part, we have $\delta * 2(k/2 - 1)$ edges required. We recall that dimensions on this part of the cycle are consumed up to $k/2 - 1$ external edges. Then, on the $d' \rightsquigarrow s$ part of the cycle, $n - \delta$ dimensions are fully consumed (i.e. up to $k/2$ external edges); it takes $(n - \delta) * 2(k/2)$ edges.

Finally, on the part $s \rightsquigarrow d'$ of the cycle, δ dimensions are consumed with only one external edge for each dimension; it takes $\delta * 2(1)$ edges. In total we have found a path between two diagonally opposed nodes of length

$$\delta * 2(k/2 - 1) + (n - \delta) * 2(k/2) + \delta * 2(1) = nk$$

which is obviously a shortest path.

3.3 Case $k \geq 3$ and k Odd

Consider an (n, k)-torus. In the case k odd, the number of edges between two diagonally opposed nodes depends on the direction used to traverse the torus to join these two nodes. For one dimension, depending on the direction used to traverse this dimension, either $\lfloor k/2 \rfloor$ or $\lceil k/2 \rceil$ edges are required to reach a diagonal node, considering only this dimension. So, in a TCC(n, k), the direction used to traverse the cycle will impact the number of external edges needed to join a diagonally opposed cycle. We can apply the same idea as in the case k even to find a path between two diagonally opposed nodes. However, we should take care to stay at a distance of 1 external edge to $C(d)$ for dimensions of $s \rightsquigarrow d'$, d' included, which can induce successive selection of internal edges to skip dimensions. Assuming that each of all dimensions is consumed in the direction requiring $(k + 1)/2$ external edges, the maximum length of a generated path is as follows.

On the $s \rightsquigarrow d'$ part of the cycle, assuming δ dimensions are consumed on this part, we have $\delta * 2((k - 1)/2)$ edges required. We recall that dimensions on this part of the cycle are consumed up to $(k - 1)/2$ external edges. Then, on the $d' \rightsquigarrow s$ part of the cycle, $n - \delta$ dimensions are fully consumed (i.e. up to $(k + 1)/2$ external edges); it takes $(n - \delta) * 2((k + 1)/2)$ edges. Finally, on the part $s \rightsquigarrow d'$ of the cycle, δ dimensions are consumed with only one external edge for each dimension; it takes $\delta * 2(1)$ edges. In total we have found a path between two diagonally opposed nodes of length:

$$\delta * 2((k - 1)/2) + (n - \delta) * 2((k + 1)/2) + \delta * 2(1) = nk + n$$

One can see that an extra cost of n edges compared to the case k even is induced. We are confident that this is of very low actual impact. Effectively, the dimension of a torus is always very small compared to its arity; for instance the Cray Titan is based on a three dimensional torus to connect hundreds of thousands of nodes: $n << k$.

So, considering any two nodes u, v of a TCC, in other words two nodes that are not necessarily diagonally opposed, we can apply the same algorithm to find a path $u \rightsquigarrow v$ that is guaranteed to be of length at most the diameter established previously.

3.4 Experimental Data, Comparison with Related Networks

We have empirically calculated the diameter of a TCC(n, k): we have established all the possible paths between all possible pairs of nodes. Considering all the paths established, we have then retained the length of the longest path, that is the diameter for this instance of n, k.

Table 1. Empirically calculated diameter of a TCC(n, k)

$n \setminus k$	2	3	4	5	6	7	8
2	5	6	8	10	12	14	16
3	7	9	12	15	18	21	24
4	10	13	16	20	24	28	32
5	13	16	20	25	30		
6	16	20	24	30	36		
7	19	23	28				
8	22	27					
9	25						
10	28						

One can see that the case $k = 2$ is indeed special as detailed in Section 3.1. For the cases $k \geq 3$, we can see that the empirical data is matching our theoretical estimations of nk in the case k even, and at most $nk + n$ otherwise.

Lastly, we summarise the TCC topology properties and compare them to those of related networks, namely (n, k)-tori (k-ary n-cubes) [15] and cube-connected cycles [11]. A cube-connected cycle CCC(d, k) is a d-cube connecting 2^d k-cycles. A CCC(d, k) with $d \neq k$ is not considered here since it is neither symmetric nor regular. So, we only consider the case $d = k$, and simply denote CCC(n). Additionally, for the sake of clarity, we consider only the case k even for a TCC(n, k).

The bisection width of a graph G is defined as the cardinality of a minimum set of edges H such that $G \setminus H$ is made of two disconnected subgraphs of same size. The bisection width is an important metric regarding fault-tolerance. One can see that the bisection width of a TCC is the same as that of an (n, k)-torus: k edges on each of the $n - 1$ dimensions are cut in two places so that the initial graph is separated into two similar entities. The results are given in Table 2.

Table 2. Comparing TCCs, CCCs and n-tori (k-ary n-cube)

	CCC(n)	TCC(n, k)	(n, k)-torus
order	$n \times 2^n$	$2n \times k^n$	k^n
degree	3	3	$2n$
diameter	$2n + \lfloor n/2 \rfloor - 2$	nk	$n \lfloor k/2 \rfloor$
bisection	2^{n-1}	$2 \times k^{n-1}$	$2 \times k^{n-1}$

4   Hamiltonian Cycle

In this section we propose an algorithm finding a Hamiltonian cycle inside a TCC. This is a fundamental routing problem which has numerous important applications. The main idea to solve this problem is to construct an Hamiltonian cycle inside a TCC of dimension 1, 2,... until n. We give a constructive proof by induction.

Let us construct a Hamiltonian cycle inside a TCC(n, k). Start by considering a TCC(2, k), that is a network of $2k$ clusters, each consisting of four nodes. Consider the two nodes $u = ([0, 0], +0), v = ([0, 0], -0)$ for dimension 0 of one of these clusters. Select the cycle $C : u = ([0, 0], +0) \rightarrow ([0, 1], -0) \rightsquigarrow ([0, 1], +0) \rightarrow ([0, 2], -0) \rightsquigarrow ([0, 2], +0) \rightarrow \ldots \rightarrow ([0, k - 1], -0) \rightsquigarrow ([0, k - 1], +0) \rightarrow ([0, 0], -0) = v \rightsquigarrow ([0, 0], +0) = u$, where $a \rightsquigarrow b$ represents the Hamiltonian path from a to b inside the cluster (i.e. k-cycle) containing a, b. We have thus constructed a cycle C including all the nodes of the k clusters $[0, i]$ ($0 \leq i \leq k - 1$). Now, inside each of these k clusters, say $[0, i]$ ($0 \leq i \leq k - 1$), consider the two nodes for dimension 1, say $x = ([0, i], +1), y = ([0, i], -1)$. Discard the edge (x, y) from C and select the path $x = ([0, i], +1) \rightarrow ([1, i], -1) \rightsquigarrow ([1, i], +1) \rightarrow ([2, i], -1) \rightsquigarrow ([2, i], +1) \rightarrow \ldots \rightarrow ([k-1, i], -1) \rightsquigarrow ([k-1, i], +1) \rightarrow ([0, i], -1) = y \rightsquigarrow ([0, i], +1) = x$. So, for each of the k clusters, we have appended to C a Hamiltonian path covering dimension 1. See Figure 7.

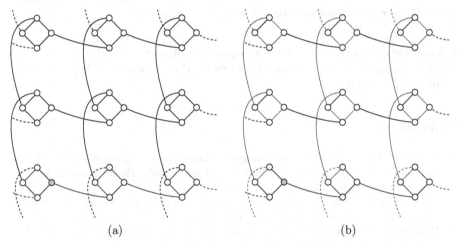

(a)   (b)

Fig. 7. (a). Constructing a cycle covering the k clusters of one particular dimension (blue edges). (b). Expanding this cycle to cover all dimensions (green edges added to the original blue cycle; red edges are discarded from the original cycle).

Assume this works for a TCC(n, k). We show it works for a TCC($n + 1$, k). Let C be a Hamiltonian cycle inside a TCC(n, k).

Expand that TCC(n, k) into a TCC($n + 1$, k); C is simply modified to include inside each cluster the unique newly added edge for dimension $n + 1$. Consider the k^n clusters of one "face" of a TCC($n + 1$, k); say the clusters $[0, i_{n-1}, \ldots, i_1, i_0]$ with $0 \leq i_j \leq k - 1$ and $0 \leq j \leq n - 1$. For each of the k^n clusters, say $[0, i_{n-1}, \ldots, i_1, i_0]$, consider the two nodes for dimension $n + 1$, say $x = ([0, i_{n-1}, \ldots, i_1, i_0], +n), y = ([0, i_{n-1}, \ldots, i_1, i_0], -n)$. Discard the edge (x, y) from C and select the path $x = ([0, i_{n-1}, \ldots, i_1, i_0], +n) \rightarrow ([1, i_{n-1}, \ldots, i_1, i_0], -n) \rightsquigarrow ([1, i_{n-1}, \ldots, i_1, i_0], +n) \rightarrow ([2, i_{n-1}, \ldots, i_1, i_0], -n) \rightsquigarrow ([2, i_{n-1}, \ldots, i_1, i_0], +n) \rightarrow \ldots \rightarrow ([k-1, i_{n-1}, \ldots, i_1, i_0], -n) \rightsquigarrow ([k-1, i_{n-1}, \ldots, i_1, i_0], +n) \rightarrow ([0, i_{n-1}, \ldots, i_1, i_0], -n) = y \rightsquigarrow ([0, i_{n-1}, \ldots, i_1, i_0], +n) = x$. So, for each of the k^n clusters, we have appended to C a Hamiltonian path covering the dimension $n + 1$, and thus C is a Hamiltonian cycle for $\text{TCC}(n + 1, k)$.

5   Conclusions

We have proposed in this paper a new topology for interconnection networks of massively parallel systems: torus-connected cycles. This topology aims at mitigating the problems faced by many network topologies proposed in the literature that hamper the actual hardware implementation of these networks. Additionally, we have shown that the diameter of a TCC is optimal in the case k even, and nearly optimal in the case k odd. Then, we have proposed a routing algorithm finding a Hamiltonian cycle inside a TCC.

Future works first include showing that the diameter of a $\text{TCC}(n, k)$ is nk for $k \geq 3$, not only k even. Then, one can think about finding algorithms solving the node-to-node and the node-to-set disjoint paths routing problems. Lastly, fault-tolerance is another possible interesting development.

Acknowledgements. This study was partly supported by a Grant-in-Aid for Scientific Research (C) of the Japan Society for the Promotion of Science under Grant No. 25330079.

References

1. TOP500: China's Tianhe-2 Supercomputer Takes No. 1 Ranking on 41st TOP500 List (June 17, 2013), http://top500.org/blog/lists/2013/06/press-release/ (last accessed August 2013)
2. Li, Y., Peng, S., Chu, W.: Metacube - a versatile family of interconnection networks for extremely large-scale supercomputers. J. Supe. 53, 329–351 (2010)
3. Bossard, A., Kaneko, K., Peng, S.: Node-to-set disjoint paths routing in metacube. In: Proc. Int. Conf. Par. Dis. Comp. Sys., pp. 289–296 (2010)
4. Ghose, K., Desai, K.R.: Hierarchical cubic networks. IEEE Trans. Par. Dis. Sys. 6, 427–435 (1995)
5. Bossard, A., Kaneko, K.: Node-to-set disjoint-path routing in hierarchical cubic networks. Comp. J. 55, 1440–1446 (2012)
6. Bossard, A., Kaneko, K.: Set-to-set disjoint paths routing in hierarchical cubic networks. Comp. J. (to appear)
7. Malluhi, Q.M., Bayoumi, M.A.: The hierarchical hypercube: a new interconnection topology for massively parallel systems. IEEE Trans. Par. Dis. Sys. 5, 17–30 (1994)
8. Wu, J., Sun, X.-H.: Optimal cube-connected cube multicomputers. J. Microcomp. Applications 17, 135–146 (1994)
9. Bossard, A., Kaneko, K., Peng, S.: A new node-to-set disjoint-path algorithm in perfect hierarchical hypercubes. Comp. J. 54, 1372–1381 (2011)
10. Bossard, A., Kaneko, K.: The set-to-set disjoint-path problem in perfect hierarchical hypercubes. Comp. J. 55, 769–775 (2012)
11. Preparata, F.P., Vuillemin, J.: The cube-connected cycles: a versatile network for parallel computation. Comm. ACM 24 (1981)

12. Seitz, C.L.: The cosmic cube. Comm. ACM 28 (1985)
13. Horiguchi, S., Ooki, T.: Hierarchical 3D-torus interconnection network. In: Proc. Int. Symp. Par. Arch. Alg. Net., pp. 50–56 (2000)
14. Al Faisal, F., Rahman, M.M.H.: Symmetric tori connected torus network. In: Proc. Int. Conf. Comp. Inf. Tech., pp. 174–179 (2009)
15. Duato, J., Yalamanchili, S., Ni, L.M.: Interconnection networks: an engineering approach. Morgan Kaufmann (2003)

Optimization of Tasks Scheduling by an Efficacy Data Placement and Replication in Cloud Computing

Esma Insaf Djebbar and Ghalem Belalem

Department of Computer Science, University of Oran, Oran, Algeria
esma.djebbar@gmail.com
ghalem1dz@yahoo.fr

Abstract. The Cloud Computing systems are in the process of becoming an important platform for scientific applications. Optimization problems of data placement and task scheduling in a heterogeneous environment such as cloud are difficult problems. Approaches for scheduling and data placement is often highly correlated, which take into account a few factors at the same time, and what are the most often adapted to applications data medium and therefore goes not to scale. The objective of this work is to propose an optimization approach that takes into account an effective data placement and scheduling of tasks by replication in Cloud environments.

Keywords: Placement of data, scheduling, optimization, clouds, large-scale.

1 Introduction

Cloud computing is the development of grid computing, parallel computing and distributed computing. It is a new pattern of business computing. Cloud computing is the large-scale datacenter resources which are more concentrated. In addition, virtualization technology hides the heterogeneity of the resources in cloud computing, cloud computing is user-oriented design which provides varied services to meet the needs of different users. It is more commercialized, and the resources in cloud computing are packed into virtual resources by using virtualization technology.

The scheduling methods implemented in the scheduler aim for better response times, by minimizing data placement. In our model, the scheduler must also take consideration by gang scheduling tasks which have the same data. The modeled system, implements a special case of parallel job scheduling called Gang Scheduling in which jobs consist of tasks that must be scheduled to run simultaneously and concurrently since they are in frequent data with each other.

The remaining parts of this paper are organized as follows. The next section briefly describes the generality of tasks scheduling in a cloud computing environment. In Sect. 3, the related works for a task scheduling and data placement in a cloud computing environment. A proposed model is illustrated in section 4 and experimentation and results is given in section 5. Section 6 concludes the paper and discusses future research directions.

J. Kołodziej et al. (Eds.): ICA3PP 2013, Part II, LNCS 8286, pp. 22–29, 2013.
© Springer International Publishing Switzerland 2013

2   Related Works

The paper [1] proposes a scheduling algorithm that addresses these key challenges scheduling task in the clouds. Incoming jobs are grouped based on the status of the task as a minimum execution time or based on the priority and minimum cost. The resource selection is made based on the constraints of using task an interesting approach. The proposed model is implemented by cloudsim simulator and the results validate the accuracy of the framework and show a significant improvement over the sequential ordering.

In [2], the authors propose a heuristic algorithm for scheduling task in which an initial task allocation will be produced at first, and then the time of completion of work can be reduced gradually by giving the initial task allocation. By adopting a comprehensive position, the algorithm can adjust data locality dynamically according to network state and workload of battery.

The paper [3] investigates the application of a group scheduling on a cloud computing model based on the architecture of cloud computing Amazon (EC2). The study takes into account the performance and cost performance while incorporating mechanisms for migration and job handling the famine tasks. The number of virtual machines (VMs) is available at any time and dynamic scales according to the demands of the tasks being maintained. The mentioned model is studied through simulation in order to analyze the performance of execution and the overall cost of group scheduling with migration and manipulation of famine. The results highlight that this scheduling strategy can be effectively deployed in the clouds, and the clouds platforms can be viable for HPC business or high performance applications.

In this paper [4], the authors propose a clustering strategy matrix k-means based on data placement for scientific applications in the cloud. The strategy contains two algorithms that group the existing datasets in k datacenters during the construction phase of workflow and dynamic data sets newly generated most appropriate datacenters based data on dependencies during the implementation phase. The simulations show that the algorithm can effectively reduce data movement during the workflow.

3   Process Used

The approach [5] includes two important steps. Each of which contains a set of operations to be performed. In addition to these two steps, we extended the strategy with a replication service that constitutes the third phase of this work. These three steps are summarized as follows:

3.1   Stage of Construction

During the construction phase, a matrix pattern will be used to represent the existing data. A pre-classification of these data is then performed by applying transformations to the matrix and distributing data across different datacenters. This distribution will represent the initial scores for the K-means algorithm, which is used during the execution stage.

Clustering the Dependency Matrix

In scientific workflows, many instances will be executed simultaneously. Some tasks use a large amount of data and produce, and several other output data. In order to perform a task, all required data must be located in the same datacenter and this may require some data movement (also called datasets). In addition, if two datasets are always used together with many tasks, they must be stored together in order to reduce the frequency of data movement.

Calculation of Dependencies

Two sets are considered, all datasets noted by D and the set of tasks rated by T. Each dataset di ∈ D has two attributes noted: (T_i, s_i) where $T_i \subset T$ is the set of tasks that use the dataset d_i, where s_i is the size of d_i. Two datasets d_i and d_j are called dependent if there are tasks that use both d_i and d_j. The amount of this dependence is equal to the number of common tasks between d_i and d_j.

Construction of the Matrix DM

Each element of the matrix DM, noted $DM_{i,j} = dependency_{ij}$. For the diagonal elements, each value DM_i, i represent the number of tasks that will use the dataset d_i. DM is a symmetric matrix of dimension n×n where n is the total number of existing Datasets.

Development of Clustered Dependency Matrix

The Bond Energy Algorithm (BEA) [6] is applied to the matrix *DM* in order to group similar values together, that is to say that large sets and small sets values together.

Two measures, BE_C and BE_L are defined for this algorithm. The permutation is done so that these measures (see Formulas 1 and 2) are maximized:

$$BE_{C_{i,j}} = \sum_{i=1}^{n} DM_{i,j} \times DM_{i,j+1} \qquad (1)$$

$$BE_{L_{i,j}} = \sum_{j=1}^{n} DM_{i,j} \times DM_{i+1,j} \qquad (2)$$

Partition and Distribution of Datasets

In this section, two important operations will be performed. These are the partitioning and distribution of datasets.

Step of Partition

All datacenters noted DC where each datacenter dc_j has a storage capacity rated cs_j. A binary partitioning algorithm is applied to the matrix CM (clustered dependency matrix) in order to get the best binary partitioning possible. A measure PM (see Formula 3) is defined for this algorithm:

$$PM = \sum_{i=1}^{P} \sum_{j=1}^{P} CM_{ij} \times \sum_{i=p+1}^{n} \sum_{j=p+1}^{n} CM_{ij} - \left(\sum_{i=1}^{p} \sum_{j=p+1}^{n} CM_{ij} \right)^{2} \qquad (3)$$

This measure means that the datasets in each partition will be higher dependencies than the datasets that are in other partitions.

Step of Distribution

In this part, we must distribute the datasets on datacenters. A parameter noted λ_{ini} is introduced for each datacenter $dc_j \in DC$. It refers to the initial use (in %) of the storage capacity of the data center; the initial size of the datasets that will be in dc_j may not exceed $cs_j \times \lambda_{ini}$. λ_{ini} value depends on the type of application running.

3.2   Stage of Execution

During the execution phase, the K-means algorithm is used to classify, dynamically a generated datasets by assigning each to one of two datacenters K obtained during the construction phase.

Scheduling and Execution of Tasks

Before worrying datasets that will be generated, first we must run existing tasks. Since the movement of datasets of a data center to another is more expensive than the scheduling of tasks to the datacenter. A job scheduling algorithm is used (Algorithm of scheduling).

Algorithm of scheduling

```
Input: T: set of tasks.
DC: set of datacenters.
Output:  All  tasks  sequenced  to  an  appropriate
datacenters.

Description:
1: for each t_i ∈ T do
2:      if datasets required by t_i are available then
3:          Schedule t_i to dc_j to be executed
4:              where dc_j has the majority of datasets
required by t_i
5:          set status_t_i=ready
6:      else status_t_i=ready
7:      end if
8: end for
9: for each t_i ∈T do
10:     if status_t_i=ready then
11:         Execute t_i
12:     end if
13: end for
```

In this algorithm, the technique used is based on the placement of datasets; the ready tasks are scheduled to the datacenter that contains the majority of the datasets required. A task is said to be ready if all required datasets belong to the set of existing datasets. Once the tasks are completed, new datasets are generated.

3.3   Stage of Replication

During the step of executing, each task will be scheduled to datacenter that has the majority of datasets required. With this approach, we will try to replicate some datasets in order to minimize their move from one data center to another and consequently reduce the response time of user requests. To do this we developed an algorithm for replication datasets.

To replicate some important datasets, the most frequently used an algorithm was established. The principle can be described as follows:

1. Given a T all tasks running in a datacenter given, we calculate the absolute majority for this set. This majority is the threshold at which the replication will take place (Line 1 of the algorithm). Thus, in each datacenter, the threshold depends of the number of tasks running in the data center (see formulas 4 and 5) if:

$$Nb_{tasks} = pair \rightarrow Threshold = (Nb_{tasks} \div 2) + 1 \quad (4)$$
$$Nb_{tasks} = odd \rightarrow Threshold = (Nb_{tasks} \div 2) \quad (5)$$

2. For each task we will mark the datasets that are not available in the datacenter recipient, that is to say that each datacenter contain its own list of marking to be established based datasets unavailable locally and which must be moved (Lines 2 and 3 and 4 and 5 of the algorithm of replication).

Algorithm of replication

Input: T: set of tasks
    K: set of datacenters results from the stage of construction
    Output: Datasets replicated
 	
Description:
1: Calculate Threshold
2: **for** each dc$_j \in$ K **do**
3:       **for** each t$_i$ $\in$ T **do**
4:          Marc d$_j$ **where** d$_j$ is required from t$_i$ but d$_j \notin$ dc$_i$ //
dc$_i$ is the datacenter destination from t$_i$
5:          **end for**
6: end **for**
7: **if** number of marking =threshold **then**
8:          Replicate d$_j$
9: **end if**
10: **for** each dc$_j$ $\in$ K **do**
11:     Update cs$_j$
12: **end** for
13: **for** each t$_i \in$T **do**
14:        Execute t$_i$
15: **end for**

3. If the majority of tasks require the displacement of the same dataset, it will be replicated to prevent displacement for each task (lines 8 and 9 of the algorithm).

4. Replication must be done at the destination datacenter on which tasks that require marked dataset will run.

5. In the case where there are multiple datasets where the marked marking has reached the threshold, replication will be done for all these marked datasets.

Once the datasets in question replicated task execution begins.

4   Experimentation and Results

We implement our simulator in java and have realized some experimentation concerning a number of displacements, response time, and the observed results are then discussed in this section.

4.1   Number of Displacements

In this first series of experiments, we measured the number of displacements of data. For this we executed the simulation with the three approaches (Without a strategy, with strategy and with replication). Simulation results were performed with the parameters described in the table 1:

Table 1. Parameters of simulation for the first experimentation

Parameters	Values
Number of tasks	1000
Size of data	3000 GO for each data
Number of datacenters	13
Capacity of storage	30000 for each data center
Number of VM	1 for each datacenter
Number of hosts	1 for each datacenter
Bandwith	10 Go/s

Figure 1 shows the resulting graph. We note with different data values, using the investment strategy reduces the number of moving data between datacenters compared to their random assignment. On the other hand, the proposed approach with replication is even better, because for some embodiments, the number of trips is equal to 0 (see Figure 1).

Number of displacements for 1000 tasks

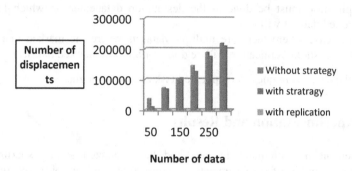

Fig. 1. Impact of a strategy with and without replication on number of displacements

4.2 Response Time

In this second series of experiments, we measured the response time. This is calculated based on the location data, that is to say, to include the latency or waiting time for data that are not found locally. For this we started the simulation with the three approaches (Without a strategy, with strategy and with replication). Simulation results were performed with the same parameters accept number of data which is 100 and number of datacenter which is 6.

Figure 2 shows the resulting graph. We note with different data values, using the investment strategy reduces the response time of tasks in relation to their random assignment. On the other hand, the proposed approach with replication is even better, because the response time is smaller.

Average response time

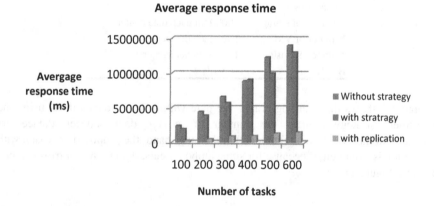

Fig. 2. Impact of a strategy with and without replication on response time

5   Conclusions

The cloud computing is emerging with rapidly growing customer demands. In case of significant client demands, it may be necessary to share data among multiple data centers fairly. In this paper, we present an efficacy data placement and tasks scheduling by replication of some data.

We managed, through this work, to implement: first, an investment strategy based data classification by the K-means algorithm, and secondly, to propose and implement an approach to data Replication for Cloud Computing environment.

To highlight the proposed and the strategy used, we conducted series of experiments by varying different input parameters approach. We used also a set of metrics such as the number of data movement, the response time and the cost incurred. The proposed approaches, as well as the strategy used, were able to improve data placement and minimize response time due to scheduling tasks to datacenters that contain the majority of the required data. For a continuation of our word we propose to integrate our process in clousim simulator and take consideration of the size of data like essential factor.

References

1. Choudhary, M., Peddoju, S.K.: A Dynamic Optimization Algorithm for Task Scheduling in Cloud Environment. International Journal of Engineering Research and Applications (IJERA) 2(3) (May-June 2012)
2. Thawari, V.W., Babar, S.D., Dhawas, N.A.: An Efficient Data Locality Driven Task Scheduling Algorithm for Cloud Computing. International Journal in Multidisciplinary and Academic Research (SSIJMAR) 1(3) (September-October) (ISSN 2278 – 5973)
3. Moschakis, I.A., Karatza, H.D.: Performance and Cost evaluation of Gang Scheduling in a Cloud Computing System with Job Migrations and Starvation Handling. IEEE (2011)
4. Yuan, D., Yang, Y., Liu, X., Chen, J.: A Data Placement Strategy in Scientific Cloud Workflows. Future Generation Computer Systems 26, 1200–1214 (2010)
5. Yuan, D., Yang, Y., Liu, X., Chen, J.: A data placement strategy in scientific cloud workflows. Future Generation Computer Systems 26(8), 1200–1214 (2010)
6. McCormick, W.T., Sehweitzer, P.J., White, T.W.: Problem decomposition and data reorganization by a clustering technique. In: Operations Research, vol. 20, ch. 1, pp. 993–1009 (1972)

A Normalization Scheme for the Non-symmetric s-Step Lanczos Algorithm

Stefan Feuerriegel[1] and H. Martin Bücker[2]

[1] University of Freiburg, 79098 Freiburg, Germany
[2] Friedrich Schiller University Jena, 07743 Jena, Germany

Abstract. The Lanczos algorithm is among the most frequently used techniques for computing a few dominant eigenvalues of a large sparse non-symmetric matrix. When variants of this algorithm are implemented on distributed-memory computers, the synchronization time spent in computing dot products is increasingly limiting the parallel scalability. The goal of s-step algorithms is to reduce the harmful influence of dot products on the parallel performance by grouping several of these operations for joint execution; thus, plummeting synchronization time when using a large number of processes. This paper extends the non-symmetric s-step Lanczos method introduced by Kim and Chronopoulos (J. Comput. Appl. Math., 42(3), 357–374, 1992) by a novel normalization scheme. Compared to the unnormalized algorithm, the normalized variant improves numerical stability and reduces the possibility of breakdowns.

Keywords: s-step Lanczos, numerical stability, synchronization-reducing.

1 Introduction

Non-symmetric eigenvalue problems arising from computational science and engineering are often large and sparse. When only a few dominant eigenvalues are needed, iterative Krylov methods enter the picture, e.g., the Lanczos algorithm [1]. When parallelizing the Lanczos method on message-passing architectures, naïve approaches focus on balancing computational load among processes, but mainly ignore communication and synchronization. These approaches essentially consist of parallelizing a known serial iterative method by parallelizing each linear algebra operation individually. Thus, the resulting implementations inherit most of the properties of the given algorithms including their serial nature. Since this often leads to poor performance, significant research effort is spent in designing new Krylov algorithms specifically for parallel computers: (i) Communication-overlapping algorithms [2, 3] aim at reducing the impact of a communication event by overlapping it with computation and/or other communication. (ii) Communication-avoiding algorithms [4, 5] rely on blocking to reduce the volume of communication. (iii) Synchronization-free algorithms [6] do not involve any synchronization of all processes at the same time. (iv) Synchronization-reducing algorithms [7–11] try to minimize the number of

J. Kołodziej et al. (Eds.): ICA3PP 2013, Part II, LNCS 8286, pp. 30–39, 2013.
© Springer International Publishing Switzerland 2013

global synchronization points (GSP), locations of an algorithm at which all information local to a process has to be globally available on all processes in order to continue the computation.

While communication-avoiding algorithms successfully reduce communication volume between processes, they do not directly focus on synchronization among processes. However, synchronization will increasingly dominate the total execution time on future extreme-scale computer systems where the number of processes will be huge. Therefore, we focus on a novel synchronization-reducing Krylov algorithm. Here, a GSP is enforced by dot product-like operations involving a reduction operation on all participating processes. When only a single GSP is enforced for s iterations of the corresponding classical algorithm, this synchronization-reducing algorithm is referred to as an s-step method [12–14]. The s-step Lanczos procedure was originally introduced for symmetric matrices [15] and later extended to non-symmetric matrices [16]. The contribution of the present paper is to derive a new variant of the algorithm [16] by extending it with a normalization scheme with an improved numerical stability. This different normalization scheme changes the underlying recurrences so that, in Sect. 2, a novel derivation of the complete algorithm is necessary. Sections 3 and 4 describe a numerical experiment and the resulting parallel performance.

Given two vectors, their dot product is denoted by $\langle v, w \rangle$. The symbol $0_{n,m}$ is used for an $n \times m$ zero matrix. Concatenation of scalar entries that form a row vector is denoted by $[x_1, \ldots, x_n]$. Concatenation of vectors or matrices that form a (block) matrix is indicated by $[v_1 \| \ldots \| v_n]$.

2 The s-Step Lanczos Method with Normalization

In the classical Lanczos algorithm [1], every iteration computes a pair of individual Lanczos vectors v_k and w_k using a GSP. In contrast, the k-th block iteration of the s-step Lanczos algorithm [16] computes a pair of blocks of s Lanczos vectors denoted by $\overline{V}_k = \left[v_k^1 \| \ldots \| v_k^s \right] \in \mathbb{R}^{N \times s}$ and $\overline{W}_k = \left[w_k^1 \| \ldots \| w_k^s \right] \in \mathbb{R}^{N \times s}$. This way, a single block iteration of the s-step Lanczos algorithm generates s iterations of the classical Lanczos algorithm using only a single GSP.

The s-step Lanczos method proceeds in two steps. First, *relaxed* Lanczos vectors are computed in a block-wise fashion. In each block iteration, a new block containing s of these vectors as columns is computed. Second, a back transformation is then applied to these vectors.

Definition 1 (s-Step Lanczos Algorithm). *Let $n = sk$ with $1 \leq n \leq N$. For a given non-symmetric matrix $A \in \mathbb{R}^{N \times N}$, the s-step Lanczos algorithm generates an upper Hessenberg matrix $\ddot{T}_n \in \mathbb{R}^{n \times n}$ as well as two additional matrices $\ddot{V}_n \in \mathbb{R}^{N \times n}$ and $\ddot{W}_n \in \mathbb{R}^{N \times n}$ such that*

$$\ddot{W}_n^T \ddot{V}_n = block\ biorthogonal\,, \tag{1a}$$

$$A\ddot{V}_n = \ddot{V}_n \ddot{T}_n + f_{k+1} v_{k+1}^1 [0, \ldots, 0, 1]\,, \tag{1b}$$

$$A^T \ddot{W}_n = \ddot{W}_n \ddot{T}_n + f_{k+1} w_{k+1}^1 [0, \ldots, 0, 1]\,. \tag{1c}$$

The upper Hessenberg matrix $\ddot{T}_n$ *is block tridiagonal*

$$\ddot{T}_n = \begin{bmatrix} \overline{G}_1 & \overline{E}_2 & & \\ \overline{F}_2 & \overline{G}_2 & \ddots & \\ & \ddots & \ddots & \overline{E}_k \\ & & \overline{F}_k & \overline{G}_k \end{bmatrix} \in \mathbb{R}^{n \times n} \text{ where each } \overline{F}_i = \begin{bmatrix} & & f_i \\ & & \\ & & \end{bmatrix} \in \mathbb{R}^{s \times s}, \quad (2)$$

each $\overline{E}_i$ *is a dense* $s \times s$ *matrix, and each* $\overline{G}_i \in \mathbb{R}^{s \times s}$ *is in upper Hessenberg form. The block-wise grouping of the relaxed Lanczos vectors is given by* $\ddot{V}_n = [\overline{V}_1 \| \ldots \| \overline{V}_k] \in \mathbb{R}^{N \times n}$ *and* $\ddot{W}_n = [\overline{W}_1 \| \ldots \| \overline{W}_k] \in \mathbb{R}^{N \times n}$ *where, for all* k, *we have* $\overline{V}_k = [v_k^1 \| \ldots \| v_k^s] \in \mathbb{R}^{N \times s}$, $\overline{W}_k = [w_k^1 \| \ldots \| w_k^s] \in \mathbb{R}^{N \times s}$, $v_k^1, \ldots, v_k^s \in \mathbb{R}^N$ *and* $w_k^1, \ldots, w_k^s \in \mathbb{R}^N$.

In an implementation, the s-step Lanczos algorithm iterates up to a block iteration $k = n/s$ yielding both $\ddot{T}_n$ and $\ddot{V}_n$. It then turns $\ddot{T}_n$ and $\ddot{V}_n$ into the corresponding matrices computed by the classical Lanczos procedure. This back transformation is sketched in the following theorem whose proof is given in [16].

Theorem 1. *Let* $\ddot{W}_n^T \ddot{V}_n$ *be a non-singular matrix and let* $\ddot{W}_n^T \ddot{V}_n = \ddot{L}_n \ddot{U}_n$ *denote its LU decomposition. Then,* $\ddot{T}_n$, $\ddot{V}_n$ *and* $\ddot{W}_n$ *can be transformed into* T_n, W_n *and* V_n, *originating from the classical Lanczos method in the absence of breakdowns, by* $T_n := \ddot{U}_n \ddot{T}_n \ddot{U}_n^{-1}$, $V_n := \ddot{V}_n \ddot{U}_n^{-1}$ *and* $W_n^T := \ddot{L}_n^{-1} \ddot{W}_n^T$.

To state computational schemes for $\overline{V}_{k+1}$ and $\overline{W}_{k+1}$, we introduce the column notation $\overline{E}_k = [e_k^1 \| \ldots \| e_k^s]$ and $\overline{G}_k = [g_k^1 \| \ldots \| g_k^s]$. Then, according to [17], the s-step basis vectors are computed as

$$\tilde{v}_{k+1}^1 := f_{k+1} v_{k+1}^1 = A v_k^s - \overline{V}_{k-1} e_k^s - \overline{V}_k g_k^s,$$
$$\tilde{w}_{k+1}^1 := f_{k+1} w_{k+1}^1 = A^T w_k^s - \overline{W}_{k-1} e_k^s - \overline{W}_k g_k^s.$$

Here, in contrast to [16], we can choose the coefficient f_{k+1} arbitrarily to transform the vectors $\tilde{v}_{k+1}^1$ and $\tilde{w}_{k+1}^1$ into normalized vectors v_{k+1}^1 and w_{k+1}^1.

To compute the remaining Lanczos vectors of the current block, [17] uses plain orthogonalization against $\overline{V}_k$ or $\overline{W}_k$ arriving at

$$\tilde{v}_{k+1}^j = A^{j-1} v_{k+1}^1 - \overline{V}_k t_k^j, \qquad \text{for } j = 2, \ldots, s, \quad (3a)$$
$$\tilde{w}_{k+1}^j = (A^T)^{j-1} w_{k+1}^1 - \overline{W}_k \hat{t}_k^j, \qquad \text{for } j = 2, \ldots, s. \quad (3b)$$

Here, the vectors t_k^j and $\hat{t}_k^j$ are determined to match the conditions $\overline{V}_{k+1} \perp \overline{W}_k$ and $\overline{W}_{k+1} \perp \overline{V}_k$ which is sufficient to enforce the block biorthogonality (1a) as stated in the following theorem whose proof is given in [16].

Theorem 2. *If* $v_1^1 = w_1^1$ *holds, then* $t_k^j = \hat{t}_k^j$ *for* $j = 2, \ldots, s$ *and the matrices* $\ddot{V}_{n+s}$ *and* $\ddot{W}_{n+s}$ *with* $n = sk$ *are block biorthogonal.*

When we implemented the original s-step Lanczos algorithm [16] in double precision floating-point arithmetic, we experienced that numerical overflows can occur. We observed that the floating-point values in $\ddot{W}_n^T \ddot{V}_n$ grew rapidly, quickly leaping the maximum value in floating-point arithmetic. To reduce the possibility of numerical overflows, we introduce the normalization scheme

$$f_{k+1} := \sqrt{|\langle \tilde{w}_{k+1}^1, \tilde{v}_{k+1}^1 \rangle|}$$

such that $\langle w_{k+1}^1, v_{k+1}^1 \rangle = \pm 1$. This differs from [16] where any normalization is avoided, corresponding to $f_{k+1} := 1$ in the new scheme.

In addition to this normalization scheme, it turns out that it is also convenient to normalize $\tilde{v}_{k+1}^j$ and $\tilde{w}_{k+1}^j$ for $j = 2, \ldots, s$ such that $\langle w_{k+1}^j, v_{k+1}^j \rangle = \pm 1$ holds. Therefore, we scale the Lanczos vectors as follows:

$$v_{k+1}^j = \tilde{v}_{k+1}^j \sigma_{k+1}^j \quad \text{and} \quad w_{k+1}^j = \tilde{w}_{k+1}^j \sigma_{k+1}^j \quad \text{for} \quad j = 2, \ldots, s \,,$$

where

$$\sigma_{k+1}^j := 1 \bigg/ \sqrt{|\langle \tilde{w}_{k+1}^j, \tilde{v}_{k+1}^j \rangle|} \quad \text{for} \quad j = 2, \ldots, s \,.$$

To compute the vectors e_k^i, g_k^i and t_k^j, we let the matrix $\overline{M}_k := \overline{W}_k^T \overline{V}_k$ be non-singular. Then, according to [17], we find these vectors as the solutions of the following $s \times s$ systems of linear equations:

$$\overline{M}_{k-1} e_k^i = c_k^i \text{ where } c_k^i = \left[\langle w_{k-1}^1, A v_k^i \rangle, \ldots, \langle w_{k-1}^s, A v_k^i \rangle \right]^T,$$

$$\overline{M}_k g_k^i = d_k^i \text{ where } d_k^i = \left[\langle w_k^1, A v_k^i \rangle, \ldots, \langle w_k^s, A v_k^i \rangle \right]^T,$$

$$\overline{M}_k t_k^j = b_k^j \text{ where } b_k^j = \left[\langle w_k^1, A^{j-1} v_{k+1}^1 \rangle, \ldots, \langle w_k^s, A^{j-1} v_{k+1}^1 \rangle \right]^T,$$

where $i = 1, \ldots, s$ and $j = 2, \ldots, s$. Computing the dot products $b_k^{i,j} := \langle w_k^i, A^{j-1} v_{k+1}^1 \rangle$, $c_k^{i,j} := \langle w_{k-1}^i, A v_k^j \rangle$, $d_k^{i,j} := \langle w_k^i, A v_k^j \rangle$ and $\overline{M}_k^{i,j} := \langle w_k^i, v_k^j \rangle$ explicitly for all $i, j = 1, \ldots, s$ is a computationally expensive task that would destroy all benefits from the s-step approach at once. Fortunately, as detailed in [17], there is a remedy to this problem consisting of computing these products recursively from the $2\,s$ dot products $\langle w_k^1, v_k^1 \rangle, \langle w_k^1, A v_k^1 \rangle, \ldots, \langle w_k^1, A^{2s-1} v_k^1 \rangle$.

Putting everything together, we now finalize the s-step Lanczos algorithm with normalization. Recall from Theorem 2 that the iteration is started with two identical vectors. We emphasize in Step 11 of the following algorithm that, for each pair of s Lanczos vectors, only a single GSP is required.

Input: Matrix $A \in \mathbb{R}^{N \times N}$, starting vectors $v_1^1 = w_1^1$.
Output: Tridiagonal matrix $T_n \in \mathbb{R}^{n \times n}$, Lanczos basis $V_n \in \mathbb{R}^{N \times n}$.
1: Initialize $\overline{V}_0 \leftarrow 0_{N,s}$ and $\overline{W}_0 \leftarrow 0_{N,s}$ and compute

$$\overline{V}_1 \leftarrow \left[v_1^1 \| A v_1^1 \| \ldots \| A^{s-1} v_1^1 \right], \qquad \overline{W}_1 \leftarrow \left[w_1^1 \| A^T w_1^1 \| \ldots \| (A^T)^{s-1} w_1^1 \right].$$

2: Compute $2s$ dot products $\langle \boldsymbol{w}_1^1, \boldsymbol{v}_1^1 \rangle, \langle \boldsymbol{w}_1^1, A\boldsymbol{v}_1^1 \rangle, \ldots, \langle \boldsymbol{w}_1^1, A^{2s-1}\boldsymbol{v}_1^1 \rangle$.

3: Initialize $\left[\boldsymbol{b}_0^1 \| \ldots \| \boldsymbol{b}_0^s \right] \leftarrow 0_{s,s}$, $\left[\boldsymbol{c}_0^1 \| \ldots \| \boldsymbol{c}_0^s \right] \leftarrow 0_{s,s}$, $\left[\boldsymbol{d}_0^1 \| \ldots \| \boldsymbol{d}_0^s \right] \leftarrow 0_{s,s}$,
$\sigma_1^1, \ldots, \sigma_1^s \leftarrow 1$, $\left[\boldsymbol{t}_0^2 \| \ldots \| \boldsymbol{t}_0^s \right] \leftarrow 0_{N,s}$, $\overline{M}_0 \leftarrow 0_{s,s}$.

4: **for** $k = 1$ **until** Convergence **do**

5:   Compute for $i, j = 1, \ldots, s$

$$\overline{M}_k^{i,j} \leftarrow \sigma_k^i \sigma_k^j \left[\langle \boldsymbol{w}_k^1, A^{i+j-2}\boldsymbol{v}_k^1 \rangle - \left(\boldsymbol{t}_{k-1}^i \right)^T \overline{M}_{k-1} \boldsymbol{t}_{k-1}^j \right] ,$$

$$\boldsymbol{c}_k^{s,j} \leftarrow \sigma_k^j \left[\boldsymbol{b}_{k-1}^{s,j+1} - \left[\boldsymbol{d}_{k-1}^{s,1}, \ldots, \boldsymbol{d}_{k-1}^{s,s} \right] \boldsymbol{t}_{k-1}^j \right] .$$

6:   Compute for $i, j = 1, \ldots, s$

$$\Omega_k^{i,j} \leftarrow \left(\boldsymbol{t}_{k-1}^i \right)^T \overline{M}_{k-1} \boldsymbol{t}_{k-1}^j , \quad \Omega_k^{s+1,j} \leftarrow \frac{\boldsymbol{c}_k^{s,s} \boldsymbol{t}_{k-1}^{s,j}}{\sigma_k^s} + \left(\boldsymbol{t}_{k-1}^s \right)^T \left[\boldsymbol{d}_{k-1}^1 \| \ldots \| \boldsymbol{d}_{k-1}^s \right] \boldsymbol{t}_{k-1}^j ,$$

$$\Xi_k^{i,j} \leftarrow \left(\boldsymbol{t}_{k-1}^i \right)^T \overline{M}_{k-1} \boldsymbol{t}_{k-1}^j , \quad \Xi_k^{i,s+1} \leftarrow \frac{\boldsymbol{t}_{k-1}^{s,i} \boldsymbol{c}_k^{s,s}}{\sigma_k^s} + \left(\boldsymbol{t}_{k-1}^i \right)^T \left[\boldsymbol{d}_{k-1}^1 \| \ldots \| \boldsymbol{d}_{k-1}^s \right] \boldsymbol{t}_{k-1}^s .$$

7:   Compute for $i, j = 1, \ldots, s$

$$\boldsymbol{d}_k^{i,j} \leftarrow \sigma_k^i \sigma_k^j \left[\langle \boldsymbol{w}_k^1, A^{i+j-1}\boldsymbol{v}_k^1 \rangle - \Omega_k^{i+1,j} - \Xi_k^{i,j+1} + \left(\boldsymbol{t}_{k-1}^i \right)^T \left[\boldsymbol{d}_{k-1}^1 \| \ldots \| \boldsymbol{d}_{k-1}^s \right] \boldsymbol{t}_{k-1}^j \right] .$$

8:   Solve $\overline{M}_{k-1} \boldsymbol{e}_k^i = \boldsymbol{c}_k^i$ and $\overline{M}_k \boldsymbol{g}_k^i = \boldsymbol{d}_k^i$ for all $i = 1, \ldots, s$.

9:   Compute $\tilde{\boldsymbol{v}}_{k+1}^1 \leftarrow A\boldsymbol{v}_k^s - \overline{V}_{k-1} \boldsymbol{e}_k^s - \overline{V}_k \boldsymbol{g}_k^s$ and $\tilde{\boldsymbol{w}}_{k+1}^1 \leftarrow A^T \boldsymbol{w}_k^s - \overline{W}_{k-1} \boldsymbol{e}_k^s - \overline{W}_k \boldsymbol{g}_k^s$.

10:   Compute $A\tilde{\boldsymbol{v}}_{k+1}^1, A^2\tilde{\boldsymbol{v}}_{k+1}^1, \ldots, A^{s-1}\tilde{\boldsymbol{v}}_{k+1}^1$ and $A^T \tilde{\boldsymbol{w}}_{k+1}^1, (A^T)^2 \tilde{\boldsymbol{w}}_{k+1}^1, \ldots, (A^T)^s \tilde{\boldsymbol{w}}_{k+1}^1$.

11:   Compute $2s$ dot products $\langle \tilde{\boldsymbol{w}}_{k+1}^1, \tilde{\boldsymbol{v}}_{k+1}^1 \rangle, \langle \tilde{\boldsymbol{w}}_{k+1}^1, A\tilde{\boldsymbol{v}}_{k+1}^1 \rangle, \ldots, \langle \tilde{\boldsymbol{w}}_{k+1}^1, A^{2s-1}\tilde{\boldsymbol{v}}_{k+1}^1 \rangle$
and wait until **global synchronization** is completed.

12:   Compute normalization coefficient $f_{k+1} \leftarrow \sqrt{\left| \langle \tilde{\boldsymbol{w}}_{k+1}^1, \tilde{\boldsymbol{v}}_{k+1}^1 \rangle \right|}$.

13:   Normalize $\boldsymbol{v}_{k+1}^1 \leftarrow \tilde{\boldsymbol{v}}_{k+1}^1 / f_{k+1}$ and $\boldsymbol{w}_{k+1}^1 \leftarrow \tilde{\boldsymbol{w}}_{k+1}^1 / f_{k+1}$.

14:   Scale the already existing matrix-by-vector products $A^1 \boldsymbol{v}_{k+1}^1 \leftarrow A^1 \tilde{\boldsymbol{v}}_{k+1}^1 / f_{k+1}$,
$\ldots, A^{s-1} \boldsymbol{v}_{k+1}^1 \leftarrow A^{s-1} \tilde{\boldsymbol{v}}_{k+1}^1 / f_{k+1}$ and
$A^T \boldsymbol{w}_{k+1}^1 \leftarrow A^T \tilde{\boldsymbol{w}}_{k+1}^1 / f_{k+1}, (A^T)^s \boldsymbol{w}_{k+1}^1 \leftarrow (A^T)^s \tilde{\boldsymbol{w}}_{k+1}^1 / f_{k+1}$.

15:   Compute

$$\langle \boldsymbol{w}_{k+1}^1, \boldsymbol{v}_{k+1}^1 \rangle \leftarrow \frac{\langle \tilde{\boldsymbol{w}}_{k+1}^1, \tilde{\boldsymbol{v}}_{k+1}^1 \rangle}{f_{k+1}^2}, \ldots, \langle \boldsymbol{w}_{k+1}^1, A^{2s-1}\boldsymbol{v}_{k+1}^1 \rangle \leftarrow \frac{\langle \tilde{\boldsymbol{w}}_{k+1}^1, A^{2s-1}\tilde{\boldsymbol{v}}_{k+1}^1 \rangle}{f_{k+1}^2} ,$$

16:   Compute normalization coefficients

$$\sigma_{k+1}^1 \leftarrow 1, \quad \sigma_{k+1}^j \leftarrow 1 \Big/ \sqrt{\left| \langle \boldsymbol{w}_{k+1}^1, A^{2j-2}\boldsymbol{v}_{k+1}^1 \rangle - \left(\boldsymbol{t}_k^j \right)^T \overline{M}_k \boldsymbol{t}_k^j \right|}, \text{ for } j = 2, \ldots, s .$$

17:   Compute for $i = 1, \ldots, s$ and $j = 2, \ldots, s+1$

$$\boldsymbol{b}_k^{i,j} \leftarrow \frac{\sigma_k^i}{\sigma_k^s} \left[\langle f_{k+1} \boldsymbol{w}_{k+1}^1, A^{i+j-s-2}\boldsymbol{v}_{k+1}^1 \rangle + \sum_{\substack{\iota = 2s \\ +3-i-j}}^{s} \frac{\sigma_k^\iota \boldsymbol{g}_k^{\iota,s} \boldsymbol{b}_k^{i-s+\iota-1,j}}{\sigma_k^{i-s+\iota-1}} \right] .$$

18:     Solve $\overline{M}_k t_k^j = b_k^j$ for $j = 2, \ldots, s$.

19:     Compute $\tilde{v}_{k+1}^j \leftarrow A^{j-1} v_{k+1}^1 - \overline{V}_k t_k^j$ for $j = 2, \ldots, s$

        and $\tilde{w}_{k+1}^j \leftarrow (A^T)^{j-1} w_{k+1}^1 - \overline{W}_k t_k^j$ for $j = 2, \ldots, s$.

20:     Normalize $v_{k+1}^j \leftarrow \tilde{v}_{k+1}^j \sigma_{k+1}^j$ and $w_{k+1}^j \leftarrow \tilde{w}_{k+1}^j \sigma_{k+1}^j$ for $j = 2, \ldots, s$.

21:     **end for**

22: Compute LU decomposition, $\ddot{L}_n \ddot{U}_n = \mathrm{diag}(\overline{M}_1, \ldots, \overline{M}_m)$.

23: Perform back transformation, $T_n \leftarrow \ddot{U}_n \ddot{T}_n \ddot{U}_n^{-1}$, $V_n \leftarrow \ddot{V}_n \ddot{U}_n^{-1}$, $W_n^T \leftarrow \ddot{L}_n^{-1} \ddot{W}_n^T$.

Table 1 compares the main computational cost for $n = sk$ iterations of the classical Lanczos algorithm and k block iterations of two variants of the s-step Lanczos algorithm. More precisely, we report the number of operations as well as vector storages of size N and neglect all corresponding costs of vectors of dimension s. Though the s-step variants slightly raise the computational cost, they reduce the number of global synchronization points by a factor of $\mathcal{O}(s)$.

Table 1. Comparison of cost for $n = sk$ iterations of the classical Lanczos algorithms and k block iterations of the s-step Lanczos variants

Operation/Storage	Classical	Unnormalized [16]	Normalized (Sect. 2)
Dot products	$2\,sk$	$2\,sk$	$2\,sk$
Vector updates	$6\,sk$	$2\,s(s-1)k + 4\,sk$	$2\,s(s-1)k + 8\,sk - k$
Matrix-vector products	$2\,sk$	$2\,sk + k$	$2\,sk + k$
Synchronization points	$\mathcal{O}(sk)$	k	k
Back transformations	—	$2k$	$2k$
Vector storage	4	$4\,s$	$4\,s$

3   Numerical Experiment

To compare the numerical behavior between the classical and the s-step Lanczos algorithm, we employ the following example taken from [16]. We consider the stationary two-dimensional convection-diffusion-reaction equation

$$-(bu_x)_x - (cu_x)_x + (du)_x + (eu)_y + fu = g \quad \text{on} \quad \Omega = (0,1) \times (0,1)$$

with $b(x,y) = e^{-xy}$, $c(x,y) = e^{xy}$, $d(x,y) = x + y$, $e(x,y) = 50\,(x+y)$, $f(x,y) = 1/(1 + x + y)$ and Dirichlet boundary condition $u_D = 0$. This partial differential equation is discretized using first-order finite differences on an $n_D \times n_D$ grid leading to a system of linear equations whose coefficient matrix A is of order $N = n_D^2 = 64^2 = 4096$ with the dominant eigenvalue $\lambda_{\max} \approx -17\,595 + 7170i$.

Figure 1 compares the Lanczos implementations. All algorithms are started with $v_1^1 = w_1^1 = [1, \ldots, 1]^T$. The upper diagram shows the convergence history of the relative accuracy of the dominant eigenvalue of A. The unnormalized 2-step variant starts to diverge at iteration 18 and breaks down at iteration 40,

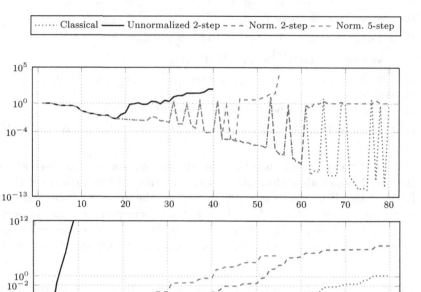

Fig. 1. Convergence history of the relative error of the dominant eigenvalue (top) and biorthogonality property (bottom) for the classical algorithm as well as for the unnormalized [16] and the normalized s-step Lanczos variant of Sect. 2

whereas the normalized 2-step variant competes well until iteration 61. However, when increasing s to $s = 5$, the divergence of the normalized variant already starts around iteration 45. The tendency for growing numerical instabilities when increasing s is well known [18, 19]. The lower diagram gives the error of the biorthogonality property and shows a similar behavior of the algorithms.

4   Parallel Performance

Previous research [16, 20, 21] already demonstrated that, compared to the classical algorithm, execution time is reduced by the unnormalized s-step algorithm. Therefore, we excluded the unnormalized s-step method from the analysis and only remark that the parallel performance characteristics of the normalized and unnormalized variants are almost identical. The focus is rather on the parallel performance of the normalized s-step Lanczos algorithm. To this end, we carried out a parallel implementation of that algorithm using PETSc [22] and included it as an additional eigenvalue solver inside SLEPc [23]. We compared the new normalized s-step variant to the classical variant implemented in SLEPc.

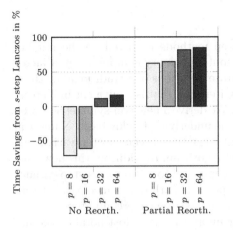
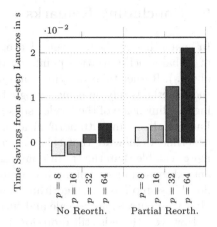

Fig. 2. Relative (left) and absolute (right) time savings per iteration, including time for reorthogonalization, when using the normalized s-step variant instead of the classical algorithm. We choose $s = 2$ and the matrix from Sect. 3 using no and partial reorthogonalization and a different number of processes p.

When spurious eigenvalues are present, the Lanczos process can converge to wrong values. This behavior appears at the same time when the Lanczos vectors start to lose biorthogonality. As a possible remedy, one can explicitly reorthogonalize the new Lanczos vector with respect to previous ones. Our normalized s-step implementations can be used along with full, local, selective, periodic, and partial reorthogonalization schemes. However, reorthogonalization can only take place once after every block iteration of the s-step method. That is, one reorthogonalizes v_{k+1}^1 and w_{k+1}^1 against V_{sk} and W_{sk} (or columns thereof) in Step 13 of the algorithm. Each reorthogonalization comes at the cost of an additional GSP.

All computations are performed on a *Nehalem*-based Cluster at RWTH Aachen University, Germany. Each node of this cluster consists of 2 sockets, each equipped with Intel Xeon X5570 quadcore processors running at 2.93 GHz. Each core has a separate L1 and L2 cache; while 4 cores share an L3 cache of size 8 MB. So, each node of this cluster is made up of 8 cores called processes hereafter. The nodes are connected by a quad data rate InfiniBand network. A synchronization with a reduction operation accounts for 0.22×10^{-4} s with 16 processes, 1.61×10^{-4} s with 32 processes, and 3.38×10^{-4} s with 64 processes.

Figure 2 compares the relative (left) and absolute (right) time savings per iteration when using the normalized s-step variant instead of the classical algorithm. In case of no reorthogonalization, the s-step algorithm performs slower than the classical algorithm for $p = 8$ and $p = 16$ processes. However, in this case it performs faster for both $p = 32$ and $p = 64$ processes. With 64 processes, for instance, the corresponding time saving per iteration accounts for 0.0042 s or 16.39 % respectively. In case of partial reorthogonalization, the s-step variant saves time for all $p = 8$, 16, 32, and 64. Here, 64 processes result in time savings of 0.0210 s or 84.92 % respectively.

5   Concluding Remarks

In sparse linear algebra, the idea of s-step methods is to reduce the number of global synchronization points on distributed-memory computers by a factor of $\mathcal{O}(s)$. Rather than carrying out s separate iterations of a traditional method, these methods rely on using a single block iteration that is equivalent in increasing the dimension of the Krylov subspace. We derive a new non-symmetric s-step Lanczos algorithm with normalization of the underlying Krylov basis. Numerical experiments indicate that this new variant—like the previous s-step variant—is more scalable than the traditional Lanczos algorithm. In addition, this new variant exhibits improved numerical accuracy compared to a previous s-step variant. So, this s-step Lanczos algorithm shows a possible path to advance parallel scalability on current large-scale and future extreme-scale supercomputers.

However, there is still room for further improvements. Most notably, the numerical stability tends to decrease with increasing s. Future work is necessary to investigate promising remedies such as residual replacement strategies or the use of a basis that is different from the monomial basis [5].

Acknowledgements. Parts of this research were conducted while the authors were in residence at the Institute for Scientific Computing, the Center for Computational Engineering Science, and the Aachen Institute for Advanced Study in Computational Engineering Science at RWTH Aachen University, D-52056 Aachen, Germany. Financial support from the Deutsche Forschungsgemeinschaft (German Research Foundation) through grant GSC 111 is gratefully acknowledged.

References

1. Lanczos, C.: An iteration method for the solution of the eigenvalue problem of linear differential and integral operators. J. Res. Nat. Bur. Stand. 45(4), 255–282 (1950)
2. Ghysels, P., Ashby, T.J., Meerbergen, K., Vanroose, W.: Hiding global communication latency in the GMRES algorithm on massively parallel machines. SIAM J. Sci. Comput. 35(1), C48–C71 (2013)
3. Ghysels, P., Vanroose, W.: Hiding global synchronization latency in the preconditioned Conjugate Gradient algorithm. In: Parallel Computing (in press, 2013)
4. Mohiyuddin, M., Hoemmen, M., Demmel, J., Yelick, K.: Minimizing communication in sparse matrix solvers. In: Proc. Conf. High Perf. Comput. Networking, Storage and Analysi, SC 2009, pp. 36:1–36:12. ACM, New York (2009)
5. Carson, E., Knight, N., Demmel, J.: Avoiding communication in two-sided Krylov subspace methods. SIAM J. Sci. Comput. 35(5), S42–S61 (2013)
6. Fischer, B., Freund, R.: An inner product-free conjugate gradient-like algorithm for Hermitian positive definite systems. In: Brown, J., et al. (eds.) Proc. Cornelius Lanczos Intern. Centenary Conf., pp. 288–290. SIAM (1994)
7. Meurant, G.: The conjugate gradient method on supercomputers. Supercomputer 13, 9–17 (1986)

8. Van Rosendale, J.: Minimizing inner product data dependencies in conjugate gradient iteration. NASA Contractor Report NASA–CR–172178, NASA Langley Research Center, Hampton, VA (1983)

9. Bücker, H.M., Sauren, M.: A Variant of the Biconjugate Gradient Method Suitable for Massively Parallel Computing. In: Bilardi, G., Ferreira, A., Lüling, R., Rolim, J. (eds.) IRREGULAR 1997. LNCS, vol. 1253, pp. 72–79. Springer, Heidelberg (1997)

10. Bücker, H.M., Sauren, M.: A Parallel Version of the Quasi-Minimal Residual Method Based on Coupled Two-Term Recurrences. In: Waśniewski, J., Dongarra, J., Madsen, K., Olesen, D. (eds.) PARA 1996. LNCS, vol. 1184, pp. 157–165. Springer, Heidelberg (1996)

11. Bücker, H.M., Sauren, M.: Reducing global synchronization in the biconjugate gradient method. In: Yang, T. (ed.) Parallel Numerical Computations with Applications, pp. 63–76. Kluwer Academic Publishers, Norwell (1999)

12. Chronopoulos, A.T.: A Class of Parallel Iterative Methods Implemented on Multiprocessors. Technical report UIUCDCS–R–86–1267, Department of Computer Science, University of Illinois, Urbana, Illinois (1986)

13. Chronopoulos, A.T., Gear, C.W.: s-step iterative methods for symmetric linear systems. J. Comput. Appl. Math. 25(2), 153–168 (1989)

14. Chronopoulos, A.T., Swanson, C.D.: Parallel iterative s-step methods for unsymmetric linear systems. Parallel Computing 22(5), 623–641 (1996)

15. Kim, S.K., Chronopoulos, A.T.: A class of Lanczos-like algorithms implemented on parallel computers. Parallel Computing 17(6-7), 763–778 (1991)

16. Kim, S.K., Chronopoulos, A.T.: An efficient nonsymmetric Lanczos method on parallel vector computers. J. Comput. Appl. Math. 42(3), 357–374 (1992)

17. Feuerriegel, S.: Lanczos-based Algorithms for the Parallel Solution of Large Sparse Linear Systems. Master's thesis, RWTH Aachen University, Aachen (2011)

18. Kim, S.K.: Efficient biorthogonal Lanczos algorithm on message passing parallel computer. In: Hsu, C.-H., Malyshkin, V. (eds.) MTPP 2010. LNCS, vol. 6083, pp. 293–299. Springer, Heidelberg (2010)

19. Carson, E., Demmel, J.: A residual replacement strategy for improving the maximum attainable accuracy of s-step Krylov subspace methods. Technical Report UCB/EECS–2012–197, University of California, Berkeley (2012)

20. Gustafsson, M., Kormann, K., Holmgren, S.: Communication-efficient algorithms for numerical quantum dynamics. In: Jónasson, K. (ed.) PARA 2010, Part II. LNCS, vol. 7134, pp. 368–378. Springer, Heidelberg (2012)

21. Kim, S.K., Kim, T.H.: A study on the efficient parallel block Lanczos method. In: Zhang, J., He, J.-H., Fu, Y. (eds.) CIS 2004. LNCS, vol. 3314, pp. 231–237. Springer, Heidelberg (2004)

22. Balay, S., Gropp, W.D., McInnes, L.C., Smith, B.F.: Efficient management of parallelism in object oriented numerical software libraries. In: Arge, E., et al. (eds.) Modern Software Tools in Scientific Computing, pp. 163–202. Birkhäuser Press (1997)

23. Hernandez, V., Roman, J.E., Vidal, V.: SLEPc: A scalable and flexible toolkit for the solution of eigenvalue problems. ACM Trans. Math. Softw. 31(3), 351–362 (2005)

Efficient Hybrid Breadth-First Search on GPUs

Takaaki Hiragushi[1] and Daisuke Takahashi[2]

[1] Graduate School of Systems and Information Engineering, University of Tsukuba
[2] Faculty of Engineering, Information and Systems, University of Tsukuba
1-1-1 Tennodai, Tsukuba, Ibaraki 305-8573, Japan
hiragushi@hpcs.cs.tsukuba.ac.jp, daisuke@cs.tsukuba.ac.jp

Abstract. Breadth-first search (BFS) is a basic algorithm for graph processing. It is a very important algorithm because a number of graph-processing algorithms use breadth-first search as a sub-routine. Recently, large-scale graphs have been used in various fields, and there is a growing need for an efficient approach by which to process large-scale graphs. In the present paper, we present a hybrid BFS implementation on a GPU for efficient traversal of a complex network, and we achieved a speedup of up to 29x, as compared to the previous GPU implementation. We also applied an implementation for GPUs on a distributed memory system. This implementation achieved a speed of 117.546 GigaTEPS on a 256-node HA-PACS cluster with 1,024 NVIDIA M2090 GPUs and was ranked 39th on the June 2013 Graph500 list.

Keywords: GPGPU, Breadth-first search, Graph500.

1 Introduction

Graph-based structures are useful for solving various problems, and processing real-world data (e.g., social network and web link network) as a graph is helpful for obtaining beneficial information. Some applications require processing of large-scale graphs. Therefore, efficient algorithms to process large-scale graphs are necessary. Graph processing is a typical data-intensive application. The Graph500 [1] benchmark has been in place since 2010 for the comparison of supercomputers based on the performance of data-intensive applications.

Breadth-first search (BFS) is an essential algorithm among the graph processing algorithms, and some complex graph processing algorithms use BFS as a sub-routine. The Graph500 benchmark uses BFS on a large-scale graph as a problem. The hybrid BFS algorithm [2] works efficiently to traverse graphs with a small-world property such as a complex network. The hybrid BFS achieved impressive speedups on CPU-based systems but the hybrid BFS implementation for GPU-based systems has not yet been evaluated. However, the concept of the hybrid BFS does not depend on target architecture, and the hybrid BFS should also work efficiently on GPU-based systems with a suitable implementation.

In the present paper, we present an implementation of a hybrid BFS that works efficiently on GPU-based systems and the result of an evaluation of the proposed implementation.

J. Kołodziej et al. (Eds.): ICA3PP 2013, Part II, LNCS 8286, pp. 40–50, 2013.
© Springer International Publishing Switzerland 2013

function breadth-first-search (root)
    frontier ← { root }
    parents ← [-1, -1, ..., -1]
    while frontier ≠ ∅
        next ← top-down-step(frontier, parents)
        frontier ← next
    end while
    return parents

Fig. 1. Procedure of level-synchronized BFS [2]

2   Hybrid Breadth-First Search

Level-synchronized BFS is a widely used method for parallel BFS. This method performs BFS using the procedure described in Fig. 1. The level of the vertices in the frontier remains constant. The level is the hop distance from a root vertex. In order to parallelize BFS, the top-down-step function is performed in parallel.

The hybrid BFS is based on level-synchronized BFS and uses two BFS approaches: top-down BFS and bottom-up BFS. The hybrid-BFS switches the approach used to process each level for efficient traversal. This algorithm is effective on a graph having a small-world property. In this section, we describe an outline of the hybrid BFS.

In top-down BFS, the computation of each iteration is performed by checking the visitation status of all vertices that neighbor any vertex in the frontier. When unvisited vertices are found in this procedure, the vertices are added to the set of the next vertices. The algorithm of top-down BFS is given in Fig. 2(a).

Unlike top-down BFS, bottom-up BFS processes each level by checking all edges not visited by its endpoint. The algorithm of the bottom-up BFS is described in Fig. 2(b). Bottom-up BFS works efficiently when many vertices are contained in a set of results of each traversal step. The sets of results for each step often contain many vertices when a target graph has a small-world property. Therefore, using bottom-up BFS may improve traversal performance.

The hybrid BFS heuristically determines which approach is used to process the next level. Traversal begins from top-down BFS and switches to bottom-up BFS when $m_f > m_u/\alpha$ is satisfied and switches back to top-down BFS when $n_f > |V|/\beta$ is satisfied, while traversing by bottom-up BFS. In those equations, m_f is the sum of the out-degrees of vertices in the frontier, m_u is the sum of the out-degrees of unvisited vertices, n_f is the number of vertices in the frontier, and α and β are heuristic parameters.

3   Single-GPU Algorithm

3.1   Graph Data Representation

The proposed implementation uses an adjacency matrix represented by compressed sparse rows (CSR) to represent graph data. It consists of offsets for

function top-down-step
(frontier, parents)
  next ← ∅
  for u ∈ frontier **do**
    for v ∈ neighbors(u) **do**
      if parents[v] = -1 **then**
        parents[v] ← u
        next ← next ∪ { v }
      end if
    end for
  end for
  return next

(a) The top-down BFS approach

function bottom-up-step
(frontier, parents)
  next ← ∅
  for v ∈ vertices
    if parents[v] = -1
      for n ∈ neighbors[v]
        if n ∈ frontier
          parents[v] ← n
          next ← next ∪ { n }
        end if
      end for
    end if
  end for
  return next

(b) The bottom-up BFS approach

Fig. 2. Single step of the top-down BFS and the bottom-up BFS approaches [2]

each row and column indices of each non-zero element. In order to treat the directed graph in bottom-up BFS, the proposed implementation also prepares a transposed graph in CSR format.

3.2 Top-Down BFS

The proposed top-down BFS implementation is based on the two-phase method presented by Merrill et al. [5]. This method divides the traversal of each level into two kernels: Expand and Contract. Expand kernel enumerates all vertices that are neighbors of any vertex in the frontier of the current level. To construct an array of the frontier efficiently, this kernel uses different methods based on the degree of vertices. Contract kernel removes duplicated vertices and previously visited vertices from the results of the expand kernel. This kernel uses visitation status bitmap, label data and some heuristic techniques to perform this task efficiently.

The original implementation of the two-phase method does not correctly maintain the visitation status bitmap to avoid atomic operations, but the proposed top-down BFS implementation uses an atomic operation to update the visitation status bitmap because efficient bottom-up BFS implementation requires a precise visitation status bitmap. Therefore, the proposed top-down BFS implementation is inefficient compared to the original two-phase implementation. Counting the number of vertices and calculating the sum of out-degrees of vertices in the frontier are needed in order to determine an approach for processing the next level. We implemented an additional kernel for the purpose of calculation.

3.3 Bottom-Up BFS

We implemented a new kernel for bottom-up traversal on a GPU. We describe this algorithm in Fig. 3. The kernel consists of four procedures.

shared prefix_scan[block_size + 1], scratch[SCRATCH_SIZE]
global_id ← block_id × block_size + thread_id
unvisited ← **not** visited[global_id]
popcnt ← population_count(unvisited)
prefix_scan ← cta_prefix_scan(popcnt)
count ← prefix_scan[block_size]
modified_vis ← 0, p ← 0, rp ← 0
while p < count
  // *Generate an Array of Unvisited Vertices*
  s_offset ← prefix_scan[thread_id] + rp − p, s_begin ← s_offset
  while rp < popcnt **and** s_offset < SCRATCH_SIZE
    shift ← 31 − count_leading_zeros(unvisited)
    scratch[s_offset] ← (global_id << 5) + shift
    unvisited ← unvisited **xor** (1 << shift)
    rp ← rp + 1, s_offset ← s_offset + 1
  end while
  syncthreads()
  remainder ← min(count − p, SCRATCH_SIZE)
  // *Check the Visitation Status of Neighbors of Unvisited Vertices*
  i ← thread_id
  while i < remainder
    v ← scratch[i], u ← 0
    cur ← transposed_rows[v], end ← transposed_rows[v + 1]
    while cur < end
      u ← transposed_colind[cur]
      if texture_fetch(tex_visited, u >> 3) **and** (1 << (u **and** 7)) ≠ 0 **then**
        break
      end if
      cur ← cur + 1
    end while
    // *Update Label and Visitation Status*
    scratch[i] ← 0
    if cur < end **then**
      scratch[i] ← (1 << (v **and** 31))
      label[v] ← u
    end if
    i ← i + block_size
  end while
  p ← p + SCRATCH_SIZE
  syncthreads()
  // *Gather the Updated Visitation Status*
  for i ∈ [s_begin, s_offset)
    modified_bits ← modified_bits **or** scratch[i]
  end for
  synthreads()
end while
next_vis[global_id] ← modified_bits

Fig. 3. Bottom-up BFS on a GPU

Generate an Array of Unvisited Vertices: First, each thread reads 32 bits from the bitmap denoting the visitation status on the global memory. Next, each thread constructs an array of unvisited vertices on shared memory from the bitset that was read. If there are too many unvisited vertices to write to shared memory, this procedure writes as many unvisited vertices as possible and writes the remaining unvisited vertices after execution of the following procedure.

Check the Visitation Status of Neighbors of Unvisited Vertices: Each thread picks an unvisited vertex from the array that is constructed in the previous procedure, and the visitation status of the neighbors of the selected vertex is checked. The selected vertex will be contained in the next frontier if any of the neighbors has already been visited.

Update Label and Visitation Status: When a thread finds a visited vertex among the neighbors of a selected vertex, the label is updated immediately by this thread, but the visitation status is tentatively written to shared memory in order to avoid atomic operation to global memory. The temporary visitation status will be written into global memory by the next procedure.

Gather the Updated Visitation Status: Each thread collects the new visitation status corresponding to vertices that are assigned in the first procedure. The 32-bit-width partial visitation bitmap is computed from the collected data and written to global memory.

3.4   Optimizations for Bottom-Up BFS

Arranging the Adjacency Matrix: The loop that checks the visitation status of neighbors can be aborted immediately when an already visited vertex is found. Therefore, checking the visitation status of vertices that have a high probability of being visited in the early part of this loop improves the traversal performance. Since the level of vertices that have large in-degree is often small, the proposed implementation checks the visitation status in descending order of in-degree.

Remove Unreachable Vertices: With the exception of the root vertex, none of the vertices can be visited when the in-degree of the vertex is 0. It is wasteful to assign threads to check their neighbors. This reduces the number of wasteful tasks by eliminating vertices that are unreachable before generating the array of unvisited vertices.

Using the Texture Cache: Checking the visitation status of neighboring vertices results in significant random accessing of the global memory. The performance of this memory accessing is improved by using cache memory. The same bitmap is also accessed by generating an array of unvisited vertices. However, the present implementation does not use the texture cache for this task, because this may result in cache pollution and may decrease the random access performance. Moreover, using cache memory for this task provides little benefit because this accessing always coalesces. Therefore, the proposed implementation does not use a cached access path for this task to improve the overall performance.

Reducing the Use of Shared Memory: The procedures presented herein use shared memory to store the unvisited vertices array and the updated visitation status. If shared memory is allocated separately for each purpose, the shared memory usage becomes large, which causes a decrease in occupancy. The shared memory usage can be reduced by eliminating unnecessary information from an array of an unvisited vertex. Since the procedure for modifying the visitation status bitmap does not use the upper bits of the vertex index, the use of arrays on shared memory for these purposes can be reduced by merging the lower bits of the vertex index and the visitation status.

3.5   Switching Between Two Approaches

The proposed implementation selects an approach for processing each level heuristically. The detail of this method is described in Section 2. This implementation uses $\alpha = 48$ and $\beta = 20$ as tuning parameters.

Top-down BFS uses an array to represent a set of vertices, whereas bottom-up BFS uses a bitmap to represent a set of vertices. Since these two approaches use different representation formats, a conversion is required for approach switching. If the visitation status bitmap is updated correctly, no conversion is required when switching from top-down BFS to bottom-up BFS. However, conversion from a bitmap to an array is required when switching from bottom-up BFS to top-down BFS. The proposed implementation uses population count instruction and prefix scan to convert from a bitmap to an array.

4   Multi-node Algorithm

The proposed hybrid BFS implementation for GPU clusters is based on the hybrid BFS algorithm proposed by Beamer et al. [4] for a distributed memory system. We modified the proposed implementation in order to use GPUs for computation. In each computation kernel, differences between the algorithm for a single GPU and the algorithm for GPU clusters are small. We added a reordering kernel and a format conversion kernel to simplify communication. In the proposed implementation, sending from device memory and receiving to device memory occurs as MPI communication. We use CUDA extensions of MVAPICH2 to overlap copying over PCI Express and MPI communication.

4.1   Top-Down BFS

Since the result of our top-down BFS kernel is represented as an array of vertices, sequences for communication can be constructed by generating sequences of their parents. Data that will be sent to the same process must be consecutive in memory in order to achieve efficient communication. However, the results of the top-down BFS kernel are unordered. Therefore, these data must be sorted according to the destination process number.

Table 1. Suite of benchmark graphs

Benchmark	Reference	Benchmark	Reference
packing-500x100x100-b050	[7] [9]	wikipedia-20070206	[7]
com-YouTube	[8]	com-LiveJournal	[8]
soc-Pokec	[8]	wiki-Talk	[8]
random.1Mv.64Me	[6]	rmat.1Mv.64Me	[6]
kron_g500-logn20	[7] [9]		

4.2 Bottom-Up BFS

Since the results of the proposed bottom-up BFS kernel are represented as a bitset, a kernel to convert from a bitset to an array is required in order to construct sequences for communication. We implemented a new kernel for this conversion that consists of an atomic add operation and conversion in a single thread block. The procedure for conversion in a single thread block is similar to the procedure for generating an array of unvisited vertices in the bottom-up BFS kernel. The visitation status bitmap is also sent by MPI communication in bottom-up BFS. No additional processing to send the visitation status bitmap is required because the visitation status bitmap is the same bitmap that is used for computation.

5 Evaluation

5.1 Single-GPU Algorithm

We evaluated the proposed single-GPU implementation by graphs listed in Table 1. These graphs are generated by GTGraph [6] or selected from the University of Florida Sparse Matrix Collection [7] and the Stanford Large Network Dataset Collection [8]. This dataset does not contain a graph that can be traversed without the use of bottom-up BFS when using the proposed implementation. We used NVIDIA Tesla M2050 for evaluation and evaluated the performance of Merrill's implementation [10] for comparison. Merrill's implementation consists only of an algorithm corresponding to top-down approach. Therefore, the most important difference between it and the proposed implementation is whether to use the bottom-up BFS.

The performance of the traversal is measured by building a BFS tree from randomly selected vertices and calculate the performance in TEPS (traversed edges per second) 64 times. The overall performance of the traversal is the median value of each measured performance. Copying from device memory to host memory is performed in order to verify the results after each construction, but the time required for this task is not included in the build time.

The overall performance for traversing each graph is shown in Fig. 4(a). The proposed implementation achieves a maximum speedup of 29x, as compared to Merrill's implementation, but does not work efficiently for some graphs. We show the ratio of the computation time of top-down BFS to the computation

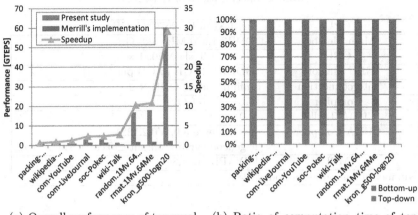

(a) Overall performance of traversal   (b) Ratio of computation time of top-down BFS and bottom-up BFS

Fig. 4. Performance characteristics of the single GPU implmentation

time of bottom-up BFS in Fig. 4(b), which indicates that the time required for top-down BFS increases when the efficiency of the proposed implementation decreases. As mentioned in Subsection 3.2, the proposed implementation of top-down BFS cannot traverse more efficiently than Merrill's implementation. This is one possible cause of the observed relative performance degradation. On the other hand, the proposed implementation works efficiently when it uses bottom-up BFS appropriately. This results shows hybrid BFS is effective for improving graph traversal performance on GPUs.

5.2   Multi-node Algorithm

We used the Graph500 benchmark to evaluate the multi-node implementation and evaluated the proposed implementation on the HA-PACS cluster. The specifications of HA-PACS are described in Table 2. Each node of HA-PACS has two CPUs and four GPUs. Each MPI process is assigned four CPU cores and one GPU, and each computation node is assigned four MPI processes. The problem scale is determined such that the number of vertices is equal to $2^{21} \times$ the number of MPI processes. We also measured the performance of the proposed hybrid BFS implementation that does not use GPUs as the target of comparison.

The overall performance of each implementation is described in Fig. 5(a). The results indicate that GPUs can accelerate the hybrid BFS. When running BFS on a multi-node system, MPI communication often takes a great deal of time. The time required for computation and communication of each implementation is shown in Fig. 5(b). This result indicates that the computation time is shortened by using GPUs, but the communication time become longer than the CPU implementation time. This difference in the communication time is thought to be due to the overhead of copying between host memory and device memory.

Table 2. Specifications of HA-PACS

CPU	Intel Xeon E5-2670 2.6 GHz × 2
Main Memory	DDR3 1,600 MHz 128 GB
GPU	NVIDIA Tesla M2090 × 4
GPU Memory	GDDR5 24 GB (6 GB per GPU)
Interconnection	InfiniBand x4 QDR × 2
Compiler	GCC 4.4.5 (-O2)
CUDA Toolkit	5.0
CUDA Compiler	nvcc release 5.0, V0.2.1221
	(-gencode arch=compute_20,code=sm_20 -O2)
MPI	MVAPICH2 1.8
Number of computation nodes	268

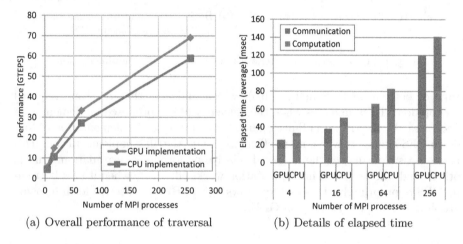

(a) Overall performance of traversal   (b) Details of elapsed time

Fig. 5. Performance characteristics of multi node implmentations

6 Related Research

On multicore systems, Agarwal et al. [3] demonstrated that using a bitmap to manage the visitation status is effective for achieving higher performance. In the GPU-based system, Harish and Narayanan [11] introduced the first implementation of BFS on a GPU. Merrill et al. [5] proposed an efficient algorithm for graph traversal on GPUs.

On the cluster system, the communication time is often longer than the computation time and often becomes a bottleneck. Satish et al. [12] presented an efficient compression algorithm and pipelined computation and communication in order to achieve good scalability. On the GPU cluster system, Bernaschi et al. [13] reported that accelerating GPU-GPU communication by APEnet+ is beneficial for BFS.

7   Conclusion

In the present paper, we presented a hybrid BFS algorithm that can improve the performance of BFS on GPU-based architecture. The proposed implementation achieves a speedup of approximately 29x compared to the existing BFS implementation for the GPU. However, the proposed implementation cannot work efficiently in some cases. Improvement of the proposed implementation so as to achieve efficient traversal in such cases will be investigated in the future.

Moreover, GPUs were demonstrated to be beneficial for traversing a graph by the hybrid BFS on a cluster system. Using GPUs requires additional time for communication but shortens the computation time to the extent that the overall performance is improved. We have not yet considered communication in the proposed implementation. Improvement of communication (e.g., data compression and pipelining) is needed in order to achieve higher performance.

Acknowledgments. This research was partially supported by Core Research for Evolutional Science and Technology (CREST), Japan Science and Technology Agency (JST).

References

1. Brief Introduction of Graph 500, http://www.graph500.org/
2. Beamer, S., Asanović, K., Patterson, D.: Direction-Optimizing Breadth-First Search. In: Proc. International Conference on High Performance Computing, Networking, Storage and Analysis, SC 2012, No. 12 (2012)
3. Agarwal, V., Petrini, F., Pasetto, D., Bader, D.A.: Scalable Graph Exploration on Multicore Processors. In: Proc. 2010 ACM/IEEE International Conference for High Performance Computing, Networking, Storage and Analysis, SC 2010, pp. 1–11 (2010)
4. Beamer, S., Buluç, A., Asanović, K., Patterson, D.A.: Distributed Memory Breadth-First Search Revisited: Enabling Bottom-Up Search. Technical Report UCB/EECS-2013-2, EECS Department, University of California, Berkeley (2013)
5. Merrill, D., Garland, M., Grimshaw, A.: Scalable GPU graph traversal. In: Proc. 17th ACM SIGPLAN Symposium on Principles and Practice of Parallel Programming (PPoPP 2012), pp. 117–128 (2012)
6. GTgraph: A suite of synthetic random graph generators, http://www.cse.psu.edu/~madduri/software/GTgraph/
7. The University of Florida Sparse Matrix Collection, http://www.cise.ufl.edu/research/sparse/matrices/
8. Stanford Large Network Dataset Collection, http://snap.stanford.edu/data/
9. 10th DIMACS Implementation Challenge, http://www.cc.gatech.edu/dimacs10/
10. back40computing - Fast and efficient software primitives for GPU computing - Google Project Hosting, http://code.google.com/p/back40computing/
11. Harish, P., Narayanan, P.J.: Accelerating Large Graph Algorithms on the GPU Using CUDA. In: Aluru, S., Parashar, M., Badrinath, R., Prasanna, V.K. (eds.) HiPC 2007. LNCS, vol. 4873, pp. 197–208. Springer, Heidelberg (2007)

12. Satish, N., Kim, C., Chhugani, J., Dubey, P.: Large-Scale Energy-Efficient Graph Traversal: A Path to Efficient Data-Intensive Supercomputing. In: Proc. International Conference on High Performance Computing, Networking, Storage and Analysis, SC 2012, No. 14 (2012)
13. Bernaschi, M., Bisson, M., Mastrostefano, E., Rossetti, D.: Breadth first search on APEnet+. In: Proc. 2012 SC Companion: High Performance Computing, Networking Storage and Analysis (SCC 2012), pp. 248–253 (2012)

Adaptive Resource Allocation for Reliable Performance in Heterogeneous Distributed Systems

Masnida Hussin, Azizol Abdullah, and Shamala K. Subramaniam

Department of Communication Technology and Networks,
Faculty of Computer Science and Information Technology,
University of Putra Malaysia, 43400 UPM Serdang, Selangor, Malaysia
{masnida,azizol,shamala}@upm.edu.my

Abstract. The rapid development of distributed systems has triggered the emergence of many new applications such as Cloud applications. Satisfaction on these systems in regards their services is an important indicator that reflect quality of IT resource management. In this paper, we address a reliability issue in the context of resource allocation that aims to improve performance of the distributed systems. We propose a heuristic scheduling by integrating different mapping and queuing strategies into allocation policy for suitably matching tasks and resources. Dynamic resource discovery and task classification are incorporated into the heuristic scheduling in pursuit of reliable decisions. Simulation experiments show that our approach achieves better response time and utilization compared to other heuristic approaches.

Keywords: Resource allocation, task-queue, reliable performance, distributed systems.

1 Introduction

The distributed systems coordinate resource sharing in dynamic environments and have been proven to be a platform of choice especially for many computationally intensive applications. While these systems providing a vast amount of computing power and communication capacity, their reliability are often hard to be guaranteed [1, 2]. Reliable performance of the distributed systems depends heavily on the quality of resource allocation [3-5]. The allocation approach in such systems required for handling service based workloads (i.e., web services) in highly efficient processing. Thus, it is necessary to have autonomous and highly dynamic resource allocation.

Specifically, our adaptive resource allocation approach is realized based on two different procedures. First, we determine available resources based on processing capacity that can satisfy the task demands. Then, we perform dynamic task queue by considerately classifying the users' tasks into different queues. A task consolidation is incorporated into the queuing process to dynamically reschedule the task for minimizing waiting time. This work evaluates in simulations with varying processing capacity and a diverse set of tasks. The results obtained from our comparative evaluation study clearly show that our resource allocation increases utilization with better response time while meeting "at-scale" processing requirements.

J. Kołodziej et al. (Eds.): ICA3PP 2013, Part II, LNCS 8286, pp. 51–58, 2013.
© Springer International Publishing Switzerland 2013

The reminder of this paper is organized as follows. A review of related work is presented in Section 2. In Section 3, we described the models used in the paper. Our strategy dealing with heterogeneous environment is presented in Section 4. Section 5 details our resource allocation policy. Experimental settings and results are presented in Section 6. Finally, conclusions are made in Section 7.

2   Related Work

The reliability has become an important issue in distributed processing for past several years. In particular, it is hard to guarantee high-reliability in distributed systems when there is involvement of unpredictable changes in processing capacity. Due to uncertainties in the resource availability and capacity, resource management mechanisms such as resource provisioning, rescheduling, migration have been extensively studied in the literature (e.g. [3, 4, 6, 7]). Their heuristic scheduling algorithms concern in assigning tasks onto computing resources according to a specified processing weight or availability such that system performance is maximized. From the authors in [3, 7] also highlighted that strategy for effective scheduling with low processing overhead is needed in the large-scale distributed systems.

The need for adaptive model in resource allocation policies are highlighted in several researchers works. The adaptive model proposed in [5] integrates two types of allocation policies are; immediate allocation with blocking and with waiting. The paper was able to minimize queue waiting times. The resource allocation policy proposed in [8] uses network delay time (i.e., short and long delay) for selecting the right resource. While their resource allocation approaches focus merely on resource capability in scheduling, our heuristic scheduling policy deals with both resources and users' tasks characteristics.

3   The Models

In this section, we describe the application and system models used in our study.

3.1   Application Model

Users' tasks considered are independent from each other (i.e. no inter-job communication or dependencies) and their arrival time at a scheduler is not known in advance. Two parameters that used to value each task are $T_i = \{w_i, status_i\}$; where w_i is the weight of tasks and $status_i$ is used by the scheduler to indicate type of task, respectively. For a given task T_i, the weight w_i is computed by the size of tasks specified by millions of instructions (MI) divided by processing capacity of a referred (the slowest) processing node. We classify two different types of tasks (i.e., $status_i$) that based on their processing requirements: special-task ($task_{ST}$) and regular-task ($task_{RT}$). The task execution time varies according to the performance of the resource on which the task is being processed. The completion time of a task i on a particular resource r denote the elapsed time from the time the task arrives into the scheduler until it completes the execution entirely:

$$CT_{(i,r)} = (wait\_t + exe\_t) \tag{1}$$

where $wait\_t$ is the elapsed time between a task submission and the start of execution, and exe_t is actual execution time of task, respectively. We assume that the task's profile is available and can be provided by the user using job profiling, analytical models or historical information [9].

3.2   System Model

The target system used in this work consists of a number of resource sites that are loosely connected by a communication network (Figure 1); given as RS_r where $r = \{1, 2..., R\}$. We form centralized scheduler to handle tasks from system users and map them onto processing nodes. Each site has a set of heterogeneous resources/processing nodes that fully interconnected and composed of a different number of cores with homogenous processing speed.

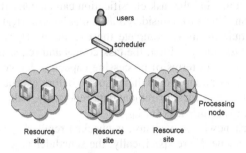

Fig. 1. The System Model

The performance of resource site affects system performance to a certain degree due to heterogeneous capacity. The processing capacity of resource r is defined as:

$$PC_r = \frac{\sum spd}{\sum p} + \left(\sum exe\_t / L\right) \tag{2}$$

where spd is relative speed of node, p is number of nodes in RS_r and L is the total number of tasks completed within some observation period, respectively. For a given nodes, its processing and availability fluctuated. The number of processing nodes in this study is assumed to be relatively less than the number of tasks to be processed. Therefore, the actual completion time of a task on a particular resource is difficult, if not impossible, to determine a prior. Hereafter, the terms resource and processing node are used interchangeably.

4   Dealing with Heterogeneity

One of the major challenges for reliable performance is the ever growing demand in processing requirement and variability in processing power that reside in distributed systems. This section begins by describing our resource discovery strategy, and then we present the formation of task classification.

4.1   Dynamic Discovery of Resource Availability

In information discovery procedure, resource availability is identified according to processing weight. This processing weight is calculated based on the processing capacity of a referred (the slowest) resource divided by number of processor of respective resource site. Then, the availability of resource r determines by comparing its average processing capacity and processing weight. The task assignment is realized when the processing capacity is satisfied (i.e., *available* = average PC_r > processing weight). The scheduler regularly checks and updates the values to maintain the accurate information of resource availability.

4.2   Task-Classification Formation

The promises of resource availability by itself cannot bring reliability to the system [2]. The scheduler then effectively scheduled users' tasks according to processing requirements. We assume that the task classification can be carried out by the scheduler prior to execution. The task considered as a *special-task* (t_{ST}) if it requires additional processing requirements to complete the execution. There are two different demands of *special-task* (task$_{ST}$). First, the task comes and requests to be executed in the most reliable resource in terms of processing capacity; denotes as task$_{ST/proc}$. The second type of demand is an input data that required before execution (task$_{ST/data}$). The data can be located in either local or remote data repository. Other than such requirements, the task is set to *regular-task* (task$_{RT}$).

The status of each newly arrived task is checked regularly in order to group the tasks into respective queue. More specifically, the scheduler tagged the status of *special-task* (task$_{ST}$) as "yes" (*status*$_i$ = *yes*) and "no" for *regular-task* (task$_{RT}$); that is proposed and used in [7].   The tasks are then queued by their submission time (i.e., first-come first serve or FCFS) in *RT-queue* or *ST-queue* (Figure 2).

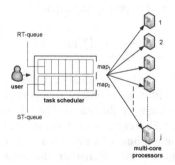

Fig. 2. Multi policies Task Scheduling

5   Multiple Queuing Policies for Dynamic Scheduling

Corresponding to two type of task queues, there are two kinds of scheduling policies i.e., *map$_1$* and *map$_2$* (Figure 2). The tasks at *RT-queue* scheduled based on a suitability/fitness value between resource r and task T_i as defined to be:

$$fit(r,i) = \frac{wait\_t}{PC_r} * w_i \tag{3}$$

where PC_r is the processing capacity (Eq. 2). A task is assigned to a processor that gives the highest suitability/fitness value fit_{max}. Meanwhile, two types of tasks in the *ST-queue* (i.e., task$_{ST/proc}$ and task$_{ST/data}$) are employed different mapping decision (i.e., map_2). The task$_{ST/proc}$ is assigned into the resource that gives the highest processing capacity and task$_{ST/data}$ randomly assigned to any available resources. For task$_{ST/data}$, in order to improve response time due to delay in data transfer time, task insertion (re)scheduling is carried out. The scheduled tasks are further inspected with respect to their expected data transfer rate dat_i for possible rescheduling. The (re)scheduling scheme allows the task to be inserted into the time slot between two consecutively scheduled tasks. The task with minimum transmission rate is scheduled first. This repeats until no further improvements in the schedule is possible.

6   Performance Evaluation

In this section, we study the performance of our resource allocation approach *Mul-policy* that is compared with three other main principles of traditional heuristic algorithms, which are *Fit-value*, *Max-max* and *Random-selection*. In *Fit-value*, the suitable resource for a particular task determined according to the highest fitness value fit_{max}. *Max-max* heuristic maps task to the resource, which gives the highest fitness value fit_{max} from its maximum list. *Fit-value* intentionally to solve the time constrained scheduling problem while *Max-max* concerning more to resource constrained scheduling. In *Random-selection*, tasks are randomly mapped to available resources.

Performance metrics used for the experiment are response time and utilization rate; given in Eq. 4 and Eq. 5, respectively.

$$response_{rate} = \sum \frac{CT_{(i,r)}}{T} \tag{4}$$

where $CT_{(i,r)}$ is defined in Eq. 1 and T is number of completed tasks.

$$utilization_{rate} = \frac{\sum exe\_t}{sumP} \tag{5}$$

where *sumP* is a total number of nodes in the system.

6.1   Experimental Settings

We have five to ten resource sites where in each of it contains a varying number of processors ranging from 4 to 10. The relative processing power (speed) of resource r is selected within the range of 1 and 7.5. Task inter-arrival times (*iat*) follow a Poisson distribution with a mean of five time units. For a given task T_i, the computational size is randomly generated from a uniform distribution ranging from 600 to 7200(MI) [23]. Estimated data transfer rate is selected randomly from the following set:

{0.01, 1.0, 3.5, 7.5, 12.5}. The inter-arrival time and data transfer time satisfy with the experiment without increasing a significant delay in task queue.

6.2   Results

Experimental results are presented in two different ways based on impact of mapping policy and task queuing on reliability.

Experiment 1: The impact of mapping policy on reliability
As shown in Figure 3, our approach *Mul-policy* outperformed others in terms of *response rate*. It also observes that *Fit-value* is comparable with *Mul-policy*. However, it indicates that *Mul-policy* works 40% better in the case of more tasks coming or being processed. This performance can be explained by the multiple mapping policies in *Mul-policy* that able to minimize waiting time although in heavy loaded situation. Figure 4 shows the utilization rate that is plotted against the number of tasks, respectively. *Mul-policy* obtains appealing utilization rate compared to three other techniques. The utilization rate in *Mul-policy* is improved greatly by about 60% on average. This indicates that prioritization of the system workload to meet the peak requirements sustains useful computing capability.

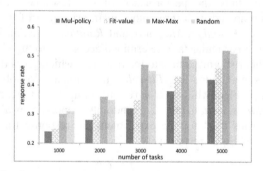

Fig. 3. Response rate with different scheduling approaches

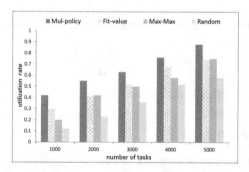

Fig. 4. Utilization rate with different scheduling approaches

Experiment 2: The impact of task queuing on reliability
We extend the analysis of *Mul-policy* corresponding to different settings in processing requirements (Table 1). This setting aims to analyze the effect of task queues in

handling varying requirements. It been set that Scenario A and B have opposite distribution of task type but each has similar distribution percentage for $task_{ST/proc}$ and $task_{ST/dat}$. Meanwhile, we set a different task distribution of special-task, $task_{ST}$ in Scenario C and D.

Table 1. Distribution of Two Different Types of Task

Scenario	Regular-task, $task_{RT}$ (%)	Special-task, $task_{ST}$ (%)	
		$task_{ST/proc}$(%)	$task_{ST/dat}$ (%)
A	60	20	20
B	40	30	30
C	50	40	10
D	50	10	40

From Figure 5, we can see that the benefit of adaptive queuing mechanism in heterogeneous system with better response rates. It demonstrates comparable results among each scenario that the differences by merely 3%. We also observed that the response rate of *Mul-policy* with Scenario A is better than Scenario B. The figure also shows that Scenario C is comparable with that in Scenario D. This is because the distributed of workload pattern in scenarios—considering the overall processing requirement relatively similar.

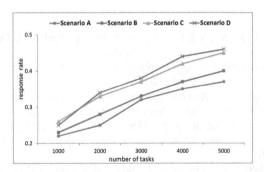

Fig. 5. Response rate of *Mul-policy* with heterogeneity in demands

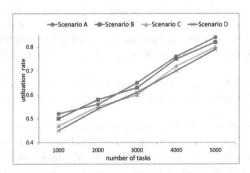

Fig. 6. Utilization rate of *Mul-policy* with heterogeneity in demands

The high resource utilization achieved using *Mul-policy* is another compelling strength (Figure 6) that reach more than 60% on average. The reason is that the tasks separated into two different queues (i.e., *RT-queue* and *ST-queue*) and simultaneously mapped to their suitable resources. Such scheduling leads to decrease resource idle time. Overall, the degree of task heterogeneity does not significantly hamper *Mul-policy* to maintain good performance.

7   Conclusion

The diverse nature of network devices/components and communication technologies greatly increases complexity in resource allocation. In this paper, we have effectively modeled adaptive scheduler that explicitly considers resource and task heterogeneity. The accurate information of both resources and tasks obtained through our discovery procedure (e.g., resource availability and task classification) plays an important role to effectively handle diversity in the system. Based on our extensive simulation results, the proposed allocation approach demonstrates robust decisions in the sense that minimum performance degradation regardless of different workload patterns. We also highlight that incorporated multiple task queues into scheduling policy yet significantly important for dependable computing in heterogeneous dynamic environments.

References

1. Raghavendra, C.S., Kumar, V.K.P., Hariri, S.: Reliability Analysis in Distributed Systems. IEEE Transaction on Computers 37, 352–358 (1988)
2. Dabrowski, C.: Reliability in Grid Computing System. Concurrency and Computation: Practice and Experience 21, 927–959 (2009)
3. Lee, Y.C., Zomaya, A.Y.: Rescheduling for reliable job completion with the support of clouds. Future Generation Computer Systems 26, 1192–1199 (2010)
4. Llorente, I., Moreno-Vozmediano, R., Montero, R.: Cloud Computing for On-Demand Grid Resource Provisioning. In: Advances in Parallel Computing, vol. 18, pp. 177–191. IOS Press (2009)
5. Hacker, T.J., Mahadik, K.: Flexible Resource Allocation for Reliable Virtual Cluster Computing Systems. Presented at the Proc. of 2011 International Conference for High Performance Computing, Networking, Storage and Analysis, Seattle, Washington (2011)
6. Hussin, M., Lee, Y.C., Zomaya, A.Y.: ADREA: A Framework for Adaptive Resource Allocation in Distributed Computing Systems. Presented at the 11th Int'l Conf. on Parallel and Distributed Computing, Applications and Technologies (PDCAT), Wuhan, China (2010)
7. Sonnek, J., Chandra, A., Weissman, J.B.: Adaptive Reputation-based Scheduling on Unreliable Distributed Infrastructures. IEEE Transaction on Parallel and Distributed Systems 18, 1551–1564 (2007)
8. Awano, Y., Kuribayashi, S.-I.: Proposed Joint Multiple Resource Allocation Method for Cloud Computing Services with Heterogeneous QoS. Presented at the The Third International Conference on Cloud Computing, GRIDs, and Virtualization, Nice, France (2012)
9. Hussin, M., Lee, Y.C., Zomaya, A.Y.: Reputation-Based Resource Allocation in Market-Oriented Distributed Systems. In: Xiang, Y., Cuzzocrea, A., Hobbs, M., Zhou, W. (eds.) ICA3PP 2011, Part I. LNCS, vol. 7016, pp. 443–452. Springer, Heidelberg (2011)

Adaptive Task Size Control on High Level Programming for GPU/CPU Work Sharing

Tetsuya Odajima[1], Taisuke Boku[1,2], Mitsuhisa Sato[1,2],
Toshihiro Hanawa[2], Yuetsu Kodama[1,2],
Raymond Namyst[3], Samuel Thibault[3], and Olivier Aumage[3]

[1] Graduate School of Systems and Information Engineering, University of Tsukuba
[2] Center for Computational Sciences, University of Tsukuba
[3] University of Bordeaux - LaBRI - INRIA Bordeaux Sud-Ouest

Abstract. On the work sharing among GPUs and CPU cores on GPU equipped clusters, it is a critical issue to keep load balance among these heterogeneous computing resources. We have been developing a runtime system for this problem on PGAS language named XcalableMP-dev/StarPU [1]. Through the development, we found the necessity of adaptive load balancing for GPU/CPU work sharing to achieve the best performance for various application codes.

In this paper, we enhance our language system XcalableMP-dev/StarPU to add a new feature which can control the task size to be assigned to these heterogeneous resources dynamically during application execution. As a result of performance evaluation on several benchmarks, we confirmed the proposed feature correctly works and the performance with heterogeneous work sharing provides up to about 40% higher performance than GPU-only utilization even for relatively small size of problems.

1 Introduction

While GPU clusters with high performance GPUs provide cost effective HPC environment, still there is a serious problem on programming for users who are forced to describe complicated codes with mixed paradigm on parallel processing and GPU computing. Recent programming codes on a modern PC cluster commonly described in a hybrid manner to combine MPI and OpenMP to exploit the parallelism of resources effectively. In addition on GPU clusters, the programmers additionally have to describe GPU manipulation. As a result, large scale parallel GPU programming on GPU clusters becomes the toughest work on parallel processing which easily causes numerous coding errors and reduces code productivity.

We have been developing a language named XcalableMP (hereinafter called XMP for short)[2], which is a directive-based PGAS (Partitioned Global Address Space) language for parallel systems with distributed memory architecture. In addition to the original XMP specification, we also proposed an extension of XMP for accelerating device programming environments such as CUDA or OpenCL, named XcalableMP-dev [3] (hereinafter called XMP-dev for short),

J. Kołodziej et al. (Eds.): ICA3PP 2013, Part II, LNCS 8286, pp. 59–68, 2013.
© Springer International Publishing Switzerland 2013

which employs the concept of XMP by supporting a feature to off-load the computation of a specified section (loop) to the target accelerating devices.

In our previous work [1], we utilized both GPU and CPU resources on each node for work sharing of the loop execution within the context of the XMP-dev language. For this purpose, we apply StarPU [4] for sub-task management and scheduling where a loop execution is divided into a number of sub-tasks for multiple GPUs and CPU cores on each computation node. Based on this concept, we implemented XcalableMP-dev/StarPU (hereinafter called XMP-dev/StarPU for short) which enables the loop-level work sharing among CPU cores and GPU on each computation node while the framework of XMP. In some cases, we confirmed that this new feature improves the performance of GPU clusters with additional power by CPU cores rather than using GPU only, with very simple and easy programming for high productivity. In many cases, however, the performance gain with GPU/CPU work sharing is not enough as estimated. The basic problem is how to decide the task size to be assigned to CPU cores and GPUs which has different characteristics on the performance.

In this paper, to solve this problem, we propose a new framework to control the task size to be dispatched to heterogeneous devices (CPU cores and GPUs) individually and dynamically. In this method, we can keep the execution time on each device as almost the same by dispatching different size of tasks to them even with a limited but moderate number of tasks according to the problem size.

2   XcalableMP, XcalableMP-dev and StarPU

2.1   Overview of XcalableMP (XMP)

XMP [5] is a PGAS language for describing large-scale scientific code on parallel systems with distributed memory architecture. For simplification for easy understanding, XMP is a directive-based parallelizing language with grammar similar to that of OpenMP. And its concept came from HPF [6] for global array distribution and work sharing on loop construction. It is possible to parallelize the target code with just a few changes on the original serial code, thus the programming effort can be significantly reduced compared with many additional lines in MPI programming.

2.2   XcalableMP-dev (XMP-dev)

In addition to XMP directives (please refer [5] in detail) which enable data/task parallelization between nodes in a distributed memory system, XMP-dev directives (please refer [3] in detail) enable further data/task parallelization between one or more acceleration devices on each node under the concept of off-loading the computation to them.

Figure 1 shows an example of XMP-dev code. When a code is written in XMP-dev, XMP directives describe the distribution of data among. On each

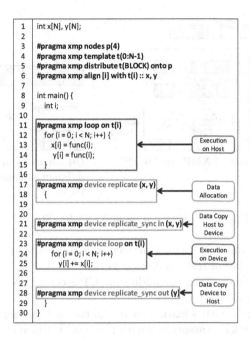

Fig. 1. An example code segment of XMP-dev

node, with XMP-dev directives (starting with "#pragma xmp device"), the user can specify the data to be allocated on GPU device, data movement between CPU and GPU, and computation offloading to GPU an shown in Figure 1. This is a large advantage for highly productive coding compared with complicated orthogonal programming with MPI and CUDA mixture, and an incremental code enhancement is possible for users as like as OpenMP.

2.3 StarPU

In this subsection, we briefly describe the concept and features of StarPU. For more details of the StarPU system, please refer [4].

StarPU is a run-time system that allocates and dispatches a collection of computations as a task to any computation resource and schedules the task execution dynamically. The target computation resources include multicore CPUs and GPUs, where each task is dispatched to a core of the multicore CPUs or to GPU device(s).

Although StarPU manages the task execution on both CPU cores and GPUs simultaneously, it is a critical issue how to decide the task size for GPUs and CPU cores to achieve high performance. The performance of recent CPUs has been increased to several hundreds of GFLOPS. However, there is still a big difference in the factor of ten between the performance of single CPU core and GPU. When there is a large number of tasks generated from a large scale data, tens or more times of tasks can be allocated to GPU device while CPU cores are

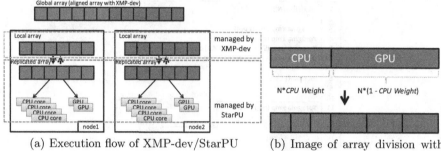

(a) Execution flow of XMP-dev/StarPU

(b) Image of array division with different amount for GPU and CPU

Fig. 2. Implementation of XMP-dev/StarPU

processing small number of them. However, it is impossible to keep the load of them when the number of tasks is limited for a small size problem, and it causes a serious situation where even the additional CPU cores become the bottleneck in total execution time.

StarPU is equipped with a feature to anneal the task size automatically when the task size (the data size associated with the task) is tuned step-by-step during the code execution in the iteration of time step simulation. However, this feature works only for cases with simple iterations of code, and it is difficult to apply this feature to a complicated execution phase of general codes. It is especially difficult when a computation node is equipped with multiple GPU devices and the performance gap between the CPU part and the GPU part is really large.

3 Dynamic Load Balancing on XMP-dev/StarPU

Our previous implementation without dynamic load balancing feature among GPUs and CPU cores are described in [1] in detail. In this section, we describe the essence of the work to understand our new feature, then introduce a dynamic load balancing feature on XMP-dev/StarPU.

3.1 Previous Implementation Strategy and Its Performance

To implement the feature of work sharing among GPUs and CPU cores for loop execution, we modified the XMP-dev compiler and the run-time system to utilize StarPU as the task scheduler and execution engine. Since the original XMP-dev/CUDA compiler is ready for data distribution and parallel execution management of basic XMP features for GPU clusters, we run StarPU on each node in the single node mode for simplicity. The XMP-dev/CUDA compiler generates a code with CUDA functions on each node, and the data distribution and synchronization among multiple nodes are performed by MPI.

Figure 2(a) shows the execution flow of XMP-dev/StarPU. The basic strategy for implementation of XMP-dev/StarPU is as follows.

- XMP-dev compiler aligns the distributed Global array to Local array for each node.
- Runtime system replicates Local array as another one named Replicated array. Local array is for communication with MPI in the context of XMP, and Replicated array is a target of task assignment and management by StarPU.
- Replicated array is allocated to StarPU's data pool and divided to a number of tasks which has the same size. Then, tasks are allocated to each device by the StarPU scheduler.
- The programmer explicitly describes the synchronization on data between Local array and Replicated array accordingly in XMP-dev syntax.

In [1], we observed that the relative performance gain by XMP-dev/StarPU to XMP-dev/CUDA is very low in many cases, at a performance with just around 45% of original XMP-dev/CUDA. This is because the task size is always constant where Replicated array on the node is always divided equally over all tasks. But the performance gap among GPU and CPU core is so large. Therefore, much larger number of tasks should be assigned to GPU than CPU core to keep the execution time balance among all computation resources. In many cases, however, there is a limit of the number of total tasks because too small size of tasks cannot be effectively executed by GPU to hide the task invocation cost including data movement between CPU and GPU. As a result, we cannot create an appropriate number of tasks to keep a good load balance between these heterogeneous resources and the efficiency of GPU execution, in a moderate size of problem. Thus, we concluded the essential problem of low performance in this work is the task size control on GPUs and CPU cores.

3.2 Improvement of XMP-dev/StarPU with Dynamic Load Balancing Feature

Previous XMP-dev/StarPU divides Replicated arrays with fixed task size whereas the performance gain by additional CPU cores to GPUs is not enough due to performance imbalance on different type of resources. We found the problem in [1] and performed a preliminary study to observe the performance behavior when the task size to be assigned CPU cores and GPUs differ to keep a good load balance. According to this study, we propose and implement a new feature for dynamic load balancing in this paper.

The key of task size control is the performance gap between CPU and GPU. In heterogeneous hybrid work sharing, CPU and GPU execution time for each task should be close or in the same order at least. On the other hand, it is required to allocate a large size of task to GPU since it has to tolerate a data transfer overhead and have a large degree of parallelism to utilize a number of cores inside the device. The best solution for this problem is to assign well balanced task size for all GPU and CPU cores in each of Replicated array to be processed in a loop.

As the answer to this problem, we introduce a parameter to decide the balance of working set size for GPU and CPU on loop work sharing, named "CPU Weight". To simplify the control of load balance on resources, we decided to apply this value to divide a Replicated array into two parts which are processed by GPUs and CPU cores before StarPU run-time system makes further subdivision of each part of array. Figure 2(b) shows the image of dividing a Replicated array where the blue part is a relatively small portion for CPU cores while the red part is a large portion for GPUs, for the total number of array elements N. This array corresponds to the Replicated array in Figure 2(a). These two parts are further divided by StarPU to smaller size of tasks. By making the data structure appropriately to bind the task data portion and computing resource in StarPU framework, we can control the task dispatch for sub-divided data portion in each side (blue or red) so as to be correctly assigned to CPU core or GPU, respectively. In Figure 2(b) for example, StarPU divides each array into three parts. In this way, we can allocate different size of tasks to heterogeneous resources to keep the load balance controlled by CPU Weight.

Since it is difficult to set the value of CPU Weight automatically by the system, we design the system where this value is decided and set by the user explicitly in the program code. It is described by new pragma "reset_weight" as "#pragma xmp device reset_weight (cpu_weight)". Here, cpu_weight provides the CPU Weight to be applied after this point until it is reset again. The user can reset CPU Weight anywhere before entering a loop construction. There are several use cases of this feature. A user may decide to set the CPU Weight statically according to his knowledge on program behavior, or he can adaptively apply it based on the program execution behavior with any hint. Since the CPU Weight is applied to divide a Replicated array linearly into just two parts for GPU and CPU as shown in Figure 2(b), it is still difficult to find the best value of it to keep perfect load balance. One of the effective ways is to find it based on dynamic profiling of execution time by GPU and CPU. Actually, it is possible to anneal the CPU Weight during multiple time steps for most of simulation codes with time development scheme.

There is an idea to imply such an adaptive optimization of CPU Weight into the run-time system to hide it from user's view, however, we think it is very sensitive parameter to role the entire load balance and it is better to pass its control to users for various applications. For example, the user can even keep several set of CPU Weight according to different loop body, and switch them to describe the "reset_weight" pragma before entering to the different loop.

4   Performance Evaluation

We use a massively GPU cluster HA-PACS in University of Tsukuba for performance evaluation. The node specification is shown below. The CPU is Intel Xeon E5-2670 2.6 GHz (8 cores * 2 sockets) with Sandy Bridge architecture, and the GPU is NVIDIA Tesla M2090 (4 GPUs/node) with Fermi architecture. All nodes are connected with dual rails of InfiniBand QDR x4 by Fat-Tree topology with full-bisection bandwidth. In this evaluation, we use just two nodes because our purpose is to observe the behavior of adaptive load balance on each node for parallel execution. Although each node has 16 CPU cores per node, the management of each GPU consumes one thread on a CPU core in StarPU. So the number of CPU cores is "16 − (Number of used GPUs)" per node.

We evaluate two benchmark codes: N-Body and MM (Matrix-Matrix Multiplication). Since the program runs on just two nodes, the communication time on MPI which is automatically generated by XMP-dev/StarPU compiler is negligible (under 1%) for both benchmarks. Thus, we evaluate the computation time on each node including data transfer overhead between CPU and GPUs, without caring MPI communication overhead.

The purpose of this evaluation is to confirm the function of dynamic load balancing based on CPU Weight works correctly and to show the potential of any dynamic load balancing algorithm by the user. Therefore, we introduce a very simple annealing algorithm to modify CPU Weight dynamically in the time step development of the simulation. In all case of evaluation, CPU Weight is changed according to the computation time of each CPU core and GPU for the outer-most loop iteration. For N-Body, the outer-most loop corresponds to the time step of physics simulation. For MM benchmark, we assume that some size of matrix-matrix multiplication such as DGEMM routine in BLAS (Gotoblas [7] for CPU kernel and MAGMA blas [8] for GPU) is executed repeatedly for larger computation. Therefore, the same size of matrix-matrix multiplication is repeated in MM and the computation time of one outer-most iteration is examined.

Based on rough estimation on sustained performance of up to four GPUs and 12 CPU cores in each node, we set the initial value of CPU Weight as 0.2. The policy to decide CPU Weight in the next time step is as follows.

$ratio = T_{CPU} / (T_{CPU} + T_{GPU})$;
if ($ratio > 0.5$) cpu_weight −= 0.01;
else cpu_weight += 0.01;

Here, T_{CPU} and T_{GPU} are the task execution time by CPU and GPU in last task execution, respectively. Those values can be directly extracted by our API function. This policy shows a very simple annealing algorithm to modify CPU Weight in step by step manner. Of course, the user can describe more sophisticated algorithm in any style.

Figures 3(a) and 3(b) show the time development of execution time (both on GPU and CPU) and CPU Weight on N-Body and MM, respectively. In both figures, blue and red bars show the execution time of one task on GPU and CPU core, respectively, and green line shows the CPU Weight applied on that time step. According to the CPU Weight adjustment policy, it is decreased constantly until the execution time of tasks on both types of resources becomes nearly equal in step by step, and finally CPU Weight keeps almost constant when they are balanced. In this way, we can achieve the best balance with adaptive control of load balance among GPUs and CPU cores where the user just provides a simple

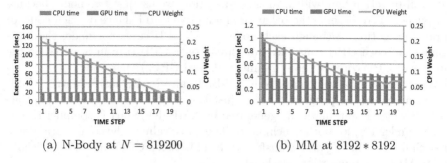

(a) N-Body at $N = 819200$ (b) MM at $8192 * 8192$

Fig. 3. Transitions of CPU Weight

notation of CPU Weight control as well as high-level PGAS programming style without any effort on describing MPI or CUDA code.

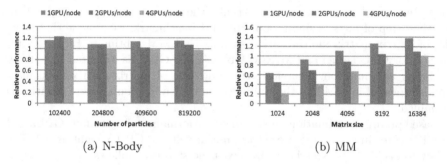

(a) N-Body   (b) MM

Fig. 4. Execution time of last time step and CPU Weight

Finally, we show the total performance gain by GPU/CPU work sharing driven by our new system compared with the performance by GPU-only. Figures 4(a) and 4(b) show the relative performance to the execution with GPU-only for various cases, on N-Body and MM benchmarks, respectively. In N-Body, GPU/CPU work sharing constantly improves the performance although the ratio of gain differs in the cases. The largest gain with up to 20% is achieved for the smallest size of problem. Basically, the performance gain is reduced when the number of GPUs increases where the usable CPU cores are decreased as mentioned before. N-body benchmark is suitable for GPU computing where the sustained performance gap between GPU and CPU is large and the effect of additional CPU cores is relatively small for larger problem size. On the other hand for MM benchmark, the performance gain by GPU/CPU work sharing increases according to the problem size where the maximum gain with approximately 40% is achieved for the largest problem size using single GPU. In MM, the task execution time for the matrix size is shorter than N-Body, and the overhead of fine task control cannot be covered by the performance of additional CPU cores.

When enough size of problem is provided, the contribution of CPU cores is great to raise the total performance of computation node.

Since current implementation of XMP-dev/StarPU compiler can handle just single dimension decomposition for multi-dimension arrays, the memory utilization and data movement efficiency is low. We think that this is one of the major factors for performance limitation. We are now developing multi-dimensional array decomposition to achieve higher performance in our system.

5   Related Works

There are several compilers for GPU accelerators, for example PGI Accelerator Compile [8] and HMPP Workbench [9]. These compilers provide a directive-based language for some accelerator including GPU. HMPP Workbench use CUDA or OpenCL for backend compiler. So, it is possible to program a hybrid work sharing with GPU and CPU, by inserting some directive in user code. However, the user has to describe additional MPI code with this complicated work sharing because the compiler just cares on a single node computation. Our XMP-dev/StarPU provides a sophisticated PGAS model programming for distributed memory system.

Also, there is a work [10] that applies StarPU to BLAS (Basic Liner Algebra Subprograms) library designed for NVIDIA GPU. This work performs work sharing with GPU and CPU on library level. In the performance aspect, this work can obtain about four times performance enhancement compared with only single GPU at Cholesky decomposition by using Intel Nehalem X5560 6 cores and 3 NVIDIA FX5800. In the XMP-dev/StarPU framework, users can write a work sharing program code more flexibly, as for the problem can be written in loop distribution basically, not just with a limited function of such a library-based approach. We need to compare the performance of our approach with native implementation of MAGMA in the same class of libraries.

As the original work by StarPU research team, the load balance issue was studied[11]. From user's view point, it is difficult to describe a code directly with StarPU for GPU/CPU work sharing. Our approach is based on high-level PGAS language (XMP-dev) using StarPU as underlying supporting system. We have not modified StarPU itself to apply to our system, and our system can work as user friendly interface for StarPU feature.

6   Concluding Remarks

In this paper, we proposed and implemented a programming environment to enable GPU/CPU work sharing on our PGAS language XMP-dev compiler and run-time system to be applied to multi-GPU equipped PC clusters. The proposed system allows users to keep the load balance among GPUs and CPU cores on each node for adaptive tuning of work sharing performance. We confirmed the effectiveness of this approach through several HPC benchmarks and achieved up to 40% of performance gain compared with original GPU-only solution.

To exploit this performance gain utilizing full computation resources on each node, the user just has to add several key directives to his original serial code to describe data distribution, loop distribution, GPU/CPU data movement and synchronization, without complicated combined paradigm of MPI and CUDA.

Our future work includes applying this system for wider variety of applications and larger systems, and also improves the performance based on multidimensional array dividing on global array handling.

Acknowledgment. This work is partially supported by a JST-ANR Joint Project entitled "Framework and Programming for Post Petascale Computing (FP3C)" and JST/CREST program entitled "Research and Development on Unified Environment of Accelerated Computing and Interconnection for Post-Petascale Era", in the research area of "Development of System Software Technologies for post-Peta Scale High Performance Computing".

References

1. Odajima, T., Boku, T., Hanawa, T., Lee, J., Sato, M.: GPU/CPU Work Sharing with Parallel Language XcalableMP-dev for Parallelized Accelerated Computing. In: Sixth International Workshop on Parallel Programming Models and Systems Software for High-End Computing (P2S2), pp. 97–106 (September 2012)
2. XcalableMP, http://www.xcalablemp.org/
3. Lee, J., MinhTuan, T., Odajima, T., Boku, T., Sato, M.: An Extension of XcalableMP PGAS Lanaguage for Multi-node GPU Clusters. In: HeteroPar 2011 (with EuroPar 2011), pp. 429–439 (2011)
4. StarPU, http://runtime.bordeaux.inria.fr/StarPU/
5. Lee, J., Sato, M.: Implementation and Performance Evaluation of XcalableMP: A Parallel Programming Language for Distributed Memory Systems. In: Third International Workshop on Parallel Programming Models and Systems Software for High-End Computing (P2S2), pp. 413–420 (September 2010)
6. High Performance Fortran Version 2.0, http://www.hpfpc.org/jahpf/spec/hpf-v20-j10.pdf
7. Texas Advanced Computing Center - GotoBlas2, http://www.tacc.utexas.edu/tacc-projects/gotoblas2
8. PGI Accelerator Compiler, http://www.softek.co.jp/SPG/Pgi/Accel/index.html
9. HMPP Workbench, http://www.caps-entreprise.com/hmpp.html
10. Agullo, E., Augonnet, C., Dongarra, J., Ltaief, H., Namyst, R., Thibault, S., Tomov, S.: Faster, Cheaper, Better - a Hybridization Methodology to Develop Linear Algebra Software for GPUs. In: GPU Computing Gems, vol. 2 (September 2010)
11. Augonnet, C., Thibault, S., Namyst, R.: StarPU: a Runtime System for Scheduling Tasks over Accelerator-Based Multicore Machines. Concurrency Computat.: Pract. Exper. (March 2010)

Robust Scheduling of Dynamic Real-Time Tasks with Low Overhead for Multi-Core Systems

Sangsoo Park

Department of Computer Science and Engineering
Ewha Womans University, Seoul, South Korea
sangsoo.park@ewha.ac.kr

Abstract. Real-time embedded systems often require the ability of adaptiveness and robustness, because their interactions with physical environments dynamically change workloads. Multi-core chips are becoming an ideal candidate hardware component for such environments, since each of them carries two or more cores on a single die, and has potential for providing execution parallelism as well as better performance at low cost. Parallelism, on the other hand, necessitates complex analysis of computation problems, such as task scheduling, while improving the realization of adaptive controls. Pfair is an optimal scheduling algorithm that can fully utilize all cores in the system, but it incurs excessive scheduling overheads which, in turn, diminishes its practicality in embedded systems. To mitigate this problem, the hybrid partitioned–global Pfair (HPGP) scheduler was proposed in previous work, which significantly reduces the number of task migrations and global scheduling points by performing global scheduling only when absolutely necessary, while still achieving full processor utilization. In this paper, the HPGP scheduler is further extended to support the adaptive controls to dynamic real-time task systems. Experimental evaluation results have shown that the extended HPGP can successfully handle dynamic task systems, thus making it suitable for embedded real-time systems.

1 Introduction

Traditional controls for embedded real-time systems focus on the behaviors of a single (sub)system under the worst-case condition, which can usually be realized by a carefully-designed *fixed* controller. However, modern embedded real-time systems often require *adaptive* controls which dynamically adjust the system configuration to deliver the specified/required performance in dynamically-changing physical environments. Such adjustments are typically achieved through control-mode changes, with different algorithms used in different modes, thus yielding different computations, communications, and performance. Adaptive controls require new software support that does not exist in today's fixed controllers. The adaptive controls for system-level functionality require collaboration among computation devices and software components running thereon.

In current practice, the lack of proper support in system software makes it difficult to implement adaptive controls in embedded real-time systems. As a result, managing dynamic workloads for adaptive controls is mainly achieved through over-design and

J. Kołodziej et al. (Eds.): ICA3PP 2013, Part II, LNCS 8286, pp. 69–76, 2013.
© Springer International Publishing Switzerland 2013

over-engineering, in which the system is designed with excessive resources and/or conservative parameters to accommodate the worst-case scenarios.

In view of its resource abundance and performance potential at low cost, a multi-core system is a promising hardware platform for implementing adaptive controls in embedded real-time systems. Carrying two or more cores on a single die, a multi-core system delivers better performance through execution parallelism with lower power consumption and reduced heat dissipation as compared to a time-sharing single-core system. However, as multi-core hardware is relatively new to embedded software developers, how to facilitate the design and maximize the benefit of multi-core systems is still un-/under-explored. One of the key research issue is to provide an effective scheduling algorithm that can better utilize the parallelism for time-critical control applications while simplifying their design.

Proportionate-fair (Pfair) scheduling[1] is an optimal algorithm among a very few algorithms for multi-core systems developed to date. However, Pfair cannot be directly applied to time-sensitive embedded systems because it incurs too much run-time overheads, such as excessive number of preemptions and system-wide locks at every scheduling point to support global scheduling.

A previous work on hybrid partitioned-global Pfair (HPGP) scheduler significantly reduces those overheads[2]. HPGP introduces a decision algorithm to choose an appropriate scheduling algorithm between low-overhead partitioned Pfair scheduler and global Pfair scheduler, based on a virtual clock. The decision algorithm calls for global scheduling only if it is absolutely necessary to minimize scheduling overheads.

In this paper, the HPGP algorithm is further extended to effectively support adaptive controls. Adaptive controls include efficient scheduling dynamic task systems such as (de)activation of tasks and adjusting invocation rate of tasks. Our evaluation results show that HPGP, like Pfair and its variants, allows dynamic changes of a task system, and at the same time, is more effective and efficient than Pfair, making it more suitable for the implementation of adaptive controls for many embedded real-time systems.

The rest of this paper is organized as follows. Section 2 provides the basic concepts of Pfair and HPGP and demonstrates how HPGP is extended to support adaptive controls in embedded real-time systems with highly dynamic task sets. Section 3 evaluates the performance of the extended HPGP scheduler, using a discrete-time simulator running on multi-core systems. Finally, we draw conclusions in Section 4.

2   The Extended Hybrid Partitioned–Global Pfair Scheduler

This section describes the previous work as well as the extension on hybrid partitioned–global Pfair (HPGP) scheduler. The system model with fixed task invocation periods is presented first, on which the design of HPGP is based and then extended to include dynamic tasks for adaptive controls.

2.1   System Model

The system under consideration for HPGP consists of N tasks running on an M-core system. All cores are assumed to have identical CPUs with synchronized clocks. Each core behaves as a single processor and can run at most one task at any given time. Tasks are assumed to be periodic, and their execution is synchronized with periodic timer ticks. To execute a task, the CPU time is allocated in a small quantum where a time quantum t represents the time interval $[t, t + 1)$.

A periodic task T is modeled as $T =< T_p, T_e >$, where T_p is the invocation period, and T_e its standalone execution time on a core. Both T_p and T_e are represented as integer multiples of the time quantum. Each task is released at the beginning of its invocation period, and must be completed within its period T_p. While tasks can be executed in parallel on different cores, there is no parallelism within a single task. Given a task T, its weight w_T is defined as $w_T = \frac{T_e}{T_p}$. A multi-core system utilization U is defined as $U = \sum^N w_T$.

A task can be divided further into a sequence of subtasks, T_i, each of which is assigned a time quantum t for execution. A subtask T_i can then be modeled as a 2-tuple $T_i =< r(T_i), d(T_i) >$, where $r(T_i)$ and $d(T_i)$ are the pseudo-release time and pseudo-deadline of T_i, respectively. Since subtasks execute in a strict sequence and T_i completes within T's period T_p, there is at most one instance of T_i running at a given time. So, all T_i's share the same period T_p, and each T_i consumes one time quantum.

The HPGP scheduler assumes the existence of both *partitioned* and *global* schedulers, which use two distinct approaches to scheduling real-time tasks on multi-core systems. A partitioned scheduler runs on each core and manages, in isolation from other cores, the execution of the allocated tasks, as the tasks arrive (or are initiated). Under this scheduler, no task migration occurs once it is assigned to a core. A global scheduler, on the other hand, dynamically determines which cores to execute which tasks, and migrates tasks from one core to another, if needed. It is also shown that an optimal scheduling algorithm can be derived using the global scheduler, such as Pfair, to achieve better processor utilization, with the schedulability condition $U \leq M$, than the partitioned scheduler [3,4].

HPGP is based on the modification and extension of Pfair which performs global scheduling using the subtasks of each task. Given an M-core system and a set of tasks in a global task queue, Pfair chooses M or fewer pseudo-released subtasks to execute at every scheduling point — i.e., the beginning of a time quantum — with each core running no more than one subtask. All chosen subtasks must belong to a set of ready tasks. The subtasks are chosen for execution according to the weights of the ready tasks, called *Pfairness*, each of which is represented by the utilization of the task that contains the chosen subtasks. Such a weight indicates the rate at which the corresponding task must be scheduled.

To achieve Pfairness, Pfair introduces the concept of scheduling error. For any given task, the scheduling error is defined as the lag of task T:

$$lag(T, t) = t \cdot w_T - S(T, t)$$

where $S(T, t)$ is the total time quanta for execution of T during the time interval $[0, t)$. Given the scheduling error $lag(T, t)$, Pfairness can be specified as $|lag(T, t)| < 1$. Pfair achieves Pfairness by running the scheduling algorithm at every time quantum, which guarantees the scheduling error caused by an improper selection of some subtask to be bounded by one time quantum for each task at any time.

As the Pfair scheduler is invoked at every time quantum, task migrations may occur very often, at every time quantum in the worst case, and thus incur high overhead. For its global scheduling, the Pfair scheduler requires tasks to synchronize their execution on all cores. During the synchronization, all the cores with their data for scheduling tasks must be locked, which may incur significant overhead. Moreover, the cores need to access a large amount of data not residing in their local cache during the task scheduling, which consequently incurs memory performance penalty.

2.2   The HPGP Scheduler

The HPGP scheduler is mainly designed to reduce the Pfair's overheads, particularly for locking cores at every time quantum and for frequent task migrations. To achieve this, we develop a light-weighted decision algorithm that runs at every time quantum to determine if the global scheduler should be invoked. With the decision algorithm, the HPGP scheduler performs global scheduling only when absolutely necessary, thus triggering only the partitioned scheduler on each core for most of the time.

The scheduler starts by distributing N tasks to M cores in a predefined order of core IDs. Each core then runs the decision algorithm to check the schedulability of the allocated tasks. To check the schedulability of a core, the decision algorithm uses the weight of $Core_i$, which is defined as its utilization, $w_{Core_i} = \sum_{T_j \in Core_i} w_{T_j}$ where T_j is a pseudo-released subtask on $Core_i$. If $w_{Core_i} \leq 1$, $Core_i$ is under-utilized for current time quantum, and all tasks on $Core_i$ are schedulable by Pfair with $M = 1$. w_{Core_i} can then be used to determine Pfairness of the task set. If $w_{Core_i} > 1$, $Core_i$ is overloaded for current time quantum and the tasks on $Core_i$ may not be schedulable. To make $Core_i$ schedulable in the case of $w_{Core_i} > 1$, $Core_i$ needs to operate w_{Core_i} times faster. Based on this, we introduce a weight-scaled virtual clock running w_{Core_i} times faster than the actual clock, to determine Pfairness.

To use Pfairness in the decision algorithm when checking the schedulablity of $Core_i$, we need to modify the lag of task T on $Core_i$ to include both under-utilized and over-loaded cases as follows:

$$lag(T, t, i) = \begin{cases} t \cdot w_T - S(T, t) & \text{if } w_{Core_i} \leq 1 \\ w_{Core_i} \cdot t \cdot w_T - S(T, t) & \text{if } w_{Core_i} > 1 \end{cases} \tag{1}$$

To achieve Pfairness, the scheduling error for task T must be less than one time quantum for every time quantum t. Therefore, to check the schedulability of $Core_i$, the decision algorithm must evaluate the satisfaction of the following condition for every T on $Core_i$ at time quantum t:

$$|lag(T, t, i)| < 1. \tag{2}$$

Note that satisfying the condition in Eq. (2) for every T alone does not guarantee the schedulability of $Core_i$, as the total workload of the task set may exceed the computing capacity of $Core_i$. The decision algorithm must also check the satisfiability of the accumulated lag condition:

$$\sum_{T \in Core_i} lag(T, t, i) \leq 0. \tag{3}$$

Using Eqs. (2) and (3), the decision algorithm on each core can determine if the allocated task set is schedulable. If schedulable, Pfair with $M = 1$ is used to schedule the tasks for the time quantum t. No task migration will occur in this case. If the decision algorithm finds the task set on any core unschedulable, it invokes the global scheduler for the time quantum t. Executing the global scheduler may result in migrating some task on $Core_i$ to a different $Core_j$. HPGP repeats the decision algorithm for every time quantum.

Compared to Pfair, HPGP reduces the scheduling overhead significantly. Although the decision algorithm runs at every time quantum, the required computation is much simpler than that involved in Pfair. Moreover, tasks are migrated only when tasks assigned to a core are not schedulable. Task migration and global scheduling are necessary to meet all task deadlines in such a case. Unlike the Pfair scheduler that uses a shared global data structure and requires the scheduling data to be locked and synchronized, the HPGP scheduler maintains its own data structure on each core, thus eliminating the blocking by the scheduler on another core when Pfair is used.

2.3 Supporting Robustness and Adaptive Controls with the HPGP Scheduler

To meet the needs of adaptive controls, the scheduler for their software implementations should be able to handle dynamic task sets. A dynamic task set contains tasks that vary in response to control mode changes. Such variations include the total number of tasks in the set and their properties, such as invocation period, computation delay, deadline, release time, and priority. In the HPGP scheduler, we focus on two dynamic changes: total number of tasks and their invocation periods.

The total number of tasks in a multi-core system changes when one or more new tasks are activated, or one or more existing tasks are terminated. In the HPGP scheduler, the task activation is determined by the collaboration between the task-distribution algorithm and the decision algorithm, while the de-activation is determined solely by the decision algorithm. When a new task arrives, the HPGP scheduler first decides which core to execute it. Given that a system with unevenly-loaded cores (with unbalanced w_{Core_i}) tends to have a larger value of accumulated lag, which may result in not satisfying Eq. (3), such a task system is unlikely to be schedulable by the decision algorithm. We, therefore, introduce a simple heuristic, which allocates each task to the core with minimum weight, in the HPGP's distribution algorithm to balance the cores' weights. On each core, the decision algorithm uses the following two conditions to activate and de-activate a task:

Activation: A task T can be activated in time quantum t **iff** $U \leq M$ at time t.
De-activation: A task T can be de-activated in time quantum t **iff** $(t + 1) \geq d(T_i) = T_p$, where T_i is T's last subtask.

When a task's invocation period changes, the new invocation period is applied to the next invocation of the task. This implies that if the task is currently executing, the new period is applied only after its current execution completes. This prevents waste of resources in generating incomplete results or simultaneously running multiple active copies of the same task.

3 Performance Evaluation

To evaluate the applicability and effectiveness of the HPGP scheduler in realizing adaptive controls, various experiments have been conducted. The Pfair scheduler was used as the baseline for comparison and a discrete-time simulator has been implemented for both the Pfair and the HPGP schedulers for the performance evaluation. To better understand and compare the performance of Pfair and HPGP schedulers, experiments with a fixed task set have been performed.

To illustrate the differences in scheduling tasks resulted from Pfair and HPGP with an extension of supporting dynamic task systems. We apply both schedulers to the system in [5] which contains a set of six tasks running on a dual-core system. These tasks are specified in the form of $T =< T_p, T_e >$ as: $T_0 = (5, 2)$, $T_1 = (15, 3)$, $T_2 = (15, 4)$, $T_3 = (6, 2)$, $T_4 = (30, 20)$, and $T_5 = (30, 6)$.

To learn the schedulers' ability of supporting adaptive controls, two cases of experiment were created: one with dynamic task activations and de-activations, and the other with dynamically-changing task invocation periods. The metrics used in our evaluation include both scheduling overhead and schedulability, represented by the total number of task migrations and the system utilization, respectively.

To evaluate the schedulers with dynamic task sets, we designed experiments to gradually swing between an under-loaded system and a fully-utilized system to mimic a control mode change. This was achieved by gradually activating the tasks in the set followed by de-activating the recently-activated tasks. Specifically, the tasks were activated every 30 time quanta in the order of their IDs from T_0 to T_5. As soon as all the tasks were activated, the system started to de-activate them one-by-one after the first invocation of each task was completed. While a new task was allowed to start its execution at any time quantum after its release, the scheduler de-activates a task only after its execution is completed.

The experimental results are plotted in Fig. 1. Both Pfair and HPGP met all task deadlines. Over a total of 177 time quanta, HPGP performed global scheduling only three times and migrated tasks on these occasions, whereas Pfair performed global scheduling at every time quantum (a total of 177 times) and migrated 39 tasks, hence showing HPGP's superiority to Pfair in reducing the scheduling overhead. The results also showed that HPGP incurred neither global scheduling nor task migrations when the system utilization is less than 1.8, regardless of the dynamic task activations/de-activations, implying that HPGP can isolate the effects of dynamic task changes and yield a stable schedule on each core.

To evaluate the schedulers with dynamically-changing task invocation periods, we designed the experiments to shorten the invocation period of T_3 from 30 to 6, at which the system became fully utilized, and then change the period back to 30.

The experimental results are plotted in Fig. 2. Similar to the case of task activations and de-activations, both Pfair and HPGP scheduled the tasks and met all of their deadlines. HPGP incurred five task migrations during more than 1049 time quanta, exhibiting a significantly lower runtime scheduling overhead than Pfair, which incurred 767 task migrations. As shown in Fig. 2, most task migrations with the HPGP scheduler

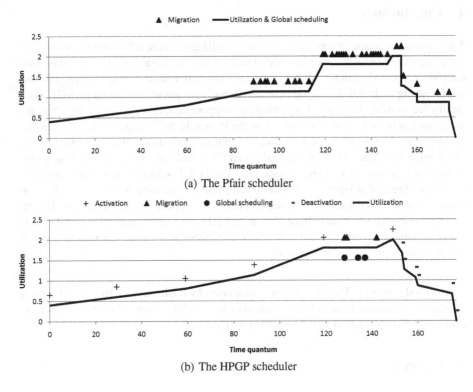

(a) The Pfair scheduler

(b) The HPGP scheduler

Fig. 1. An example of task activations/de-activations

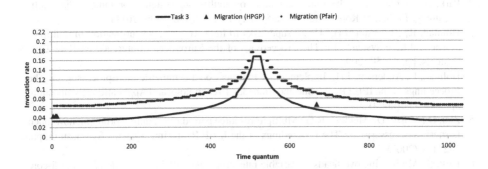

Fig. 2. An example of changing the invocation rate of a task

happening at the system startup. This implies the unbalanced initial core weights used in the task distribution algorithm, which, in turn, causes a less partitioned system to effectively apply the partitioned schedulers [6].

4   Conclusions

The support for adaptive controls poses new challenges to the scheduler in an underlying computing platform. In an embedded real-time system that interacts with the external physical world changing dynamically, the scheduler must manage a dynamic task set, including their activations, de-activations, and changes of invocation periods. Since multi-core systems have great potentials to support adaptive systems with changing workloads, scheduling solutions based on the Pfair scheduling algorithm have been receiving considerable attention for adpative control applications. We have proposed an extension to the Pfair scheduler—called the HPGP scheduler—to improve the capability of handling dynamically-changing task sets. The HPGP scheduler combines the partitioned and the global versions of Pfair to reduce the scheduling overheads, and adopts the distribution and decision algorithms modified to support dynamic task sets. The experimental evaluation results have shown that HPGP yields improved schedules with lower scheduling overheads and fewer task migrations and global scheduling instants, when the task sets change dynamically.

Acknowledgements. This research was supported by Basic Science Research Program through the National Research Foundation of Korea (NRF) funded by the Ministry of Education, Science and Technology (2011-0013422).

References

1. Baruah, S.K., Cohen, N.K., Plaxton, C.G., Varvel, D.A.: Proportionate progress: a notion of fairness in resource allocation. Algorithmica 15(6), 600–625 (1996)
2. Park, S.: A real-time scheduling technique on multi-core systems for multimedia multi-streaming. Journal of Korea Multimedia Society 14(11), 1478–1490 (2011)
3. Holman, P., Anderson, J.H.: Using supertasks to improve processor utilization in multiprocessor real-time systems. In: The Proceedings of the Euromicro Conference on Real-Time Systems, pp. 41–50 (2003)
4. Holman, P., Anderson, J.H.: Implementing Pfairness on a symmetric multiprocessor. In: The Proceedings of the IEEE Real-Time and Embedded Technology and Applications Symposium, pp. 544–553 (2004)
5. Zhu, D., Mossé, D., Melhem, R.G.: Multiple-resource periodic scheduling problem: how much fairness is necessary? In: The Proceedings of the IEEE Real-Time Systems Symposium, pp. 142–151 (2003)
6. Park, S.: Minimizing overheads of variable rate streaming with hpgp scheduler on multi-core processors. In: The Proceedings of the International Conference on Multimedia Information Technology and Applications (2012)

A Routing Strategy for Inductive-Coupling Based Wireless 3-D NoCs by Maximizing Topological Regularity

Daisuke Sasaki[1], Hao Zhang[1], Hiroki Matsutani[1],
Michihiro Koibuchi[2], and Hideharu Amano[1]

[1] Keio university, Japan
[2] National Institute of Informatics, Japan
blackbus@am.ics.keio.ac.jp

Abstract. Inductive-coupling is a 3D integration technique that can stack more than three known-good-dies in a System-in-Package (SiP) without wire connections. To make the best use of wireless property, the 3D ICs would have a great flexibility to customize the number of processor chips, SRAM chips, and DRAM chips in a SiP after the chip fabrication.

In this work, we design a deadlock-free routing protocol for such 3-D chips in which each chip has different Network-on-Chip (NoC) topologies. We classify two-surface NoC of each chip into is 2D mesh and irregular structure in order to apply the custom routing algorithm to its topology. In mesh topologies, X-Y routing is used for well traffic distribution, while Up*/Down* routing is applied for reduced path hops in irregular topologies. Evaluation results show that the average number of hop count in uniform traffic can be improved by up to 11.8%, and the average hop count in neighbor traffic can be improved up to 6.1%.

1 Introduction

Due to the increasing design cost of custom System-on-Chips (SoCs) in recent process technologies, System-in-Packages (SiPs) or 3D ICs that can select and stack necessary known-good-dies in response to given application requirements have become one of hopeful design choices.

Various interconnection techniques have been developed to connect multiple chips in a 3D IC package: wire-bonding, microbump [1], wireless (e.g., capacitive-coupling and inductive-coupling) [2,3] between stacked dies, and through-silicon via (TSV) [2] between stacked wafers. Although many recent studies on 3D IC architectures focus on the TSV, here we focus on inductive-coupling that can connect more than three known-good-dies without wired connections.

It is expected to build target 3D ICs after fabricated dies with a small cost. In the future, by using developing techniques on power transmission using inductive coupling transceiver [4], it will be possible to add, remove, and swap chips in cards by users, e.g. chip stacks just before a parallel application executes. That is, chip level reconfiguration is possible.

J. Kołodziej et al. (Eds.): ICA3PP 2013, Part II, LNCS 8286, pp. 77–85, 2013.
© Springer International Publishing Switzerland 2013

In such chips, we cannot expect any pre-determined network topology for each intra-chip communication; this makes it difficult to establish deadlock-free routing paths in such ad-hoc 3D CMPs. One solution is to use a simple ring as 3D networks and bubble flow control which is a topology independent deadlock free routing [5]. Although this approach is simple and suitable for small systems, performance is limited. Another method is introducing deadlock-free routing for irregular networks based on conservative acyclic graph using spanning trees [6]. However, it ignores topological regularity of the vertical dimension of such chips when attempting path search.

From the practical viewpoint, most of networks in a chip would be two dimensional mesh. The regularity of topologies is a key concern to increase the performance of deadlock-free routing. Here, we design a deadlock-free routing protocol for such 3D chips. To optimize routing paths to topological structure of each chip, we classify two-surface NoC of each chip into is 2D mesh and irregular structure. In mesh topologies, X-Y routing is used for well traffic distribution, whereas Up*/Down* routing is applied for reduced path hops in irregular topologies.

2   Wireless 3D CMPs

2.1   Inductive Coupling Technique

An inductive coupling based wireless 3-D connection [2,7,8,3] is attractive because of the following properties: first, dies can be connected after fabrication, that is, only verified dies can be used. Second, a number of dies can be stacked so performance is much increased by adding more dies. Moreover, no special process technology is needed. The inductor can be built by normal CMOS wiring layers. It is interestingly reported that the inductive coupling technology has achieved more than 8GHz with a low energy dissipation and a low bit-error rate (BER$< 10^{-14}$) [3].

2.2   3D CMP Systems

The flexibility of wireless inter-chip communication is attractive for designing 3D CMPs, because a CMP is collection of heterogeneous hardware components, such as processor, cache and memory chips. Their resource utilization highly depends on the target application set. It is desirable to change the stack chips when attempting target applications are switched.

It becomes possible to change chip composition freely according to the required performance of application by using wireless connection with CMP. For example, more processor chips can be added for computation-bound applications, while more cache chips will be useful for memory-bound applications. However, it means that it is difficult to decide what kind of chips incorporated in the CMP in advance.

In such CMPs we cannot expect any pre-determined network topology for each intra-chip communication; this makes it difficult to establish efficient deadlock-free routing paths in such ad-hoc 3D CMPs.

This is just a problem to be mitigated in this work. In particular, we assume target CMPs that consist of 2D mesh NoCs and partially irregular NoCs whose two-dimensional coordinates of routers are the same as those in 2D mesh for composing the vertical links.

3 Mixed Routing

3.1 Assumption

In order to stack chips for building a 3D NoC, the position of coils that makes a vertical link must has the same two-dimensional coordinate in all chips. We assume that coils are provided in each chip with a certain intervals. A router is directly connected with each coil to transfer data from/to the intra-chip network. A three dimensional coordinates (x,y,z) is given to the router which is connected to the coil (x,y) of the z'th chip. Here, we only care about the routing between such routers connected to the coil, although there may be other routers used only for intra-chip network. The routing between the numbered routers and routers for only intra-chip network will be done depending on the topology and the local rule of the intra-chip network.

Logically, the 3D links can be treated just a linear network. Since the switching the receiver and transceiver can be done quickly in wireless interconnection network, here, a half duplex bi-directional communication is assumed on the linear network. Since each chip has different size of cores, it is difficult to provide a inductive coupling link at all (x,y) positions in a chip. Moreover, some vertical links have to be shut down for reducing the power consumption of Networks [9,10]. Besides, some vertical links may encounter faults. Thus, these vertical links cannot work. All the above reasons make the vertical direction network an irregular one. However, of course, each chip must have a connectivity between upper and lower chips with some links.

Since various type chips can be stacked, various intra-chip networks are connected. Here, we make the following assumption for each intra-chip network: (1) all nodes on the chip are reachable only with the intra-chip network, and (2) an intra-chip network of each chip has a deadlock-free routing method. If the intra-chip network of the stacked chip can work by itself, these assumptions are naturally satisfied.

According to the detected topology, the standard routing algorithms described in the following subsections are applied in the intra-chip network. Note that both algorithms can be deadlock free without virtual channels.

3.2 Recognition of the Mesh

In an NoC by using wireless inductive coupling links, various chips with their own intra-networks can be stacked, and it is difficult to fix the routing information beforehand. Also, considering faults, automatic topology recognition algorithm is advantageous.

Here, it is necessary to detect which is the topology of each chip, mesh or irregular. When the system boots, each node checks the neighboring nodes and layer information to detect the topology and the three-dimensional node number. Here, the topology is detected according to the following simple algorithm.

——— Algorithm of Mesh Recognition ———

1. Find a minimum mesh consisting of four nodes connected with a ring structure.
2. A minimum mesh is treated as a 2nd-level node whose links are edges which are shared by other minimum meshes.
3. When such four nodes form a ring structure, it is treated as a 3rd-level node, and it is repeated until no ring structures is found or every node in the plane is included.

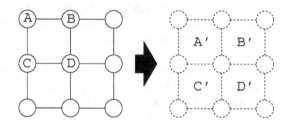

Fig. 1. Example of Topology detection flow

The left side of Fig. 1 shows an example of 3×3 topology. First, it is confirmed whether node A connects with the node of the east side. If it is connected, the node on the east will be named as node B. Node B, node C, and node D are checked in the same way. If it checks being connected, the node A, B, C, and D form the minimum mesh A'. It is carried out repeatedly and forms small meshes A', B', C', and D' as shown in the right side of Fig. 1.

Next, the meshes A', B', C', and D' are treated as a 2nd-level nodes and examined whether they are connected in the same way. In this case, the 3rd-level node becomes a 3×3 squire mesh.

This process is applied for XY plane, YZ plane, and ZX plane. If the mesh structure in all planes can be connected, they will be treated as a 3D mesh.

3.3 Mixed Routing

The general way for routing in a network consisting of various types of sub-networks is treating it as an irregular topology, and apply Up*/Down* routing.

However, of UP*Down* routing is commonly less effective than topology dependent routing like dimension order routing in the mesh even by using the optimized root node selection algorithm[11] . By using the mesh recognition algorithm shown before, we can identify whether the source node and destination node belong to the same mesh, independent meshes or not.

Here, the following simple Mixed routing is proposed to make the use of regularity as possible:

Mixed Routing

Assume that the source router S (s_x, s_y, s_z) wants to send a packet to destination router D (d_x, d_y, d_z).

1 If the source and destination are in the same chip $(s_z = d_z)$, use the intra-chip routing depending on the topology of the chip.
2 If the source and destination are in the same mesh topology, use the dimension-order routing in the mesh.
3 If both the source and destination are not on any mesh topologies, use the Up*/Down* routing.
4 If either the source and destination is in a mesh topology, use the dimension order routing in the mesh and Up*Down* in other parts. We call this routing "topology switching routing".

Topology Switching Routing

Here, we switches the topology from mesh to irregular or irregular to mesh only once and each router provides two virtual channels.

1 If the source node belongs to a mesh and destination node dose not belong the same mesh, the packet is routed to the relay-node at the edge of the mesh by dimension order routing. Then, the virtual channel is changed. From the relay-node to the destination node, Up*Down* routing is applied.
2 If the source node does not belong to any mash, Up*Down* routing is used to the relay node at the boundary of the mesh to which the destination node belongs. Then, the virtual channel is changed. From the relay-node to the destination node, dimension order routing is used.

The relay-node is selected so as to minimize the hop of the total route. This selection is can be done easily, since the number of candidate nodes on the boundary are limited.

Mixed routing is deadlock free. It is obvious because of the following reason:

- In each network, Up*Down* routing or dimension order routing, each of which is deadlock-free in each topology are used.
- When the routing algorithm is switched, the virtual channel number is changed.

Here, the routing algorithm is switched only once, since we assume two virtual channels. Thus, Up*Down* routing is applied around the destination nodes if it belongs to the different meshes as the source node belongs to. Adding more virtual channels will increase the flexibility if the system becomes large.

4 Evaluation Results

In this section, the proposed Mixed routing is compared with a baseline irregular routing, in which the whole 3D network is treated as an irregular topology and Up*/Down* routing is used to route packets. The spanning tree roots for Up*/Down* routing are optimized so as to minimize the average hop count of each application based on an exhaustive search for fair comparisons.

4.1 Network Simulation

Simulation Setup. To evaluate hop count of Mix routing and irregular routing, we used a network simulator called Irre_sim [12]. Irre_sim is a cycle-accurate simulator of interconnection networks written in C++. Although the traffic is artificially generated, the operation of routers are based on the real hardware design. Here, a standard three-stage wormhole router and 5-flit (1-flit header + 4-flit body) packets are used.

We evaluated network configurations in Table 1 with the network simulator. Topology (x, y, z) denotes a wireless 3D CMP that consists of z chips where each chip consists of $x \times y$ nodes.

Here, we use a number of chips with irregular topology as a parameter. Irregular topologies are automatically generated from 2D mesh network by randomly removing horizontal links. In addition, the number of vertical links (Z links) has been changed randomly as shown in the table. In order to keep connectivity of the network, removal which makes isolated nodes is prohibited.

Table 1. Target architecture for network simulator

	T444	T448
Topology	(4,4,4)	(4,4,8)
Number of Nodes	64	128
Number of Z links	48 — 42 — 36	112 — 98 — 84

Traffic patterns of uniform used for the simulation. Uniform trrafic is randomly selected source and destination node.

Evaluation Results of Network Simulation. Fig. 2, 3 show average hop count of Mixed routing and irregular routing at uniform traffic.

Each topology in the graph is based on the configuration shown in Table 1 with the number of irregular chips as a parameter. The meaning of link 48 is to have 48 Z links.

In Fig. 2, the hop count of Mixed routing is improved by 6.6% compared to that of irregular routing when irregular 1 with link 36 in uniform trrafic. Similarly, in Fig. 3, it is improved by 11.8% when irregular 1 with link 36.

Fig. 4, 5shows the average hop count at neighber traffic.

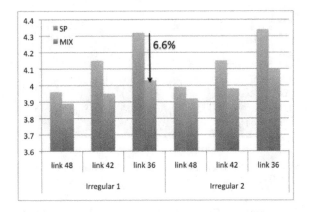

Fig. 2. Average hop count of Mixed routing and irregular routing at uniform traffic (T444)

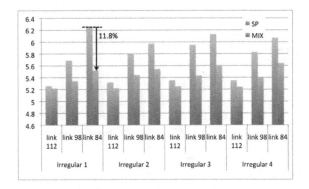

Fig. 3. Average hop count of Mixed routing and irregular routing at uniform traffic (T448)

In Fig. 4, the hop count of Mixed routing is improved by 3.3% compared to that of irregular routing when irregular 2 with link 36 in uniform trrafic. Similarly, in Fig. 5, it is improved by 6.1% when irregular 3 with link 98.

The hop counts is increased as the number of chips with irregular network increases. However, when Mixed routing is used, the increasing ratio in uniform and neighber trrafic is much suppressed by using a small number of 2D mesh is used efficiently.

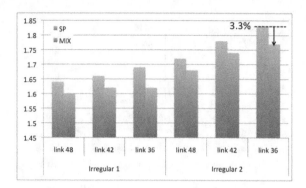

Fig. 4. Average hop count of Mixed routing and irregular routing at neighber traffic (T444)

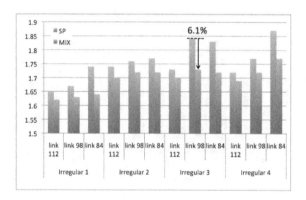

Fig. 5. Average hop count of Mixed routing and irregular routing at neighber traffic (T448)

5   Conclusions

A routing method for wireless 3D CMPs consisting of chips with various intra-chip networks is proposed and evaluated. Although the effect is depending on the number of 2-D mesh in the 3-D network, network simulation results revealed that Mixed Routing improved performance of irregular routing up to 6.0%. By using the full-system simulator, the execution time of parallel application programs is compared, and except a few cases, the performance with Mixed Routing overcomes that of irregular routing.

Now, Mixed Routing simply uses layers which includes the source node or destination node. This strategy may cause the traffic congestion when a specific chip (e.g. processor) generates a lot of packets. Selecting the light traffic chips and switching the route is our next improvement policy in future work.

References

1. Black, B., et al.: Die Stacking (3D) Microarchitecture. In: Proceedings of the International Symposium on Microarchitecture (MICRO 2006), pp. 469–479 (December 2006)
2. Rhett Davis, W., et al.: Demystifying 3D ICs: The Pros and Cons of Going Vertical. IEEE Design and Test of Computers 22(6), 498–510 (2005)
3. Miura, N., et al.: A 0.14pJ/b Inductive-Coupling Inter-Chip Data Transceiver with Digitally-Controlled Precise Pulse Shaping. In: Proc. of ISSCC 2007, pp. 358–359 (February 2007)
4. Radecki, A., Chung, H., Yoshida, Y., Miura, N., Shidei, T., Ishikuro, H., Kuroda, T.: $6W/25mm^2$ inductive power transfer for non-contact wafer-level testing. In: Proc. IEEE Int. Solid-State Circuits Conf. Digest of Technical Papers (ISSCC), pp. 230–232 (February 2011)
5. Matsutani, H., et al.: A Vertical Bubble Flow Network using Inductive-Coupling for 3-D CMPs. In: Proc. of the 5th ACM/IEEE International Symposium on Networks-on-Chip (NOCS 2011), pp. 49–56 (May 2011)
6. Flich, J., et al.: A Survey and Evaluation of Topology Agnostic Deterministic Routing Algorithms. IEEE Trans. on Parallel and Distributed Systems 23(3), 405–425 (2012)
7. Kanda, K., et al.: 1.27-Gbps/pin, 3mW/pin Wireless Superconnect (WSC) Interface Scheme. In: Proc. of ISSCC 2003, pp. 186–187 (February 2003)
8. Miura, N., et al.: A 1Tb/s 3W Inductive-Coupling Transceiver for Inter-Chip Clock and Data Link. In: Proc. of ISSCC 2006, pp. 424–425 (February 2006)
9. Zhang, H., Matsutani, H., Take, Y., Kuroda, T., Amano, H.: Vertical Link On/Off Control Methods for Wireless 3-D NoCs. In: Herkersdorf, A., Römer, K., Brinkschulte, U. (eds.) ARCS 2012. LNCS, vol. 7179, pp. 212–224. Springer, Heidelberg (2012)
10. Zhang, H., Matsutani, H., Koibuchi, M., Amano, H.: Dynamic power on/off method for 3D NoCs with wireless inductive-coupling links. In: Proceedings of the 16th IEEE Symposium on Low-Power and High-Speed Chips (Cool Chips XVI), pp. 1–3 (2013)
11. Matsutani, H., et al.: A Case for Wireless 3D NoCs for CMPs. In: Proceedings of the 18th Asia and South Pacific Design Automation Conference (ASP-DAC 2013) (January 2013)
12. Jouraku, A., Koibuchi, M., Amano, H.: An Effective Design of Deadlock-Free Routing Algorithms Based on 2-D Turn Model for Irregular Networks 18(3), 320–333 (March 2007)

Semidistributed Virtual Network Mapping Algorithms Based on Minimum Node Stress Priority

Yi Tong, Zhenmin Zhao, Zhaoming Lu, Haijun Zhang,
Gang Wang, and Xiangming Wen

Beijing Key Laboratory of Network System Architecture and Convergence,
Beijing University of Posts and Telecommunications, Beijing
shine1114@bupt.edu.cn

Abstract. Network virtualization has been regarded as a fundamental paradigm that extenuates the ossification of the current network. In a virtualization-enabled networking infrastructure, numbers of diverse virtual networks (VNs) can coexist on a shared physical substrate. In this regard, an important challenge is the allocation of substrate network resources to instantiate multiple VNs. To address this challenge, we propose a semidistributed approach and a balanced VN assigning procedure focusing on balancing the substrate node stress. Besides, numerical experiment results show that the proposed approach has a better performance in terms of node stress and messages exchanges.

Keywords: Network Virtualization, Node Stress, Semidistributed Approach.

1   Introduction

Over the course of past three decades, the Internet has demonstrated its innumerable value by becoming a fundamental component of the modern world, especially proved in modeling the way we access and exchange information. Nonetheless, with the rapid growth of the network size diversified application demands are emerging gradually. This diversification highlights the inherent problems that exist in the current Internet architecture, such as low scalability, poor diversity, weak manageability and lacking service quality assurance etc. To break the impasse, the network virtualization concept has been proposed as a potential solution for constructing the next-generation Internet architecture by allowing multiple architectures or experiments to run on a shared physical substrate simultaneously [1, 2]. In a network virtualization environment, the traditional Internet Service Provider (ISP) has been decoupled into two independent entities [3]: infrastructure provider (InP), who maintains and manages the physical infrastructure; service provider (SP), who creates virtual networks to offer end-to-end services by renting resources from multiple infrastructure providers.

As shown in Figure 1, each virtual network is a group of virtual nodes interconnected via a set of virtual links over substrate network. The problem of mapping virtual resources to substrate resources in an optimal way is commonly known as the Virtual Network Mapping problem. However, due to the combination of constraint

J. Kołodziej et al. (Eds.): ICA3PP 2013, Part II, LNCS 8286, pp. 86–93, 2013.
© Springer International Publishing Switzerland 2013

upon nodes and links, the VN Mapping problem is NP-hard, though kinds of mapping requests are acknowledged in advance.

Motivated by it, we proposed a novel VN mapping method to involve the entire mapping execution .The rest of this paper is organized as follows. Section 2 discusses the related work. Section 3 presents the network model and formalizes the VN assignment problem. Section 4 gives the Semidistributed approach and the algorithms related to our mapping procedure respectively. Section 5 evaluates the proposed VN assignment algorithms and compare to the other existing algorithms or models. Then Section 6 concludes the paper and states the possible future work.

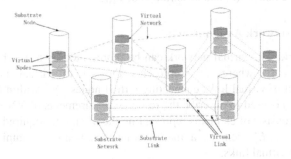

Fig. 1. Network Virtualization

2   Related Work

To address the challenging VN Mapping issue, a number of proposals and heuristic algorithms have been put forward.

1) In centralized approach, all the functions are incorporated into the responsibilities of the central coordinator such as collecting information, choosing substrate topology, conducting actual mapping operation and updating information etc. Inconsistencies and conflicts may be avoided during resource allocation. But its advantages also bring high latency, serious delays and scalability limitation [4, 5].

2) In distributed approach, every substrate node runs intelligence agent which can exchange messages and cooperate to execution of the specified algorithm [6]. Despite the fact that distributed approach yields good performance with limited information, but the overhead of message exchange increases linearly as the network grows in size.

Thus we propose semidistributed VN mapping algorithms which is aimed to exploring a trade-off between centralized and fully distributed mapping models.

3   Network Model and Problem Description

3.1   Network Model

Substrate Network: The substrate network is modeled as a weighted undirected graph and it is denoted as $G_s = (N_s, L_s)$, where N_s is the set of substrate nodes and

Ls is the set of substrate links. Each substrate node $n_s \in N_s$ is associated with several parameters: $C(n_s)$ indicates the total CPU capacity; $C^i(n_s \to n_v)$ indicates the CPU resource allocated to the virtual node during the life time of a specific VN; $R(n_s)$ indicates the residual CPU capacity.

$$R(n_s) = C(n_s) - \sum_{1 \le j < i} C^j(n_s \to n_v), \quad (i, j \in N) \tag{1}$$

Equally, each substrate link also has some attributes metrics: $B(l_s(e, f))$ indicates the available bandwidth capacity of the link $l_s(e, f) \in L_s$, where e, f means the link between substrate node $n_s(e)$ and substrate node $n_s(f)$.

3.2   Virtual Network Assignment

Virtual Network: The virtual network can be represented by a weighted undirected graph $G_v^i = (N_v^i, L_v^i)$, where N_v^i represents the set of virtual nodes and L_v^i represents the set of virtual links connecting virtual nodes N_v^i within life time VN i. $req = (G_v^i, V_v^i, E_v^i)$ is used to describe the resource requirements of VN i: V_v^i denotes a vector which consists of elements representing the minimum required capacity of all the virtual nodes; E_v^i denotes a matrix whose elements are minimum required bandwidth of all virtual links.

VN Mapping Problem: The assignment of a virtual network onto the substrate network can be denoted as: $M : G_v \xrightarrow{req = (G_v^i, V_v^i, E_v^i)} G_s$. The mapping process can be naturally decomposed into node mapping and link mapping:

1) Node mapping: note that in many previous VN mapping algorithms, a group of virtual nodes from same VN request can be mapped to a same substrate node. In our algorithms, two virtual nodes from the same virtual network are generally mapped in different physical nodes for the consideration of load balancing. It is formalized as:

$$M_N : N_v^i \xrightarrow{V_v^i} N_s \tag{2}$$

$$M_N(n_v^i(e)) \in N_s, \forall n_v^i(e), n_v^i(f) \in N_v^i, \forall n_v^j(f) \in N_v^j \tag{3}$$

$$M_N(n_v^i(e)) = M_N(n_v^i(f)), e = f \tag{4}$$

$$M_N(n_v^i(e)) = M_N(n_v^j(f)), i \ne j \tag{5}$$

2) Link mapping: link mapping process assigns the virtual links to substrate paths that satisfy the virtual link bandwidth restriction. It can be formalized as:

$$M_L : L_v^i \xrightarrow{E_v^i} L_s, M_L(l_v^i(e, f)) \in L_s \tag{6}$$

3.3   Measurement of Substrate Network Node Stress

In [4, 7], they use number or occupied CPU resources of the embedded virtual nodes to define the node stress. Contrarily, greedy algorithm only takes the residual capacity of CPU resources into account. However, neither of them gives a comprehensive expression of the substrate node state. In this paper, we adopt the concept node stress which can denote both the occupied ratio and load condition of the underlying physical resource. We define node stress as follows:

$$S_N(n_s) = \frac{\sum_{0 \le j < i} C^j(n_s \to n_v)}{C(n_s)}, \forall n_s \in N_s \tag{7}$$

In this paper, it is supposed that VN requests are predefined and notified in advance.

4   Balanced Virtual Network Mapping Algorithm

The aim of our semidistributed virtual network mapping approach is to exploit the advantages of both centralized and fully distributed models. So the quantity of our processing entity is doubled comprising center unit and root nodes. The balanced VN mapping algorithms are carried out in a collaborating procedure and the whole mapping task is allocated as follows:

- *The center unit: a.* maintain global information; *b.* conduct the VN decomposition operation; *c.* select root nodes from substrate nodes; *d.* calculate node stress according to the latest node capacity; *e.* execute node stress sorting algorithm; *f.* act as a controller in center-root communicating interaction etc.
- *The root nodes: a.* gather the sub-region information within star topology; *b.* carry out our improved shortest path tree algorithm; *c.* pick up candidates nodes from the rest substrate nodes; *d.* execute node and link mapping in practical.

4.1   Sub-VN Decomposition Algorithm

Since the virtual network topology may become quite large, considering the whole VN topology and its constraints tends to be a tough task. It is a classic method that the VN is divided into many connected sub-VNs. To simplify the problem, we decompose the VN and assume that it is constituted by interconnected star (hub-and-spoke) clusters:

Table 1. Sub-VN Decomposition Algorithm

Algorithm 1: Sub-VN Decomposition Algorithm
INPUT: $G_v^i = (N_v^i, L_v^i)$
OUTPUT: $G_v^i(j) = (N_v^i, L_v^i)_j, j = 1, 2, \ldots$

i. Sort the virtual node $n_v^i \in N_v^i$ with the highest capacity requirement $C(n_v^i)$ to make it the hub of the cluster $Hub_{G_v^i(j), j=1,2\ldots}$

ii. Determine the neighboring virtual nodes directly connected to the hub node to represent the spoke nodes $Spokes_{G_v^i(j), j=1,2\ldots}$

iii.Remove the $N_v^i \in G_v^i(j)$ (hub and spoke nodes) as well as their corresponding links $L_v^i \in G_v^i(j)$ from the VN topology.

iv. Select the next hub-and-spoke cluster, then go to i.

4.2   Node-Stress-Sorting Algorithm

As mentioned above, our work focuses on considering the node stress. Upon receiving a mapping request from a sub-VN cluster, the center unit starts to run the sorting algorithm to find the lightest-stress node. The node with minimum utilization i.e. the relative free substrate node is selected to be the root nodes performing following mapping.

4.3   Center-Root Communicating Protocol

The protocol is based on five types of messages which are sent and received asynchronously between the center unit and root nodes. These messages are used to organize the Main VN mapping algorithm iterations. The protocol is described in Fig.2.

Table 2. Node-Stress-Sorting Algorithm

Algorithm 2: Node-Stress-Sorting Algorithm
INPUT: $n_s \in N_s$, $R(n_s)$, $S_N(n_s)$
OUTPUT: $n_s^{Root} \in N_s$
i. Find a set of nodes $A = \{n_s \in N_s \mid R(n_s) \ge \min C(Hub_{G(j)})_{j=1,2..}\}$ which are able to support the hub node $Hub_{G(j),j=1,2...}$
ii. Sort these substrate nodes $n_s \in A$ according to $S_N(n_s)$.
iii. Assign the substrate node with lightest stress $\min S_N(n_s)$ to be the root node $n_s^{Root} \in A$.
iv. If substrate node $n_s(e)$ and node $n_s(f)$ have the same stress rate, $S_N(n_s(e)) = S_N(n_s(f))$, $n_s(e), n_s(f) \in A$, resort them by their residual capacity $R(n_s(e)), R(n_s(f))$, then assign node with higher residual capacity to be the root node $n_s^{Root} \in A$.
v. Receive the next sub-VN request, go to *i*.

Message	Demomstration
START	This message is used to activate a new mapping process sent by center unit . Only the root node who is selected by center unit can receive it.
HMD	This message is sent out by the root node who just finished the hub mapping. Once received, the center unit passes a node list which contains all substrate nodes meeting the hub capacity requirement down to root node after calculating.
SMD	Having accomplished the spokes node mapping, root node confirms the success message by sending SMD to center unit and by the way upload the latest node capacity of capacity-changed nodes.
LM	This message is used for acknowledging the root node to start the sub-VN's link mapping.
AD	After fulfilled all the mapping of the small sub-VN, root node send AD to center unit to stop the execution of Main VN Mapping Algorithm.

Fig. 2. Ceter-Root Communicating Protocol

Table 3. Main VN Mapping Algorithm

Algorithm 3: Main VN Mapping Algorithm

INPUT: $G_s = (N_s, L_s)$, $req = (G_v^i(j), V_v^i(j), E_v^i(j)) j = 1,2,..., S_N(n_s)$, $n_s \in N_s$

OUTPUT: $M : G_v^i(j) \xrightarrow{req=(G_v^i, V_v^i, E_v^i)} G_s(j)_{i=1,2}$

---

i. Upon receiving a sub-VN request, center unit chooses the root node to send START massage according to Node-Stress-Sorting Algorithm. Once the root node received it, it maps itself to hub node $M_N(Hub_{G_v^i(j)}) = n_s^{Root} \in G_s(j)_{j=1,2...}$

ii. Then the root node n_s^{Root} send the HMD message to the center unit.

iii. Upon receiving the HMD message, center unit sends a node list. It consists of a set of substrate nodes meeting the capacity requirement of the spokes nodes $B = \{n_s \in N_s, Spokes_{G_v^i(j)} \in G_v^i(j)_{j=1,2...} \mid R(n_s) \geq \min C(Spokes_{G_v^i(j)})_{j=1,2.}\}$; According to the list, the root node n_s^{Root} determines the candidate substrate nodes based on Improved Shortest Path Tree Algorithm.

iv. At last, the root node maps the candidate nodes $n_s \in B$ to spokes nodes $M_N(Spokes_{G_v^i(j)}, j=1,2...) = n_s \in G_s(j)_{j=1,2...}$ in a specific order that node with highest residual capacity is mapped to the highest-capacity-required spokes node, and so on. It is not terminated until the mapping procedure is finished.

v. Send SMD to the center unit, and update available capacity to the center unit.

vi. Center unit sends the LM message to the root node, then maps the spokes links.

vii. Send AD to center unit.

4.4　Main VN Mapping Algorithm

The VN mapping process can be viewed as a cooperative interaction. Center unit executes the sorting algorithm and information exchange protocols, meanwhile root nodes carry out sub-VN mapping algorithm. Due to overall scheduling, conflicts can be effectively avoided and multiple VN requests can be undertaken simultaneously.

4.5　Improved Shortest Path Tree Algorithm

Improved Shortest Path Tree Algorithm ran by root node n_s^{Root} is implemented through using the Dijkstra algorithm. It calculates a path from the root node to any other node belonging to the matrix B up to the weights. However, the weights are neither the distance nor the costs of the link. Different from them, we use the stress rate of the end node of the path to represent the weights. So we expectedly elect the sub-region with a comparatively lower stress from the candidate region.

5　Simulation Results and Analysis

The performance of our proposed algorithms is evaluated through detailed simulation experiments. The substrate network is 100 nodes 500 links generated by the GT-ITM

[8]. The computing capacity at substrate nodes and bandwidth capacity on the links are 100 and 10000, separately. The VN topologies are random and can be decomposed into many small one hub four spokes star sub-VNs. The size is uniformly distributed from 10 to 50. In view of the powerful function library, we use Matlab to complete our simulation. In order to make the results more accurate, simulation runs five times, and the average results of all experiments are adopted.

1) The value and distribution of the node stress to some extent reflect the whole network load balanced status. Under different number of VN requests, we made a comparison between our algorithms and greedy algorithm. Figure.5shows node stress of our balanced mapping procedure is relatively smaller than greedy algorithm.

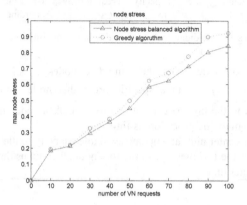

Fig. 3. Maximum node stress under different number of VN Requests

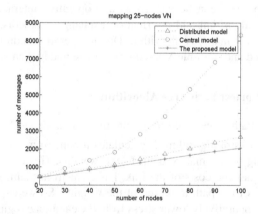

Fig. 4. Number of messages exchanged within mapping a VN

2) Looking into the fact, the mapping efficiency is closely related to message exchanges; huge message exchange may lead to high latency further to influence the ability of underlying network to access more VNs. Figure.6 illustrates the number of messages exchanged to map 25-nodes VN. The performance results are compared

with the centralized approach and the distributed approach. It is clearly shown that the proposed approach has less message exchange. So in a practical process, it will gain a possibly higher efficiency.

6   Conclusions

In this paper, we propose a novel virtual network mapping method called Semidistributed virtual network mapping approach. Undertakers involved in this mapping procedure have been defined. And the whole mapping task has been partitioned and allocated explicitly. Based on VN decomposition, Node-Stress-Sorting Algorithm and Improved Shortest Path Tree Algorithm have been developed additionally with the ultimate goal to balance the node stress. Main VN Mapping Algorithm executing entire mapping process through handling communicating protocol between center unit and root nodes has been presented. Evaluation results suggest that the proposed approach and algorithms yield better performance.

In the future, we plan to investigate VN mapping problems through providing more intelligent algorithms in further.

References

1. Fischer, A., Botero, J., Beck, M., De Meer, H., Hesselbach, X.: Virtual network embedding: A survey. IEEE Communications Surveys Tutorials PP(99), 1–19 (2013)
2. Wang, A., Iyer, M., Dutta, R., Rouskas, G., Baldine, I.: Network virtualization: Technologies, perspectives, and frontiers. Journal of Lightwave Technology 31(4), 523–537 (2013)
3. Belbekkouche, A., Hasan, M.M., Karmouch, A.: Resource discovery and allocation in network virtualization. IEEE Communications Surveys Tutorials 14(4), 1114–1128 (2012)
4. Zhu, Y., Ammar, M.: Algorithms for assigning substrate network resources to virtual network components. In: Proceedings of the 25th IEEE International Conference on Computer Communications, INFOCOM 2006, pp. 1–12 (2006)
5. Fan, J., Ammar, M.: Dynamic topology configuration in service overlay networks: A study of reconfiguration policies. In: Proceedings of the 25th IEEE International Conference on Computer Communications, INFOCOM 2006, pp. 1–12 (2006)
6. Houidi, I., Louati, W., Zeghlache, D.: A distributed and autonomic virtual network mapping framework. In: Fourth International Conference on Autonomic and Autonomous Systems, ICAS 2008, pp. 241–247 (2008)
7. Chowdhury, M., Rahman, M., Boutaba, R.: Vineyard: Virtual network embedding algorithms with coordinated node and link mapping. IEEE/ACM Transactions on Networking 20(1), 206–219 (2012)
8. Zegura, E., Calvert, K., Bhattacharjee, S.: How to model an internetwork. In: Proceedings of Fifteenth Annual Joint Conference of the IEEE Computer Societies, Networking the Next Generation, INFOCOM 1996, vol. 2, pp. 594–602 (1996)

Scheduling Algorithm Based on Agreement Protocol for Cloud Systems

Radu-Ioan Tutueanu, Florin Pop, Mihaela-Andreea Vasile, and Valentin Cristea

University *Politehnica* of Bucharest
Computer Science Department, Faculty of Automatic Control and Computers
{radu.tutueanu,mihaela.vasile}@cti.pub.ro,
{florin.pop,valentin.cristea}@cs.pub.ro

Abstract. Task scheduling algorithms have a huge impact by handling and executing users' requests in a data-center that serves a Cloud System. A problem very close to the industry is the capability to estimate costs, especially when switching from one provider to another. In this paper we introduce an agreement-based scheduling algorithm, aimed to bring an adaptive fault tolerant system. For the agreement protocol we proposed a 3-Tier structure of resources (hosts and VMs). Then an adaptive mechanism for agreement establishment is described. The scheduling algorithm considers workload distribution, resources heterogeneity, transparency, adaptability and also the ease to extend by combining with other scheduling algorithms. Based on simulation experiments, we can draw the conclusion that an agreement based algorithm improves both scheduling in Cloud and the mapping of SLAs at lower levels, possibly ensuring the same cost on data-centers belonging to different providers.

Keywords: Scheduling Algorithm, Agreement, Adaptive Distributed Systems, Fault Tolerant Systems, Cloud Computing.

1 Introduction

Cloud is used everywhere now, supporting email applications, video-streaming, online working environments, file sharing (especially photos and videos), government services or socializing online - everything can be done and kept in the Cloud. So, tasks scheduling become critical for SLA assurance. Sometimes resource and service providers use hybrid solution based on special agreements. The white paper [1] states that even though Big Data is relative to the organization we're talking about, we are definitely in the Big Data era and it is increasing fast throughout a vast number of fields: research, financial services, media, healthcare, defence, human resources and marketing. More and more companies are faced with the challenge of storing and managing huge quantities of data (many PetaBytes, and the order is growing). An important task is transforming that data into information, and that is why Cloud Computing is so important right now. A prediction made by the International Data Corporation [2] says that PaaS industry will see an explosion, as industry public platforms will increase tenfold by 2016 from the number at the end of 2012, many in the domains.

J. Kołodziej et al. (Eds.): ICA3PP 2013, Part II, LNCS 8286, pp. 94–101, 2013.
© Springer International Publishing Switzerland 2013

We propose in this paper an agreement based algorithm for task scheduling in Cloud environments with fault tolerance support. We propose a 3-Tiers agreement protocol that enables the scheduling algorithm to use about all of the systems already developed in data-centres or in inter-Clouds. The algorithm adds advantages like: workload distribution, heterogeneity, transparency, adaptability and also the ease to extend by combining with other algorithms.

The paper is structured as follows. Section 2 presents related work in the field. In Section 3 we describe the Agreement based Scheduling Algorithm and in Section 4 we presents the experimental results obtained using simulation. Conclusions and future work are presented in Section 5.

2   Related Work

With cost effectiveness, performance, flexibility and low power consumption in mind, scheduling is a very important part in cloud computing and it has been given the attention it deserves by researchers and the industry [3], [4].

Modified Critical Path is a scheduling algorithm for tasks with dependencies, using Latest Possible Start Time to map tasks to resources [5]. Here, the agreement is made between processors that allow the execution for tasks with the earliest start time. The paper [6] presents a heuristics based genetic algorithm that tries to solve the NP-complete problem of mapping meta-tasks to machine using heuristics like giving priority to the task that can be completed the earliest, combined with a well defined genetic algorithm [7]. The algorithm manages to minimize the completion time and increase the throughput of the system. Another example of bio-inspired applications in this domain is presented in [8], which proposes a scheduling algorithm based on reinforcement learning. This method aims at finding an optimal configuration setting for VMs and software running in those VMs and the experimental results prove the approach's effectiveness. Another approach is self-adaptive distributed scheduling platform composed of multiple agents implemented as intelligent feedback control loops to support policy-based scheduling and expose self-healing capabilities [9] [10].

3   Agreement Based Scheduling Algorithm

We start by describing formally all the elements involved. These are nodes, an abstraction of a VM capable of running on demand tasks, the task itself, the execution time together with dependencies and requirements.

A **node** is an abstraction of VM capable of running on demand tasks. It can have one or more cores, it belongs to a domain - which can be a zone of the same provider or a different provider. The model is $N_i(\alpha_i, \beta_i, c_i, a_i, z_i, r_i, q_i)$, where: α_i - execution factor, relative to a reference processor speed $\alpha_i = \frac{ProcSpeed(N_i)}{refSpeed}$; β_i - current usage factor ($\beta = [\beta_{core_1}, \beta_{core_2}, \ldots, \beta_{core_n}]$); c_i - cost per execution unit; a_i - architecture; z_i - zone/domain the host belongs to; r_i - current available resources; and q_i - current task queue.

A **task** is defined as $T_i(a_i, p_i, d_i, B_i)$, where: a_i - arrival time; p_i - estimated processing time on the reference processor; d_i - deadline; and B_i - budget.

The **estimated execution time** of a task on a specific node is the product between the task estimate processing time on the reference processor: $ET(t_i, n_j)$ - Estimated execution time of task i on node j: $ET(T_i, N_j) = \alpha_j p_i$. The **dependencies** are modeled as $e_{ij} = (T_i, T_j)$: T_i finishes before T_j starts running.

Requirements. We have identified the following requirements related to the duration of the agreement, deadlines and the estimated execution time. For task T_i running on node N_j we have: $a_i + ET(T_i, N_j) \leq d_i$. A **strong agreement requirement** is $\max\{a_i + ET(T_i, N_j)\} \leq T_A$. A **light agreement requirement** (where $0 \leq f < \frac{1}{n}$ and $n \geq 1$) is $\max\{d_i\} \leq T_A + f * T_A$.

3.1   3-Tier Structure

We propose a 3-Tier structure considering the following reasons: we have a distributed algorithm and distributing the processing and message passing should show an increase in performance, especially when messages are short; we have machines with different characteristics (OS, architecture) and we could extend the algorithm and specialize those machines with different scopes, for example Tier 1 machines specialized on different tasks.

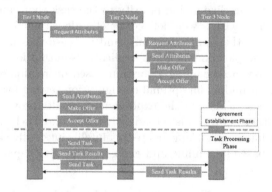

Fig. 1. Overall view of communication between a node on each Tier in the proposed algorithm. The two phases are highlighted: agreement establishment and task processing. Here, both nodes accept the offer and are then sent task(s) according to that offer.

The *Tier 1 - Tier 2* separation is inspired from a load balancing system, Tier 2 nodes being in charge of distributing tasks to the machines they have an agreement with, distributing the scheduling process and limiting the number of messages that Tier 1 computers send. The *Tier 2 - Tier 3* separation comes from current solutions in the industry, we have machines that distribute tasks and machines that run them. Here, Tier 1 and Tier 2 machines distribute tasks, and both Tier 3 and Tier 2 machines run them. In order to minimize the number of messages used, we added proxy servers between the Tiers. This enables the sender node to send a message containing all the destination nodes, the proxy splitting the message and grouping the resulting messages by destination.

3.2 Agreement and Prerequisites

Agreement. An agreement has two participants: *Initiator* and *Acceptor*. It contains details about the resources reserved and their availability. An agreement is established in two steps for each participant: *Initiator*: 1. Request attributes; 2. Make offer and *Acceptor*: 1. Send attributes; 2. Accept/Refuse offer.

We chose an agreement based algorithm due to the many advantages it brings to scheduling in Cloud. One of the first advantages that comes to mind is *workload distribution*, functioning as a load balancer and making sure resources on all machines are evenly utilized. It is scientifically proven that machines with a high workload do not function as well and this could lead to unwanted results. Another advantage is *heterogeneity transparency*, the type of VM and the OS being of no importance for the end user. Another feature of the overall system is its *adaptability*, because agreements can change all the time, so when a host is identified as not working properly, agreement establishment with a faulty node can be avoided. This makes the algorithm *fault tolerant*.

Prerequisites. The hosts are referred to as Nodes, each Tier having one or more Nodes. The Nodes know at start up (using a configuration file) which Tier they belong to. In terms of agreement participants, Tier 1 Nodes are Initiators, Tier 3 Nodes are Acceptors and Tier 2 Nodes handle both roles sequentially. They are first Initiators, and after completing agreements with Tier 3 Nodes, they become acceptors for Tier 1 Nodes. Tier 1 Nodes have a mission to fulfil: they need to complete agreements to cover the list of resources needed. Tier 3 Nodes complete agreements on a first come, first serve basis, while Tier 2 Nodes need to match resources with requirements (see Fig. 1). The following prerequisites are considered already established: (1) each node has a list with all the other nodes and is aware of which Tier they belong to; (2) A 3-Tier structure has been previously created; (3) Tier 1 nodes have a list of resources they need to provide, derived from the tasks that need to be run.

3.3 Agreement Establishment, Task Scheduling and Fault Tolerance

Agreement Establishment. Tier 1 Nodes first ask Tier 2 Nodes for a list of their attributes (processing power, memory, storage, VM type). Because our model assumes that Tier 1 Nodes have a list with the tasks that need to be run beforehand, Tier 1 Nodes have a way to estimate the resources needed (Alg. 1).

First, it sends a request to all nodes from Tier 2. They respond to this request with their available resources and resources of nodes they have completed an agreement with, named in the algorithm attributes. Then, they check their estimation of resources needed and make an offer to the respective node, using the smallest number between that of resources needed and that of resources

Algorithm 1. Tier 1 Agreement establishment

---

for each none N in `myNodesList` where Tier(N) = 2 **do**
    Request Attributes (N);
    Add attributes (Node, Resource, Quantity) to `AttList`;
end for
for each set of attributes (N, R, Q) in `AttList` **do**
    Get (from `myResourcesToProvideList`) the needed resources → (myR, myQ);
    (Resource, Quantity) = Compare(R, Q, myR, myQ)
    Make Offer (Node, Resource, Quantity)
    if Offer is Accepted **then**
        Withdraw(Resource, Quantity) from `myResourcesToProvideList`;
        Add(N, Resource, Quantity) to `myResourcesList`;
    end if
end for
SendTasks(); {tasks are assigned to each node (see Algorithm 3)}
for each Task T failed from node N **do**
    Add N to `faultList`; Resend T;
end for
for each node N in `myNodesList` **do**
    SendFaultlist(N);
end for

---

available of that node. After all agreements are established, tasks are assigned to nodes, as described in Alg. 3. Failed tasks are logged, machines are flagged as faulty and the tasks resent to other machines. The list of faulty machines is sent to all other nodes, to prevent further agreements to be established. This uses a 3 strike algorithm, as in an algorithm is considered faulty after three errors.

Algorithm 2. Tier 3 Agreement establishment

---

if AttributeRequest has been received from node N (from Tier 2) **then**
    SendAttributes(N, myResourceList);
end if
if (Offer O is received) AND ($N \notin$ `faultList`) **then**
    AcceptOffer(O);
    remove(O.Resource, O.Quantity) from `myAvailableResourcesList`;
end if

Tier 2 Nodes establish agreements with Tier 3 Nodes similar with the Alg. 1. They send a request for their available resources, attributes in the algorithm, and then they make offers to them. Tier 2 nodes have a constant defined, MAX, that represents the maximum number of Tier 3 nodes they can establish an agreement with. When an agreement is established, they add the respective node's resources to their list. Alg. 2 describes the way Tier 3 nodes establish agreement. They send a list with their available resources when receiving a request, and they accept offers on a FCFS basis. Establishing Tier 1 - Tier 2 agreements from a

Tier 2 Node's perspective are made as follow: Tier 2 nodes receive requests for info about their resources and add those requests on a waiting list, until they have established all Tier 3 agreements. Only after that they answer to those requests. When receiving an offer, they accept it on a FCFS basis.

Algorithm 3. Agreement based task scheduling

---

for each task T **do**
  scheduled = **false**;
  for each Agreement A **do**
    if $A.getAvailableRes() > T.getNecessaryRes()$ **then**
      sendTask(T, A); *scheduled* = **true**; break;
    end if
  end for
  if *scheduled* is **false then**
    A = get a new agreement for T; sendTask(T, A);
  end if
end for

Task Scheduling. The assignment of tasks to resources is done by the Tier 1 nodes. To keep the algorithm of low complexity, we schedule the tasks on a FIFO basis. This can be easily changed, wither by using advanced scheduling algorithm at this pace or by making sure the resources are requested in increments that would not make a task have to split to two or more nodes. To avoid adding work for Tier 2 nodes without a purpose, Tier 1 nodes send tasks directly to the node that runs it (Alg. 3).

Fault Tolerance. We consider the following faults: (i) for *Task* we can have node incompatibility resulting in a processing error, so the task is rescheduled on a different node or even a different platform; (ii) *Node* N_i is down, so all tasks scheduled on N_i should be rescheduled; and (iii) $ET(T_i, N_j)$ takes more than initially computed. Allocate more resources(extend agreement) or, if this is not possible, give task to another node. In terms of fault tolerance, this agreement based algorithm has the potential to use all the systems already in place at the PaaS level. In particular, the algorithm retries a failing task on a different machine. It also logs which machine had failed, creating a faulty machines list. The list is used to avoid agreements with machines, if they have failed more that a predefined number of times, three would be a good number in the general case.

4   Experimental Results

We were interested in comparing our algorithm with the base algorithm on time it took for tasks completion and we are expecting similar results. We compared our 3-Tier Agreement Based Algorithm with a 2-Tier Based Algorithm, with the scope of observing the number of messages in between hosts. We are expecting to see an increased number of messages for 3-Tier algorithms. However, the advantage of a 3-Tier algorithm over a 2-Tier algorithm lies not in the total number of messages, but in the fact that they are distributed over the network.

For simulation tests in CloudSim [11], we used a VM:host ratio of 6:1. We used 4000 independent tasks (simulated as cloudlets) with a number of VMs starting from 120 to 720 using a 100 increment. We used 2 brokers in both cases and we were interested to see the average finishing time. The ratio of Tier 2 Nodes to Tier 3 Nodes was 1:6 (see Fig. 2(left)). As the algorithm that we compared (FCFS) our implementation with iterates through VMs and assigns them a Task in order and keeping in mind that our tasks are homogeneous, the fact that the finishing time is so close to it means that we did not loose any machines and comes to validate our algorithm. The agreements are correctly established and tasks are evenly distributed between them.

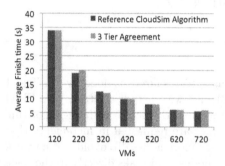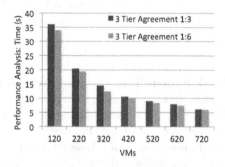

Fig. 2. (left) Comparison between proposed algorithm with a Tier 2 - Tier 3 nodes ratio of 1:6 and the default CloudSim scheduling algorithm; (right) Comparison between the average termination time of 4000 tasks with different Tier 2 - Tier 3 ratios

Next, we analyzed two 3-Tier Agreement Based Algorithms, both of them with two Tier 1 nodes(brokers), but with different ratios for Tiers 2 and 3. Thus, the first one has three Tier 3 nodes for each Tier 2 node (a ratio of 1:3), whereas the former has a ratio of 1:6. Fig. 2(right) shows a compared average termination time for 4000 tasks, starting from 120 VMs to 720 using a 100 increment. We can observe that the two approaches offer close result, partly because the tasks are homogeneous, but the algorithm with more nodes on Tier 3 performs better.

5   Conclusion

We proposed an agreement based algorithm to enhance the task scheduling process and make it more flexible, transparent and extendible. The algorithm is adaptive, fault tolerant, with workload distribution and large extension capabilities. We tested proposed algorithm using CloudSim with different numbers of nodes on each Tier. Evidence showed that it is better to have more nodes on the last Tier than on the second, with the 6:1 ratio giving the best results. For future work we propose: defining cost awareness policies for the agreement and extending the (re)negotiation protocol based on that; combining Tier 1 Nodes with a evolutionary algorithm in order to specialize Tier 1 Nodes.

Acknowledgment. The research presented in this paper is supported by projects: *"SideSTEP - Scheduling Methods for Dynamic Distributed Systems: a self-* approach"*, ID: PN-II-CT-RO-FR-2012-1-0084; *"ERRIC - Empowering Romanian Research on Intelligent Information Technologies"*, FP7-REGPOT-2010-1, ID: 264207; and by a grant of the Romanian National Authority for Scientific Research, CNDI-UEFISCDI, project number 47/2012.

References

1. Davies, K.: Best practices in big data storage. Tabor Communications Custom Publishing Group (2013) (accessed May 20, 2013)
2. Gens, F.: Idc predictions 2013: Competing on the 3rd platform. Int. Data Corporation (2012) (accessed May 25, 2013)
3. Frincu, M.E., Craciun, C.: Multi-objective meta-heuristics for scheduling applications with high availability requirements and cost constraints in multi-cloud environments. In: Proc. of the 2011 Fourth IEEE Int. Conf. on Utility and Cloud Computing, UCC 2011, pp. 267–274. IEEE Computer Society (2011)
4. Wang, L., Chen, D., Ranjan, R., Khan, S.U., Kolodziej, J., Wang, J.: Parallel processing of massive eeg data with mapreduce. In: Proceedings of the 2012 IEEE 18th International Conference on Parallel and Distributed Systems, ICPADS 2012, pp. 164–171. IEEE Computer Society, Washington, DC (2012)
5. Hagras, T., Janeek, J.: Static vs. dinamic list-scheduling performance comparison. Acta Polytechnica 43(6) (2003)
6. Kaur, K., Chhabra, A., Singh, G.: Heuristics based genetic algorithm for scheduling static tasks in homogeneous parallel system. Int. Journal of Computer Science and Security 4(2), 183–198 (2010)
7. Kolodziej, J., Khan, S.U.: Multi-level hierarchic genetic-based scheduling of independent jobs in dynamic heterogeneous grid env. Inf. Sci. 214, 1–19 (2012)
8. Xu, C.Z., Rao, J., Bu, X.: Url: A unified reinforcement learning approach for autonomic cloud management. J. Parallel Distrib. Comput. 72(2), 95–105 (2012)
9. Frincu, M.E., Villegas, N.M., Petcu, D., Muller, H.A., Rouvoy, R.: Self-healing distributed scheduling platform. In: Proc. of the 2011 11th IEEE/ACM Int. Symp. on Cluster, Cloud and Grid Computing, CCGRID 2011, pp. 225–234. IEEE Computer Society, Washington, DC (2011)
10. Wang, L., Khan, S.U., Chen, D., Kolodziej, J., Ranjan, R., Xu, C.Z., Zomaya, A.: Energy-aware parallel task scheduling in a cluster. Future Gener. Comput. Syst. 29(7), 1661–1670 (2013)
11. Calheiros, R.N., Ranjan, R., Beloglazov, A., De Rose, C.A., Buyya, R.: Cloudsim: a toolkit for modeling and simulation of cloud computing environments and evaluation of resource provisioning algorithms. Soft.: Pract. and Exp. 41(1), 23–50 (2011)

Parallel Social Influence Model with Levy Flight Pattern Introduced for Large-Graph Mining on Weibo.com

Benbin Wu, Jing Yang*, and Liang He

Department of Computer Science and Technology, East China Normal University,
200241 Shanghai, P.R. China
bbwu@ica.stc.sh.cn, {jyang,lhe}@cs.ecnu.edu.cn

Abstract. With a suitable method to rank the user influence in micro-blogging service, we could get influential individuals to make information reach large populations. Here a novel parallel social influence model is proposed to face to these challenges. In this paper, we firstly propose impact factors named Social Network Centricity and Weibo Heat Trend, describe a general algorithm named ActionRank to calculate the user influence based on these factors and the user-weibo behavior graph. Secondly, we introduce the Levy flight pattern into ActionRank, for the random large distance jumping phenomenon and the power-law distribution of the retweet cascade hops on Weibo.com meet its requirement. Thirdly, the parallel ActionRank is proposed with the help of MapReduce for large-scale graphs. Experiment results demonstrate that ActionRank on Levy flight pattern outperforms other algorithms and show the consistency of parallel ActionRank on datasets with sizes ranging from 20M to 1100 M edges.

1   Introduction

Studying influence patterns can help us understand how to help marketers design more effective campaigns[1]. We will do our social influence analysis base on Weibo.com, which is the largest twitter-like social network in China. In this paper, a general method named ActionRank is presented to assess users' influence. Using a large amount of data gathered from Weibo.com, we analyze the behavior between user and his tweets, i.e., follow, post, retweet. Furthermore, we are interested in message propagation over multiple hops. Here we need to formally define message propagation.

If a user u_0 posts a message M to a set of users U = { u_1, u_2, u_3,...}, we say M is originated by u_0 and propagated to U. If a user u_1 also retweet M after receiving it from u_0 and another user $v \notin$ U receives from u_1, then M is propagated by two hops, i.e., $u_0 \rightarrow u_1 \rightarrow v$. Each hop increases the chance for M to reach more users.

Common social network analysis are based on single-computer systems as sequential applications on small to medium size datasets, and struggle with datasets due to large memory consumption and long execution times. There is a clear need for high performance and distributed social network analysis to enable scenario with

J. Kołodziej et al. (Eds.): ICA3PP 2013, Part II, LNCS 8286, pp. 102–111, 2013.
© Springer International Publishing Switzerland 2013

large-scale graph mining. The MapReduce approach has been proved to be successful for handling the analysis of large data in parallel on huge clusters of computers. Motivated by these challenges, we provide a parallel social influence model using Hadoop, the open source implementation of MapReduce here.

Also, different from many prior studies in this field, an interesting phenomenon is found on Weibo.com in this work that a certain number of users retweet the originals posted by user u, even though they have no connection with u. Messages sometimes do not propagate along the link relation, even jumping a random large distance. It is in line with Levy flight pattern instead of the random walk pattern discussed in [2, 3, 4], and we will discuss this phenomenon in Section 4.

The rest of this paper is organized as follows. Section 2 mentions the related work. Our general model ActionRank and the parallel one are proposed in Section 3. Section 4 describes how we collect the data on Weibo.com and shows why we introduce Levy flight pattern to ActionRank base on the analysis of real-world data. Experiments and evaluations are shown in Section 5. Finally Section 6 ends with the conclusions.

2   Related Work

Many scholars have studied in how to assess the user influence in micro-blogging service, and propose the corresponding influence models in three categories as follow.

- Models based on the PageRank thought. Weng proposes an PageRank-like topic-similarity influence model based on the nodes and edges in the social network[5]. [6] applies an algorithm based on PageRank to produce influence ranking of users of a Java Developer bulletin board. But it's insufficient that they consider only the follow/followed relation to rank users' influence for the existence of robot fans.
- Models based on user behavior. Considering behavior of follow, retweet and mention, Cha assess the corresponding influence in [1]. Ye divides the social influence into follower, reply and retweet influence, and considers the ranking by most reply users as the stable standard for social influence ranking[7]. Although user behavior is considered by these scholars, it has limitations that they only choose single factor (i.e., number of retweet messages) or some statistics to assess the influence.
- Models based on both PageRank and user behavior. In current micro-blogging service, Twitter or Weibo.com, it is the retweeting behavior that contributes to the information dissemination. Kwak et al. considers "retweet tree", but they do not use them as a measure of influence[8]. Eytan et al. discuss the user influence using the "information propagation tree" that constructed by the retweet of originals, but they do not take the interaction between user and tweets into consideration[9]. Yuto et al. propose the TURank model[2] based on both their proposed user-tweet graph and the ObjectRank[3] that improved from PageRank. TURank analyzes the user behavior of follow, post and retweet tweets. Although it not only explores the interaction between users and tweets, also makes good use of social network and the information propagation pattern, TURank is still inadequate in the following respects.

1)In information propagation process, it is considered in TURank that user influence can only spread to one hop distance;2)It is also somewhat limited by the fact that the initial influence of users is equaled to each other in the network in TURank model.

To address these deficiencies, this work builds on previous contributions in two respects. Firstly, we proposes two factors Social Network Centrality (SNC) and Weibo Heat Trend (WHT), then a user influence model ActionRank is proposed. Secondly, the Levy flight pattern is introduced in ActionRank instead of random walk pattern.

3   User Behavior Influence Model

In this section, we construct user-weibo behavior graph and propose the two factors definitions firstly, then the general ActionRank model and the parallel one are shown.

3.1   User-Weibo Behavior Graph

Reference to TURank, we describe the user-weibo scheme graph used in our model firstly, as shown in Fig.1. Then the user-weibo behavior graph is discussed.

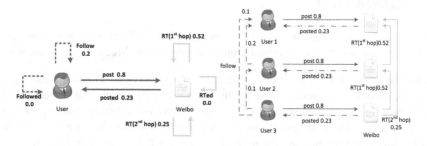

Fig. 1. User-Weibo schema graph   **Fig. 2.** User-Weibo behavior graph

A user-weibo scheme graph $UWG_s = (V_s, E_s)$ defines the structure and edge weights of the user-weibo behavior graph. Here V_s is the node set consisting of user nodes and tweet nodes, and E_s is the edge set consisting of post, posted, follow, followed, RT(1st hop), RT(2nd hop), and RTed edges. According to Fig. 1, the scores' calculation of each user for subsequent ranking is based on Eq. (1).

$$\vec{r} = dA\vec{r} + \frac{(1-d)}{|V|}\vec{e} \qquad (1)$$

Different from the user-tweet scheme graph in TURank, user-weibo scheme graph includes not only the RT edge in one hop, but also the RT edge in two hops. Fei et al. take the Sum of Neighbor's Degree(SND) into consideration[10] and show that the user influence is affected by the users' in two hops.

The weight $w(e_s)$ is set to $e_s \in E_s$ in accordance with the following two methods: firstly, edges' weight of follow/followed is set as the same to TURank. Secondly, we refer to the studies of Nicholas et al. in [11] to set the weight of retweet edges. So we use statistics in [12] as edge weight to assign to the retweet edges as Fig.1. Note that the sum of all outdegree weights of every node must be less than or equal to 1.

On the basis of user-weibo scheme graph, we construct the corresponding user-weibo behavior graph UWG=(V, E) in Fig.3., here V is the node set consisting of user nodes and tweet nodes, and E is the set of all edges with non-zero weight. The weight w(e) set to the edge $e \in E$ from node $u \in V$ is calculated by Eq. (2).

$$w(e) = \frac{w(e_s)}{OutDeg(u, e_s)} \tag{2}$$

where $e_s \in E_s$ is the edge of the same type as e, and $OutDeg(u, e_s)$ is the number of outgoing edges of type e_s from node u.

3.2   Definition

Definition 1. Social Network Centricity(SNC). SNC means one's position in the social network and is defined as Eq. (3). The more bidirectional edges one has, the stronger his connection in the network and the larger SNC he/she has, for these bidirectional edges may make his/her move from the periphery to the center of the social network. To measure one's SNC, we should consider the bidirectional edges not only between one and his friends, but also between the friends of his friends[10].

$$SNC_i = \frac{f_i + s_i}{\max\{f_j + s_j\}} (0 < i \le N, j = 1 \cdots N) \tag{3}$$

where N is user number, f_i and s_i are the number of bidirectional edges between one and his friends, his friends and their friends respectively.

Definition 2. Weibo Heat Trend(WHT). WHT shows the average retweet heat trend of a tweet from the posted day, it is defined as Eq. (4).

$$Trend(i) = \frac{1}{D} \sum_{t=1}^{D} \frac{|V_{i,j}| - \mu_i}{\sigma_i} (0 < i \le N, 0 < t \le D) \tag{4}$$

where i is the tweet index, D is the days to count, $|V_{i,j}|$ means the number of retweeted tweets after original i posted. μ_i and σ_i is the average number and the variance of retweeted tweets in D days respectively.

3.3   General ActionRank Model

Based on discussions above, we present our user influence general algorithm named ActionRank here. Every tweet becomes a quintuple of the form: f = (v, t, w, o, h), where t is the time user v posts a tweet w to retweet o, h is w's retweet hops from o.

On Weibo.com, if user v post tweet w to retweet o and the retweet hops of w is no less than 2 from o, the text of w contains form"//@user", which means that o reach v through the user. Retweet hops can be comuted by counting the number of this form. Here shows the general ActionRank process.

STEP 1. Initialize the users' influence by their scores of SNC;
STEP 2. With Eq. (1), calculate the influence of user and tweet iteratively based on the user-weibo behavior graph and WHT of every tweets.

3.4 Parallel ActionRank Model

MapReduce is a programming framework for distributed processing of large data sets. In the map stage, each machine(called a process node) receives a subset of data as input and produces a set of intermediate key/value pairs. In the reduce stage, each process node merges all intermediate values associated with the same intermediate key and outputs the final computation results. Generally, a map function is specified to process a key/value pair to generate a set of intermediate key/value pairs, and a reduce function to merge all intermediate values associated with the same interme- diate key.

Here we use Hadoop , an open source implementations of the MapReduce fram- work , to launch the MapReduce task of parallel ActionRank model. We first partition the large social network graph into subgraphs and distribute each subgraph to a process node. A subgraph is constructed by three forms: users and their friends, origi- nal tweets and the tweets that retweet them, users and their posted tweets. Note that each edge e_{ij} has a node score value r_i, thus, the map function is defined as for every key/value pair e_{ij} / r_i, it issues an intermediate key/value pair $e_{i*} /(r_i + w_{ij} * r_j)$.

In the reduce stage, each process node collects values associated with an intermediate key e_{i*} to generate new r_{i*} according to Eq. (1) and all intermediate values associated with the same key e_{i*} to generate new r_i according to Eq. (4). So the one time map- reduce process corresponds to one iteration in the parallel ActionRank model.

4   Data Prepare and Data Analysis

In this section, we firstly discuss about the real-world datasets crawled from Wei- bo.com. Secondly, the reason why Levy flight pattern is applied to ActionRank is presented according to the analysis on Weibo.com.

4.1   Data Collection

With the APIs provided on Weibo.com, we get four datasets in domains of technolo- gy, real estate, entertainment and sports respectively over the period 1/1/2013- 2/28/2013. Basic statistics of these four datasets is shown in Table 1.

Consistent with previous work[2, 3, 9], both the indegree ("followers") and outde- gree ("friends") distributions are highly skewed, which reflects the passive and one- way nature of the "follow" action on Weibo.com.

Table 1. Basic statistics of four datasets

Datasets	Technology	RealEstate	Entertainment	Sports
#Nodes	23243281	11758207	8930453	3256366
Mean outdegree	3236.93	6787.28	6420.97	5263.46
Mean Indegree	16826.38	47922.82	238331.6	18179.86
#Edges	1098154665	657843258	20196876	30223596

4.2 Data Analysis

There are many reasons why individuals may choose to pass along the messages other than considering identity of the users from whom they received it[7]. A tweet with useful content can influence others to pass along and make itself spread to larger cascade hops. Here we give a definition to the term retweet cascade hops.

Definition 3. Retweet Cascade Hops(RCH). RCH is the largest hops one original can spread to. Fig.3 shows the statistical distribution of RCH in four datasets.

In Fig.3, the RCH of most of originals is 0, it means that most of originals aren't retweeted, nevertheless, some originals' RCH is larger than 20. Note that the user influence discussed in this work is mostly based on retweet behavior, originals with 0 RCH couldn't feedback to the influence of their promulgators according to user-weibo behavior graph in Fig.2. So we ignore these originals in this work.

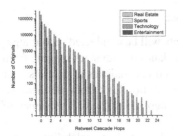

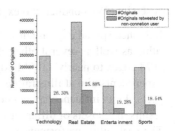

Fig. 3. Distribution of RCH in datasets   **Fig. 4.** Analysis of originals retweeted at 1st hop

Base on the analysis of retweet behavior of the first hop in four datasets, an interesting large-distance behavior phenomenon is found on Weibo.com that the mean 22.75% of the originals are retweeted by users who have no connection to originals' promulgators, and the phenomenon is shown and discussed as below.

Large-Distance Behavior Phenomenon

The retweet behavior at the first hop of originals is analyzed in Fig.4. It tells that average 22.75% of originals are retweeted by users who have no connection to originals' promulgators , which is the large-distance behavior phenomenon on Weibo.com.

Power-Law of the Retweet Cascade Hops(RCH)

Fig.5 shows the power-law distribution of RCH in four datasets. In other words, the larger the retweet cascade hops has, the less the number of originals is and vice versa.

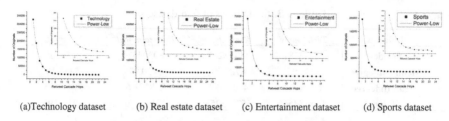

| (a)Technology dataset | (b) Real estate dataset | (c) Entertainment dataset | (d) Sports dataset |

Fig. 5. Power-law distribution of hops in four datasets

The existence of random large distance and the power-law distribution of RCH meet the theorem of Levy flight pattern, The Levy flight random jump probability is:

$$d = \frac{l^{-u}}{C} = \frac{l^{-u}}{\sum_{k=r+1}^{D} k^{-u}} (1 < u \le 3) \tag{5}$$

where C is normalization coefficient, l is the retweet cascade hops of a tweet, u is the exponent of the power-law equation that retweet cascade hops meet. D is the largest RCH empirically and r is 1.0 in social network.

5   Experiments and Evaluations

In this section, We conduct two experiments as below:

a)   Influence spread experiments. These experiements will be conducted on our algorithm as well as several other algorithms on four datasets with sizes ranging from 20M edges to nearly 1100M edges. Table 3 shows other statistics of datasets. Our experiments aim at illustrating the performance of ActionRank from the these aspects: 1) its influence spread comparing to other algorithms, 2) its consistency of results in datasets of different size.

b)   The scalability performance experiments. We further conduct scalability experiments with our parallel ActionRank model to evaluate the speedup of the distributed mining algorithm on the 5 computer nodes using the dataset selected from Technology datasets, with the edge size is {20M, 60M, 100M, 150M, 200M}

Table 2. Statistics of four datasets

Datasets	Technology	RealEstate	Entertainment	Sports
Mean #bidirections	416.17	371.46	271.61	298.89
Mean #originals	54.68	5.54	41.43	42.11

5.1   Random Jump Probabilities in ActionRank

Since ActionRank proposed in Section 4 is a general model with nonuniform random jump probability. In experiment a), we use Levy flight pattern and random walk pattern respectively to express the probability. So ActionRank on Levy flight pattern is named as ActionRankLF, and ActionRank on random walk pattern as ActionRankRW.

5.2   Experiments and Metrics

In influence spread test, we compare ActionRankLF and ActionRankRW to the algorithms of TURank, PageRank and Random. And Random is the baseline comparison. For each user influence ranking from these five algorithms, we select the top N individuals who get the highest influence scores as the seeds and check the individuals' number who retweet seeds' originals simulating the size influence can spread to. And N is assigned with values{30, 50, 100, 130, 150, 200, 250, 300, 400, 500}.

5.3   Evaluations

Fig. 6(a)-(d) show the results on influence spreads of five algorithms in different experimental networks. Fig. 6(a) and Fig. 6(b) show the similar results on technology and real estate datasets, two large network with exceed 600 million edges. These two figures show that ActionRankLF produces the best influence spread and has a large winning margin over ActionRankRW. But ActionRankRW is close to TURank: its influence spread essentially covers that of TURank and is only 0.63% larger. Comparing to other algorithms, ActionRankLF and ActionRankRW perform better than PageRank and Random. Random has a worst influence spread, indicating that a careful seed selection is indeed important to effective viral marketing results.

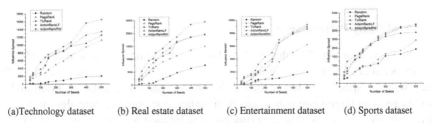

(a)Technology dataset   (b) Real estate dataset   (c) Entertainment dataset   (d) Sports dataset

Fig. 6. Influence spread experiment results

Fig. 6(c) and Fig. 6(d) show the results of entertainment and sports datasets with 20M edges and 30M edges respectively. In these two graphs, ActionRankLF still outperforms other methods and reaches larger influence spread size. But the advantage from ActionRankLF and ActionRankRW has narrowed obviously. We finds from the rankings that the top individuals are almost famous singers, actors/actresses in entertainment dataset and popular athletes, sports stars, sports commentators in sports dataset, who have plenty of followers. As Fig. 4 has shown, only 19.28% and 19.54% of the originals are retweeted by non-connection individuals in entertainment and sports datasets, but most of which are not posted by these top N seeds. In this case, ActionRankLF is nearly to ActionRankRW and get similar influence spread results, although it is still better than TURank resulting from the impact of SNC and WHT factors in ActionRank. In these two figures, ActionRankRW matches the influence spread of TURank in some cases, likewise, ActionRankLF, ActionRankRW and TURank still outperform PageRank and Random. Differently, the curves of PageRank and Random cross each other in Fig. 6(c) and Fig. 6(d), but not in Fig. 6(a) and Fig. 6(b), because of the randomness of Random algorithm, it is reasonable that some seeds with high influence scores are selected by Random to have a larger spread than PageRank.

Overall, ActionRankLF outperforms other algorithms in four datasets, and exhibits a trend that it could reach the same large influence spread size with at a larger speed than other algorithms from the beginning. But the more seeds are added, the lower the influence scores of new seeds have, it appears that the growth of the influence spread tends to slow down. Considering the algorithm performance when the number of seeds ranges from 30 to 150, Fig. 6(c) shows that although ActionRankLF reaches the largest influence spread size, but its speed to get the a larger influence spread size is slower than that in other datasets, since the individuals in entertainment dataset post least originals in Table 3. Analysis on the singers' and actors' originals, which are mainly about the mood description, then the factor WHT of ActionRank gets a smaller value in entertainment dataset than in other ones and ActionRankLF is near to ActionRankRW, though better than TURank for the impact of SNC, which seeks the people having a large number of bidirectional connections to help the information diffusion.

Fig. 6 also demonstrates that our ActionRank algorithm outperforms other ones in datasets with different large-size, and shows the consistency of ActionRank in these experiments, meanwhile, the ActionRank on Levy flight pattern is also better than that on random walk pattern, and is more suitable for Weibo.com.

5.4   Scalability Performance

It can be seen from Fig. 7(a) that as the edge size of dataset raises to nearly 150 M, the distributed social influence mining algorithm starts to show a good parallel efficiency with the speedup is larger than 2. It confirms that the parallel ActionRankLF model is good on large-scale datasets as many other distributed mining algorithms.

Fig. 7(b) shows our speedup experiments on a Hadoop platform using 1 to 5 computer nodes using Real Estate dataset (657 M edge size). This figure also tells the reasonable parallel efficiency and gets a larger speedup than 3 while using 5 nodes.

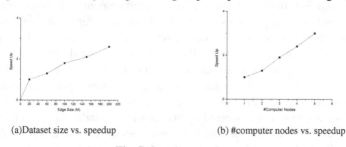

(a)Dataset size vs. speedup   (b) #computer nodes vs. speedup

Fig. 7. Speed up results

6   Conclusions and Future Work

In this paper, we firstly propose two impact factors named SNC and WHT, then based on these factors and the user-weibo behavior graph, general ActionRank is presented. Secondly, we introduce the Levy flight pattern to the ActionRank in this work. Facing to the challenges of large-scale graph mining on the social network, we finally extends the ActionRank to a parallel one based on the MapReduce framework and show the scalability and efficient of the parallel one.

The general problem of social influence analysis represents a new and interesting research direction in social network mining. There are many potential future directions of this work. One interesting issue is to extend the ActionRank to the text analysis and the topic model of users and tweets, and another interesting issue is to design the ActionRank model as a (semi-)supervised learning.

Acknowledgement. This work is supported by Opening Project of Shanghai Key Laboratory of Integrate Administration Technologies for Information Security(AGK 2011005), and grants from the Shanghai Science and Technology commission International Cooperation Foundation(No. 11530700300, No. 12dz1500205).

References

1. Cha, M., Haddadi, H.: Measuring user influence in twitter: the million follower fallacy. In: Proc. of Conf. AAAI on Weblogs and Social Media, Washington, pp. 11–13 (2010)
2. Yamaguchi, Y., Takahashi, T., Amagasa, T., Kitagawa, H.: TURank: twitter user ranking based on user-tweet graph analysis. In: Chen, L., Triantafillou, P., Suel, T. (eds.) WISE 2010. LNCS, vol. 6488, pp. 240–253. Springer, Heidelberg (2010)
3. Andrey, B., Vagelis, H., Yannis, P.: ObjectRank: authority-based keyword search in database. In: Proc. of the 30th VLDB Conference, Toronto, pp. 564–575 (2004)
4. Chen, W., Wang, C., Wang, Y.: Scalable influence maximization for prevalent viral marketing in large-scale social networks. In: Proc. of Conf. KDD, USA, pp. 1029–1038 (2010)
5. Weng, J., Lim, E., Jiang, J.: Twitterrank: finding topic-sensitive influential twitterers. In: Proc. of the 3rd Conference on Web Search and Data Mining, USA, pp. 261–270 (2010)
6. Zhang, J., Ackerman, M.S., Adamic, L.: Expertise networks in online communities: structure and algorithms. In: Proc. of Conf. WWW, Canada, pp. 221–230 (2007)
7. Ye, S., Wu, S.F.: Measuring message propagation and social influence on twitter.com. In: Proc. of Conf. SocInfo, China, pp. 221–230. IEEE Press (2010)
8. Kwak, H., et al.: What is twitter, a social network or a news media? In: Proc. of Conf. WWW, USA, pp. 591–600. ACM Press (2010)
9. Bakshy, E., Hofman, J.M.: Everyone's an influencer: quantifying influence on twitter. In: Proc. of Conf. WSDM, China, pp. 65–74. ACM Press (2011)
10. Fei, H., Chen, M., Zhu, C.: Discovering influence users in micro-blog marketing with influence maximization mechanism. In: Proc. of Conf. Globecom, USA, pp. 488–492 (2012)
11. Christakis, N.A., et al.: Dynamic spread of happiness in a large social network: longitudinal analysis over 20 years in the Framingham heart study. Medical Journal (2008)
12. Chen, Y.: Influence assess model analysis on weibo. FuJian Computer, 6–25 (2012)

Quality Control of Massive Data for Crowdsourcing in Location-Based Services

Gang Zhang and Haopeng Chen

REINS Group, School of Software
Shanghai Jiao Tong University
Shanghai, P.R. China
{infear,chen-hp}@sjtu.edu.cn

Abstract. Crowdsourcing has become a prospective paradigm for commercial purposes in the past decade, since it is based on a simple but powerful concept that virtually anyone has the potential to plug in valuable information, which brings a lot of benefits such as low cost and high immediacy, particularly in some location-based services (LBS). On the other side, there also exist many problems need to be solved in crowdsourcing. For example, the quality control for crowdsourcing systems has been identified as a significant challenge, which includes how to handle massive data more efficiently, how to discriminate poor quality content in workers' submission and so on. In this paper, we put forward an approach to control the crowdsourcing quality by evaluating workers' performance according to their submitted contents. Our experiments have demonstrated the effectiveness and efficiency of the approach.

Keywords: crowdsourcing, massive data, quality control, location-based services (LBS).

1   Introduction

The proposal of "Crowdsourcing" paradigm was first defined as "a company or organization outsources their tasks to those who are not specific in the form of free voluntary (and usually large public networks.)" [1]. In today's Web 2.0 world, the concept of crowdsourcing, that virtually anyone has the potential to plug in valuable information is extended to wiki and other collaboration tools [2].Recently this paradigm has also flourished in location-based service (LBS) [3], in which the smart-device users contribute information about their surroundings, thereby providing a collective knowledge about the physical world. In some cases, these services rely on mapping software such as Google Maps. For example, CROWDSAFE [4], a novel convergence of Internet crowdsourcing and portable smart devices to enable real time, location based crime incident searching and reporting. In addition, there are also many other indoor LBS based on the Access Points (AP), which is called "wifi-type" service. But no matter which kind of LBS，the quality of service completely depends on the crowdsourcing quality. In this paper, indoor LBS is our research background.

J. Kołodziej et al. (Eds.): ICA3PP 2013, Part II, LNCS 8286, pp. 112–121, 2013.
© Springer International Publishing Switzerland 2013

The paper is structured as follows.Sec.2 gives a quick overview of the concept of crowdsourcing and the research already done in the area. In Sec.3, we present our main design about how to solve the questions mentioned above. Detailed implementation would be involved in Sec.4 and experience results would be analyzed in Sec.5. In Sec.6, we would do conclusion and some discussion about our future work.

2   Related Work

In crowdsourcing paradigm, there are two roles, employer and worker as is shown in Fig.1. People called employer submit tasks, evaluate worker's submitted results and pay workers, while workers pull and complete tasks, get pays from employers.[5]

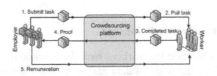

Fig. 1. Crowdsourcing scheme

Generally, crowdsourcing task is simple but needs large amount of resource. But now we can now harness human resource in near-real time from a vast and ever-growing, distributed population of online Internet users [6]. In this way, crowdsourcing brings low cost and high efficiency. But if exists cheating, the quality of tasks would be influenced. Meanwhile, it cost a lot that validating whether a worker is cheating in the task.

Some researches consider that inaccurate acceptance or rejection would affect not only current task, but also possibly drive a new wave of fraudsters, because those who have cheated do not receive any punishment. For example, Matthias et al. raise "Majority Decision Approach" [5] to judge whether worker's submission is correct in simple tasks, and using "Control Group Approach" method in complicated cases. Besides, Petros and Hector propose "Gold Standard Performance" to detect one worker's performance before the crowdsourcing task starts [7]. In addition, it is also a hot topic that to balance the task quality and rewards cost. For instance, in 2009, Yahoo's research institute made a quantitative analysis on the relationship between "Financial Incentives" and "Performance of Crowds" [8], and found that higher rewards can accelerate the accomplishment of the task, but cannot improve its quality. In this paper, we would discuss about the task quality from a new aspect.

3   System Design

The goal of our system is to locate all Access Points (AP) accurately in an area, thus providing value-added services later. While one's smart-device is access to one AP, he could submit a record contains the information about it to server as a worker's task in crowdsourcing. On the server side, the system would filter and aggregate these submitted records as an employer's job. As is shown in Fig.2, there are three phases in our system design: *Filtering, Aggregating,* and *Feedback.*

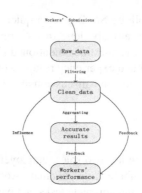

Fig. 2. System design

3.1   Filtering: Refine Submitted Contents

We call the records set submitted by workers **raw data**, since it is necessary to prepro-
cess these records to reduce the scale of data and make our later work more accurate.

First, the records with wrong formats or values are rejected. In our design, each
record is composed of a tuple like this: (*wid, apid, bid, fid, rid, lx, ly*). We use a 32-bits
positive integer to denote each worker's id(*wid*), AP's id (*apid*) and AP's position
which consists of a building (*bid*), a floor (*fid*), a room (*rid*) and a pair of coordinates
(*lx, ly*) in the room respectively. So it is easy to eliminate those records with wrong
formats or values. Second, we detect cheating workers. For instance, one worker may
submit same records frequently during a period (i.e.10 seconds) in a crowdsourcing
task. This is supposed to be a kind of cheating like that in "Page Rank" [9]. So we
retain the records earliest submitted and discard the remainder.

After filtering, the scale of records set is trimmed first, which can accelerate our
later work. Meanwhile, we make the records more meaningful, which would improve
our aggregation. The records set after filtering is called **clean data**.

3.2   Aggregating with Quality Table

It is realistic that the position of AP is comparatively fixed during a short period such
as one day. Then, we periodically aggregate the clean data to locate the position AP in
this phase, which can be divided into two parts:

First, we define *ar* ("Accept Rate") to describe each worker's overall performance
which is summarized from his history task. It is also used to judge the probability that
the worker's submitted records would be accepted in his next task. Here, Quality Table
[10] is introduced to denote such probability. For example, in Fig. 3, if one's *ar* is
close to 1 or 100%, all records he submits in next task would be regarded as quality of
his *ar* and accepted completely. On the other side, if one's *ar* is close to 0, the quality
of his submission may be also poor and thus, discarded. In addition, one's submission
would be accepted partly. This case would be introduced in detail in the Sec.4.

Second, we do aggregation on the result of the previous step with "Majority Decision Approach". For example, for AP whose *apid* is 10, there exist 100
records(including the generated ones) that show the position of it is ($bid_1, fid_1, rid_1, lx_1,
ly_1$) and another 60 records that tell ($bid_2, fid_2, rid_2, lx_2, ly_2$).Then, the first result is
more trustable.

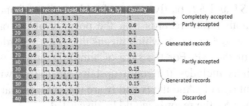

Fig. 3. Quality Table

3.3   Feedback on Workers' Performance

In this phase, we update one's *ar* according to his contribution in the current task and his history performance, which is kind of feedback on *ar*.

First, for each worker, we count the number of the records in his submission which match our aggregated results, which is named, *hit*. It demonstrates one's contributions in the tasks during a short period. For example, one worker submits 100 records one day and 80 of them match the aggregated results, his *hit* is 80/100=80%.For the sake of accuracy, these three values (*match records number*, *submitted records number*, *hit*) would be all retained for future use. It has to be noted that the clean data is used as our input but not the results after the first step of the aggregate phase, since it is more reasonable.

Then, we update each worker's *ar* according to his contribution in the current task and previous ones. Here, two approaches are introduced; **Static Period Analysis** and **Sliding Window Analysis**. The details would be involved in Sec.4.

4   Implementation

In this Sec, we discuss about our system implementation in detail, particularly in algorithms. Due to limited space, we focus on the algorithms part of aggregating and feedback phases.

4.1   Aggregating with Mapreduce Model

As mentioned in the design part, the clean data is aggregated periodically. We donate: [*t1*, *t2*] as such period, and assume there are n workers who involved in the task during the period. Besides, we have follow arguments as input:

- *S*: clean data set derived from workers' submitted records during this period [t_1, t_2]. The format of each record is (*apid, bid, fid, rid, lx, ly, wid*).
- *A= {ar₁...arₙ}*: the latest *ar* of each worker. It is supposed to be fixed during the period [t_1, t_2].
- *S1, S2:* two thresholds used to judge how worker's submission would be accepted. There are three cases according to the value of *ar*:
  — *ar* is greater than *S1*:accepted completely with quality of one's *ar*.

— *ar* is between *S1* and *S2*: partly accepted with quality of one's *ar*. Meanwhile, we generate another four records near the position of the origin one and give each one quality *_q*= $(1-ar)/4$, which means that these records are also the possible positions of the AP. For the sake of simplification, it is assumed that the possible positions includes the room upstairs (*fid*+1), downstairs (*fid*-1), left (*rid*-1) and right (*rid*+1).And the *lx* and *ly* are the same as that of the origin one.

— *ar* is smaller than *S2*:the records would be discarded.

Since the records set may be too large to handle, we use HADOOP framework here to improve performance of data processing. So our algorithm can be divided to mapper part and reducer part. The Mapper procedure is as follows:

```
Algorithm1: Aggregating Mapper
Input: Records Set S consists of records. Accept Rate Set A= {ar₁...arₙ}
describe each one's honesty.S1 and S2 act as ar thresholds.
Output: Record Set S'. Each record owns an extra element quality de-
scribes the accuracy of this record.


For each record = (apid, bid, fid, rid, lx, ly, wid) in S:
      ar = A[wid]
      If ar > S1
            // completely accepted
            Output (apid, bid, fid, rid, lx, ly, ar)
      Else if ar > S2:
            //partly accepted, quality=ar.
            Output (apid, bid, fid, rid, lx, ly, ar)
            _q = (1 - ar) / 4 //generate records of positions around.
            Output (apid, bid, fid+1, rid, lx, ly, _q)
            Output (apid, bid, fid-1, rid, lx, ly, _q)
            Output (apid, bid, fid, rid+1, lx, ly, _q)
            Output (apid, bid, fid, rid-1, lx, ly, _q)
      Else:
            Continue next loop. // discarded
```

Now we do reduce job. Since each record in S' contains an *apid*, position information (*bid, fid, rid, lx, ly*) and a quality, we could first count the total quality of each tuple (*apid, bid, fid, rid, lx, ly*) and group them by *apid* later. Finally, we sort them by the quality each one has in each group and the max one is our aggregation result, for most workers think that this position is the most accurate one where the AP is located.

```
Algorithm2: Aggregating Reducer
Input: Records Set S' consists of the records whose format is (apid,
bid, fid, rid, lx, ly, quality).
Output: Each AP's id and its accurate position.

quality_table = {}
```

```
result_table = {}
For each r in S':
      k = (r.apid, r.bid, r.fid, r.rid, r.lx, r.ly)
      v = r.quality
      If k in the keyset of quality_table:
            Update its value by adding v
      Else:
            Insert (k, v) into quality_table
For each (k, v) in quality_table:
      If k.apid in the keyset of result_table:
            k' = (k.id, result_table[k.apid])
            v' = quality_table[k']
            If v'>v:
                  Update by set result_table[k]=v'
      Else:
            k' = k.apid
            v' = (k.bid, k.fid, k.rid, k.lx, k.ly)
            Insert (k', v') into result_table
For each (k, v) in result_table:
      output (k, v)
```

4.2   Feedback: Static Period Analysis and Sliding Window Analysis

Here, we present two approaches: *Static Period Analysis* and *Sliding Window Analysis*, which are used to evaluate each worker's performance (*ar*). We regard one day as the minimum unit to do aggregation and calculate each one's hit.

Static Period Analysis

The approach is called "*Static Period Analysis*", for we consider each one's performance keeps stable within a comparatively short period such as one week. During the period, one's last updated *ar* is always used to judge how his submission would be accepted (completely or partly accepted or rejected). As usual, we calculate hit every day for future use. At the end of this period, his up-to-date *ar* would be summarized according to these hits. It would come into effect in next period.

Given the period *p* days, we have:

- (arc_i, rc_i, hit_i), i=1...p: tuples denote one's contribution in the task every day. It contains:
  - arc_i: count of accurate records in one's submission.
  - rc_i: counts of all records in one's submission.
  - hit_i: the proportion of *arc* in *r*.

Then, the up-to-date *ar* would be calculated as follows:

$$ar = \frac{\sum_1^p arc_i}{\sum_1^p rc_i} \qquad (1)$$

Since one's performance is supposed to be stable during a short period, it is considered that each worker's ar keeps constant during p days. This would make one's performance not sensitive to his contribution every day. It has to be noted that we make use of the weighted average here, since it is more accurate.

Sliding Window Analysis

Static Period Analysis could reflect one worker's performance periodically and also time efficient. But it does not take one's history performance into account. Besides, one's ar would not ascend no matter how great his contribution is during the period. Relatively speaking, "*Sliding Window Analysis*" is more flexible and accurate.

Here, we introduce the following definitions:

- SW_i, $i \in N$: A sliding window denotes the i_{th} dynamic period $[t_{1i}, t_{2i}]$. Here the length of SW is p days for example and we mark each day as an integer from 1. So first SW is [1, p] and it would slide to right by increasing both t_{1i} and t_{2i} by 1. For instance, the third SW would be [3, p+2] and the n_{th} SW is [n, n+p-1].

- H_i, $i \in N$: The set contains one's contribution every day during the current SW_i period. Each contribution is a tuple (*arc, rc, hit*).

- ar_i, $i \in N$: worker's ar on the i_{th} day.

- w: impact factor which denotes one's history performance influence.

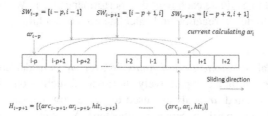

Fig. 4. Sliding Window

Then, the ar_i is calculated by:

$$ar_i = w * ar_{i-p} + (1 - w) * \frac{\sum_{i-p+1}^{i} arc_j}{\sum_{i-p+1}^{i} ar_j} \qquad (2)$$

First, we take the worker's history performance into account by giving ar_{i-p} a certain weight, regarding that it would influence one's later performance (ar_i) to some extent. Second, arc and rc are still used instead of hit here for accuracy. Last but not least, we also do periodically analysis like that in Static Period Analysis which would not suffer from the case in which one's contribution varies dramatically from day to day.

With *Sliding Window Analysis*, we combine one's history performance and contributions in recent tasks together, which is more persuasive and thoughtful. Meanwhile, it is also not sensitive to one's contribution each day. But the cost on time is also higher.

5   Experiments and Evaluation

To evaluate the effectiveness of our approach, we generate massive data set to simulate the submitted records under crowdsourcing model. The data set has the characteristics of that in crowdsourcing in reality. We would see the improvements as using our approaches. Time consuming and the aggregated results' accuracy are the points.

5.1   Filtering and Quality Table

In this part, the effectiveness of aggregating with filtering and quality table is evaluated. Given 1000 workers and 1500 Access Points (AP), we generate data of 1GB size to simulate the records that submitted by workers in crowdsourcing every day during a period of 30 days. We pick up a piece of period (5 days) of the results. *Static Period Analysis* is used here with 5 days ($p = 5$). In addition, we also have:

- Two thresholds: $S1$=0.8, $S2$=0.3.
- Each worker's initial *ar* is 1 or 100%.

And four cases :

- None: without filtering and quality table.
- Filtering only: only using filtering.
- Aggregating only: only aggregate with quality table.
- Both: using both filtering and quality table to aggregate.

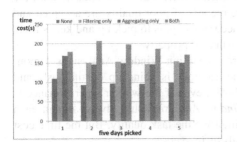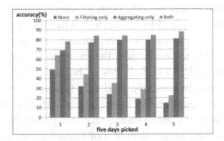

Fig. 5. Time cost and Accuracy in different cases

As is shown in the Fig.5 without filtering and quality table, the accuracy of the aggregated result is lower than 30%, which is an unacceptable value in practical applications. In addition, as time goes on, the accuracy is going down continuously (include the case of Filtering only), since more workers submit records of low quality.

On the other side, although the time cost of aggregating that utilize filtering and quality table is higher (2~3 times more than case of None), its accuracy is very satisfied (more than 80% at last). Since each worker's performance tends to be stable, it would be more and more accuracy to validate one's submission quality. Besides, aggregating with quality table would bring more continuous improvements than filtering.

In conclusion, though time cost is a bit higher, our approach, particularly the aggregating with quality table, performs well on quality control of workers' submission.

5.2 Static Period Analysis and Sliding Window Analysis

We would still compare the difference of these two approaches from two aspects, performance and accuracy. The arguments *S1*, *S2* and the period length are set the same as those in the previous experiment.

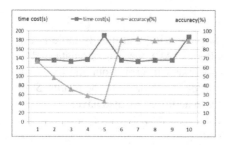 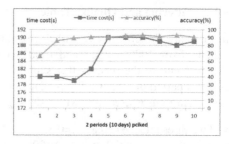

Fig. 6. Static Period Analysis and Sliding Window Analysis ($w=0.25$)

In Fig.6, the performance of approach Static Period Analysis is evaluated. As the period is 5 days long, the feedback phase is always called at the end of each period, such as the 5_{th} and 10_{th} day. Therefore, the time cost keeps stable during each period and ascend dramatically on these days. On the other hand, the accuracy is continuously going down during the first period, since each worker's *ar* is not updated until the end of the period. Thereby, more and more records of poor quality are accepted and the task quality is affected. After that, the accuracy begins to pick up and keeps high, for all the workers' performance has been evaluated properly.

On the other side, the evaluation of approach Sliding Window Analysis is demonstrated in Fig.6. It has to be noted that the accuracy is going up continuously and tends to be stable gradually (above about 90%), even if the worker's performance is very changeable in the period. *Sliding Window Analysis* could always obtain each worker's performance accurately, thereby improve the task quality. But the time cost is 30% higher than that of Static Period Analysis in average.

On the whole, if workers' performance keeps stable, it is efficient and acceptable to take the approach Static Period Analysis. Otherwise, Sliding Window Analysis is more preferred for its flexibility and accuracy.

6   Conclusion and Future Work

In crowdsourcing, the contents submitted by workers are always large and inaccuracy. So it is essential to control the quality of the contents. Here, we regard indoor LBS as research background and discuss how to qualify these data efficiently and accurately. It has to be noted that our approach can be applied to many other applications such as the detection of malicious comments on E-commerce sites, since it is irrelevant to the semantic of the contents. Our focus is each worker's contribution within all workers.

Our next work will focus on data refreshing in crowdsourcing. As times goes on, the scale of the data would be too massive to retain. So it is necessary to have a mechanism to eliminate those data with low value or freshness [11].

Acknowledgement. This paper is supported by Shanghai Municipal Science and Technology Commission under Grant No. 11dz1502500.

References

1. Howe, J.: The Rise of Crowdsourcing, Wired (June 2006), http://www.wired.com/wired/archive/14.06/crowds.html
2. Greengard, S.: Following the crowd. Communications of the ACM 54(2), 20–22 (2011)
3. Alt, F., Sahami, A., Schmidt, S.A., Kramer, U., Nawaz, Z.: Location-based crowdsourcing: extending crowdsourcing to the real world. In: 6th Nordic Conference on Human-Computer Interaction: Extending Boundaries, pp. 13–22
4. Shah, S., Bao, F., Lu, C.-T., Chen, I.-R.: CROWDSAFE: crowdsourcing of crime incidents and safe routing on mobile devices. In: 19th ACM SIGSPATIAL International Conference on Advances in Geographic Information Systems, pp. 521–524
5. Hirth, M., Hoßfeld, T., Tran-Gia, P.: Cost-Optimal Validation Mechanisms and Cheat-Detection for Crowdsourcing Platforms. In: 5th International Conference on Innovative Mobile and Internet Services in Ubiquitous Computing, pp. 316–321
6. Lease, M., Yilmaz, E.: Crowdsourcing for information retrieval. Newsletter ACM SIGIR Forum Archive 45(2), 66–75 (2011)
7. Venetic, P., Garcia-Molina, H.: Quality control for comparison microtasks. In: The 1st International Workshop on Crowdsourcing and Data Mining, pp. 15–21
8. Mason, W., Watts, D.J.: Financial incentives and the "performance of crowds". ACM SIGKDD Explorations Newsletter 11(2), 100–108 (2009)
9. Chen, Z., Ma, J., Cui, C., Rui, H., Huang, S.: Web page publication time detection and its application for page rank. In: 33rd International ACM SIGIR Conference on Research and Development in Information Retrieval, pp. 859–860
10. Cheng, R., Chen, J., Xie, X.: Cleaning uncertain data with quality guarantees. Journal VLDB Endowment 1(1), 722–735 (2008)
11. Bouzeghoub, M.: A framework for analysis of data freshness. In: 2004 International Workshop on Information Quality in Information Systems, pp. 59–67 (2004)

Part II
International Workshop on Big Data Computing (BDC 2013)

Towards Automatic Generation
of Hardware Classifiers

Flora Amato, Mario Barbareschi, Valentina Casola,
Antonino Mazzeo, and Sara Romano

Università degli Studi di Napoli "Federico II",
Dipartimento di Ingegneria Elettrica e Tecnologie dell'Informazione,
Via Claudio 21, 80125, Napoli, Italia
{flora.amato,mario.barbareschi,casolav,mazzeo,sara.romano}@unina.it

Abstract. Nowadays, in a broad range of application areas, the daily
data production has reached unprecedented levels. This data origins from
multiple sources, such as sensors, social media posts, digital pictures and
videos and so on. The technical and scientific issues related to the data
booming have been designated as the "Big Data" challenges. To deal
with big data analysis, innovative algorithms and data mining tools are
needed in order to extract information and discover knowledge from the
continuous and increasing data growing. In most of data mining methods the data volume and variety directly impact on computational load.
In this paper we illustrate a hardware architecture of the decision tree
predictor, a widely adopted machine learning algorithm. In particular we
show how it is possible to automatically generate a hardware implementation of the predictor module that provides a better throughput that
available software solutions.

1 Introduction

In many application areas the daily data production has reached unprecedented
levels. According to recently published statistics, in 2012 every day 2.5 EB (Ex-
abyte) were created, with 90% of the data created in the last two years [7]. This
data origins from multiple sources: sensors used to gather climate information,
social networks, digital pictures and video streaming, and so on. Moreover, the
size of this data is growing exponentially due to not expensive media (smartphones and sensors), and to the introduction of big Cloud Datacenters. The
technical and scientific issues related to the data booming have been designated
as the "Big Data" challenges and have been identified as highly strategic by major research agencies. Most definitions of big data refer on the so-called three Vs:
volume, variety and *velocity*, referring respectively to the size of data storage, to
the variety of source and to the frequency of the data generation and delivery. To
deal with big data analysis, innovative approaches for data mining and processing are required in order to enable process optimization and enhance decision
making tasks. To achieve this, an increment on computational power is needed
and dedicated hardware can be adopted. There are two main classes of solutions: 1) using general purpose CPUs as multi-core processors and/or computer

J. Kołodziej et al. (Eds.): ICA3PP 2013, Part II, LNCS 8286, pp. 125–132, 2013.
© Springer International Publishing Switzerland 2013

clusters to run the data mining software; 2) using dedicated hardware (special purpose) to compute specific parts of an algorithm, reducing the computational effort. Indeed special purpose machines may not be suitable as they are not programmable and many classification systems need tuning and reprogramming to achieve high accuracy. Nevertheless Field Programmable Gate Array (FPGA) can be adopted for the low costs and the re-configuration properties.

At this aim, in this paper, we have focused our attention on FPGA for the classification task. In particular, we adopt an FPGA architecture implementing a predictor, built by the C4.5 decision tree algorithm, widely adopted for classification tasks in many application areas [1]. Exploiting hardware characteristics, this architecture is designed to maximize the throughput, making the classification task suitable for very large amount of data characterized by an high number of features in input and a high number of classes in output. Indeed in literature some FPGA based solutions exist, nevertheless our focus is on the automatic generation of an optimized hardware description that provides higher throughputs than available solutions. In particular we show how it is possible the automation of the hardware accelerator generation process, starting from the data model. We illustrate its applicability in two real case studies (URL malicious detection and event detection with sensor networks) obtaining performance that are 4 orders of magnitude greater than software implementation.

The reminder of the paper is structured as follows: in Section 2 we describe related work to both C4.5 algorithm and data mining algorithm implemented on FPGAs; in Section 3 we introduce some details on the C4.5 algorithm describing the learning and prediction phases and illustrating the improvements achieved with hardware implementation. In Section 4 we present the process that automatize the hardware synthesis. In Section 5 two case studies are presented to demonstrate the advantages of the proposed solution. Finally, in Section 6 some conclusion and future work are drawn.

2   Related Work

As mentioned above, FPGAs are very suitable to implement classification algorithm as they need deep re-programming during the tuning phase. Several FPGA-based classification architectures have been proposed in order to *speed up* the classification processes [11,12]. In [13] two FPGA architectures were proposed to classify packets traffic. Both architectures use a programmable classifier exploiting the C4.5 algorithm. Using NetFPGA, in [9] the authors proposed a traffic classifier by using C4.5. The main architectural characteristic is the programmability by the software, without loss of service, using memories that store the classifier.

The C4.5 classification algorithm is very promising for big data analysis, it performs very well in many application domains as the predictor works on the tree structure built during the learning phase. It was presented by Quinlan in [10] and soon was adopted in a broad range of applications such as image recognition, medical diagnosis, fraud detection and target marketing.

In [4] and [8] the C4.5 algorithm was adapted within the framework of differential privacy in distributed environments. In [5] the authors show the power of C4.5 for classifying the Internet application traffic, due to the discretization of input features done by the algorithm during classification operations. The authors of [14] extended the traditional decision tree based classifiers to work with uncertain data.

The results presented in these papers are very interesting, but they did not provide any automatic tool to automatically generate the hardware architecture from the prediction model. In this paper we intend to propose an automatic generation tool and we will describe the results of two case studies.

3   The Classification Algorithm

To characterize and classify big data, we exploit the C4.5 decision tree algorithm widely adopted for classification tasks in several application areas. C4.5 is based on decision-tree induction approach, which directly constructs a classification model from the training database, following a top-down and divide-and-conquer paradigm. This classifier is made of a learner for building the predictive model, named training phase, and a predictor for performing data classification.

Algorithm 1. Description of the algorithm for building a decision tree model Classifier

---

Data: Training Set T, Output Class $C = C_1, ..., C_k$
Result: Prediction Model outputted by learner
/* Base Case   */
if T ʄ T *contains one or more examples, all belonging to the same class* C_j **then**
  Create a single leaf in which all the sample having label C. /* The
     decision tree for T is a leaf identifying class C$_j$ */

if $T = \emptyset$ **then**
  Creates a single leaf that has the label of the most frequent class of the
     samples contained in the parent node /* heuristic step leading to
     misclassification rates   */

/* Recursive Case   */
if T *contains samples that belong to several classes* **then**
  foreach *Feature f* **do**
     Find the normalized information gain by splitting on f, based on an
     Entropy Test Value
  Let f$_i$ be the attribute with the highest normalized information gain; Create
     a decision node that splits on f$_j$;/* node associated with the test
     */
  Create a branch for each possible outcome of the test; Execute the
     algorithm on each branch (corresponding to a subset of sample)
     /* partitioning of T in more subsets according to the test on
     the attribute obtained by splitting on f$_j$ */

During the training phase, a domain expert builds a training set, i.e. a subset of data records that have been previously classified, which will be used to tune the predictor and define the predictor parameters. The predictor decision rules are modeled as a tree, the nodes represent classes associated to events to be detected and branches represent conjunctions of conditions that define a path that leads to a class. Periodically, or when some samples are mis-classified, the learner can recalculate the parameters on the basis of a new training set, in order to refine the behavior of the classifier, excluding in this way the predictor behaviors that leads to the mis-classifications. As this activity requires re-programming the classifier, we have implemented the predictor with a re-programmable hardware. As illustrated in Algorithm 1, the algorithm recursively works on data taken from the training set. At each step, the data set is split, based on conditions of a chosen feature that are defined by thresholds. The selection of the feature is performed by using an *entropy test*.

Let T be the set of samples, $freq(C_j, T)$ the number of samples in T that belong to class C_j, the entropy of T is defined as:

$$Info(T) = -\sum((freq(C_j, T)/T) \cdot log_2(freq(C_j, T)/T))$$

The algorithm computes the value of *Info* for all T_i partitioned in accordance with n conditions on a feature f_i:

$$Info_{f_{i(T)}} = \sum((T_i/T) \cdot Info(T_i))$$

The features that maximize the following Gain value are selected for the splitting:

$$Gain(f_i) = Info(T) - Info_{f_{i(T)}}$$

In order to be properly processed, the input information must be represented by a proper data model. For the selected dataset, proper features must be chosen, in order to obtain effective classification for the data of the targeted applications. In the proposed case studies, the candidate features will be selected in order to obtain high accuracy in the classification results, even if the huge dimension of dataset requires that the features are computed with low computationally cost.

4   The Synthesis Process to Generate the Classifier

The predictor module is based on the tree-like model defined by the learner and the tree visit is usually executed in a sequential way. Each tree node contains a predicate that represents a condition, while leaves are labeled with classes the samples belong to. The predictor hardware implementation, intrinsically concurrent, is able to elaborate in parallel the conditions of the nodes of the tree.

We designed a fully automatic process to synthesize the decision tree hardware starting from the training set. The process flow is reported in Figure 1; it is made of three different steps that produce in output three standard artifacts. The goal of the *Data Processing* is to automatically structure data coming from heterogeneous sources into a common schema, a data-preprocessing tool extracts

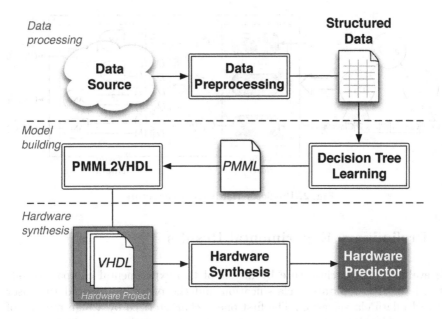

Fig. 1. Process flow from data source to the hardware implementation of decision tree

the only relevant information to build a common schema and it implements the methodology proposed by Amato et al. in [2,3]. This artifact, stored in a tabular format, is given in input to the *Model Building* step. It implements C4.5 learning algorithm, the output of this step is the predictor model coded into PMML (Predictor Model Markup Language), a standard XML schema for predictors. At this step, exploiting the PMML formalization, we developed a tool, PMML2VHDL, that parses the decision tree predictor model and generates an optimized hardware description for the predictor [1]. We formalized it in VHDL but other descriptions can be adopted. Finally, in the last step, the *Hardware Synthesis*, we used the VHDL as input for the hardware synthesizer in order to obtain a working version of the predictor.

As for the hardware architecture, we implemented the tree visiting algorithm as a multi-output boolean function: 1) we pre-evaluated all conditions (nodes) in parallel using configurable components called *Decision Boxes*, that are implemented as comparators; 2) we performed the visiting as a boolean function, implemented with a component called *Boolean Net*.

In Figure 2 we report an example of decision tree and the corresponding hardware scheme. As illustrated, each tree path leads to a class, so the *AND* of decisions along the path can be represented by a boolean minterm, and the multitude of paths that lead to the same class may be represented as a boolean function in SOP form. Due to space limitations, we cannot report the details of the hardware implementation, in next section we will present some preliminary experimental results on different case studies.

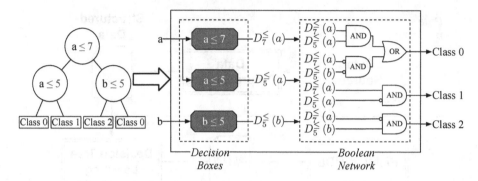

Fig. 2. Predictor Hardware architecture

5   Preliminary Experimental Results

We evaluated the architecture by means of two experimental campaigns, one related to URL reputation classification and the other one related to sensor networks data classification. The first one is characterized by a high number of features, while the second one is an interesting case study with a high number of classes.

Malicious URL Detection: we chose the dataset proposed by [6], created to detect the malicious web sites from the URLs. The dataset contains about 2.4 million records and 3.2 million host-based features, coded in floating point. In order to handle this data we performed a pre-processing activity and we applied a feature filter based on the entropy test. We discarded features having a value less than a threshold defined for this case study. Thanks to this filtering process, we reduced the number of significant features to 51. From this data collection we built the C4.5 predictor tree model. In order to evaluate the accuracy of the predictor we applied a cross validation technique which breaks the dataset in 10 sets: 7 sets are used as training set and 3 sets are used for testing. The overall accuracy of the system was evaluated as the average accuracy over 10 iterations, in which samples for training and testing were randomly chosen. Using KNIME framework, we obtained a predictor tree with 624 nodes, 32 levels and 98.647% of accuracy. Once built the predictor model, we classified 4 million records with the KNIME software version in order to compare it with our proposal. As for the proposed architecture, we automatically obtained the VHDL project from the KNIME PMML file by using PMML2VHDL tool. The experiments were done using a Xilinx Virtex5 LX110T-2 and the results are reported in the first column of Table 1.

The interesting result is that the computation time is 11.28 ms, while the classification of the same 4 million records with KNIME on an Intel Core $i7-3770$ $(3.40GHz)$, with 16Gb RAM requires, in average, about 124,834.45 ms ($\sim$ 2 min). The gain obtained in terms of elaboration time by introducing the hardware classifier is about of 10,000 times the software implementation.

Table 1. Classification results for malicious URL detection and sensor network dataset

	malicious URL detection	sensor network event detection
Features	51	12
Classes	2	24
Accuracy (%)	98.647	98.994
Throughput (Gbps)	578.93	126.48
Slices	2777	1546
Computation Time (ms)	11.28	7.59

Event Detection over Sensor Network: this case study is focused on sensor networks data classification to detect different events, for instance temperature and acceleration exceeding nominal values. We referred to a sensor network deployed in [1] and running for several days, we collected data and manually labeled the training set in 24 thresholds, representing 24 alarm classes. Following the same steps described for the first case study, we obtained a predictor tree with 329 nodes and 20 levels with an accuracy of 98.994%. The computation time for the classification of 2.5 million samples was in average 75,770 ms using KNIME. The hardware synthesis results of this decision tree are reported in the second column of Table 1. Even in this case we obtained a gain of 10,000. Furthermore we can see that the throughput of the second case is lower than the first one, although we have less nodes and less levels.

In conclusion we can observe that in the both case studies the computation time gain is very high, and the proposed architecture seems very suitable for big data applications.

6   Conclusion and Future Work

The adoption of FPGA in big data analysis seems very promising. In this paper we proposed a process to implement in hardware a reconfigurable decision tree classifier. In particular, we proposed an innovative architecture to fasten the classificator that is made of *Decision Boxes* to compute in parallel all decisions and a *Boolean Net*, to effectively compute the classification. We evaluated the proposal with two different case studies, putting in evidence the great performance obtained with the hardware implementation. Many optimization are still possible, in future work we intend to enhance the proposal by introducing pipelining mechanism into the available hardware implementation, furthermore we want to prove the scalability of the proposed approach.

Acknowledgments. This work was partially supported by FARO 2012 project "Un sistema elettronico di elaborazione in tempo reale per l'estrazione di informazioni da video ad alta risoluzione, alto frame rate e basso rapporto segnale rumore" founded by the University of Naples "Federico II".

References

1. Amato, F., Barbareschi, M., Casola, V., Mazzeo, A.: An FPGA-based smart classifier for decision support systems. In: Zavoral, F., Jung, J.J., Badica, C. (eds.) Intelligent Distributed Computing VII. SCI, vol. 511, pp. 289–299. Springer, Heidelberg (2014)
2. Amato, F., Casola, V., Mazzeo, A., Romano, S.: A semantic based methodology to classify and protect sensitive data in medical records. In: 2010 Sixth International Conference on Information Assurance and Security (IAS), pp. 240–246. IEEE (2010)
3. Amato, F., Casola, V., Mazzocca, N., Romano, S.: A semantic-based document processing framework: A security perspective. In: International Conference on Complex, Intelligent and Software Intensive Systems, pp. 197–202 (2011)
4. Friedman, A., Schuster, A.: Data mining with differential privacy. In: Proceedings of the 16th ACM SIGKDD International Conference on Knowledge Discovery and Data Mining, pp. 493–502. ACM, New York (2010)
5. Lim, Y.S., Kim, H.C., Jeong, J., Kim, C.K., Kwon, T.T., Choi, Y.: Internet traffic classification demystified: on the sources of the discriminative power. In: Proceedings of the 6th International Conference on Emerging Networking EXperiments and Technologies, pp. 9:1–9:12. ACM, New York (2010)
6. Ma, J., Saul, L.K., Savage, S., Voelker, G.M.: Identifying suspicious URLs: an application of large-scale online learning. In: Proceedings of the 26th Annual International Conference on Machine Learning, pp. 681–688. ACM (2009)
7. Mayer-Schönberger, V., Cukier, K.: Big Data: A Revolution That Will Transform How We Live, Work, and Think. Houghton Mifflin Harcourt (2013)
8. Mohammed, N., Chen, R., Fung, B.C., Yu, P.S.: Differentially private data release for data mining. In: Proceedings of the 17th ACM SIGKDD International Conference on Knowledge Discovery and Data Mining, pp. 493–501. ACM, New York (2011)
9. Monemi, A., Zarei, R., Marsono, M.N.: Online NetFPGA Decision Tree Statistical Traffic Classifier. Computer Communications (2013)
10. Quinlan, J.R.: C4.5: programs for machine learning. Morgan Kaufmann Publishers Inc., San Francisco (1993)
11. Schadt, E.E., Linderman, M.D., Sorenson, J., Lee, L., Nolan, G.P.: Computational solutions to large-scale data management and analysis. Nature Reviews Genetics 11(9), 647–657 (2010)
12. Skoda, P., Medved Rogina, B., Sruk, V.: FPGA implementations of data mining algorithms. In: MIPRO, 2012 Proceedings of the 35th International Convention, pp. 362–367. IEEE (2012)
13. Tong, D., Sun, L., Matam, K., Prasanna, V.: High throughput and programmable online traffic classifier on FPGA. In: Proceedings of the ACM/SIGDA International Symposium on Field Programmable Gate Arrays, pp. 255–264. ACM (2013)
14. Tsang, S., Kao, B., Yip, K., Ho, W.S., Lee, S.D.: Decision trees for uncertain data. IEEE Transactions on Knowledge and Data Engineering 23(1), 64–78 (2011)

PSIS: Parallel Semantic Indexing System - Preliminary Experiments

Flora Amato[1], Francesco Gargiulo[2], Vincenzo Moscato[1],
Fabio Persia[1], and Antonio Picariello[1]

[1] University of Naples "Federico II", Dipartimento di Ingegneria Elettrica e
Tecnologie dell'Informazione, via Claudio 21, 80125, Naples, Italy
[2] Centro Italiano Ricerche Aereospaziali "CIRA" Via Maiorise, 81043,
Capua (CE), Italy

Abstract. In this paper, we address the problem of defining a semantic indexing techniques based on RDF triples. In particular, we define algorithms for: i) defining clustering techniques of semantically similar RDF triplets; ii) defining algorithms for inserting, deleting and searching on a K-d based semantic tree built on the base of such clusterings; iii) defining a parallel implementation of the search algorithms. Preliminary experiments runned on a GRID-based parallel machines are designed and preliminary implemented and discusses, showing the performances of the proposed system.

1 Introduction

In this paper, we describe a semantic indexing technique based on RDF (Resource Description Framework) representation of the main concepts of a document. With the development of the Semantic Web, in fact, a large amount of RDF native documents are published on the Web and, for what digital documents concerns , several techniques could be used to transform a text document into a RDF model, i.e. a set of subject, verb, object triples [1]. Thus, in our approach we propose to capture the semantic nature of a given document, commonly expressed in Natural Language, by retrieving a number of RDF triples stored into a graph database and to semantically index the documents on the base of meaning of the triples' elements. The proposed index can be hopefully exploited by actual web search engines to improve the retrieval effectiveness with respect to the adopted query keywords or for automatic topic detection tasks.

The paper is organized as in the following. In the next section we report the state of the art in Graph Databases Systems. In Section 3 we illustrate our proposal for RDF based semantic index discussing indexing algorithms and providing some implementation details. Section 4 contains experimentation aiming at validating the effectiveness and efficiency of our proposal. Finally, some conclusions are outlined in Section 5.

J. Kołodziej et al. (Eds.): ICA3PP 2013, Part II, LNCS 8286, pp. 133–140, 2013.
© Springer International Publishing Switzerland 2013

2   State of the Art

The declarative query language SQL has been used for many decades in Relational Database systems (sets of large tables containing strongly connected data). Nowadays, a high interest is growing around NoSQL systems, such as Google's BigTable or Facebook's Cassandra, CouchDB, Project Voldemort, and Dynamo. Because of the graph's efficacy in modeling objects and interactions, because of their importance in computer science, in representation of social network, of web site link structures, or even of metabolic networks, chemical structure and genetic maps, it is easy to understand why many applications need a system able to store and query those graphs. For what Graph Database field concerns, the necessity to manage large information with graph-like nature has incremented the relevance of this area. Graph Database models are conceptual tools used to represent the real-world entities and the relationship among them [7] but the term also represents structured types of data and mathematical frameworks . Graph DB appears as an evolution of Object-oriented DB-models and attempt to overcome the limitations of traditional database models with the goal of capture the inherent graph structure of data appearing in applications in which the interconnectivity of data is an important aspect (i.e. Hypertext or Geographical Information Systems). Graph Databases are characterized by the following three features:

1. Data and the schema are represented by graph or by data structures generalizing the notion of graph as Hypergraphs or Hypernodes.
2. Manipulation of data is expressed by graph transformations like graph-oriented operations and type constructors.
3. Integrity constraints enforce data consistency.

Introducing graphs as a modeling tools for areas where data and relations between the data are at the same level (and information about interconnectivity is more important as the data itself), has many advantages: first of all, it facilitates the modeling of data, because graph structures can be manipulated directly by users. All the information about an entity is contained in a single node and related information is showed in nodes connected to it by arcs [8] . Second, the queries can refer directly to the graph structure and is not important to require full knowledge of the structure to express meaningful queries[9] . At least, graph databases provide special graph storage structure and efficient graph algorithms for specific implementations [10] . The Resource Description Framework (RDF), a recommendation of the W3C, is an infrastructure that enables the encoding, exchange and reuse of structured metadata. As far as the RDF Stores are concerned, Byrne[11] research project must be mentioned. It refers, indeed, the development of a data querying application based on the Jena RDF store. Although in the context of the Semantic Web (SW) holding data in graph format could mean to be able to find shortest paths between nodes, compare the degree of nodes, and do k-neighbourhood queries, a great part of the SW tools do not support graph searching algorithms [14], [15]. One of the RDF central benefits is its capability to interconnect resources in an extensible way. In that context, basic graph theory's concepts, like "node" ,"edge" ,"path" ,"neighborhood" or "connectivity", are crucial. A triple consisting of a subject, a predicate and an object (resource, property and property value) represent the RDF atomic expression, more technically, it constitute a relationship statement between the subject and the object. An RDF Graph is a set of such triples. As regards the languages for querying RDF data, one can't go on without mentioning SPARQL, a proposal of a protocol and query language designed for easy access to RDF stores. A simple query is based on graph patterns, and query processing consists of the binding of variables to generate pattern solutions. There are many graph data management applications or libraries, and in [16], the authors compare four of the most popular Graph Databases: *(i)* Neo4j: it is a GDB designed for network oriented data that does not rely on a relations layout of the data, but on a network model storage that store nodes, relationships and attributes. *(ii)* HypergraphDB: it is designed for artificial intelligence and semantic web projects, stores also hypergraph structures(graph with hyperedges, arcs that connect more than two nodes). *(iii)* Jena (RDF): it stores the graph as a set of tables and indexes: the node table stores a map of the nodes in the graph, but the information about the RDF triplets are stored in the "triple indexes", that describes the structure of the graph. *(iv)* Dex: it is a GDB implementation based on bitmap representation of the entities. Nodes and Edges are encoded as collections of objects that have a unique logical identifier.

In [17] the Authors' experiment use the HPC Scalable Graph Analysis Benchmark, designed to capture the most representative graph operations. Results show that for small graphs all four databases have reasonable performances for most operations, but only Dex and Neo4j are able to load the largest benchmark sizes. In particular, Dex achieved the best performance for most operations and close to Neo4j, in those where Neo4j was the fastest. A comparison between MySQL (a RelationalDB) and Neo4j has been realized by Vicknair [18]. It involved objective benchmarks and subjective comparisons; it was based on system documentation and experience .

3 Parallel Semantic Index

The parallel semantic index relies on the data structure for RDF triples obtained as described in [4]. In this paper, the author proposed a semantic index based on K-d trees. Each node of the K-d tree contains an RFD triple previously mapped in a point of a $k - dimensional space$. They defined a semantic similarity measure d over the set S of RDF triples such that (S, d) is a metric space. The mapping between the metric space (S, d) of RDF triples and the k-dimensional space is built ensuring that the triples that are (semantically) close in RDF space are also close in the $k - dimensional$ one.

Once all RDF triplets have been mapped in a point of R_k, every point is inserted in a K-d tree. The problem of similarity search - i.e. the process of finding and retrieving triples that are similar to a given triple or set of triples - corresponds to a nearest neighbors or range query problem.

The goal is the parallelization of search in K-d tree in order to increase performance. The basic idea is to split the K-d tree **T** into p partitions $C1, ..., Cp$ and assign each partition to a job and then assign jobs to nodes of the parallel grid. The partition of a tree is a special case of the problem of partition of a graph. Consider a graph $G = (V, E)$ with n vertices labeled by $1, 2, ..., n$. G is a not directed and connected graph. A partition of G is a partition of its vertices into disjointed subset named components. We consider only connected partitions of G, that is, those with components that contain connected subgraph of G. Denote:

- p the number of components of a partition $1 \le p \le n$;
- $\Pi_p(G)$ the set of all possible partitions (connected) of G into p non-empty components;
- $\pi = (C1, C2, ..., Cp)$ a generic partition in $\Pi_p(G)$.

A p-partition of G is a partition $\pi \in \Pi_p(G)$. The goal of partitioning can be stated as an appropriate function funzione $f : \Pi_p(G) \to R^+$ called objective function. The optimal value of the objective function f is denoted with f^*. A partition $\pi \in \Pi_p(G)$ such that $f(\pi) = f^*$ is an optimal partition and is denoted by π^*; in general, it is not unique. Given a graph $G = (V, E)$ and an integer $1 \le p \le |V|$, the partitioning problem with objective function f is solved finding the optimal value $f : \Pi_p(G) \to R^+$.

In order to distribute the computational load uniformly over the grid, we consider K-d tree partition whose components have approximately the same number of vertices. The search for this partition is an instance of the problem of equipartition of a graph in which each vertex is assigned a unit weight and the objective function in one of the following:

$$L_1 = f(\pi) = \sum ||C_k| - \mu| \tag{1}$$

$$L_2 = f(\pi) = \sum (|C_k| - \mu)^2 \tag{2}$$

$$L_\infty = f(\pi) = max||C_k| - \mu| \tag{3}$$

$$MaxMin = f(\pi) = minC_k \tag{4}$$

$$MinMax = f(\pi) = maxC_k \tag{5}$$

Where $1 \le k \le p$ and $\mu = |V|/p$. If f is $L1$ problem is NP-hard for trees and it can be solved in polynomial time for special classes of trees such as stars, paths and caterpillars (Aparo et al. 1973, DeSimone et al. 1990). Becker et al, (Schach et al. 1982), propose shifting algorithms that solve in polynomial time problems of equipartition of trees, with objective functions (4) and (5). When the graph to be partitioned is a tree the computational complexity of the problem seems to depend strongly on the objective function. The case of the trees is borderline between graph paths and graphs. It is as the watershed between problems solvable in polynomial time and problems that an approximate solution must be found.

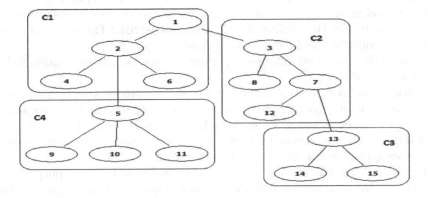

Fig. 1. A p-partition of a tree with p = 4 components (subtrees)

The K-d tree has been partitioned with the algorithm proposed by Schach (Schach et al. 1982) in p components $C1, ..., Cp$ with $p = 50$. The configuration of the grid is: 8 hosts each one with 8 CPUs (Scope[1]). Each component is assigned to a job J_i. Each job J_i knows jobs connected to it, for example job J_1, with the component $C1$ of the 1, knows that elaboration from the vertex 1 will continue, if necessary, in job J_2 and from vertex 2 in J_4. Each job also knows a special job, named *End*, to send the results. The *m-nearest neighbors* and *range* queries are executed from the root of the K-d tree . If during its elaboration, a job found the complete answer to the current query then it the returns the results to the *End* job otherwise it sends a message to the appropriate job connected to it and then elaboration will continue in the next job according to the well-known K-d tree search algorithm. The message contains the objective of search (the type of query, the arguments of the query, etc.) and the partial results, if exists, already achieved by job performed previously. Since the components of the partition must be connected, they are obtained by cutting some edge of the tree, for example the $C2$ partition in fig. 1 is obtained by cutting the edges *(1, 3)* and *(7, 13)*. In addition, each partition contains a vertex, named component root, from which all others vertices cam be reached. Obviously a partition may not contain all vertices contained in the subtree of the root component, such as the $C2$ partition does not contain vertices of $C3$. When a job receives a message the K-d tree search at the root of its component starts. Because all jobs are allocated on separate nodes of the grid, they can be executed in parallel, and then multiple K-d tree searches can be started and executed simultaneously on the same tree. This approach do not improve the performance of the single K-d tree query but improves the performance of the execution of a very large number of queries by means the parallelization.

---

[1] http://scopedma-wn.dma.unina.it

4 Preliminary Experimental Results

In this section, we describe the adopted experimental protocol, used to evaluate the efficiency and the effectiveness of our indexing structure, and discuss the obtained preliminary experimental results. Regarding the triples collection, we selected a subset of the **Billion Triple Challenge 2012 Dataset**[2], in which data are encoded in the *RDF NQuads* format.

We used the *context* information to perform a correct semantic disambiguation of triple elements[3][5],[6].

In particular, as evaluation criteria in the retrieval process using our semantic index, we measured from one hand the *index building time* and *average search time* as a function of indexed triples, and from the other one the *success rate*, that is the number of *relevant*[4] returned triples with respect to several k-nearest neighbors queries performed on the data collection.

Figure 2 shows the average index building and search times (purple-line), and the related comparisons with the theoretical lower (red) and upper (green) bounds. In all the considered case studies, the times exhibit logarithmic trends (respectively $O(nlog(n))$ and $O(log(n))$, n being the number of triples), as we theoretically expected.

For obtaining running times, we used SCOPE [5] as Parallel Computing Environment and MPI (Message Passing Interface) as Parallel Programming Model. SCOPE is an infrastructure provided by the Information System Center of University of Naples, composed by about 300 computing nodes (64 bit Intel Xeon with 8 GB RAM)[12],[13]. In particular, we used a number of processors equal to the number of partitions.

For what the effectiveness concerns, we have computed a sort of average precision of our index in terms of relevant results with respect to a set of query examples (belonging to different semantic domains).

In particular, a returned triple is considered *relevant* if it belongs to the same semantic domain of the query triple. We obtained an average success rate greater than 75% varying the result set size in the case of 50 queries performed on the entire dataset (about 1000000 triples) as reported in Table 1.

---

[2] http://km.aifb.kit.edu/projects/btc-2012/

[3] The Billion Triple Challenge 2012 dataset consists of over a billion triples collected from a variety of web sources in the shape $< subject >< predicate >< object >< context >$ (e.g. $<Jorge\ Mario\ Bergoglio>$, $<elect>$, $<Pope><religion>$). The dataset is usually used to demonstrate the scalability of applications as well as the capability to deal with the specifics of data that has been crawled from the public web.

[4] A result triple is considered relevant if it has a similar semantics to the query triple.

[5] www.scope.unina.it

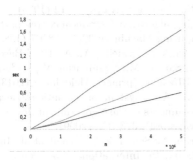 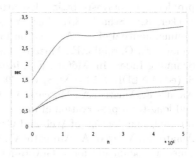

(a) Index Building Times   (b) Search Times

Fig. 2. Average Index Building Times and Search Times

Table 1. Average Success Rate

Number of Triples	Success Rate
50	100%
75	92%
100	88%
150	81%
200	75%

5   Conclusion and Future Works

In this paper, we have designed a semantic index based on RDF triples, in order
to catch and manage the semantics of documents. We have described the data
structures, the algorithms for building the index and its use for semantic queries.
Several preliminary experiments have been carried out using the standard Billion
Triple Challenge 2012 Data Set, showing good performances both for efficiency
and for effectiveness. We are planning to extend our paper in several directions:
i) the use of domain based linguistic ontologies, instead or in addition to the used
WordNet; ii) the use of different similarity distance measures; iii) to compare our
algorithms with the several ones produced in the recent literature and iv) try
other partitioning strategies.

References

1. d'Acierno, A., Moscato, V., Persia, F., Picariello, A., Penta, A.: iwin: A summarizer
   system based on a semantic analysis of web documents. In: 2012 IEEE Sixth International Conference on Semantic Computing (ICSC), pp. 162–169. IEEE (September 2012)

2. Aparo, E.L., Simeone, B.: Un algoritmo di equipartizione e il suo impiego in un problema di contrasto ottico. Estratto da Ricerca Operativa (6), 1–12 (1973)
3. Becker, R.I., Schach, S.R., Perl, Y.: A shifting algorithm for min-max tree partitioning. Journal of the Association for Computing Machinery 29(1), 58–67 (1982)
4. Amato, F., Gargiulo, F., Mazzeo, A., Moscato, V., Picariello, A.: An RDF-Based Semantic Index. In: Métais, E., Meziane, F., Saraee, M., Sugumaran, V., Vadera, S. (eds.) NLDB 2013. LNCS, vol. 7934, pp. 315–320. Springer, Heidelberg (2013)
5. Amato, F., Mazzeo, A., Moscato, V., Picariello, A.: A system for semantic retrieval and long-term preservation of multimedia documents in the e-government domain. International Journal of Web and Grid Services 5(4), 323–338 (2009)
6. Amato, F., Mazzeo, A., Moscato, V., Picariello, A.: Semantic Management of Multimedia Documents for E-Government Activity. In: International Conference on Complex, Intelligent and Software Intensive Systems, CISIS 2009, pp. 1193–1198. IEEE (March 2009)
7. Silberschatz, A., Korth, H.F., Sudarshan, S.: Data models. ACM. Comput. Surv. 28(1), 105–108 (1996)
8. Paredaens, J., Peelman, P., Tanca, L.: G-log: a graph-based query language. IEEE Trans. Knowl. Data Eng. 7(3), 436–453 (1995)
9. Abiteboul, S.: Querying semi-structured data. In: Afrati, F.N., Kolaitis, P.G. (eds.) ICDT 1997. LNCS, vol. 1186, pp. 1–18. Springer, Heidelberg (1996)
10. Guting, R.H.: GraphDB: modeling and querying graphs in databases. In: Proceedings of the 20th International Conference on Very Large Data Bases (VLDB), pp. 297–308. Morgan Kaufmann (1994)
11. Byrne, K.: Tethering cultural data with RDF. In: Proceedings of the Jena User Conference (2006)
12. Moscato, F., Vittorini, V., Amato, F., Mazzeo, A., Mazzocca, N.: Solution workflows for model-based analysis of complex systems. IEEE Transactions on Automation Science and Engineering 9(1), 83–95 (2012)
13. Cilardo, A., Gallo, L., Mazzeo, A., Mazzocca, N.: Efficient and scalable OpenMP-based system-level design. In: Design, Automation Test in Europe Conference Exhibition (DATE), pp. 988–991 (2013)
14. Angles, R., Gutierrez, C.: Querying RDF data from a graph database perspective. In: Gómez-Pérez, A., Euzenat, J. (eds.) ESWC 2005. LNCS, vol. 3532, pp. 346–360. Springer, Heidelberg (2005)
15. Stuckenschmidt, H.: Towards an RDF query language-comments on an emerging standard. SIG SEMIS (Semantic Web and Information Systems) (2005)
16. Dominguez-Sal, D., Urbón-Bayes, P., Giménez-Vañó, A., Gómez-Villamor, S., Martínez-Bazán, N., Larriba-Pey, J.L.: Survey of graph database performance on the HPC scalable graph analysis benchmark. In: Shen, H.T., et al. (eds.) WAIM 2010. LNCS, vol. 6185, pp. 37–48. Springer, Heidelberg (2010)
17. Bader, D., Feo, J., Gilbert, J., Kepner, J., Koetser, D., Loh, E., Madduri, K., Mann, B., Meuse, T., Robinson, E.: HPC Scalable Graph Analysis Benchmark v1.0. HPC Graph Analysis (February 2009)
18. Vicknair, C., Macias, M., Zhao, Z., Nan, X., Chen, Y., Wilkins, D.: A comparison of a graph database and a relational database: a data provenance perspective. In: Proceedings of the 48th Annual Southeast Regional Conference, p. 42. ACM (2010)

Network Traffic Analysis Using Android on a Hybrid Computing Architecture

Mario Barbareschi, Antonino Mazzeo, and Antonino Vespoli

Università degli Studi di Napoli "Federico II",
Dipartimento di Ingegneria Elettrica e Tecnologie dell'Informazione,
Via Claudio 21, 80125, Napoli, Italia
{mario.barbareschi,mazzeo,antonino.vespoli}@unina.it

Abstract. Nowadays more and more smartphone applications use internet connection, resulting, from the analysis point of view, in complex and huge generated traffic. Due to mobility and resource limitations, the classical approaches to traffic analysis are no more suitable. Furthermore, the most widespread mobile operating systems, such as Android, do not provide facilities for this task. Novel approaches have been presented in the literature, in which traffic analysis is executed in hardware using the Decision Tree classification algorithm. Although they have been proven to be effective in accelerating the classification process, they typically lack an integration with the remaining system. In order to address this issue, we propose a hybrid computing architecture which enables the communication between the Android OS and a traffic analysis hardware accelerator coexisting on the same chip. To this aim, we provide an Android OS porting on a Xilinx Zynq architecture, composed of a dual-core ARM-based processor integrated with FPGA cells, and define a technique to realize the connection with programmable logic components.

1 Introduction

Data traffic is reaching unprecedented volume. Network infrastructures are growing in order to provide high bandwidth. In the foreseeable future the internet traffic will amount to 165×10^{15} bytes per hour [9]. In this context the mobile domain plays a crucial role due to the widespread use of smartphones. In fact, in 2017 the mobile 4G communication standard will reach 45% global traffic and 10% global connections [8]. Network technology lags development compared to those forecasts, therefore the need for network monitoring grows. On the one hand, the task of traffic monitoring is becoming a basic activity in designing new network infrastructures and managing the existing ones. On the other hand, the emerging architectures will need new techniques to support traffic analysis, due to the huge amount of traffic that could result in packet loss and analysis failures.

Traffic analysis is the basic task to network management, such as flow prioritization for QoS, traffic policing, traffic diagnostic, and so on. Moreover, traffic analysis is a powerful tool to acquire information about incoming flow for the detection of anomalous behaviors, viral infections, hacking attempts, phishing

J. Kołodziej et al. (Eds.): ICA3PP 2013, Part II, LNCS 8286, pp. 141–148, 2013.
© Springer International Publishing Switzerland 2013

and SPAM. This operation typically requires a high computational effort and power consumption, and therefore is not well suited for the resource constrained mobile devices, that are particularly subject to attacks.

Several solutions have been proposed in the network infrastructure domain to provide high throughput traffic analysis techniques, mostly based on hardware approaches, that are able to guarantee the same efficiency of a software implementation, but with higher throughput [3]. Although they have been proven to be effective in accelerating the classification process, they typically lack an integration with the whole system.

In this paper we propose a general solution for the integration of a hardware accelerator for efficient traffic analysis, within a mobile operating system. The architecture we propose can be successfully adopted in a variety of applications, such as traffic monitoring for security purposes.

In order to create an experimental platform, we adopt a hybrid computing architecture which enables the communication between the Android OS, one of the most popular mobile OSs, and a generic custom traffic analysis hardware accelerator, coexisting on the same chip. To this aim, we provide an Android OS porting on a Xilinx Zynq architecture, composed of a dual-core ARM-based processor integrated with FPGA cells. We show how the OS interacts with the traffic classifier, implemented on the custom logic part, using the interrupt mechanism.

The reminder of the paper is structured as follows: in Section 2 we will describe related work for traffic analysis and for smartphone security issues; in Section 3 we will give details about traffic analysis and our implementation on the Android OS; in Section 4 we will show how to implement the proposed architecture, and in particular how to run Android on the Zynq platform; in Section 5 we will show some preliminary results; at the end in Section 6 some conclusion and future work are drawn.

2   Related Work

Smartphone traffic analysis has been recently addressed by several research papers, aimed at profiling the involved application protocols. In [6] the authors proposed a method to collect raw information about traffic using an application installed on the end terminals. The aim is to collect data to infer offline characteristics about the smartphones' traffic. This approach diverges from others, such as [10] and [7], in which the traffic analysis is performed directly on the network infrastructure, as it allows to combine local information, such as battery level, with the globally collected traffic trends.

As for security issues, several approaches have been proposed to provide smartphones with intrusion detection features. [13] described a security framework applied to the smartphone architecture. Each security issue was covered by a specific module of the proposed framework. The authors devised the introduction of an IDS for network monitoring activities against policy violations, but did not provide any implementation of this module. Similarly, the authors of [14] proposed an IDS tailored for smartphones (SIDS), that runs directly on mobile devices to improve the protection for some security threats. Even in this case, no details were given about the implementation, nor on the impact on the smartphone systems. In this scenario, the architecture we propose could represent the enabling technology to prove the feasibility of an IDS implementation on mobile devices.

3   Traffic Analysis Process

Traffic analysis is the basic task to network management, such as flow prioritization for QoS, traffic policing, traffic diagnostic, and so on. Furthermore, researchers use the traffic analysis to design and plan the future network architectures, especially in the mobile domain. Also, an accurate analysis provides some benefits to the network security in intrusion detection and access control.

Online analysis can also improve the smartphones' security, enabling mechanisms to avoid attacks. Attackers get unauthorized access to the mobile devices using the Internet: in fact they publish malwares through the apps or the websites. Once infiltrated in the device, a malware attempts to get the resource control, collects, redirects or deletes data from the memory [18].

The simplest way to analyze traffic is to classify the packets. We can distinguish some kinds of classification techniques for the traffic: DPI (Deep Packet Inspection), port number-based, heuristic-based and machine learning-based. Recently, in the research community, the machine learning-based classification has been receiving a lot of attention, because it provides a high accuracy in classification and a great adaptability in dynamic context, such as the traffic analysis [2,5,12]. Since smartphones continuously receive information from the Internet, a software approach is too expensive for the limited computational resources.

Hence we propose a hardware approach to the traffic analysis that allows to save computational resources for other tasks. The analysis task is split into two parts:

- Background mode: a hardware accelerator continuously analyzes the incoming traffic flow to detect anomalies or intrusion attempts;
- Foreground mode: when the hardware detects an insecure event, it calls the OS to catch the anomaly.

This approach is less intrusive than a purely software approach, because the traffic analysis does not require the execution of an algorithm for each received packet.

We apply this paradigm to the Android operating system, as illustrated in figure 1. The Internet traffic passes through a traffic analyzer and the communication between the application layer and the hardware accelerator is arbitrated by a Linux driver.

In the next section, we illustrate the whole architecture, by showing a prototype developed on Xilinx Zynq FPGA architecture.

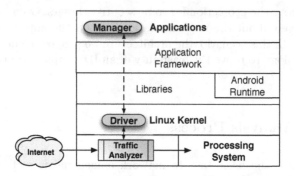

Fig. 1. Hardware traffic analysis architecture using Google Android Operating System

4   Architecture Implementation: Google Android on Xilinx Zynq

In order to provide a prototype of the proposed architecture, we developed the Zedroid project ([4]) in which we realized a hardware version of traffic analyzer and the Google Android Operating System porting on Xilinx Zynq.

In particular, for the prototype, we used the Avnet ZedBoard, a complete development kit that includes: a Xilinx Zynq-7000, 512 MB DD3, 256 Mb Flash, SD Card support, 10/100/1000 Ethernet, USB OTG 2.0 and multiple display standards. The Zynq architecture is composed of a programmable logic, based on FPGA technology, and of a processing subsystem. It allows the combination of a general purpose process with custom hardware peripherals in the same chip.

4.1   Implementation of the Hardware Traffic Analyzer

The figure 2 shows an instance of the proposed approach. We used the Ethernet wired interconnection, as Zynq does not provide a wireless one. Note that from the analysis point of view there are no differences between these kinds of communication as we are only interested in the packets' content.

As shown in figure 2, we can consider two parts: the top section represents the Zynq processing system, while the bottom shows the custom traffic analyzer implemented in the programmable logic part. The two sections communicate by using the AXI interfaces, that represent the general purpose ports of the AMBA 3.0 standard [1]. Normally, the *Ethernet DMA* copies the received packets directly to the system memory. In this specific case instead, we configured the DMA at system boot to redirect all traffic packets to the Programmable Logic (PL) section, where they are analyzed by a hardware accelerator. The main block is the *Classifier*, that detects malicious packets by using their features, properly extracted by the *Feature Extractor* component. In order to reduce the latency of the approach, we separated each packet into *header* and *payload*. Indeed, the custom peripheral separates the headers from the payloads, copying the former into the level-2 (L2) cache and the latter into the main memory: this way, packet headers will always be available in the high speed L2 cache for the Linux specific tasks[19].

As said in the previous section, several approaches exist to perform packets classification. Among them, the Decision Tree algorithm is the most used for the traffic classification, and several works have been proposed in the literature, that provide a hardware implementation of it[3,15,17,11]. One of these implementations could be used in our scheme to realize the classifier component. Note that out approach is generic and could support any kind of classifier that provides the compliant functionalities.

In the following subsection we are going to give some details about the Android porting process.

4.2   Google Android Operating System Porting Process

The Google Android Operating System porting is a process that involves adapting the software stack of the OS to a given platform. Android needs a set of minimum hardware requirements [16]. Since the ZedBoard has the minimum requirements for Android 2.2 (Froyo), we opened a project, called *Zedroid* [4], in which we reported a complete guide to obtain a working system on the board with the Google OS. The project aim is to support the research community in prototyping and in studying Android on a reconfigurable hardware. We report in the following the main porting process steps:

1. Minimal hardware configuration;
2. Linux configuration, patching and compilation;
3. Android compilation;
4. Filesystem configuration.

The hardware configuration is a step executed by Xilinx Platform Studio. This tool allows to configure the system, in terms of both hard and soft peripherals. The output of this phase is a bitstream file that will configure the Zynq FPGA.

The Android stack is composed of a Linux kernel. It has to be adapted accordingly to the underlying hardware. This phase is carried out by configuring some files of the Linux source code and applying patches before compilation. For instance, Android requires configuration of some Linux software components, such as: ANDROID_BINDER_IPC, ANDROID_LOW_MEMORY_KILLER and USB_ANDROID to be run. As for the patches, Google provides a Git repository in which any developer can choose the most suitable one based on the available Linux kernel version. The compilation phase requires an ARM toolchain to be completed. The result is a compressed version of the kernel, that will be loaded in memory at boot.

In order to complete the software stack, Android has to be compiled too. Since Android is an open-source project, it can be downloaded, configured and compiled. The result is a filesystem containing the files for the boot phase. All the files (bitstream, linux kernel and Android) could be stored into an SDCard, to enable the Zedboard to perform automatic self-programming of the FPGA. The programming task is made of two steps: (i) First Stage Bootloader, in which the FPGA automatically loads the bitstream from the SDCard, in order to configure both programmable logic and processing system; (ii) Second Stage Bootloader, in which the compressed Linux kernel is loaded into memory to be executed by the processing system. After the whole kernel has been loaded, the Android OS is up and running.

4.3   Hardware Traffic Analysis Architecture

The Android OS interfaces the hardware using the system libraries. To handle new peripherals, Android requires new libraries. Since they are written in C, an Android app can use them by properly implementing the function calls in NDK (Native Developing Kit). For this reason we introduced a new library to manage the traffic analysis task from the operating system.

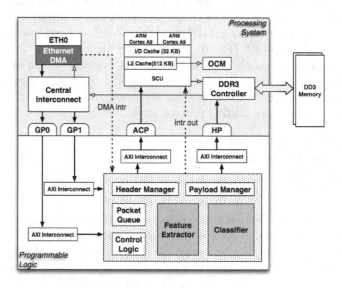

Fig. 2. Hardware traffic analysis architecture using Google Android Operating System

5   Preliminary Experimental Result

For brevity sake, we synthetically report some main results in terms of latency and throughput to prove the effectiveness of the proposed approach. In order to create a working example of the proposed architecture, we implemented the schema pictured in Figure 2. In this section we focus on the feature extractor and classifier, because the other components are not relevant for our purposes. As for the feature extractor, we implemented it as sequential machine that extracts 7 features, such as: protocol, source and destination ports number, average, maximum, minimum and variance of the size of the last N received packets. For the classifier, we adopted the C4.5 algorithm to obtain the predictor tree model in order to classify if the analyzed flow is malicious or not. The synthesis of this block was done using the tool developed in [3]. To maximize the accuracy of the generated predictor, we used the last 4 packets in feature extracting, obtaining 98.42% accuracy. The feature extractor has a throughput of 15.56 Gbps and the classificator has 20.62 Gbps; they both have 4 clock cycles latency. We generated in loop, by using an Android app, a 1024 byte packets flow traffic in order to measure the global delay in packet traversal through the programmable logic, with and without the traffic analyzer, into the cache. Without the analyzer we obtained in average 6.70 ms and using it the delay increased by 87.98 ns. The delay in packet traversal through the central interconnection is 7.3 ms. This counterintuitive result is the consequence of the packet splitting and the direct copying of the header into the L2 cache. Indeed the required time in reading the cache is constant, as a function of ethernet headers' bytes, because no cache flushing is required. Obliviously, we noted that during Android running, the traffic analysis task did not generate extra workload on the CPU.

6   Conclusion and Future Work

The growing of network traffic and related security issues by new generation devices, such as the smartphones, are recent open issues. Traffic analysis plays a very important role to improve security mechanisms in the future communication models and dedicated hardware solutions for the traffic analysis are needed.

Mobile devices can be used to this task, but their capabilities are very limited in terms of computational power and available memory: for these reasons we exploited the possibility of using a hardware accelerator to overcome these limitations.

In this paper we presented an architecture for traffic analysis using Google Android Operating System on a hybrid computing system. We provided an experimental platform in which we had Android running on dual-core ARM processing system and a hardware traffic analyzer embedded in the same chip. We argued that the proposed solution offers very high performance in terms of system load, as the traffic analyzer does not load the Android OS system resources, but runs on dedicated hardware; this feature will enable an easy integration of a dedicated analyzer in future smartphones' architectures. Furthermore, in future work we will show the feasibility of the approach, in terms of throughput and latency as a function of traffic rate and we will evaluate the energy consumption compared with available software solutions.

References

1. Akhila, P.: Design of amba 3.0 (axi) bus based system on chip communication protocol. International Journal (2013)
2. Alshammari, R., Zincir-Heywood, A.N.: Machine learning based encrypted traffic classification: identifying ssh and skype. In: Proceedings of the Second IEEE International Conference on Computational Intelligence for Security and Defense Applications, CISDA 2009, pp. 289–296. IEEE Press, Piscataway (2009)

3. Amato, F., Barbareschi, M., Casola, V., Mazzeo, A.: An FPGA-based smart classifier for decision support systems. In: Zavoral, F., Jung, J.J., Badica, C. (eds.) Intelligent Distributed Computing VII. SCI, vol. 511, pp. 289–299. Springer, Heidelberg (2014)
4. Barbareschi, M., Mazzeo, A., Vespoli, A.: Zedroid: Android 2.2 (froyo) porting on zedboard (2013),
   http://wpage.unina.it/mario.barbareschi/zedroid/index.html
5. Bernaille, L., Teixeira, R., Akodkenou, I., Soule, A., Salamatian, K.: Traffic classification on the fly. SIGCOMM Comput. Commun. Rev. 36(2), 23–26 (2006)
6. Falaki, H., Lymberopoulos, D., Mahajan, R., Kandula, S., Estrin, D.: A first look at traffic on smartphones. In: Proceedings of the 10th ACM SIGCOMM Conference on Internet Measurement, pp. 281–287. ACM (2010)
7. Hur, M., Kim, M.S.: Towards smart phone traffic classification. In: APNOMS, pp. 1–4 (2012)
8. Cisco Visual Networking Index: Global mobile data traffic forecast update, 2010-2015. Cisco white paper (2011)
9. Cisco Visual Networking Index-Forecast: Methodology 2007–2012. Cisco System (2008)
10. Lee, S.W., Park, J.S., Lee, H.S., Kim, M.S.: A study on smart-phone traffic analysis. In: 2011 13th Asia-Pacific Network Operations and Management Symposium (APNOMS), pp. 1–7. IEEE (2011)
11. Li, J., Chen, Y., Ho, C., Lu, Z.: Binary-tree-based high speed packet classification system on FPGA. In: 2013 International Conference on Information Networking (ICOIN), pp. 517–522. IEEE (2013)
12. Lim, Y.S., Kim, H.C., Jeong, J., Kim, C.K., Kwon, T.T., Choi, Y.: Internet traffic classification demystified: on the sources of the discriminative power. In: Proceedings of the 6th International COnference, Co-NEXT 2010, pp. 9:1–9:12. ACM, New York (2010)
13. Luo, H., He, G., Lin, X., Shen, X.: Towards hierarchical security framework for smartphones. In: 2012 1st IEEE International Conference on Communications in China (ICCC), pp. 214–219 (2012), doi:10.1109/ICCChina.2012.6356880
14. Salah, S., Abdulhak, S.A., Sug, H., Kang, D.K., Lee, H.: Performance analysis of intrusion detection systems for smartphone security enhancements. In: 2011 International Conference on Mobile IT Convergence (ICMIC), pp. 15–19. IEEE (2011)
15. Schadt, E.E., Linderman, M.D., Sorenson, J., Lee, L., Nolan, G.P.: Computational solutions to large-scale data management and analysis. Nature Reviews Genetics 11(9), 647–657 (2010)
16. Shanker, A., Lal, S.: Android porting concepts. In: 2011 3rd International Conference on Electronics Computer Technology (ICECT), vol. 5, pp. 129–133. IEEE (2011)
17. Skoda, P., Medved Rogina, B., Sruk, V.: FPGA implementations of data mining algorithms. In: 2012 Proceedings of the 35th International Convention, MIPRO, pp. 362–367. IEEE (2012)
18. Wang, Y., Streff, K., Raman, S.: Smartphone security challenges. Computer, 52–58 (2012)
19. Xilinx: Zynq-7000 ap soc redirecting ethernet packet to pl for hardware packet inspection tech tip (2013), http://www.wiki.xilinx.com/Zynq-7000+AP+SoC+Redirecting+Ethernet+Packet+to+PL+for+Hardware+Packet+Inspection+Tech+Tip

Online Data Analysis of Fetal Growth Curves

Mario A. Bochicchio[1], Antonella Longo[1], Lucia Vaira[1], and Sergio Ramazzina[2]

[1] Department of Engineering for Innovation, University of Salento, Lecce, Italy
{mario.bochicchio,antonella.longo,lucia.vaira}@unisalento.it
[2] Alba Project srl, Lecce, Italy
sergio.ramazzina@albaproject.it

Abstract. Fetal growth curves are considered a critical instrument in prenatal medicine for an appropriate fetal well-being evaluation. Many factors affect fetal growth including physiological and pathological variables, therefore each particular population should have its own reference charts in order to provide the most accurate fetal assessment. In literature a large variety of reference charts are described but they're up to five decades old and consider hospital-based samples, so they're not suitable for the current population and furthermore they don't address the ethnicity, which is an important aspect to take into account. Starting from a detailed analysis of the limitations that characterize the current adopted reference charts, the paper presents a new method, based on multidimensional analysis for creating dynamic and customized fetal growth curves. A preliminary implementation based on open source software, shows why Big Data techniques are essential to solve the problem.

Keywords: Reporting, Personalized Analytics, Multidimensional Analysis.

1 Introduction

In obstetrics and gynecology specific medical tests are often used to evaluate the fetal growth and eventually diagnose possible fetal anomalies. Throughout pregnancy, the mother is subject to different ultrasound scans in order to track fetal growth and to assess fetal health. The main evaluated fetal biometric parameters are: Biparietal Diameter (BPD), Head Circumference (HC), Abdominal Circumference (AC), Femur Length (FL), Crown to Rump Length (CRL). To detect whether growth parameters lay within normal ranges, they are compared to particular reference charts, which show average values of such parameters as a function of the gestational age and allow detecting potential fetal pathologies. These curves have been proposed more than five decades ago by Lubchenco et al. [10], Usher and McLean [16] and Babson and Brenda [1]. They are supported by a huge amount of scientific literature, which at the same time clearly shows its main constraints:

- the patients' number (some thousandth) is low with respect to the number of newborn per year (about 160 ML) in the world;

J. Kołodziej et al. (Eds.): ICA3PP 2013, Part II, LNCS 8286, pp. 149–156, 2013.
© Springer International Publishing Switzerland 2013

— the patients are not representative of the variety of anthropometrical factors related to ethnicity and other relevant factors;
— the commonly used growth curves are not updated for the current population, so they are not suitable to investigate temporal trends in fetal growth curves.

Fetal growth is influenced by a variety of factors, racial, social and economic among others, as well as specific medic conditions that may pre-exist or that may develop during pregnancy. Hence, it's not surprising that fetal biometric parameters show a degree of variation from country to country and from area to area within the same country. Beyond ethnicity, others factors affect fetal growth including fetus gender, physiological and pathological variables, maternal height and weight, drug or tobacco exposure, genetic syndromes, congenital anomalies and placental failure ([8], [11], [12], [15]). Some authors addressed these issues providing an increasing number of fetal growth charts for specific groups and subgroups of population, but their studies suffer from a considerable methodological heterogeneity making them difficult to extend on the large scale. Other authors, such as Gardosi [4] in 1992, proposed to adjust growth curves for most of the influential factors and introduced the idea of individualized fetal growth charts according to specific maternal and fetal characteristics. After about 20 years the interesting proposal, based on proprietary software and on centralized applications, did not produce results documented in the scientific literature. From a theoretical point of view the development of personalized reference charts for fetal growth curves can be formulated as a multidimensional analysis problem on the biometric dataset, routinely collected by doctors for fetal health assessment during pregnancy. Parameters (ethnicity, maternal sizes, familial aspects etc.) impacting the fetal growth can be modeled as cubes dimensions and each homogeneous group of patients (with respect to a given set of dimensions) can be considered as a subcube of the above mentioned biometric dataset [7]. In the multidimensional analysis the requirement of personalized chart can be also expressed in the form: "which is the normal range associated to the X biometric parameter of a Y-weeks old fetus belonging to the subcube defined by the Z dimensional parameters?".

In order to design a system able to dynamically answer to these questions, an important constraint comes from the problem size, which is a function of the number of newborns per year. In this case, considering the storage space needed for the biometric dataset and for the other related data (order of magnitude of some PB), the distributed nature of the system and the number of operations per newborn (order of magnitude of millions or more) we will demonstrate that Big Data techniques must be adopted to satisfy its requirements.

The paper is organized as follows: Section 2 and 3 present the background and the problem; afterwards we show how a conventional open source data warehouse (DW) system can be used to compute the personalized fetal growth curves (Section 4). Then, we show why DW systems are insufficient to effectively manage the whole dataset needed to supply the "Personalized Fetal Growth Curves" service on global scale, and how the problem can be overcome using Big Data techniques (Section 5). Section 6 is for conclusions and future works.

2   Background and Related Works

After the pioneering works of Lubchenco et al. [10], Usher and McLean [16] and Babson and Brenda [1], fetal growth assessment is a well established and mature research field in obstetrics and gynecology ([2], [3], [5], [6]). The proliferation of studies on specific subgroups of patients ([17], [18], [19], [20], [21]) was characterized by a considerable methodological heterogeneity, which made them difficult to normalize and generally reuse for diagnostic purposes. As a consequence, in clinical practice generic reference charts are preferred to specific ones. To preserve the simplicity of the approach without loss of diagnostic power, some authors proposed the adoption of purposely developed software tools (Web and Mobile Applications) to create customized growth charts ([4], [5]) based on a regression model fitted to a very large group of newborns. GROW software[1] by Gardosi can be used as a web application or stand alone. Once inserted parameters such as weight, height, gender and ethnicity, it produces an ideal fetal growth curves using the GROW (Gestation Related Optimal Weight) method. Another widely used software is EcoPlus by Thesis Imaging[2], an information system which allows comprehensive management of medical records by typing fetal biometric parameters, which are directly compared with the reference values for gestational age, with the display of the growth curve percentile. X-Report OstGyn[3] processes ultrasound parameters in real time, displaying graphics of the acquired data, and comparing them with those of previous scans. The software offers the possibility of adopting different references for the growth curves. Since the reference values are often based on tables and formulas not easy-to-interpret, patients are increasingly making use of web applications or even mobile applications (Apps) preferring the simplicity and immediacy of reading rather than the scientific and methodological correctness. Among the best known applications there are iFetus[4] uses the most recent and updated biometric tables of the Caucasian race (valid for both European and North American populations); Fetal Ultrasound Calculator2[5] and Percentile Growth Charts[6] that let patient know the percentiles based on World Health Organization (WHO) standards and to design custom charts. These applications address the problem of positioning data on chart used as reference standard for the construction of growth curves, but WHO standards are dated, they are still based on generic reference charts and don't differentiate by ethnic origin, so they are unsuitable to assess the biometric parameters in several cases of practical interest.

---

[1] http://www.gestation.net

[2] http://www.tesi.mi.it:8080/TesiSito/products.php

[3] http://www.gsquared.it/X-Report.html

[4] http://appfinder.lisisoft.com/app/ifetus.html

[5] http://appfinder.lisisoft.com/app/fetal-ultrasound-calculator2.html

[6] https://play.google.com/store/apps/details?id=com.endyanosimedia.ipercentiles&hl=it

To our knowledge, big data techniques for approaching the issue of personalized growth chart have not yet been explored, even if it is clear the benefits which they could bring, as proved in [22] dealing with large volumes of data.

3   Multidimensional Modeling and Analysis for Creating Personalized Charts

The detailed analysis of the fetal intrauterine growth monitoring is out of the scope of this paper but, in summary, the essential idea is that: a) fetuses at the same gestational age, with similar genetic nature (like ethnicity) and in similar environmental conditions (food, smoke, ...) are subject to similar growth curves. This kind of fetuses will be referred, in the following of the paper, as Homogeneous Fetal Groups (HFG); b) a fetus having growth parameters different from those of its HFG is potentially pathologic. Monitoring is performed measuring the main biometric parameters (the above cited BPD, HC, AC, FL and CRL) by means of maternal trans-abdominal ultrasound pictures. All HGFs can be dynamically extracted from the whole dataset by means of multidimensional queries where fetal biometric parameters are the measures while the dimensions are the parameters (ethnicity, maternal weight and height, familial aspects, foods etc.) impacting the fetal growth.

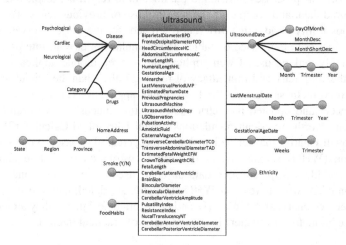

Fig. 1. Dimensional Fact Model of an ultrasound test

As shown in Fig. 1, in collaboration with a research group of obstetrics and gynecologists we identified 9 main dimensions of analysis which lead to more than 10.000 Homogeneous Fetal Subgroups that the system must be able to identify and continuously update by adding the new fetal sizes when they arrive from the hospitals or directly from the patients (20 ML per year, about 2 every 3 seconds). It means that this problem largely exceeds the computation capabilities of a classic multidimensional analysis system (such as the one included in the Pentaho BI suite). In order to produce updated HFG in a reasonable time, specific techniques must be investigated.

4 Data Layer Design

For the purposes of this paper, test data (both fetal and maternal) has been created by means of a purposely-designed data generator. In a real scenario, instead, fetal growth data come from a number of heterogeneous sources (hospitals, EHR repositories, patients etc.) through different channels (web services, web applications, mobile applications etc.) and in different formats (HL7 or proprietary formats). The normalized data model we designed to collect and integrate fetal growth data coming from the above mentioned sources, named DB4GO (DataBase for Gynecology and Obstetrics), is based on the "HL7 Reference Information Model" [9], on the "Universal Data Model for Healthcare" [13] and on the "HL7 Harmonization Process for the integration phase" [9]. The same DB4GO database is used as data warehouse to build the multidimensional data cubes (data marts) needed for the personalized fetal growth diagnoses.

To correctly size this repository and the computational power needed to compute the personalized growth curves, we should consider that each year 160 millions of newborn come to the World (4.4 from US and 5.5 from Europe). Considering a Fetal Growth Tracking (FGT) online-service able to follow 50% of newborns from Europe and US, a record size of 10 KB for each pregnant woman plus 2 KB for each fetus and a running window of 6 year to track mothers with 2 or more children, the global storage space sum up to about 360 GB of online multidimensional data (about 1.5 PB including also ultrasound images).

From the computational point of view, to generate the custom growth charts for Italy, the FGT system should run about 20 millions (5 millions pregnant women x 4 tests) multidimensional queries per year, i.e. about 2 queries each 3 seconds, which largely exceed the capabilities of a standard business intelligence suite (normally adopted for multidimensional analysis) such as Pentaho BI. Existing Big Data solutions focus on addressing the Volume aspect of the 3-V's of Big Data [23]. Specialized technologies including distributed databases [24], Hadoop [25] and NoSQL ([26], [14]) have been developed to support scalable data storage and on-demand querying over large volumes of data. These systems usually provide high performance for data that has been persisted and properly indexed.

5 Test Architecture

To have a first indication about the resources consumption needed to the FGT service, and about how they scale with the problem size, we created 7 different dataset representative of different nationalities (American, Arabian, English, Italian, Norwegian, Pakistani, Thai and Turkish). The dataset, including respectively 1000, 10000, 100.000, 200.000, 500.000, 700.000 and 1.000.000 records, have been produced by means of a biometric parameters generator, which produces a significant number of samples starting from the fetal growth curves reported in literature for the different populations, according to its statistics (mean values and standard deviations of the Gaussian distributions related to each gestational week).

The computational tests have been performed on a standard Pentium 5 machine running at 2.5 GHz with 8 GB of RAM and 2 TB of storage space (SATA Disks). All tests have been based on Saiku V2.1 (a software component of the Pentaho suite), running a "template query", which shows the Head Circumference mean value (50th percentile) according to the different nationalities. The average processing times are shown in Fig. 2. They clearly demonstrate that even with a small fraction (about 3%) of the records to be processed in the fully working system, a single machine is far from satisfying the temporal constraints of processing 2 queries each 3 seconds defined in the previous section. Moreover, since the database is characterized by a large number of concurrent users asking for different queries, acceleration strategies based on suitable caching strategies are not effective and cloud (or grid) based solutions are required. Two more options, aimed to contain the overall computational power required to solve the problem are under evaluations:

— the adoption of a different processing strategy, based on the clustering of multidimensional dataset with Hadoop, as described in [22];
— the adoption of tensor-based computation, which is a very effective way to manage multidimensional datasets on distributed and parallel machines.

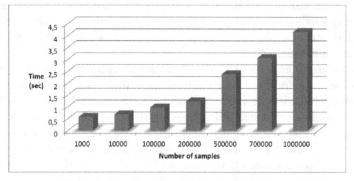

Fig. 2. Processing time with respect to the patients' number

6   Conclusions and Future Works

The fetal growth assessment is a relevant problem since it concerns about 160 ML of newborns per year. Due to the *"ethnicity reshufflement"* of the population, it's by nature a global phenomena which can benefit from the adoption of Big Data techniques and cloud infrastructures. The goal is to obtain personalized Fetal Growth Curves' computation within a given timeframe (< 1.5 s) over a given dataset (from about 360 GB to several TB) of multidimensional data. In order to have some preliminary figures about the resources consumed by FGT service we performed an experiment based on Saiku Suite V2.1. The first results show that the problem can be solved at a reasonable cost and in an acceptable time with cloud (or grid) based techniques.

More promising results came from the adoption of 2 advanced approaches based parallel clustering algorithm and on tensor-based computation. In the future we plan to adopt the Pentaho Community Distributed Cache (CDC), which allows clearing the cache of only specific Mondrian cubes (so it allows updating each single HFG without impacting on the other cubes). Another approach can explore advanced clustering techniques for multidimensional datasets based on MapReduce Framework, as in [22], which demonstrated the be very effective to solve the problem at a reasonable price by means of Big Data techniques running on cloud infrastructure.

References

1. Babson, S.G., Benda, G.I.: Growth graphs for the clinical assessment of infants of varying gestational age. J. Pediatr. 89, 814–820 (1976)
2. Bonellie, S., Chalmers, J., Gray, R., Greer, I., Jarvis, S., Williams, C.: Centile charts for birth-weight for gestational age for Scottish singleton births. BMC Pregnancy Childbirth 8, 5–14 (2008)
3. Fenton, T.R.: A new growth chart for preterm babies: Babson and Brenda's chart updated with recent data and a new format. BMC Pediatr. 3, 13–22 (2003)
4. Gardosi, J., Chang, A., Kalyan, B., Sahota, D., Symonds, E.M.: Customised antenatal growth charts. Lancet 339, 283–287 (1992)
5. Gardosi, J., Mongelli, M., Wilcox, M., Chang, A.: An adjustable fetal weight standard. Ultrasound Obstet. Gynecol. 6, 168–174 (1995)
6. Giorlandino, M., Padula, F., Cignini, P., Mastrandrea, M., Vigna, R., Buscicchio, G., Giorlandino, C.: Reference interval for fetal biometry in Italian population. J. Prenat. Med. 3(4), 62–65 (2009)
7. Golfarelli, M., Rizzi, S.: Data Warehouse - Teoria e pratica della progettazione. McGrow-Hill (2006)
8. Groveman, S.A.: New Preterm Infant Growth Curves Influence of Gender and Race on Birth Size. Masters thesis. Biotechnology and Bioscience, Drexel University, Philadelphia, PA (2008)
9. HL7 Reference Information Model, Health Level Seven, Inc., http://www.hl7.org/v3ballot/html/infrastructure/rim/rim.htm
10. Lubchenco, L.O., Hansman, C., Boyd, E.: Intrauterine growth in length and head circumference as estimated from live births at gestational ages from 26 to 42 weeks. Pediatrics 37, 403–408 (1966)
11. Niklasson, A., Albertsson-Wikland, K.: Continuous growth reference from 24th week of gestation to 24 months by gender. BMC Pediatr. 8, 8–32 (2008)
12. Oken, E., Kleinman, K.P., Rich-Edwards, J., Gillman, M.W.: A nearly continuous measure of birth weight for gestational age using a United States national reference. BMC Pediatr. 3, 6–15 (2003)
13. Silverston, L.: The Data Model Resource Book, Revised Edition. A Library of Universal Data Models by Industry Types, vol. 2. John Wiley and Sons, New York (2001)
14. Stonebraker, M.: NoSQL and enterprises. Commun. ACM 54(8), 10–11 (2011)
15. Thomas, P., Peabody, J., Turnier, V., Clark, R.H.: A new look at intrauterine growth and the impact of race, altitude, and gender. Pediatrics 106(2) (2000), http://www.pediatrics.org/cgi/content/full/106/2/e21
16. Usher, R., McLean, F.: Intrauterine growth of live-born Caucasian infants at sea level: standards obtained from measurements in 7 dimensions of infants born between 25 and 44 weeks of gestation. J. Pediatr. 74, 901–910 (1969)

17. Mongelli, M., Gardosi, J.: Longitudinal study of fetal growth in subgroups of a low-risk population. Ultrasound in Obstetrics & Gynecology 6(5), 340–344 (1995)

18. Kramer, M.S., Platt, R.W., Wen, S.W., Joseph, K.S., Allen, A., Abrahamowicz, M., Blondel, B., Breart, G.: A new and improved population-based Canadian reference for birth weight for gestational age. Pediatrics 108(2), e35 (2001)

19. McCowan, L., Stewart, A.W., Francis, A., Gardosi, J.: A customised birthweight centile calculator developed for a New Zealand population. Aust N. Zeal. J. Obstet. Gynaecol. 44(5), 428–431 (2004)

20. Salomon, L.J., Duyme, M., Crequat, J., Brodaty, G., Talmant, C., Fries, N., Althuser, M.: French fetal biometry: reference equations and comparison with other charts. Ultrasound Obstet. Gynecol. 28(2), 193–198 (2006)

21. Verburg, B.O., Steegers, E.A., De Ridder, M., Snijders, R.J., Smith, E., Hofman, A., Moll, H.A., Jaddoe, V.W., Witteman, J.C.: New charts for ultrasound dating of pregnancy and assessment of fetal growth: longitudinal data from a population-based cohort study. Ultrasound Obstet. Gynecol. 31(4), 388–396 (2008)

22. Cordeiro, R.L.F., Traina Jr., C., Traina, A.J.M., Lopez, J., Kang, U., Faloutsos, C.: Clustering very large multi-dimensional datasets with mapreduce. In: Proceedings of the 17th ACM SIGKDD International Conference on Knowledge Discovery and Data Mining. ACM (2011)

23. Laney, D.: 3D data management: Controlling data volume, velocity, and variety. Technical report, META Group (2001)

24. Garcia-Molina, H., Ullman, J.D., Widom, J.: Database systems: The complete book. Prentice Hall Press, NJ (2008)

25. Shvachko, K., Kuang, H., Radia, S., Chansler, R.: The Hadoop distributed file system. In: 2010 IEEE 26th Symposium on Mass Storage Systems and Technologies (MSST), pp. 1–10 (2010)

26. Han, J., Haihong, E., Le, G., Du, J.: Survey on nosql database. In: 2011 6th International Conference on Pervasive Computing and Applications (ICPCA), pp. 363–366 (2011)

A Practical Approach for Finding Small {Independent, Distance} Dominating Sets in Large-Scale Graphs

Liang Zhao[1,2,*], Hiroshi Kadowaki[1], and Dorothea Wagner[2]

[1] Graduate School of Informatics, Kyoto University, 606-8501, Japan
[2] Institute of Theoretical Informatics, Karlsruhe Technology of Informatics,
D-76128 Karlsruhe, Germany
liangzhao@ieee.org

Abstract. Suppose that in a network, a node can dominate (or cover, monitor, etc) its neighbor nodes. An interesting question asks to find such a minimum set of nodes that dominate all the other nodes. This is known as the *minimum dominating set* problem. A natural generalization assumes that a node can dominate nodes within a distance $R \geq 1$, called the minimum *distance* dominating set problem. On the other hand, if the distance between any two nodes in the dominating set must be at least $z \geq 1$, then the problem is known as the minimum *independent* dominating set problem. This paper considers to find a minimum distance-R independence-z dominating set for arbitrary R and z, which has applications in facility location, internet monitoring and others. We show a practical approach. Empirical studies show that usually it is very fast and quite accurate, thus suitable for Big Data analysis. Generalization to directed graphs, edge lengths, multi-dominating are also discussed.

1 Introduction

Dominating Set (DS) is a well-known combinatorial optimization problem. For many years, researchers studied it and its variants in numerous fields, most from theoretical aspect (see, e.g., [1,4,6,7,9,12]). Empirical studies [10,11,13,15,16] are limited to either small-size instances or problem formulation. The purpose of this paper is to provide a practical algorithm to a general formulation.

Let $R \geq 1$ and $z \geq 1$ be two (fixed) integers. Given an undirected graph $G = (V, E)$ with a set V of nodes and a set E of edges, a set $D \subseteq V$ is said an (R, z)-DS if $\forall v \in V$, $\exists d \in D$, $\text{dist}(d, v) \leq R$, and $\text{dist}(d_1, d_2) \geq z$, $\forall d_1, d_2 \in D$, $d_1 \neq d_2$, where dist denotes the distance (length of a shortest path) between two nodes. We consider to find a minimum (R, z)-DS for a given graph.

This problem has applications in sensor networks (where a node monitors its neighbor nodes), internet monitoring ([15], where a node monitors its neighbor links), facility location ([16], where a node serves its neighbor nodes) and others. Unfortunately it is hard to solve. Even for the simplest $(1, 1)$-DS problem, no

---

* Corresponding author.

J. Kołodziej et al. (Eds.): ICA3PP 2013, Part II, LNCS 8286, pp. 157–164, 2013.
© Springer International Publishing Switzerland 2013

algorithm can achieve an approximation factor better than $c \log |V|$ for some constant $c > 0$ unless P = NP ([14]). On the other hand, $(1, 2)$-DS cannot be approximated within factor $|V|^{1-\epsilon}$ for any $\epsilon > 0$ unless P = NP ([5]). Therefore we need efficient approximation algorithms or heuristics in practice ([11]).

For that purpose, we can treat the min-$(R, 1)$-DS problem as a Set Cover problem by thinking that a node covers all nodes within distance R. Thus the well-known *greedy algorithm* [8] gives a $1 + \log |V|$ approximation, almost matches the best bound $c \log |V|$. However, this approach requires $O(|V||E|)$ running time and $\Omega(|V|^2)$ space (only for $R = 1$ both are $O(|V| + |E|)$), thus it is not suitable for large instances except when $R = z = 1$. For a more *practical* approach, Sasaki et al. [15] and Wang et al. [16] proposed a simple heuristic Sieve and reported that it can treat as many as 10^8 nodes and is quite accurate in practice.

For the case of $z = 2$, there exists a 5-approximation algorithms for unit disk graphs ([9]), and an empirical study [10] considered small instances with less than 1500 nodes. As far as we know, there is no empirical study for $z \geq 3$.

In this paper, we combine the works [15,16] and the greedy approach. The idea is to repeatedly select a node v with the largest *residual degree*, which is the number of neighbors of v that have not been dominated so far. Notice that for $R = 1$, this is nothing but the greedy algorithm. For $R \geq 2$, however, they are different. An interesting observation is that any two nodes selected in this way must be of distance R or more, hence it is an (R, z)-DS algorithm for all $z \leq R$. We also show how to handle the cases when $z > R$.

The rest of the paper is organized as follows. In Section 2 we give a description of our Quasi-Greedy heuristic (QGreedy) for $(R, 1)$-DS. Then in Section 3 we show how to treat (R, z)-DS, $z \geq 2$. In Section 4 we show empirical results. Finally in Section 5 we conclude and discuss further extensions.

2   Quasi-Greedy Heuristic (QGreedy) for $(R, 1)$-DS

2.1   Overview

Let us first give the outline of the heuristic. Let $n = |V|$ and $m = |E|$. For simple notation, we will not distinguish a set $\{v\}$ and the element v in the following.

For two sets $U, W \subseteq V$, let $\text{dist}(U, W) = \min\{\text{dist}(u, w) \mid u \in U, w \in W\}$ denote the (minimum) *distance* from U to W in G. Let

$$\Gamma_r(U) = \{v \in V \mid \text{dist}(v, U) \leq r\}$$

denote the set of nodes that can be reached from U via at most r edges. Since $z = 1$, we are just asked to find a smallest set $D \subseteq V$ such that $\Gamma_R(D) = V$ with no independence requirement. For that purpose, a simple idea is to repeatedly find a node that dominates some un-dominated node(s), see Table 1.

Clearly how to select d is important. We have three strategies:

(1) Maximize $|\Gamma_R(d) - \Gamma_R(D)|$. This is the greedy algorithm (Greedy), which requires quadric time and quadric space for all $R \geq 2$. Only for $R = 1$, however, it can be done in linear time, since $\sum_{v \in V} |\Gamma_1(v)| = n + 2m$.

Table 1. A general framework to construct an $(R, 1)$-DS D

```
1   D = ∅
2   while |ΓR(D)| < n do
3       select a node d ∈ V such that ΓR(d) − ΓR(D) ≠ ∅
4           D = D ∪ {d}
5   end while
```

(2) Choose any d such that $\Gamma_R(d) - \Gamma_R(D) \neq \emptyset$. This is the Algorithm Sieve [15,16]. For a good solution, Sieve checks nodes in the fixed *degree-descending* order, which can be determined at the beginning by a bucket-sort in $O(m + n)$ time. Sieve also has a labeling method to complete other tasks in a total $O(R(m+n))$ time, with a reverse-delete step to make the solution minimal. We note that R is fixed and usually small in practice.

(3) Maximize the *residual degree* $|\Gamma_1(d) - \Gamma_R(D)|$. This is our approach Quasi-Greedy heuristic (QGreedy), as it is somehow greedy but not exactly (however, when $R = 1$, it is greedy). Unlike Greedy, our algorithm can be done in linear time by combining a (bucket-based) priority queue and the labeling method in [15,16]. Let us explain the detail in the next subsection.

2.2 Detail of QGreedy

We explain how to maximize $|\Gamma_1(v) - \Gamma_R(D)|$. We use adjacent lists to store the graph. Then, different from Sieve, we employ a priority queue to store the unselected nodes v with key $|\Gamma_1(v) - \Gamma_R(D)|$. A standard bucket-based priority queue can do this efficiently. Since keys are no more than the maximum degree plus 1 and never increase, the whole operations (**insert**, **deletemax** and **decreasekey**) take $O(n + m)$ time, each operation $O(1)$ and at most $n + m$ operations.

On the other hand, updating $\Gamma_R(D)$ and $|\Gamma_1(v) - \Gamma_R(D)|$ in a total of linear time is not trivial. Fortunately we can extend (in fact, simplify) the labeling method in [15,16]. Let us define a label $\ell(v)$ for each node v. At the beginning, $D = \emptyset$ and $\ell(v) = 0$ for all v. Then $D \neq \emptyset$ and we define

$$\ell(v) = \max \left\{ 0, \ R + 1 - \min_{d \in D} \text{dist}(d, v) \right\}.$$

Therefore a node v is dominated by D if and only if $\ell(v) \geq 1$. On the other hand, the priority $key(v)$ of a node v is defined as $|\Gamma_1(v) - \Gamma_R(D)|$. At the beginning, $key(v) = |\Gamma_1(v)|$ can be calculated in $O(n + m)$ time. Now suppose that $|\Gamma_R(D)| < n$ and a node d maximizing $key(d)$ was selected (Line 3 in Table 1). Notice that $key(d) \geq 1$. To update $\ell(v)$, we do a bounded breadth-first search (BFS) starting from d with maximum depth R. In the BFS, when we meet a node v, we compare $\ell(v)$ with $\ell'(v) = R + 1 - \text{dist}(d, v)$. If $\ell'(v) > \ell(v)$, then we update the label of v to $\ell'(v)$ and continue; otherwise *we do not search* v. If the old label is 0, i.e., v was not dominated before, we increment $|\Gamma_R(D)|$.

It is easy to see that the running time is $O(R(m + n))$, since a node or an edge is checked by at most R times (notice $\ell(v) \leq R + 1$). This is the same as Sieve. For the performance ratio, when $R = 1$, (as it is the same as Greedy) the solution is a $1 + \log n$ approximation; otherwise the ratio can be $\Omega(n)$.

2.3   Finding Lower Bounds

We discuss how to find lower bounds, which will be used in the empirical study.

The min-$(R, 1)$-DS problem is an Integer Programming to minimize $\sum_{v \in V} x_v$ under constraints $\sum_{v \in \Gamma_R(u)} x_v \geq 1, \forall u \in V$, and $x_v \in \{0, 1\}, \forall v \in V$. A dual Integer Programming of it would be to maximize $\sum_{u \in V} y_u$ under constraints $\sum_{v \in \Gamma_R(u)} y_u \leq 1, \forall v \in V$, and $y_u \in \{0, 1\}, \forall u \in V$. The weakly duality theorem says that any feasible solution of the dual is a lower bound of the primary. Therefore any $(\infty, 2R + 1)$-DS is a lower bound of the minimum $(R, 1)$-DS.

Finding a maximum $(\infty, 2R + 1)$-DS, also known as the distance-$(2R + 1)$ independent set problem, however, is NP-hard even for bipartite planar graphs of maximum degree three or chordal graphs ([2]). Moreover, $\forall \epsilon > 0$, approximating it within factor $n^{1/2 - \epsilon}$ is also hard (i.e., impossible unless P = NP) even for bipartite graphs ([2]). Nevertheless, we can calculate a maximal $(\infty, 2R + 1)$-DS greedily, as first proposed in [15,16]. An interesting observation in our experiments is that the gap is usually not so big in practice.

3   Extension to (R, z)-DS, $z \geq 2$

We observe that QGreedy only select nodes of label 1 or 0 (since $key(d) = |\Gamma_1(d) - \Gamma_R(D)| \geq 1$ when d was selected). This implies that the distance between any pair of the selected nodes is at least R. Hence actually by QGreedy we find an (R, z)-DS for all $1 \leq z \leq R$. This observation is also used in constructing a lower bound (i.e., a maximal $(\infty, 2R+1)$-DS) for $(R, 1)$-DS with slightly different way to select nodes. We note that neither the greedy algorithm nor Sieve has this feature. They cannot construct a distance dominating set with independence.

For $z > R$, we can use another label $s(v) = \max\{0, z + 1 - \min_{d \in D} \text{dist}(d, v)\}$ and only adopt node d if it maximizes $key(d)$ and $s(d) \leq 1$. Label $s(v)$ can be updated similarly as $\ell(v)$ in a total $O(z(m + n))$ running time. Therefore the total running time is $O((R + z)(m + n))$. This extension, however, may fail to find a feasible solution. For example, consider the min-$(1, 3)$-DS problem for a graph with four nodes a, b, c, d and three edges (a, b), (b, c), (c, d). The only solution is $\{a, d\}$, whereas the QGreedy (of course the greedy algorithm too) first finds b or c and then stops without finding a feasible solution. Details are omitted due to the limit of paper.

4   Empirical Study

We study the performance of QGreedy by comparing it with an exact algorithm (Exact), the greedy algorithm (Greedy, [8]) and Sieve ([15,16]). Exact simply uses

an Integer Programming solver GLPK (http://www.gnu.org/software/glpk/).
All tests were done on a laptop Fujitsu Lifebook SH76/HN with Intel Core i5-
3210M CPU and 8GB RAM running Linux. We implemented Greedy, Sieve and
QGreedy in C language and complied them by gcc 4.7.2.

First we test the algorithms with random graphs, which were generated by
GTgraph (http://www.cse.psu.edu/~madduri/software/GTgraph/) with parameters $m = 10n$. Since the graph are directed and have multi-edges, we added
missing edges to get an undirected graph and removed multi-edges. The final
number of edges are about $20n$.

Table 2. Sizes of the random graphs used in experiments

n	100	110	120	130	140	150	160	170	180	190	200
m	1,812	1,992	2,180	2,408	2,628	2,824	2,974	3,202	3,402	3,600	3,786

n	1,000	10,000	100,000	1,000,000
m	19,824	199,798	1,999,792	19,999,798

We also test many other different kinds of networks. Due to the limit of pages,
we only show the results for the following networks: USA-road-d.E from 9th DI-
MACS http://www.dis.uniroma1.it/challenge9/download.shtml and others from SNAP http://snap.stanford.edu/data/.

Table 3. Sizes of some different kinds of networks used in experiments

name	description	n	m
ca-AstroPh	Collaboration network of Arxiv Astro Physics	37,544	792,320
com-youtube	Youtube online social network	1,134,890	5,975,248
USA-road-d.E	road network of the east of USA	3,598,623	8,778,114
as-skitter	Internet AS graph	1,696,415	22,190,596

For small random graphs, we show the results in Fig. 1. For larger instances,
we report the calculation results in Table 4. For other types of networks, we show
the results in the following figures. It can be observed that usually both Sieve and
QGreedy perform quite well. The gap from the lower bounds is usually not big.
We remark that the running time of QGreedy is usually two times faster than
Sieve, because we have no reverse delete step. Usually it is at most four times of
a pure breadth-first-search (less than 3s for all the instances), almost constant
to all R for all the instances tested (despite of our analysis of $O(R(m + n))$).

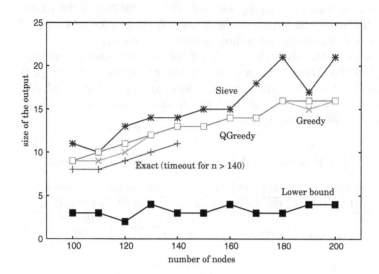

Fig. 1. $(1,1)$-DS results for the small random graphs with time limit 180s. We can see that the gap between the lower bounds and the optimal is quite big. QGreedy and Greedy are better than Sieve. We remark that the running time of all algorithms except Exact is 0.00s. For $R \geq 2$, since the diameters of these small instances are either 1 or 2, all algorithms find an optimal or a near optimal solutions in almost 0s.

Table 4. $(R,1)$-DS results for larger random graphs, shown as s/t where s is the size of the output and t is the running time in seconds. As before, we consider the lower bounds are too weak for random graphs. We remark that QGreedy finds (R,R)-DS.

n	1,000	10,000	100,000	1,000,000
Greedy, $R=1$	85/0.00	844/1.22	memory out	
Greedy, $R=2$	7/0.04	72/1.38	memory out	
Greedy, $R=3$	1/0.10	6/5.52	memory out	
Sieve, $R=1$	109/0.00	1,013/0.00	10,243/0.06	103,037/0.70
Sieve, $R=2$	8/0.00	89/0.00	906/0.06	9,181/0.88
Sieve, $R=3$	1/0.00	7/0.00	70/0.06	679/0.92
QGreedy, $R=1$	84/0.00	843/0.02	8,469/0.12	84,691/2.38
QGreedy, $R=2$	13/0.00	122/0.00	1,149/0.14	11,638/2.48
QGreedy, $R=3$	1/0.00	12/0.00	113/0.14	1,104/2.66
Lowerbound, $R=1$	20/0.00	191/0.02	1,891/0.10	18,965/1.66
Lowerbound, $R=2$	1/0.00	2/0.00	13/0.10	147/1.82
Lowerbound, $R=3$	1/0.00	1/0.00	1/0.04	2/0.96

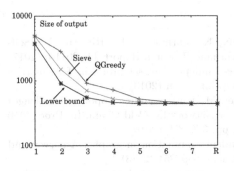

Fig. 2. Results for ca-AsAstroPh

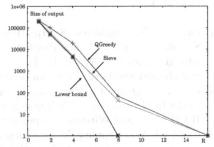

Fig. 3. Results for com-youtube

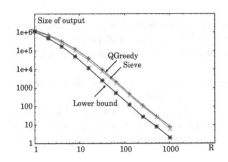

Fig. 4. Results for USA-road-d.E

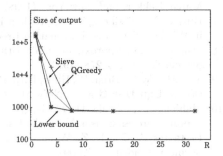

Fig. 5. Results for as-skitter

5   Conclusion

In this paper, we gave a Quasi-Greedy heuristic QGreedy for finding small (independent) distance dominating sets. Experimental results show that the running time is usually less than four times of a pure BFS, and the solutions are only a few times worse than the lower bounds. Comparing to a previous algorithm Sieve ([15,16]), QGreedy is faster with competitive sizes of solutions, and has the advantage of independence, which is considered important in many area (e.g., wireless sensor network [7,10], parallel computing [1], etc).

We remark that it is not difficult to extend the heuristic to edge-lengths, multi-dominating and node-different dominating radius. See [16] for a different but similar work. As a future work, it would be interesting to give theoretical analysis and extend the algorithm to other Dominating Set problems.

Acknowledgement. This work was supported by JSPS KAKENHI Grant Number 23700018, 25330026.

References

1. Datta, A.K., Devismes, S., Heurtefeux, K., Larmore, L.L., Rivierre, Y.: Self-Stabilizing Small k-Dominating Sets. Verimag Research Report TR-2011-6 (2011)
2. Eto, H., Guo, F., Miyano, E.: Distance-d independent set problems for bipartite and chordal graphs. J. Combinatorial Optimization (2013)
3. Gupta, A., Diallo, C., Marot, M., Becker, M.: Understanding Topology Challenges in the Implementation of Wireless Sensor Network for Cold Chain. In: Proc. 2010 IEEE Radio and Wireless Symposium, pp. 376–379 (2010)
4. Goddard, W., Henning, M.A.: Independent domination in graphs: A survey and recent results. Discrete Mathematics 313(7), 839–854 (2013)
5. Halldorsson, M.M.: Approximating the minimum maximal independence number. Inform. Process. Lett. 46, 169–172 (1993)
6. Haynes, T.W., Hedetniemi, S., Slater, P.: Fundamentals of domination in graphs. Marcel Dekker, Inc., New York (1998)
7. Hurink, J.L., Neiberg, T.: Approximating Minimum Independent Dominating Sets in Wireless Networks. Information Processing Letters, 155–160 (2008)
8. Johnson, D.S.: Approximation algorithms for combinatorial problems. J. Comput. System Sci. 9, 256–278 (1974)
9. Marathe, M.V., Breu, H., Hunt, H.B., Ravi, S.S., Rosenkrantz, D.J.: Simple Heuristics for Unit Disk Graphs. Networks 25(2), 59–68 (1995)
10. Mahjoub, D., Matula, D.W.: Experimental Study of Independent and Dominating Sets in Wireless Sensor Networks Using Graph Coloring Algorithms. In: Liu, B., Bestavros, A., Du, D.-Z., Wang, J. (eds.) WASA 2009. LNCS, vol. 5682, pp. 32–42. Springer, Heidelberg (2009)
11. Molnar Jr., F., Screenivasan, S., Szymanski, B.K., Korniss, G.: Minimum Dominating Sets in Scale-Free Network Ensembles. Scientific Reports 3, 1736 (2013)
12. Poghosyan, A.: The probabilistic method for upper bounds in domination theory, doctoral thesis, University of the West of England (2010)
13. Potluri, A., Negi, A.: Some Observations on Algorithms for Computing Minimum Independent Dominating Set. In: Aluru, S., Bandyopadhyay, S., Catalyurek, U.V., Dubhashi, D.P., Jones, P.H., Parashar, M., Schmidt, B. (eds.) IC3 2011. CCIS, vol. 168, pp. 57–68. Springer, Heidelberg (2011)
14. Raz, R., Safra, S.: A sub-constant error-probability low-degree test, and sub-constant error-probability PCP characterization of NP. In: Proc. 29th STOC, pp. 475–484 (1997)
15. Sasaki, M., Zhao, L., Nagamochi, H.: Security-aware beacon based network monitoring. In: 11th IEEE International Conference on Communication Systems, Guangzhou, China, pp. 527–531 (2008)
16. Wang, J., Gim, J., Sasaki, M., Zhao, L., Nagamochi, H.: Efficient Approximate Algorithms for the Beacon Placement and its Dual Problem (Abstract). In: International Conf. on Computational Intelligence and Software Engineering (CiSE), Wuhan, China, pp. 1–4 (2009)

Part III
International Workshop on Trusted Information in Big Data (TIBiDa 2013)

Part III

Robust Fingerprinting Codes for Database

Thach V. Bui[1], Binh Q. Nguyen[1], Thuc D. Nguyen[1],
Noboru Sonehara[2], and Isao Echizen[2]

[1] University of Science, Ho Chi Minh City, Vietnam
{bvthach,nqbinh,ndthuc}@fit.hcmus.edu.vn
[2] National Institute of Informatics, Tokyo, Japan
{iechizen,sonehara}@nii.ac.jp

Abstract. The purchasing of customer databases, which is becoming more and more common, has led to a big problem: illegal distribution of purchased databases. An essential tool for identifying distributors is database fingerprinting. There are two basic problem in fingerprinting database: designing the fingerprint and embedding it. For the first problem, we have proven that Non-Adaptive Group Testing, which is used to identify specific items in a large population, can be used for fingerprinting and that it is secure against collusion attack efficiently. For the second problem, we have developed a solution that supports up to 262,144 fingerprints for 4,032 attributes, and that is secure against three types of attacks: attribute, collusion and complimentary. Moreover, illegal distributor can be identified within 0.15 seconds.

Keywords: Database Distribution, Fingerprinting Codes, Group Testing, Error Correcting Codes.

1 Introduction

1.1 Database Distribution

The growing practice of purchasing customer databases has led to growing concern about privacy protection. Many countries and organizations have thus taken steps to protect privacy. For example, the European Union enacted the EU Directive on Data Privacy in 1995, and the United Kingdom enacted the Data Protection Act (DPA) three years later. These laws require the control of information in the processing of personal data, i.e., data about a living and identifiable individual. They require that personal data be used only for authorized and lawful purposes. This means that any other use of such data, such as retention for longer than necessary, use for other purposes without permission, and redistribution, should be detected to enable punishment of the offender. Much research has been done on protecting data privacy [7–9], and most of it has focused on preventing the identification of individuals from the information contained in the data. The rapid development of the Internet has led to people sharing a lot of personal information, e.g., preferences, online without realizing it. For example, Facebook encourages its members to list their favorite

J. Kołodziej et al. (Eds.): ICA3PP 2013, Part II, LNCS 8286, pp. 167–176, 2013.
© Springer International Publishing Switzerland 2013

books and movies and promises that such information will be kept confidential (www.facebook.com/help/privacy). Therefore, when it sells such member information to third parties, it must ensure that its members cannot be identified from the data. The data is very useful to make companies orientate their new products. Therefore, selling customer databases is a potential business.

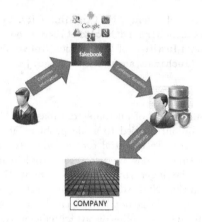

Fig. 1. The model of database distributing

Although their purpose is to protect customer privacy, the EU Directive on Data Privacy and the DPA sill allow companies to sell customer databases. We call this practice *database distribution*. A crucial problems is thus to prevent a purchaser from illegally distributing the database. If a purchased database is illegally distributed, the distributor must be identified. Since there is no physical way of preventing a purchaser from distributing the database, our problem is to identify distributors. Willenborg and Kardaun [1] proposed adding fingerprints to the database to enable identification of an illegal distributor. A various versions of the database to be distinguished. However, the algorithm used to create fingerprints is not deterministic and can be used only for identifying specific records.

Therefore, we have to guarantee two requirements before selling a customer database: the privacy and fingerprints for the database. In this paper, we only concentrate on fingerprints for database.

1.2   Related Work

There are basic components of the fingerprinting process: designing and embedding. Boneh-Shaw (BoSh) [2] designed a system for fingerprinting digital data. Their system is aimed at collusion attacks (in which purchasers combine several copies of the same content but with different fingerprints in attempt to remove the original fingerprints or to frame innocent purchasers). If their system has up to d colluders with an ϵ-secure error and supports N owners, their code length is about $t = O(d^4 \log(N/\epsilon) \log(1/\epsilon))$. This is not an optimal code. Tardos [3] used probability to construct a fingerprinting code with a length of $t = O(d^2 \log(N/\epsilon))$. However, it takes a time of $O(tN)$ if we want to identify the colluders.

Various groups of researchers [4–6] proposed schemes for embedding finger-prints into databases. However, these schemes are effective only for *numeric attributes*. Since customer information is **string, numeric and text data**, these schemes are not applicable to database fingerprinting.

1.3 Group Testing

During World War II, U.S. authorities drafted millions of citizens into the armed forces. The infectious diseases posing serious problems at that time included gonorrhea and syphilis. The cost of testing each person to determine who was infected in terms of time and money. They want to detect who was infected as fast as possible with the lowest cost. Dorfman [14], a statistician working for U.S. Army, designed such a system. In this system, N blood samples are collected from N inductees, mixed together, and then tested. If a combined sample is free of infection, the all of the contributors to that sample can be considered infection-free. This idea led to the creation of a new research field: Group Testing (GT). There are two kinds of GT: Adaptive Group Testing (AGT) and Non-Adaptive Group Testing (NAGT). Group Testing has been applied to a variety of problems. For example, it can effectively detect *hot items* [16] in a data stream. It can also be applied in Data Forensics [15] and Wireless Sensor Networks [17].

Our Contribution: Our main contributions are proving that NAGT can be used for fingerprinting and for embedding fingerprints into a database on the basis of the database attributes (not its tuples) for both text and numeric data. We propose a technique for fingerprinting that is based on NAGT and that is secure against three types of attacks: attribute, collusion and complimentary. An attribute attack is one in which the attacker tries to change and/or delete one or more attributes of the database, and a complimentary is one in which the attacker tries to combine many copies of a database in order to get the original database. Moreover, if a database is illegally distributed, the distributor can be identified in $O(\texttt{number of attributes})$. In particular, our solution can support up to 262,144 fingerprints for 4,032 attributes, is effective against three types of attacks and can identify an illegal distributor in less than 0.15 seconds.

Outline of the Paper: The rest of this paper is organized as follows: Section 2 presents the preliminaries. Section 3 describes our proposed solution. The next Section describes the security, effectiveness, and testing of our solution. The last Section summarizes the key points and mentions future work.

2 Preliminaries

2.1 Non-Adaptive Group Testing

This section addresses two crucial problems in NAGT: construction and decoding. NAGT can be represented by a $t \times N$ binary matrix M. If M can detect up to d infected samples in N samples, we say that M is d-disjunct with t tests. Formally, a binary matrix is said to be d-disjunct if and only if (iff) the union of any d columns does not contain other columns.

There are two ways to construct d-disjunct matrices. With the deterministic construction, $t = O(d^2 \log N)$ [22]; scheme using this construction does not generate the column we want. Indyk-Ngo-Rudra [10] propose a strongly explicit construction, e.g. any entry in M could be computed in time $poly(t)$, that gets $t = O(d^2 \log N)$. Since schemes using these constructions based on probability, whether or not a d-disjunct matrix is obtained is unknown. With the strongly explicit construction, Kautz and Singleton [13] do not use randomness and get $t = O(d^2 \log^2 N)$. Therefore, there is a tradeoff between random construction and nonrandom construction in terms of the number of tests.

The other problem is decoding time. The N infected/disinfected samples are considered as a vector $X = (x_1 \ x_2 \ ... \ x_N)^T$, where $x_j = 1$ iff the jth sample is infected. An outcome vector, or an outcome of testing, is equal to $C = (c_1 \ c_2 \ ... c_t)^T = MX$. It is easy to map $c_i \geq 1$ to the ith test that is infected. The decoding time C using a naive algorithm [13] is $O(tN)$. In 2010, Indyk-Ngo-Rudra [10] proved that a d-disjunct matrix can be decoded in $poly(d) \cdot t \log^2 t + O(t^2)$ time. Although it is remarkable result, it also takes at least $poly(d) \cdot t \log^2 t + O(t^2)$ time to determine whether a person is infected. Thuc D. Nguyen et. al. [17] did this in $O(t)$ time. Cheraghchi [11] also could decode d-disjunct matrices in time $poly(t)$. Although Group Testing was developed in 1943, the product of matrix-vector M and x has until now been a Boolean operations. In 2013, Thach V. Bui et. al. [12] raised variant of NAGT so that this product is dot product.

2.2   Reed-Solomon Codes and Concatenated Codes

G.D. Forney [18] described the basic idea of *concatenated codes*. Concatenated codes are constructed by using an *outer code* $C_{out} : [q]^{k_1} \to [q]^{n_1}$, where $q = 2^{k_2}$, and a binary *inner code* $C_{in} : \{0,1\}^{k_2} \to \{0,1\}^{n_2}$. Suppose we have two codes: C_{out} of length n_1, dimension k_1 and distance Δ_1 and C_{in} of length n_2, dimension k_2 and distance Δ_2. Suppose further that the alphabet of the second codes is 2 and the alphabet of the first codes is 2^{k_2}. The concatenated codes $C = C_{out} \circ C_{in}$, as defined in the above subsection, has length $n = n_1 n_2$ with message length $k_1 k_2$ of a minimum distance at least $\Delta_1 \Delta_2$. C's size is $(n_1 n_2) \times 2^{k_1 k_2}$.

Reed-Solomon (RS) codes, named after the two inventors, I.S. Reed and G. Solomon [19], are widely used in many fields [21]. They are not only q-nary codes but also *maximum distance separable* codes. A $[n, k]_q$-code C, $1 \leq k \leq n \leq q$, is a subset $C \subseteq [q]^n$ of size q^k. Parameters n, k, and q represent *block length, dimension*, and *alphabet size*. In this model, we choose C_{out} as $[q - 1, k]_q$-RS code and C_{in} as an identity matrix I_q. A d-disjunct matrix ($d = \lfloor \frac{n-1}{k-1} \rfloor$) is achieved from $C = C_{out} \circ C_{in}$ by setting all $N = q^k$ codewords as columns of the matrix. According to Kautz and Singleton [13], given d and N, if we set $q = O(d \log N)$ and $k = O(\log N)$, the resulting matrix is $t \times N$ d-disjunct, where $t = O(d^2 \log^2 N)$.

2.3 Error Correcting Codes (ECCs)

Suppose we have two codes: C_{out} and C_{in} as defined in Subsection 2.2. A code is called e-error detecting if it can detect up to e errors in the outcome vector. In other words, the minimum Hamming distance between any two codewords of it and the outcome vector is at least $e+1$. A code is called e-error correction if it can correct up to e errors in the outcome vector. In other words, the minimum Hamming distance between any two codewords code of it and the outcome vector is at least $2e+1$. Since the minimum Hamming distance of $C = C_{out} \circ C_{in}$ is at least $\Delta_1 \Delta_2$, C is $\frac{\Delta_1 \Delta_2 - 1}{2}$-error correcting. If we set C_{out} as $[n, k, n-k+1]_q$-RS codes and $C_{in} = [q, q, 1]_2$ (I_q), C is $\frac{n-k}{2}$-error correcting. Using the *naive decoding algorithm* for concatenated codes [18] and the Berlekamp - Massey algorithm [20], we can decode any code word x of C in $O(n^2) + O(t) = O(t^2/q^2) + O(t) = O(t)$ time (since $n \leq q$ and $t = nq$) by implementing the following algorithm:

Algorithm 1. The algorithm for decoding a codeword

Step 1. (Initiation) Let $x = 0_{1 \times t}$ and $y = 0_{1 \times n}$.
Step 2. (A naive algorithm for concatenated codes)
for $i = 1 : 1 : n$ do
  if $x(1, i+1 : i*q) = I_q(j, :)$ then
    $y(i) = j$;
  else
    $y(i) = 1$; This is an error of our codeword.
  end if
end for
Step 3. (Berlekamp - Massey algorithm) Using this algorithm [20] to decode y.

2.4 Collusion Attack

Definition 1. *A collusion attack is an attack against digital fingerprinting in which several copies of the same content but with different fingerprints are combined in an effort to remove the original fingerprints or to frame innocent owners.*

The binary codes constructed by Tardos [3] for fingerprinting for N owners are ϵ-secure against d pirates (colluders) and have length $t = O(d^2 \log (N/\epsilon))$. His algorithm can identify some of the colluders in $O(tN)$ time with a probability of at least $1 - \epsilon^{d/4}$. Since a binary matrix is d-disjunct iff the union of any d columns (fingerprints) does not contain other columns, a d-disjunct matrix is secure against an attack by up to d colluders. With the construction in Subsection 2.2, our code has length $t = O(d^2 \log^2 N)$. Moreover, our weakness is to detect up to 1 colluder if this attack occurs. However, a colluder can be identify in $O(t)$ time, which is better than that of Tardos [3].

Furthermore, a code length of $t = O(d^2 \log N)$, less than that of Tardos' construction, can be obtained by using the technique proposed by Indyk-Ngo-Rudra [10], with a time to decode a codeword of $poly(d) \cdot t \log^2 t + O(t^2)$. Once again, only one colluder can be detected. The detection of all colluders using a d-disjunct matrix remains for future work.

3   Proposed Solution

3.1   Embedding Fingerprinting Codes

Assume that our database has t attributes and m tuples. Our fingerprinting code is a d-disjunct $M_{t \times N}$ matrix. The number of columns (N) is the maximum owners supported. The jth user corresponds to M_j, and M_j is embedded into the database using the following rule: if $M_j(i) = 1$, anonymize the ith attribute of the database.

For example, assume we have a matrix $M_{9 \times 12}$ (our fingerprinting codes) and the following database (Table 1)

Table 1. Original database

Birthday	Weight	Height	School	Gender	Country	Blood type	Religion	Condition
23.5.1982	50	1.72	High school	M	Vietnam	A	Buddhism	Headache
11.7.1965	70	1.67	Grad.	M	Japan	B	None	Stomachache

If we choose two columns, $M_9 = (1\,1\,1\,0\,0\,0\,0\,0\,0)^T$ and $M_{10} = (0\,0\,0\,1\,1\,1\,0\,0\,0)^T$, we can generate two corresponding databases (Table 2):

Table 2. First and second databases

Birthday	Weight	Height	School	Gender	Country	Blood type	Religion	Condition
5.1982	100	1	High school	M	Vietnam	A	Buddhism	Headache
7.1965	100	1	Grad.	M	Japan	B	None	Stomachache
Birthday	Weight	Height	School	Gender	Country	Blood type	Religion	Condition
23.5.1982	50	1.72	University	Human	Asia	A	Buddhism	Headache
11.7.1965	70	1.67	University	Human	Asia	B	None	Stomachache

3.2   Decoding Fingerprinting Codes

If we have a database with t attributes, we identify the owner by using the following algorithm:

Algorithm 2. Algorithm for decoding a fingerprint

Step 1. (Initiation) Let $x = 0_{1 \times t}$

Step 2. (Get owner's fingerprint) If jth attribute differs from jth attribute of original database for at least 50% of positions, $x(j) = 1$.

Step 3. (Decoding procedure) Use the algorithm in Subsection 2.3 to decode x.

Note that the number of levels for which an attribute is anonymized is not counted. We will discuss about security and efficiency in Section 4.

4   Security and Efficiency

4.1   Attribute Attack

We ignore tuple deletion attacks since our database has millions of tuples. Each owner is represented by a unique fingerprinting code. Although an attacker may not know the exact values, he can create fake values. For example, the original birthday might be 17.09.1990, and the birthday of owner's database is 9.1990. However, the attacker could distribute his database with a fake value of 20.05.1990. Our proposed solution would count this attribute as 0. Therefore, it gives us an incorrect fingerprinting code. For example, suppose the original code was $x = (1\ 1\ 1\ 0\ 0\ 0)$ and the code we received after attack was $y = (1\ 1\ 1\ 0\ 1\ 0)$. Since our codes are $ECCs$ (Subsection 2.3), if the attacker changes up to $e = \frac{n-k}{2}$ attributes, the original code can be recovered from the incorrect code.

4.2   Collusion Attack

As described above, a collusion attack is an attack against digital fingerprinting which several copies of the same content but with different fingerprints are combined in an effort to remove the original fingerprints or to frame innocent owners. If the intention is the former, the matter is handled as described above. If the intention is the latter, our solution handles it as follows. Each owner is assinged a unique column in d-disjunct matrix M. According to the definition of this matrix, if we combine up to d columns, we can not create another columns. Therefore, an attacker can not frame innocent owners if he has up to d copies. Our code length is $t = O(d^2 \log^2 N)$ while that of Li et. al. [4] uses fingerprinting codes proposed by Boneh-Shaw [2], is approximately the square of ours.

4.3   Complimentary Attack

As described above, a complimentary attack is an attack in which an attacker tries to combine many copies of a database in order to get the original database. Given that fingerprinting codes $M_1, M_2, \ldots, M_j$ are assigned to the $1st, 2nd, jth$ owner, respectively, we define $wt(M_1, M_2) = wt(M_1 \cup M_2) = \sum_{i=1}^{t} 1 - M_1(i) * M_2(i)$. $wt(M_1, M_2, \ldots, M_j) = t$ to mean that if we combine the database versions corresponding to these codes, we can get the original database. Our goal is to determine the probability of $wt(M_1, M_2, \ldots, M_j) = t$. Since $M_i = C_{out}^i \circ I(i)$, $wt(M_{j_1}, M_{j_2}) = t$ iff $wt(C_{out}^{j_1}, C_{out}^{j_2}) = t$. Therefore, the probability of $wt(M_1, M_2, \ldots, M_j) = t$ is:

$$1 - \left(1 - \frac{1}{q^{j-1}}\right)^n = 1 - \left(1 - \frac{1}{q^{j-1}}\right)^{q-1} = 1 - \left(1 - \frac{1}{q^{j-1}}\right)^q \cdot \frac{q^{j-1}}{q^{j-1}-1} \tag{1}$$

$$> 1 - e^{-j+1} \cdot \frac{q^{j-1}}{q^{j-1}-1} > 1 - \frac{e^{-j+1}}{q} \tag{2}$$

4.4 Effectiveness

The time it takes to identify an illegal database distributor is the time it takes to decode a d-disjunct matrix. According to Subsections 2.2 and 2.3, it takes $O(t)$ ms to do this, where t is the number of database attributes. We compare our proposed solution to those of Boneh-Shaw [2] and Tardos [3] in Table 3:

Table 3. Comparison of solutions

	Attribute attack	Collusion attack	Complimentary attack	Efficiency
Boneh-Shaw [2]	√	√	x	x
Tardos [3]	x	√	x	x
Our solution	√	√	√	√

4.5 Experiment

We implemented our solution by using MATLAB on an Acer Aspire 4740-432G32Mn. Parameters n, k, q, d, and N were defined as in Section 2. For simplicity, we set C_{out} to $[n, k]_q$ RS codes and C_{in} to identity matrix I_q. To increase the number of tolerated errors (number of changed attributes), we set $k = 3$. Since the database attributes of Forest Cover Type (available at http://kdd.ics.uci.edu/databases/covertype/covertype.html) are 61, we use this dataset for the first experiment. The other experiments are tested by random data. As shown in Table 4, it took less than 0.15 seconds to identify an illegal distributor.

Table 4. Experimental results for proposed solution

n	k	q	d	No. attributes of database	N Max No. FCs	Max no. tolerant errors	No. changed Attributes	Tracing time (seconds)
7	3	8	3	56	512	2	0	0.0232
							1	0.0241
							2	0.0242
15	3	16	7	240	4096	6	0	0.0297
							1	0.0309
							6	0.0300
31	3	32	15	992	32768	14	0	0.0519
							1	0.0529
							14	0.0520
63	3	64	31	4032	262144	30	0	0.1186
							1	0.1198
							30	0.1213

5 Conclusion

We have showed that Non-Adaptive Group Testing can be used for fingerprinting a database containing numeric and/or text data on the basis of its attributes. This scheme is secure against attribute, collusion, and complimentary attacks. Furthermore, an illegal distributor of the database can be quickly identified. It can thus be used by a database seller ensure the privacy of customers and to prevent illegal distribution. This work did not consider the degree of privacy achieved with the proposed solution. Future work thus includes efforts to guarantee customer privacy when a database is distributed and to identify the best approach to generating fingerprints for protecting databases.

References

1. Willenborg, L., Kardaun, J.: Fingerprints in microdata sets. In: CBS (1999)
2. Boneh, D., Shaw, J.: Collusion-secure fingerprinting for digital data. IEEE Transactions on Information Theory 44(5), 1897–1905 (1998)
3. Tardos, G.: Optimal probabilistic fingerprint codes. J. ACM 55(2), 10 (2008)
4. Li, Y., Swarup, V., Jajodia, S.: Fingerprinting relational databases: Schemes and specialties. IEEE Transactions on Dependable and Secure Computing 2(1), 34–45 (2005)
5. Guo, F., Wang, J., Li, D.: Fingerprinting relational databases. In: Proceedings of the ACM Symposium on Applied Computing, pp. 487–492. ACM (2006)
6. Agrawal, R., Kiernan, J.: Watermarking relational databases. In: Proceedings of the 28th International Conference on VLDB, pp. 155–166 (2002)
7. El Emam, K., et al.: A globally optimal k-anonymity method for the de-identification of health data. Journal of the American Medical Informatics Association 16(5), 670–682 (2009)
8. Samarati, P.: Protecting respondents identities in microdata release. IEEE Transactions on Knowledge and Data Engineering 13(6), 1010–1027 (2001)
9. Sweeney, L.: Achieving k-anonymity privacy protection using generalization and suppression. International Journal of Uncertainty, Fuzziness and Knowledge-Based Systems 10(05), 571–588 (2002)
10. Indyk, P., Ngo, H.Q., Rudra, A.: Efficiently decodable non-adaptive group testing. In: Proceedings of the Twenty-First Annual ACM-SIAM Symposium on Discrete Algorithms, pp. 1126–1142. SIAM (2010)
11. Cheraghchi, M.: Noise-resilient group testing: Limitations and constructions. In: Kutyłowski, M., Charatonik, W., Gębala, M. (eds.) FCT 2009. LNCS, vol. 5699, pp. 62–73. Springer, Heidelberg (2009)
12. Bui, T.V., Nguyen, O.K., Dang, V.H., Nguyen, N.T.H., Nguyen, T.D.: A variant of non-adaptive group testing and its application in pay-television via internet. In: Mustofa, K., Neuhold, E.J., Tjoa, A.M., Weippl, E., You, I. (eds.) ICT-EurAsia 2013. LNCS, vol. 7804, pp. 324–330. Springer, Heidelberg (2013)
13. Kautz, W., Singleton, R.: Nonrandom binary superimposed codes. IEEE Transactions on Information Theory 10(4), 363–377 (1964)
14. Dorfman, R.: The detection of defective members of large populations. The Annals of Mathematical Statistics 14(4), 436–440 (1943)
15. Goodrich, M.T., Atallah, M.J., Tamassia, R.: Indexing information for data forensics. In: Ioannidis, J., Keromytis, A.D., Yung, M. (eds.) ACNS 2005. LNCS, vol. 3531, pp. 206–221. Springer, Heidelberg (2005)
16. Cormode, G., Muthukrishnan, S.: What's hot and what's not: tracking most frequent items dynamically. ACM Transactions on Database Systems (TODS) 30(1), 249–278 (2005)

17. Nguyen, T.D., Bui, T.V., Dang, V.H., Choi, D.: Efficiently Preserving Data Privacy Range Queries in Two-Tiered Wireless Sensor Networks. In: 2012 9th International Conference on Ubiquitous Intelligence & Computing and 9th International Conference on Autonomic & Trusted Computing (UIC/ATC), pp. 973–978. IEEE (2012)
18. Forney Jr., G.D.: Concatenated codes. DTIC Document (1965)
19. Reed, I.S., Solomon, G.: Polynomial codes over certain finite fields. Journal of the Society for Industrial and Applied Mathematics 8(2), 300–304 (1960)
20. Massey, J.: Shift-register synthesis and BCH decoding. IEEE Transactions on Information Theory 15(1), 122–127 (1969)
21. Wicker, S.B., Bhargava, V.K.: Reed-Solomon codes and their applications. Wiley-IEEE Press (1999)
22. Porat, E., Rothschild, A.: Explicit non-adaptive combinatorial group testing schemes. In: Aceto, L., Damgård, I., Goldberg, L.A., Halldórsson, M.M., Ingólfsdóttir, A., Walukiewicz, I. (eds.) ICALP 2008, Part I. LNCS, vol. 5125, pp. 748–759. Springer, Heidelberg (2008)

Heterogeneous Computing vs. Big Data: The Case of Cryptanalytical Applications

Alessandro Cilardo

Department of Electrical Engineering and Information Technologies
University of Naples Federico II
acilardo@unina.it

Abstract. This work discusses the key opportunities introduced by Heterogeneous Computing for large-scale processing in the security and cryptography domain. Addressing the cryptanalysis of SHA-1 as a case-study, the paper analyzes and compares three different approaches based on Heterogeneous Computing, namely a hybrid multi-core platform, a computing facility based on a GPU architecture, and a custom hardware-accelerated platform based on reconfigurable devices. The case-study application provides important insights into the potential of the emerging Heterogeneous Computing trends, enabling unprecedented levels of computing power per used resource.

1 Motivation: The Emerging Heterogeneous Computing Trends

Heterogeneous Computing refers to systems that use a variety of different computational units, such as general-purpose processors, special-purpose units, i.e. digital signal processors or the popular graphics processing units (GPUs), co-processors or custom acceleration logic, i.e. application-specific circuits, often implemented on Field-Programmable Gate Arrays (FPGAs). Heterogeneous Computing is today emerging as a new important direction in computer architecture and high-performance programming. According to the market research firm IDC, 30% of all high-performance computing (HPC) sites use accelerators. In particular, three of the first ten supercomputers are currently heterogeneous computers using accelerators. Traditional high-end supercomputing is however only a part of the emerging scenario, where distributed, loosely-coupled, cloud-based access to high-performance computing as a service is increasingly materializing as a clear trend. In fact, an increasing number of research organizations from disparate fields (e.g. life sciences, engineering, physics, healthcare) are moving to cloud-based platforms [1], providing high-performance Heterogeneous Computing as a service [2]. There are already numerous ongoing projects and initiatives on Heterogeneous Computing, most being focused on GPU-based architectures[3, 4]. However, heterogeneous platforms are increasingly extending their range. For a variety of applications, in fact, the highest performance boost comes from dedicated hardware acceleration, i.e. the design of custom

J. Kołodziej et al. (Eds.): ICA3PP 2013, Part II, LNCS 8286, pp. 177–184, 2013.
© Springer International Publishing Switzerland 2013

circuits and systems embedded in the computing platform executing performance critical kernels. Field-Programmable Gate Arrays (FPGAs) offer a way to achieve such hardware-based, application-specific performance without the time and cost of developing an Application-Specific Integrated Circuit (ASICs) directly on silicon [5–7]. Not surprisingly, during the very recent years several innovative companies have headed to FPGA-based heterogeneous platforms. Some of the prominent examples include Convey, Maxeler, SRC, Nimbix [2].

The availability of massively parallel, hybrid, application-specific computing resources, possibly accessed through a loosely-coupled, distributed, cloud-based infrastructure, poses important challenges and introduces new opportunities for a range of complex applications [8] dealing with large datasets or inherently relying on massive processing. An important example is the security and cryptography domain, as the (un)availability of suitable computing resources is an essential underlying assumption for many cryptographic algorithms. The paper presents the key opportunities for large-scale processing in the security and cryptography domain. In particular, we analyze a case-study application, i.e. the cryptanalysis of the SHA hash function family, which is vital to many security infrastructures. We compare three different approaches based on Heterogeneous Computing, namely a hybrid multi-core platform, a computing facility based on a GPGPU architecture, and a custom hardware-accelerated platform based on reconfigurable devices. The case-study applications provide important insights into the potential of the emerging trends towards Heterogeneous Computing, enabling unprecedented levels of *computing power per used resource* for cryptanalytical applications, as demonstrated in the following sections.

2   A Case-Study Application

Cryptographic processing usually requires massive computation and often relies on special-purpose hardware solutions exhibiting much better performance / cost ratios than off-the-shelf computers [9, 10]. Clearly, the emerging wave of Heterogeneous Computing introduces a whole range of new opportunities for this application domain. This work addresses the cryptanalysis of hash functions, namely the SHA-1 primitive, to demonstrate this potential. We chose the SHA-1 function as it is a popular hash primitive adopted by a number of security protocols. In fact, the robustness of cryptographic hash functions has recently become a hot topic in the field of information security [11–13] since it is critical to all applications which involve hashing as a security-critical step.

2.1   The SHA-1 Cryptographic Hash Function

Standardized by NIST as a Federal Information Processing Standard [14], the function takes a message of length less than 2^{64} bits and produces a 160-bit hash value. The input message is padded and then processed in 512-bit blocks in the Merkle-Damgård iterative structure. Each iteration invokes a so-called *compression function* which takes five 32-bit chaining values along with a 512-bit message block and uses them to compute five new 32-bit values summed word-wise with the input 32-bit numbers to produce the subsequent five chaining values. The compression function is made of 80 consecutive *rounds* where some Boolean and arithmetic operations are applied to the internal variables sequentially to obtain the chaining values. Although we cannot provide here the details of SHA-1 cryptanalysis, we introduce some high-level concepts which are relevant to the computational aspects of the cryptanalysis process. For more details, please refer to [15]. The essential aim of an attack to SHA-1 is to find two colliding messages, i.e. to different messages having the same hash value. The idea behind the attack to SHA-1 is to constrain the values of the messages and the internal variables processed by the compression function in order to reach a collision with a certain probability. Such set of bit-level constraints on the difference of two messages is called *differential characteristic*. In essence, the collision search proceeds by setting the degrees of freedom available in the input messages (which can be controlled by the attacker) and evaluating pairs of messages whose differences comply with a given characteristic. The computation of each of the 80 rounds within the compression function is called an *Elementary Operation* (EO). On a pure hardware platform, the cost in terms of clock cycles of an EO can be as low as one clock cycle, while on a processor the cost will of course be higher as it will involve several instructions. To quantify the overall cost of an attack, we introduce the concept of *Mean number of EOs for a collision* (MEOC). Notice that this parameter only depends on the algorithm used for the collision search process. As mentioned earlier, the execution times in terms of clock counts $C(i)$ for each round i depend on the implementation and, thus, the MEOC is not necessarily proportional to the total clock count for a collision. The *Mean Clock Count to Collision* (MCCC), rather, should be computed as the weighted sum of the EO counts $N(i)$, i.e. $MCCC = \sum N(i) \cdot C(i)$. Since the times $C(i)$ depend on the different architectural optimizations employed for a given computational platform, a good metric for the quality of an implementation is the $MEOC/MCCC$ ratio, called here *EO per clock cycle* (EOC). For a single, basic core performing a sequence of EOs, the ideal bound for EOC is 1.

2.2 Attack to SHA-1 Relying on a Hybrid Multi-core HPC Platform

A software program for fast collision search, first presented in [16], was implemented as a HPC application run on a hybrid supercomputing facility, namely the Maricel multi-core cluster hosted at the Barcelona Supercomputing Center. The cluster is based on 72 QS22 blades, each including 2x Cell/B.E. processors at @3.2Ghz and 8 GBytes of RAM. The total number of cores is 1296 for a peak performance of 10 TFlops. The Cell/B.E. is a heterogeneous processor composed of one main general purpose processor (PPU) and eight specialized cores (SPUs) with software-managed local stores (see Figure 1). The implementation of the collision search application exploited several effective techniques, including pruning and early stop techniques, which shrink the search space by several orders of magnitude, as well as Auxiliary Paths [15]. Furthermore, the HPC application was highly optimized to leverage the SIMD architecture of the SPU cores.

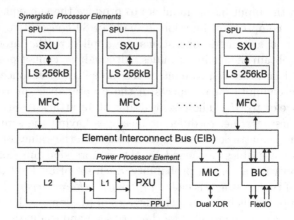

Fig. 1. Architecture of the Cell/B.E. processor

Four characteristics are processed concurrently by the four slots in a lock-step fashion, achieving a reasonably high SIMD speed-up ($3.03X$ for a 4-way SIMD parallelization) in spite of the relatively complex control structure of the search process. Based on the above techniques, we were able to show the feasibility of an attack against a reduced version of SHA-1 as large as 71 rounds [16] (against the standard 80-round SHA-1). We were able to complete the search process with a relatively small computational workload, equal to approximately 2500 Cell/B.E. machine-hours per block.

2.3   Attack to SHA-1 Relying on a GPU-Based Supercomputer

This work also considers for comparisons a solution [17] relying on a super-computer based on Graphics Processing Units (GPUs), currently one of the most popular approaches to data-intensive computing problems. Namely, [17] exploited the GPU facility available in the Lomonosov supercomputer, one of the most powerful HPC center in the world. Each GPU node of Lomonosov has 2 NVidia Fermi X2070 GPUs, each having 6 GB of memory. The architecture of the NVIDIA Fermi GPU is shown in Figure 2. As usual, the collision search process was divided in two blocks, the second one involving most of the computation effort. The whole computation is distributed over the available GPU processors, each relying on 448 internal CUDA cores working in parallel and running at 1.15 GHz. According to the results provided in [17], the highly-optimized GPU application run on the Lomonosov supercomputer achieves an EOC of 0.0126 for the first block and 0.00977 for the second block (which takes most of the overall execution time). The work uses a characteristic targeted at a 75-round collision, for which a taylored version of our prototypical FPGA platform reaches an EOC of 0.84.

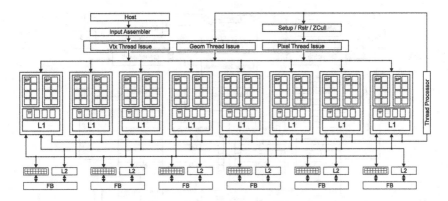

Fig. 2. Architecture of the NVIDIA Fermi GPU

2.4 Attack do SHA-1 Relying on a FPGA-Based Parallel Machine

Finally, the analysis presented in this work addresses the opportunities provided by Field-Programmable Gate Arrays (FPGAs). A key advantage enabled by FP-GAs is that they enable the implementation of hardware-accelerated computing platforms at marginal non-recurring engineering costs. Furthermore, both static and dynamic circuit specialization, enabled by reconfigurable devices, can play a key role, since it is normally possible to identify a large number of optimizations that are specific to the input parameters of a given algorithm, e.g. the differential characteristic for SHA-1 collision search. These optimizations can be taken into account when physically implementing the design on an FPGA device. Figure 3 shows the architecture of the FPGA-based *SHA-1 collision search core* used for supporting the algorithmic exploration [15] as well as accelerating the collision search process. We designed the architecture of a parallel machine made of FPGA nodes, where each FPGA in the platform contains a number of such collision cores. Namely, we targeted the low-end, inexpensive devices of the Xilinx Spartan3A family [18]. Many innovative techniques were used for speeding up the collision search process. For example, we implemented ad-hoc logic circuits depending on the input characteristic controlling the selective bit-flipping related to Auxiliary Path enumeration, we relied on segmented incrementers [19], we decided to only check a digest of the characteristic for compliance, in order to save test cycles, we carefully balanced the use of LUTs and flip-flops for maximizing the efficiency in resource utilization, etc. The EOC measured for the above SHA-1 collision core was very close to the ideal bound, precisely EOC= 0.84.

3 Comparisons and Discussion

We essentially rely on two metrics to assess and compare the profitability of the different approaches: the *computational density*, i.e. amount of delivered computation per hardware unit, and the *absolute collision time* under a given cost

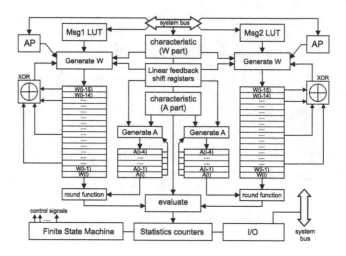

Fig. 3. The architecture of an FPGA core used to speed-up SHA-1 collision search

budget to implement the cryptanalysis computing platform. The computational density can be measured by means of the EOC of the SHA-1 cryptanalytical machine. Looking at the proposal in [16], a highly optimized SIMD application running on the CellBE cores was able to reach an EOC = 0.026, referred to one SPU. Taking into account the difference in the clock frequency, that means that a single SHA-1 collision core in the FPGA-based platform is able to find a collision in a comparable time, precisely only around 1.19 times larger than a single SPU core in the multi-core supercomputer used in [16], However, the extremely low cost per core for the FPGA solution allows much higher levels of parallelism. Looking at the GPU-based solution, based on the results provided in [17], a single FPGA-based SHA-1 collision core is able to find a collision 4.79 times faster than a CUDA core in the Lomonosov supercomputer for the first block, and 6.18 times faster for the second block. To assess the solutions in [16] and [17] taking into account the absolute time-to-collision in addition to the EOC, we estimated the performance of a large-scale parallel FPGA cluster relying on the SHA-1 collision cores, built under a similar cost budget as the facilities used in [16] and [17]. Conservatively this corresponds to a number of collision cores in the order of one hundred thousand (i.e., less than $4,800$ XC3SD3400A low-end devices). The resulting performance data for 71- and 75-round characteristics are displayed in Table 1. For a uniform comparison, the same number of Elementary Operations is assumed to be executed on the compared platforms for each characteristic. The table indicates the actual system frequency, the EOC, and the absolute estimated time-to-collision as determined by the level of parallelsim of each solution. The time achieved by the approach based on FPGAs is one order of magnitude less, at least, compared to the alternatives based on HPC facilities, confirming the potential impact of reconfigurable technologies to enable profitable solutions in the cryptanalysis domain. Interestingly, the reported execution times and the system frequencies also provide an indication of

Table 1. Comparisons of approaches to SHA-1 cryptanalysis

Approach	Collision	EOC	Frequency [GHz]	Estimated Time [hours]
HPC based on CellBE	71 rounds	0.026	3.2	16.7
HPC based on GPU	75 rounds	0.0098	1.15	532
reconfigurable hardware	71 rounds	0.84	0.083	0.026
reconfigurable hardware	75 rounds	0.84	0.083	72.4

the electrical energy consumed by the computation, a crucial constraint for high-performance applications, which is likely to be at least two orders of magnitude less for the FPGA case compared to the conventional HPC facilities.

4 Conclusions

This paper presented a case for the role of Heterogeneous Computing for high-performance cryptanalytic applications. Addressing the cryptanalysis of SHA-1 as a case-study, the paper compared three different approaches based on Heterogeneous Computing. In particular, under the same cost budget, the times for a collision reached by the FPGA platform are at least one order of magnitude lower than other heterogeneous HPC facilities, reaching the highest performance/cost ratio for SHA-1 collision search and providing a striking confirmation of the impact of the new trends in Heterogeneous Computing.

References

1. Paranjape, K., Hebert, S., Masson, B.: Heterogeneous computing in the cloud: Crunching big data and democratizing HPC access for the life sciences. Technical report, Intel White Paper (2012)
2. Nimbix: HPC in the cloud. Technical report (2013), http://www.nimbix.net/cloud-supercomputing/
3. Kessler, C., Dastgeer, U., Thibault, S., Namyst, R., Richards, A., Dolinsky, U., Benkner, S., Larsson Träff, J., Pllana, S.: Programmability and performance portability aspects of heterogeneous multi-/manycore systems. In: Proceedings of Design Automation and Test in Europe, DATE (2012)
4. Alves, A., Rufino, J., Pina, A., Santos, L.P.: clOpenCL - supporting distributed heterogeneous computing in HPC clusters. In: Caragiannis, I., et al. (eds.) Euro-Par Workshops 2012. LNCS, vol. 7640, pp. 112–122. Springer, Heidelberg (2013)
5. Cilardo, A., Gallo, L., Mazzeo, A., Mazzocca, N.: Efficient and scalable OpenMP-based system-level design. In: Design, Automation Test in Europe Conference Exhibition (DATE), pp. 988–991 (2013)
6. Cilardo, A., Gallo, L., Mazzocca, N.: Design space exploration for high-level synthesis of multi-threaded applications. Journal of Systems Architecture (2013)
7. Cilardo, A., Fusella, E., Gallo, L., Mazzeo, A.: Automated synthesis of FPGA-based heterogeneous interconnect topologies. In: 2013 International Conference on Field Programmable Logic and Applications, FPL (2013)

8. Moscato, F., Vittorini, V., Amato, F., Mazzeo, A., Mazzocca, N.: Solution work-flows for model-based analysis of complex systems. IEEE Transactions on Automation Science and Engineering 9, 83–95 (2012)
9. Cilardo, A., Mazzeo, A., Mazzocca, N., Romano, L.: A novel unified architecture for public-key cryptography. In: Proceedings of the Design, Automation and Test in Europe, vol. 3, pp. 52–57 (2005)
10. Cilardo, A., Mazzeo, A., Romano, L., Saggese, G.: Exploring the design-space for FPGA-based implementation of RSA. Microprocessors and Microsystems 28, 183–191 (2004)
11. Wang, X., Yin, Y.L., Yu, H.: Finding collisions in the full SHA-1. In: Shoup, V. (ed.) CRYPTO 2005. LNCS, vol. 3621, pp. 17–36. Springer, Heidelberg (2005)
12. De Cannière, C., Mendel, F., Rechberger, C.: Collisions for 70-step SHA-1: On the full cost of collision search. In: Adams, C., Miri, A., Wiener, M. (eds.) SAC 2007. LNCS, vol. 4876, pp. 56–73. Springer, Heidelberg (2007)
13. Sotirov, A., Stevens, M., Appelbaum, J., Lenstra, A., Molnar, D., Osvik, D., de Weger, B.: MD5 considered harmful today: Creating a rogue CA certificate. In: 25th Chaos Communications Congress (2008)
14. NIST: Federal information processing standard, FIPS-180-2. Secure hash standard (2002)
15. Cilardo, A., Mazzocca, N.: Exploiting vulnerabilities in cryptographic hash functions based on reconfigurable hardware. IEEE Transactions on Information Forensics and Security 8, 810–820 (2013)
16. Cilardo, A., Esposito, L., Veniero, A., Mazzeo, A., Beltran, V., Ayguadé, E.: A CellBE-based HPC application for the analysis of vulnerabilities in cryptographic hash functions. In: Proceedings of the 12th Conference on High Performance Computing and Communications (HPCC 2010), pp. 450–457. IEEE (2010)
17. Adinetz, A.V., Grechnikov, E.A.: Building a collision for 75-round reduced SHA-1 using GPU clusters. In: Kaklamanis, C., Papatheodorou, T., Spirakis, P.G. (eds.) Euro-Par 2012. LNCS, vol. 7484, pp. 933–944. Springer, Heidelberg (2012)
18. Xilinx: Spartan-3A FPGA family data sheet DS529. Technical report, Xilinx (2010), http://www.xilinx.com
19. Cilardo, A.: The potential of reconfigurable hardware for HPC cryptanalysis of SHA-1. In: Proceedings of Design, Automation, and Test in Europe (DATE), pp. 998–1003 (2011)

Trusted Information and Security in Smart Mobility Scenarios: The Case of S²-Move Project*

Pietro Marchetta[1], Eduard Natale[1], Alessandro Salvi[1], Antonio Tirri[1],
Manuela Tufo[2], and Davide De Pasquale[2]

[1] University of Napoli - Federico II, Via Claudio 21, 80125 Napoli, Italy
{pietro.marchetta,alessandro.salvi}@unina.it,
{ed.natale,an.tirri}@studenti.unina.it
[2] University of Sannio, Piazza Guerrazzi 1, 82100 Benevento, Italy
manuela.tufo@unisannio.it, davide.depasquale@studenti.unisannio.it

Abstract. Smart cities and smart mobility represent two of the most significant real use case scenarios in which there is an increasing demand for collecting, elaborating, and storing large amounts of heterogenous data. In urban and mobility scenarios issues like data trustiness and data and network security are of paramount importance when considering smart mobility services like real-time traffic status, events reporting, fleets management, smart parking, etc. In this architectural paper, we present the main issues related to trustiness and security in the S²-Move project in which the contribution is to design and implement a complete architecture for providing soft real-time information exchange among citizens, public administrations and transportation systems. In this work, we first describe the S²-Move architecture, all the actors involved in the urban scenario, the communication among devices and the core platform, and a set of mobility services that will be used as a proof of the potentialities of the proposed approach. Then, considering both architecture and the considered mobility services, we discuss the main issues related to trustiness and security we should taken into account in the design of a secure and trusted S²-Move architecture.

1 Introduction

Today more than 50% of people around the world live in an urban area and by 2050 this percentage will grow up to 70%[1]. While cities are becoming more and more the center of the economic, political and social life, an efficient, effective and secure mobility remains a non-trivial key challenge to face. In this new social scenario, the citizen has the opportunity to share geo-referenced information acting such as human sensors network thanks to a deep interconnected network.

---

* The activities described in this paper are funded by MIUR in the field of Social Innovation of the program with the grant number PON04a3_00058. We would like to thank (i) University of Napoli Federico II for providing SincroLab and ArcLab laboratories for lodging some S²-Move activities; (ii) the industrial partners collaborating in the project; (iii) Dario Di Nocera, Antonio Saverio Valente, and Luca Iandolo for their valuable work and support.

J. Kołodziej et al. (Eds.): ICA3PP 2013, Part II, LNCS 8286, pp. 185–192, 2013.
© Springer International Publishing Switzerland 2013

This innovative citizen-centric vision of the city is behind S^2-Move [2, 3], a 36-months long project funded by MIUR, started in June 2012. The aim of the project is to create a link between the digital and the real world, changing the way in which cities interact with the population. To provide the previous opportunity a number of challenges arose when considering trustworthiness and security of a smart mobility scenario both as a black box and as related to each technological brick [4]. For example, issues related to users privacy [12], secure communications among all the entities involved in the S^2-Move scenario (users, cars, devices, etc) [9, 10], vehicular and ad hoc networks security [25–32], cyber attack events involving malware/worms [5, 6] and botnets [7, 8], cloud infrastructures [11]. In this architectural paper, we first briefly describe the S^2-Move architecture, then considering both architecture and mobility services, we discuss the main issues related to trustiness and security we have taken into account in the design of the S^2-Move architecture.

2 S^2-Move

The main idea of S^2-Move is to supply soft real-time information exchange among citizens, public administrations and transportation systems. S^2-Move uses customized maps as the most user-friendly and intuitive approach to supply urban mobility services based on urban probes real-time information.

Urban probes represent a heterogeneous set of devices/sensors deployed in the urban environment to detect different real-time information. They range from simple sensors to sophisticated devices, such as smartphones or tablets. S^2-Move exploits urban probes as well as a new prototype of On Board Unit (OBU). This is a smart electronic device, connected with the vehicle CAN bus, able to collect in-vehicle information (e.g. speed, pedals pressure, fuel consumption, etc.) as well as to process data and to communicate with a Central Processing System (CPS)[1]. The OBU is also responsible for both vehicle-to-vehicle (V2V) and vehicle-to-infrastructure (V2I) communications. Crossing the data provided by multiple sources of information the S^2-Move system can both monitor the urban environment and provide services to the citizens and the social community. CPS is the S^2-Move architecture core and it is composed by three main layers: *data layer* (responsible for data storage and low-level computation); *core layer* (to manage user authentication, customized maps, data exchange with the urban probes and raw data preservation); *presentation layer* (for the interaction among final users and administrator).

While the platform can be easily used to provide a widespread of urban information-based services, the project currently focus on two exemplar case of study: traffic monitoring and fleet management. Traffic monitoring aims at determining real-time knowledge of traffic jam exploiting the information collected from the urban environment. Note that, traditional traffic monitoring systems are based on data collected through heterogeneous sensors [13] (inductive loops,

---

[1] While the CPS represents a single logic unit, it is distributely implemented for coping with scalability and robustness issues.

magnetic sensors, video cameras, infrared sensors, etc.). The usage of those sensors is very expensive, hence new monitoring technologies, based on GPS have been recently proposed [13, 14]. The S^2-Move aims to implement traffic monitoring services by using GPS and information provided by the OBU devices to infer the traffic condition by observing the speed of the monitored vehicles along the urban routers. To this end, a data collection module hosted on the OBU device samples and filters kinematics information coming from the CAN bus. Once collected and filtered, data is sent to the CPS where they are processed to infer the traffic information [14]. Fleet management has two main aims: Fleet Monitoring and Fleet Control. Fleet monitoring can be meant as the tracking of a group of vehicles moving in the urban environment. Fleet Control allows the coordinate motion of a group of vehicles traveling with a common velocity and a predefined intra-vehicular distance (platooning [15]). Platooning is based on the design of decentralized control algorithm that funds on reliable V2V and V2I communication. To this aim heterogeneous wireless communication technologies and their performance must be carefully taken into account [16–19]. A first attempt to platooning design within the S^2-Move context is described [2, 3], while the design of more sophisticated control approaches embedding adaptive mechanisms [20–23] is currently under development.

3   Trusted Information and Security in S^2-Move: An Architectural View

In this section we first review both (a) secure and trusted fleet and traffic management and (b) users and vehicles communications privacy, then we describe an architectural solution we should follow in the S^2-Move project.

Secure and Trusted Fleet and Traffic Management. There are different kinds of attacks, performed against the exchanged messages. In [25], authors analyzed different types of attacks, including *Fabrication Attack*, *Replay Attack* and *Sybil Attack*. During a *Fabrication Attack*, false information is transmitted. In this case, for example, a vehicle belonging to the fleet can change the speed of the fleet itself or other parameters of cruise. In addition, a malicious agent can create problems in traffic management reporting vehicle collisions that are not true, or signaling a free road, in presence of an incident, to aggravate the situation. In [24], authors described the IEEE 1609.2 protocol for message authentication and security at the data link layer. This protocol uses IEEE 802.11p protocol for data transmission, which does not provide any kind of security, since it is based on a communication outside the BSS (Basic Service Set) context. The IEEE 1609.2 protocol uses a Public Key Infrastructure (PKI). To allow the physical implementation of this type of infrastructure, each vehicle will come with a Trusted Platform Module (TPM) that works with the OBU. In the PKI paradigm, each vehicle is equipped with two keys, one public and one private, and a certificate that proves its identity, validating the public key held. Since TPMs are resistant to software attacks (but not to physical tampering), they are used to ensure the storage of cryptographic keys and certificates, and to implement the required cryptographic mechanisms. In addition to this new hardware device, the implementation of the PKI requires the presence of a Certification Authority (CA) that deals with the release and management of certificates to the members of the network, vehicles in the case of S^2-Move. This type of infrastructure is able to ensure *Authenticity*, *Integrity* and optionally *Confidentiality* to the messages that are in transit in the network. Moreover, it is possible to prevent different kinds of attacks (like the *Sybil* attack) that may make unusable the traffic management system presented in this work. In fact, in order to perform a *Sybil* attack, a malicious vehicle pretends the presence of a traffic jam, sending out at the same time several messages and using for each of them a different identity. But for each of these identities there is the need to use a valid certificate, making very complex and virtually impossible this type of attacks. The authentication procedure provided by the IEEE 1609.2 protocol operates as follows. If a vehicle wants to send a message in the network, it has to sign it with its private key and then it attaches its certificate provided by the CA. This certificate contains the public key associated with the private key used. In order to sign the message is used the *Elliptic Curve Digital Signature Algorithm (ECDSA)*, an encryption algorithm with 224 or 256 bits asymmetric keys. This algorithm requires a heavy use of computational resources, guaranteed on the vehicle by the TPM mentioned before. The recipient of the message will reach the sender's public key using the certificate attached to the message. To verify the authenticity of the certificate, the recipient will see, using the public key of the CA, the signature contained in the authentication of the certificate, signed by the CA with its private key. In the case of information needed for the traffic management, there is no need to make the transmissions confidential, as it would introduce only overhead. The confidentiality of information can become crucial in the implementation of additional features such as vehicle platooning or an online payment system for parking. In this regard, the IEEE 1609.2 protocol also provides an encryption algorithm, given by a combination of symmetric and asymmetric encryption. The symmetric encryption algorithm used is the AES-CCM, while the asymmetric one is the *Elliptic Curve Integrated Encryption Scheme (ECIES)*. [24] However, the use of the IEEE 1609.2 protocol does not guarantee the solution to all the security problems listed above and that arise from the implementation of our project. In fact, the possession of a certificate by a vehicle does not necessarily imply its correct behavior. Moreover, there are also privacy issues. In fact, the use of certificates, even if multiples, makes the vehicle recognition and tracking even easier. As widely reported in [25] it is necessary to combine the IEEE 1609.2 protocol with other mechanisms that can adequately identify suspicious vehicles in order to protect the privacy of the users. In cases in which a vehicle performs suspicious actions, the CA has the power to revoke its certificate. To do this, it can submit a *Revocation of the Trusted Component (RTC)* to a vehicle requiring the deletion of all the cryptographic material that it keeps in its TPM. In cases where this message does not reach the TPM because the attacker is able to block it, the CA recurs the use of *Certificate Revocation List (CRL)*, a list of all revoked certificates.

The CPS will also preserve the CRL and will send it periodically to the *Road Side Unit (RSU)*. Then the RSU will forward it to the vehicles. A vehicle will discard a received message if signed with a revoked certificate.

Users and Vehicles Communications Privacy. Another key issue is to protect the privacy of users that moves in the city and that use S^2-Move vehicles equipped with OBUs. In this case it is possible to follow two different paths: use of aliases or adopting the group keys (signatures) that may be especially effective in the fleet management [26]. The first solution is to associate the certificates to aliases associated with vehicles. Each alias must still be due to the vehicle to enable the authorities to any checks. To ensure this form of anonymity, vehicles must be equipped with the *Electronic License Plate (ELP)* and the CA will associate aliases to the ELP. Therefore, the authorities will be able to trace the identity of the owner of the vehicle through the ELP. The creation of aliases with the associated keys can occur both by the CA and by the vehicle itself. In the first case, the CA will create offline all the necessary information that will be transferred to the vehicle during annual revisions, while in the second case the vehicle will create all the necessary information thanks to the TPM. In fact, the TPM will send the alias and the public key of the CA, which will reply by sending the certificate to the vehicle. The second approach is preferable because the aliases can be changed more frequently and, in addition, the security offered will be greater, as the private key related to the alias will never be disclosed by the TPM. Each vehicle will not be equipped with an individual certificate, but with a large number of certificates, each valid only for a short period. Changing certificate frequently (every 5-10 minutes) ensure greater privacy to the user because the messages appear to come from different sources. Moreover, if an attacker could take the cryptographic information in the TPM of a vehicle, he would have access to a large number of certificates (in the order of 10^5) and could easily lead to a *Sybil* attack without this kind of trick. The second solution is, as previously mentioned, the use of signatures group [27]: the vehicles of the network are divided into groups and each group member has its own secret key together with the public key of the group. A vehicle of the group, instead of authenticate their messages using their private key associated with the certificate, will use its secret key group member. This will protect the anonymity to the members of the group, anonymity that must still be resolved by the competent authorities. To make the anonymity resolvable, there are entities called Group Manager. The Group managers have a group manager secret key, which allows the identification of the message sender. As proposed by [31], a solution can be the use a symmetric structure key to reduce the overhead due to the asymmetric encryption algorithms and eliminate the need to contact the CA for the establishment of asymmetrical group keys. In this approach the group leader (that is the leader of the fleet in our case) is responsible for generating a symmetric key and distribute it to each of the members of the group by encrypting it with their corresponding public keys (previously sent in broadcast with the relevant certificate). At this point, all the members can sign messages with the public key of the group, so that they can make confidential communications. To allow the propagation of the messages between the S^2-Move fleets and provide a mechanism for checking the validity of the information contained in the message, it is necessary that the geographic areas of the groups overlap. In that way, a vehicle placed in the shared area (the first and the last of the fleet) has the keys of both groups and will send the message to the next group using its key. This is a solution based on symmetric keys and does not provide the message non-repudiation and it is not designed to protect the privacy of users as it allows communication only within the group or with adjacent groups. On the other hand, it allows the management and the creation of groups without the need to contact the CA. To ensure a wide non-repudiation policy for the message, it is necessary to create a unique group key pair (public and private keys) for the whole group by contacting the CA. In that way, the CA will assign each vehicle of the fleet with a recognition ID, which will be included in the message signature. Since the ID is sent in the signature of a message, this kind of implementation does not guarantee the privacy of users, that can only be ensured by the approach previously presented and proposed in [27]. The CA can revoke the certificate to a vehicle in the event of its suspicious behavior. It is necessary, however, an additional security mechanism that allows all vehicles to decide autonomously whether the information received from a vehicle are correct, or if they should be discarded even if it has a valid certificate. They are used trust models that, in vehicular environments, such as the present, which must take into account some factors due to the particular structure of vehicular networks. In [32], authors proposed the assignment of this trustiness value directly to the groups rather than to the individual entities. However, this is not possible as the groups (fleets) in the case of S^2-Move can be short-lived. In practice, data-oriented trust models are used to assign the value of trust directly to the received message and to the information contained therein. In assigning this trust value, it will consider two kinds of factors: a type of factors of the static type, such as a trust value that can be assigned a priori to the sender entity based on the type of vehicle (police car, bus, etc.) and a type of factors of the dynamic type, such as the spatial or temporal proximity to the logged event. By grouping different reports about the same event, and applying the theory of *Dempster-Shafer* taking into account the factors listed above, it will be possible to assess the level of trust of the event in question. Considering separately each event shows off the downside of this approach: as the trust relationships must be evaluated from the scratch for each event, if the network is sparsely populated this model will be inapplicable, having an insufficient number of alerts [28, 29], c. However, it is possible to use hybrid trust models, which mostly provide a mechanism of opinion piggybacking [28, 30].

The Case of S^2-Move. The solutions previously described could be profitably applied in S^2-Move. Since the CPS is always available, it can be used as a certification server, in addition to the functionalities of data collection and processing. It would be possible to assign a group key to the fleets that are formed over time. At the same time, the Group Manager (which does not correspond to the leader of the fleet, but acts only as a secure entity) could handle multiple group keys and different fleets in the reference area (via the RSU), allowing the establishment of group member secret keys for each member of the fleet. S^2-Move has been designed in such a way to make the architecture independent from the possible presence of the RSU. While this design choice has brought significant advantages in terms of extensibility of services offered by the platform freeing the interaction between the actors of the urban landscape by the presence of RSU, the solution proposed in literature based on the RSU, regarding the conservation of CRL lists but also for the groups management, is not currently applicable. An alternative approach would be the preparation of the CRL lists by the CPS (that will be sent to all the vehicles) and the embedding of the Group Management logic within the CPS itself. Moreover, the benefits of an approach based on symmetric-key communications are significant when compared to other implementations presented. In S^2-Move the RSU are not necessarily present, and then the connection to the CPS may not be constant due to the availability of a cellular network. Therefore, in this case, an implementation based on asymmetric keys may create problems in the management of the security of the fleet, which may not be able to get a pair of valid key (being not able to contact the group manager). For this purpose, the following resolving hypothesis is considered: when the network is not available, it is possible to use symmetric keys to ensure the authenticity and integrity of messages transmitted within the fleet. In this way, vehicles not belonging to the fleet cannot send invalid information to the fleet vehicles. At the time when the network becomes available again, matching the Group Manager with the CPS (and consequently with the systems CA), it is possible to ask for the establishment of a group key and private keys for the members of the group, ensuring the anonymity and security in the transmissions.

4 Discussion and Conclusion

Trusted information and security (at different layers) represent really important aspects to carefully consider when designing and planning smart mobility platforms. In this architectural paper we have discussed the S^2-Move architecture, its main components and applications, and we have provided a review of the main challenges related to trusted information and security of the entire architecture. Finally, we have reported some potential solutions to trusted communications and privacy in the S^2-Move architecture and services. Experimental evaluation is left for future work.

References

1. United Nations Department of Economic and Social Affairs Population Division, World Urbanization Prospects: The 2011 Revision (2012)
2. Marchetta, P., et al.: S^2-MOVE: Smart and Social Move. In: IEEE GIIS (2012)
3. Marchetta, P., et al.: Social and Smart Mobility for Future Cities: the S2-Move project. In: AICA 2013 (2013)
4. Abdullahi, A., Brown, I., El-Moussa, F.: Privacy in the age of Mobility and Smart Devices in Smart Homes. In: PASSAT, SocialCom 2012 (2012)
5. Dainotti, A., Pescapé, A., Ventre, G.: Worm traffic analysis and characterization. In: IEEE Inter. Conference on Communications, ICC (2007)
6. Colleen, S., Moore, D.: The spread of the witty worm. IEEE Security & Privacy 2(4) (2004)

7. Dainotti, A., King, A., Claffy, K., Papale, F., Pescapé, A.: Analysis of a /0 stealth scan from a Botnet. In: ACM IMC (2012)
8. Barford, P., Vinod, Y.: An inside look at botnets. In: Malware Detection, vol. 27, pp. 171–191. Springer, US (2007)
9. Landman, M.: Managing smart phone security risks. In: Information Security Curriculum Development Conference. ACM (2010)
10. Chourabi, H., et al.: Understanding smart cities: An integrative framework. In: HICSS (2012)
11. Wayne, J., Grance, T.: Guidelines on security and privacy in public cloud computing. NIST special publication (2011)
12. Armac, I., et al.: Privacy-friendly smart environments. In: NGMAST (2009)
13. Barbagli, B., et al.: A real-time traffic monitoring based on wireless sensor network technologies. In: IWCMC (2011)
14. Hadachi, A.: Travel time estimation using sparsely sampled probe GPS data in urban road network, Ph.D. Thesis, Normandie University (2013)
15. Hedrick, J.K., Tomizuka, M., Varaiya, P.: Control issues in automated highway systems. IEEE Control Systems 14(6) (1994)
16. Bernaschi, M., Cacace, F., Pescapé, A., Za, S.: Analysis and Experimentation over Heterogeneous Wireless Networks. In: TRIDENTCOM 2005, Trento, Italy (2005)
17. Iannello, G., Pescapè, A., Ventre, G., Vollero, L.: Experimental Analysis of Heterogeneous Wireless Networks. In: Langendoerfer, P., Liu, M., Matta, I., Tsaoussidis, V. (eds.) WWIC 2004. LNCS, vol. 2957, pp. 153–164. Springer, Heidelberg (2004)
18. Karrer, R., Matyasovszki, I., Botta, A., Pescapé, A.: Experimental evaluation and characterization of the magnets wireless backbone. In: WINTECH, pp. 26–33 (2006)
19. Botta, A., Pescapé, A., Ventre, G.: Quality of Service Statistics over Heterogeneous Networks: Analysis and Applications. EJOR 191(3) (2008)
20. di Bernardo, M., et al.: Model reference adaptive control of discrete-time piecewise linear systems. International Journal of Robust and Nonlinear Control 23(7) (2013)
21. di Bernardo, M., Montanaro, U., Santini, S.: Canonical forms of generic piecewise linear continuous systems. IEEE TAC 56(8) (2011)
22. di Bernardo, M., et al.: Experimental implementation and validation of a novel minimal control synthesis adaptive controller for continuous bimodal piecewise affine systems. Control Engineering Practice 20(3) (2012)
23. Di Bernardo, M., Montanaro, U., Santini, S.: Novel switched model reference adaptive control for continuous piecewise affine systems. In: CDC 2013 (2008)
24. Kenney, J.B.: Dedicated Short-Range Communications (DSRC) Standards in the United States (2011)
25. Raya, M., Papadimitratos, P., Aad, I., Jungels, D., Hubaux, J.-P.: Eviction of Misbehaving and Faulty Nodes in Vehicular Networks (2007)
26. de Fuentes, J.M., Gonzalez-Tablas, A.I., Ribagorda, A.: Overview of Security issues in Vehicular Ad-hoc Networks (2010)
27. Malina, L., Hajny, J.: Group Signatures for Secure and Privacy Preserving Vehicular Ad Hoc Networks
28. Raya, M., Papadimitratos, P., Gligor, V.D., Hubaux, J.: On Data-Centric Trust Establishment in Ephemeral Ad Hoc Networks (2007)
29. Zhang, J.: A Survey on Trust Management for VANETs (2011)
30. Dotzer, F., et al.: VARS: A Vehicle Ad-Hoc Network Reputation System (2005)
31. Raya, M., Aziz, A., Hubaux, J.: Efficient Secure Aggregation in VANETs (2006)
32. Tajeddine, A., Kayssi, A., Chehab, A.: A Privacy-Preserving Trust Model for VANETs (2010)

A Linguistic-Based Method
for Automatically Extracting Spatial Relations
from Large Non-Structured Data

Annibale Elia[1], Daniela Guglielmo[1], Alessandro Maisto[2], and Serena Pelosi[2]

[1] Department of Political, Social and Communication Science - SemanticItaLab,
University of Salerno
via Giovanni Paolo II 132, 84084, Fisciano, Italy
{elia,dguglielmo}@unisa.it
[2] Department of Electric Engineering and Information Technologies,
University of Naples "Federico II"
via Claudio 21, 80125 Napoli, Italy
{maisto.ale,serenapelosi}@gmail.it

Abstract. This paper presents a Lexicon-Grammar based method for automatic extraction of spatial relations from Italian non-structured data. We used the software *Nooj* to build sophisticated local grammars and electronic dictionaries associated with the lexicon-grammar classes of the Italian intransitive spatial verbs (i.e. 234 verbal entries) and we applied them to the Italian text Il Codice da Vinci ('The Da Vinci Code', by Dan Brown) in order to parse the spatial predicate-arguments structures. In addition, Nooj allowed us to automatically annotate (in XML format) the words (or the sequence of words) that in each sentence (S) of the text play the 'spatial roles' of Figure (F), Motion (M) and Ground (G). Finally the results of the experiment and the evaluation of this method will be discussed.

1 Introduction

Nowadays, every electronic device we use generates a large amount of data. That enormous volume represents just a part of the problem: the age of Big Data, in fact, makes it necessary to explore an immense and various quantity of large-sized non-structured data and to transform them in structured information as soon as possible. That leads us to another problem, the velocity: the data high speed of obsolescence forces us to compress the data management time [1], [2], [3]. In that context, the most suitable software are perhaps those able to quickly analyse the data, extracting value from chaos [4]. However, data must not only be processed in real time but also accurately analysed from the point of view of their semantic content. The semantic information hidden in the data poses, in fact, several challenges to Natural Language Processing [5], [6].

One of the harder task is how to automatically capture *semantic roles* from texts. Semantic roles express the relation between the predicate (i.e. the verb) and its

J. Kołodziej et al. (Eds.): ICA3PP 2013, Part II, LNCS 8286, pp. 193–200, 2013.
© Springer International Publishing Switzerland 2013

arguments in a sentence, and can be of different types depending on the nature of the semantic predicate (dative, spatial, communication, etc.). With respect to **spatial relations**, many studies have dealt with the question of the expression of motion in language [7]. However, the way motion event, spatial relations and spatial roles should be handled by parsers and automatically detected is still controversial [8], [9], [10].

NLP systems for acquiring spatial semantics use, in fact, either statistical methods or hybrid ones whereas linguistic-based methods are noticeably lacking.

This paper explores a linguistic-based method for automatically extracting spatial relations from Italian text corpora. In particular, we present a Semantic Predicates System for accurately assigning "spatial roles" to the syntactic arguments involved into a spatial relation, i.e. to perform a *spatial role labeling* task. The NLP software used for this purpose is **Nooj** (www.nooj4nlp.net), a linguistic development environment that includes large-coverage electronic dictionaries and local grammars (i..e automata and transducers), to parse corpora in real time and transform non-structured data (texts in natural language) in semi-structured data (texts in XML format). Given the text *Il Codice da Vinci* (the "The da Vinci Code", 140.000 word forms) electronic dictionaries and local grammars, built within Nooj, allow us to automatically detect and annotate the "location" (i.e. GROUND entity) and the "subjects" or the "objects" of the story that move, are moved or remain stationary with respect to that location (i.e. FIGURE entity). The text tagged in XML will be suitable to be queried on its contents in natural language (i.e. *Where is the Figure*?) We obtained this result on the basis of the syntactic information and argument requirement(s) attached to the motion verbs and encoded into a lexicon-grammar matrix of 234 intransitive spatial verbs [11].

Section 2 gives a preliminary remark on the Semantic Role Labeling; Section 3 describes the semantic predicates system developed by the Lexicon-Grammar and the syntactic sentences under study; Section 4 presents the semantic model chosen for the task and the syntactic-semantic mapping built; Section 5 describes the experiment carried out within the software Nooj. Finally, Section 6 outlines our manual evaluation of the method and discusses the results (i.e. precision and recall).

2   Semantic Role Labeling

Semantic Roles (SR) (or theta or thematic roles) correspond to the well-known notion of lead: "Who did What to Whom, How, When and Where" [12], [13]. Automatic Semantic Role Labeling is defined as a shallow semantic parsing which consists of recognition of the semantic arguments associated with the predicate of a sentence [14]. The main task of an SRL system is to map free text sentences to the semantic representation, by identifying all the syntactic functions of clause-complements and labeling them with their semantic roles [15], [16]. To work, an SRL system needs a computational lexicon in which all the predicates and their relative semantic arguments are specified: the most important computational lexicon was created by Frame Net project and Prop Bank [17], [18], [19].

3 Lexicon-Grammar of Spatial Verbs

Within the framework of Lexicon-Grammar (LG) we argue that the semantic predicates can be completely inferred and derived from the lexicon-syntactic behaviour of the operator verbs [20], [21]. Up to now, the semantic predicates identified in Italian are those involving the intuitive notion of 'exchange' or 'transfer' and are for this reason called **Transfer Semantic Predicates** [22], [23].

The NLP experiment carried out here is based only on spatial verbs collected in the classes 7D, 7P, 7DP, 7S, 8 [11], equal to a total of some 234 intransitive constructions sharing the N_0 V Loc (E + Loc N_2) base sentence structure.[1] In particular, the constructions that we aim at locating here are of the following types: i) **class 7DP**: *Il treno va da Napoli a Milano* "The train goes from Napoli to Milan"; ii) **class 7P**: *L'acqua esce dalla stanza* "The water comes out from the room", iii). **class 7D**: *L'aereo atterrò in città* "The plane landed in the city"; iv). **class 8**: *La barca naufraga in mare* "The boat shipwrecks at sea"; v) **class 8**: *Elia abita a Parigi* "Elia lives in Paris"

4 Syntactic-Semantic Mapping: Figure, Motion, Ground

The next stage was the mapping of the spatial lexicon-grammar built so far (i.e. the lexicon-grammar of spatial verbs) onto a spatial semantic model. The semantic model chosen for our task is the **Motion Event Semantics** as theorized by Talmy [24].[2] In other words we gave a semantic interpretation to the verb and the arguments occurring in the intransitive spatial constructions by assigning different spatial semantic category or 'spatial roles' to them. According to [24] the two main entities related to each other in a motion event are: the **Figure** (F) that is the entity that move or is moved, remain stationary or is located with respect to larger entity called **Ground** (G), i.e. the localization space. The following sentences exemplify these categories:

(1) *La penna* (F) *giaceva sul tavolo* (G)   "The pen lay on the table"
(2) *La penna* (F) *cadeva sul tavolo* (G)   "The pen fell on the table"

In both of them *la penna* (the pen) specifies the "object" that functions as Figure and *il tavolo* (the table) the "object" that functions as Ground. The following formula represents Talmy's motion event:

[**Figure Motion** (MOVE/BELOC) [Path (PATH/SITE) **Ground**]PLACE] MOTION EVENT.

---

[1] The class 57 is not accounted here and will be addressed in a future work. The spatial semantic class encodes, in total, 711 verbal entries.

[2] Any other theoretical framework and notational system concerning the semantic interpretation of the relational entities involved in the motion event would be also suitable for the purpose of our experiment.

Thus, following this motion event schema, we diagrammed the sentences (1) and (2) as follow:

[[*La penna*]FIGURE [*giaceva*]MOTION [[*sul*]SITE [*tavolo*]GROUND]PLACE]MOTION EVENT
[[*La penna*]FIGURE [*cadeva*]MOTION [[*sul*]PATH [*tavolo*]GROUND]PLACE]MOTION EVENT

Here the whole syntactic sequence, i.e. elementary sentence (S), corresponds semantically, to a single motion event (ME)[3] and the syntactic components N0 V N1 received respectively the "semantic roles" of Figure, Motion and Ground. This can be represented by a predicative relation between Figure (F) and a Ground (G), with the Motion (M) as a pivot element playing the role of **semantic predicate** (PRED), i.e. M $_{PRED}$ (F, G). All the sentences collected in the LG tables of intransitive spatial verbs received in other word the same semantic representation M $_{PRED}$ (F, G) independently from the syntactic position that their arguments fill in the sentence.[4] At this preliminary stage the identification task was limited only to capturing automatically the Ground from texts and not to distinguishing the exact nature of it (Source, Goal, Scenery).[5] The main aim of our experiment, in fact, was answer to the following generic question: *where is the Figure?*

5   Nooj Grammars and Corpus Analysis

Nooj is a rule-based linguistic engine used to formalize linguistic phenomena and to parse texts. It allows for automatically annotating large text corpora by applying in tandem electronic dictionaries and local grammars [25]. We can use them to formalize languages or, in the NLP context, to locate patterns and to retrieve information from texts. Electronic dictionaries are lists of lemmas associated with morpho-syntactical, syntactical and semantic codes and with inflectional and derivational paradigms. For the purpose of our task we built sophisticated locals grammars and electronic dictionaries associated with the intransitive spatial verbs of the intransitive classes 7D, 7P, 7DP, 7S, 8 in order to recognize them and assign predicate/argument structures to the natural language sentences in which they occur. By making use of variables and metanodes, a grammars net has been built to automatically annotate the words (or the sequence of words) that in each sentence of the text (ME)[6] play the 'spatial roles' of Figure (F), Motion (M) and Ground (G).

---

[3] Talmy's motion event covers dynamic configurations as well as static ones.

[4] We have simplified the representation for illustrative purposes. Verbs of the class 7DP such as *cadere* selects for both a provenance and a destination complement, so that their semantic representation includes two Grounds. It is of the following type: M (F, G1, G2).

[5] In a future work we will work on that.

[6] On the basis of the syntactic-semantic mapping pointed out in the Section 2 we assumed that an elementary spatial sentence (S), i.e. the sequence of spatial verb (V) plus its selected arguments (N0, Loc N1) corresponds semantically to a single motion event (ME).

The Fig. 1 is a simplified version of a more complex net of grammars (correlated to the classes 7D, 7P, 7DP, 7S, 8) used to identify and annotate Figure, Motion and Ground from corpora.

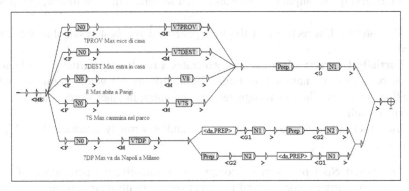

Fig. 1. Nooj Grammar to recognize and annotate spatial relations

The Da Vinci Code Corpus (i.e. 140.000 word forms) has been automatically annotated by applying the dictionaries of the spatial verbs and the Nooj grammar discussed above (see Figure 1). We obtained as a result more than 1400 concordances, converted into XML format. Below we present an example of XML annotated sentence:

(1)   <ME> <F>*Gli uomini*</F> <M>*entrarono*</M> *nell'* <G>*ingresso principale*</G> </ME>
       <ME> <F>The men</F> <M>came</M> in <G>the main entrance</G> </ME>

In addition to concordances and texts in XML format, Nooj also offers the opportunity to visualize the output (i.e. annotations produced by the grammar) within **Structural Trees**. Given the annotated sentence in (1), we obtain for it the following semantic representation (Fig. 2):

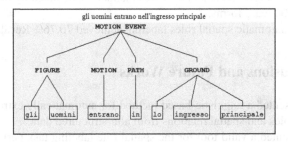

Fig. 2. Structural Tree

6   Results and Evaluation of the Tool

This section presents the evaluation of the parsing and annotation tasks carried out with Nooj. More than 1400 annotated concordances (then converted into XML format) were found.[7] Then a random sample of some 1000 concordances (72, 4%) was manually checked by three persons. In order to evaluate the performance of the tool we calculated the percentage of Precision (P) generated by the automatic annotation by classifying the output (i.e. each annotated sentence) into the following types:

1. **Completely Correct:** when the tool generated the best result that we could achieve.

2. **Partially Correct:** when our tool generates a result only partially satisfactory, that can be smoothly improved, in future, by modifying the whole grammar and/or expanding the nodes. The tool recognizes and annotates, in other words, only a part of the correct result.

3. **Incorrect:** when our tool misrecognizes and/or wrongly annotates both Figure and Ground.

We evaluated Nooj precision by computing, separately, the percentage of completely correct, partially correct, and incorrect output (with their sub-cases) with respect to the 1000 automatically annotated concordances of the sample. Table 1 presents the quantitative results of our evaluation:

Table 1. Evaluation of results

False Negative	False Positive	Recall	Precision
29,2%	**27,2%**	**70,8%**	72,2%

Out of 1000 concordances, automatically annotated with the spatial categories or tags <F>, <M>, and <G>, 36, 8% were completely correct; 35,8% were only partially correct and, finally, 27,2% were completely incorrect or **false positive** (**FP**). Since the partially correct outputs are easily improvable, we are very satisfied with the results obtained by Nooj. As a matter of fact, '**completely correct**' and '**partially correct**' amount to 72,8% Precision (P). Recall was manually calculated by three persons on a sample of 38.000 word forms.

Overall our automatic spatial roles labeling achieved 70,76% Recall (R).

7   Conclusions and Future Works

This study presented a linguistic-based method for automatically extracting and annotating spatial roles and spatial relations from non-structured data.

Nooj represented a valid tool for the spatial role labeling task performed here. The precision of about 73% and the recall of about 71% were very satisfactory results for us. However, more work has to be done. In future, we aim at reducing the percentage of false positives (27,2 %) and false negatives (29,2%) by adding a more careful transformational analysis of the Italian spatial verbs, on the basis of an in-deep error

---

[7] Each concordance corresponds to a sentence (S) containing spatial relations (i.e. a motion event), S=ME.

and silence analysis. In particular, our team at SemanticItaLab is equipped with the lexical and syntactic resources useful to handle with the main sources of error. We are able, on other words, to filter out from the total output all the semi-fixed and fixed expressions (e.g. *tornare in mente*), all the temporal expressions (e.g. *in quel momento*) and many lexical and syntactic ambiguities (e.g. *ricorrere a casa vs. ricorrere a testimoni*) which caused noise during the experiment described here. We are also able to correctly detect verb-particle constructions such as *andare via di casa* and all the unrecognized word forms (e.g. *Audi*) by automatically update our name entities dictionaries (which contain, up to now, 3327 PERSON names and 1113 LOCATION names).

Finally we are also able to improve our local grammar net by formalising all the nominalisations of Italian spatial verbs such as *fare ritorno a Roma* where the spatial predicate is actualized in a nominal predicative form (e.g. *ritorno*) rather than in a canonical verbal form (e.g. *ritornare*). We estimate to reduce the percentage of false positive of 10% and the percentage of false negatives of 15%.

The main goal will be to build an automatic semantic role system for all the complements of a single clause. We are equipped with 8 different semantic predicates classes of containing some 5000 verbs of Italian [21], with which we can identify and annotate all the semantic roles occurring in text and create a semantic tagged corpus of the Italian language.

The idea to assign semantic roles to the argument of a verb (i.e. semantic role labeling) is a way to add useful semantic information to the non-structured and large texts and to answer queries like who, when, where or what happened. This is useful in systems that require the comprehension of sentences, like dialogues systems, information retrieval, information extraction or automatic translation.

References

1. Russom, P.: Big data analytics. TDWI Best Practices Report, Fourth Quarter (2011)
2. McAfee, A., Brynjolfsson, E.: Big data: the management revolution. Harvard Business Review 90(10), 60–66 (2012)
3. Villars, R.L., Olofson, C.W., Eastwood, M.: Big data: What it is and why you should care. White Paper, IDC (2011)
4. Ganz, J., Reinsel, D.: Extracting value from chaos. In: Gunn, J. (s.d.) IDC, Libraries in Science Fiction (2011)
5. Amato, F., Mazzeo, A., Moscato, V., Picariello, A.: A system for semantic retrieval and long-term preservation of multimedia documents in the e-government domain. International Journal of Web and Grid Services 5(4), 323–338 (2009)
6. Amato, F., Mazzeo, A., Moscato, V., Picariello, A.: Exploiting cloud technologies and context information for recommending touristic paths. In: Zavoral, F., Jung, J.J., Badica, C. (eds.) Intelligent Distributed Computing VII. SCI, vol. 511, pp. 281–287. Springer, Heidelberg (2014)
7. Beavers, J., Wei, T.S., Levin, B.: The typology of motion expressions revisited. Journal of Linguistics 46, 331–377 (2009)
8. Bateman, J.A.: Language and space: a two-level semantic approach based on principles of ontological engineering. International Journal of Speech Technology 13(1), 29–48 (2010)

9. Li, H., Zhao, T., Li, S., Zhao, J.: The extraction of trajectories from real texts based on linear classification. In: Proceedings of NODALIDA 2007 Conference, pp. 121–127 (2007)
10. Kordjamshidi, P., Van Otterlo, M., Moens, M.: Spatial Role Labeling: Towards Extraction of Spatial Relations from Natural Language. ACM Journal 5 (2011)
11. Bocchino, F.: Lessico-Grammatica dell'Italiano: le costruzioni intransitive. Ph.D Thesis in General Linguistics, University of Salerno (2006)
12. Palmer, M., Gildea, D., Xue, N.: Semantic Role Labeling. Morgan and Claypool (2010)
13. Baptista, J., Talhadas, R., Mamede, N.: Semantic Roles for Portuguese Verbs. In: Proceedings of the 32nd Conference on Lexis and Grammar, Faro, September 10-14, University of Algarve, Portugal (2013)
14. Palmer, M., Gildea, D., Kingsbury, P.: The proposition bank: An annotated corpus of semantic roles. Computational Linguistics 31(1), 71–106 (2005)
15. Rahimi Rastgar, S., Razavi, N.: A System for Building Corpus Annotated With Semantic Roles. Doctoral dissertation, Jönköping University (2013)
16. Monachesi, P.: Annotation of semantic role. Utrechet University, Netherlands (2009)
17. Ruppenhofer, J., Ellsworth, M., Petruck, M.R., Johnson, C.R., Scheffczyk, J.: FrameNet II: Extended theory and practice (2006)
18. Basili, R., De Cao, D., Lenci, A., Moschitti, A., Venturi, G.: Evalita 2011: the frame labeling over italian texts task. In: Evaluation of Natural Language and Speech Tools for Italian, pp. 195–204 (2013)
19. Giuglea, A.M., Moschitti, A.: Semantic role labeling via framenet, verbnet and propbank. In: Proceedings of the 21st International Conference on Computational Linguistics and the 44th Annual Meeting of the Association for Computational Linguistics, pp. 929–936 (2006)
20. Gross, M.: Les bases empiriques de la notion de prédicat sémantique. In: Langages, Larousse, Paris, vol. (63) (1981)
21. Elia, A.: On lexical, semantic and syntactic granularity of Italian verbs. In: Kakoyianni - Doa, F. (ed.) Penser le Lexique Grammaire: Perspectives Actuelles, Honoré Champion, Paris, pp. 277–286 (2013)
22. Elia, A., Vietri, S., Postiglione, A., Monteleone, M., Marano, F.: Data Mining Modular Software System. In: Proceedings of SWWS 2010 – The International Conference on Semantic Web and Web Service, Las Vegas, Nevada, USA (2010)
23. Vietri, S.: The Construction of an Annotated Corpus for the Analysis of Italian Transfer Predicates. In: Linguisticae Investigationes. Benjamins, Amsterdam (2013)
24. Talmy: Toward a Cognitive Semantics. Typology and process in concept structuring vol. II. The MIT Press, Cambridge (2000)
25. Silberztein, M.: Nooj manual (2003), http://www.nooj.com

IDES Project: A New Effective Tool
for Safety and Security in the Environment

Francesco Gargiulo[1], G. Persechino[1], M. Lega[2], and A. Errico[1]

[1] CIRA - Italian Aerospace Research Centre, Italy
{f.gargiulo,g.persechino,a.errico}@cira.it
[2] Department of Environmental Sciences - University of Naples Parthenope, Italy
lega@uniparthenope.it

Abstract. In the region of Campania in south-west Italy there is growing evidence, including a World Health Organization (WHO) study of the region, that the accumulation of waste, illegal and legal, urban and industrial, has contaminated soil, water, and the air with a range of toxic pollutants including dioxins. An effective environmental monitoring system represents an important tool for an early detection of the environmental violations. The IDES Project is a Geo-environmental Intelligence System developed by the CIRA with the contribution of universities and other government bodies and it aims at implementing an advanced software and hardware platform for image, data and document analysis in order to support law enforcement investigations. The IDES main modules are: *Imagery Analysis Module* to monitor land-use and anthropogenic changes; *Environmental GIS Module* to fuse geographical and administrative information; *Epidemiological domain Module*; *Semantic Search Module* to discover information in public sources like: Blog, Social Network, Forum, Newspapers; This paper focuses on Semantic Search Module and aims to provide the greatest support to the extraction of possible environmental crimes collecting and analyzing documents from online public sources. Unlikely people denounce criminal activity to the authorities. On the other hand many people through blogs, forums and social networks every day expose the status of land degradation. In addition, journalists often, have given the interest of the public, documenting the critical environmental issues. All this unstructured information are often lost due to the difficulty to collect and analyse. The IDES Semantic Search Module is an innovative solution for aggregating of the common uneasiness and thoughts of the people able to transform and objectify the public opinion in human sensors for safety environmental monitoring. In this paper we introduce methods and technologies used in some case studies and, finally, we report some representatives results, highlighting innovative aspects of this applied research.

Keywords: Illegal dumping, Landfills monitoring, interoperability, Text semantic search, Information retrieval, Geographical Information Systems.

1 Introduction

A recent census of the Italian illegal dumping sites estimates the presence of 4866 illegal dumping. Only 21% of surveyed landfills have been reclaimed and more than

J. Kołodziej et al. (Eds.): ICA3PP 2013, Part II, LNCS 8286, pp. 201–208, 2013.
© Springer International Publishing Switzerland 2013

700 contain hazardous waste [1]. The citizens' exposure to toxic waste is a major public health problem, therefore, the responsible public authorities have the need to act as soon as possible in the identification of such environmental issues. Identifying the problem, as soon as it occurs, would reduce reclamation costs. So it is necessary a more frequent and more targeted monitoring of large areas. On the other hand, public authorities do not have large budgets, so the required solution must also be economically feasible. Many employers and gears are involved in territory control requiring high costs for this activity. But control of the territory is a necessary action for the prevention of such unlawfully. It is a difficult challenge to perform long-term environmental monitoring with today's manned aircraft because of vehicle, cost, and mission limitations. Moreover, where there are small sources of pollution and contamination over a wide area, the illegal dumping is very difficult to detect. The use of satellite monitoring exceeds the current limits of traditional methods of detection. The satellite images are able to continuously monitor, in terms of space and time, large part of the territory. Early intervention on the waste accumulation is the only way to prevent its transformation in illegal landfill. The continuous satellite scanning allows the detection of anomalies connected to the dumping area employing a smaller number of operators. In this way the operators can arise only in aimed interventions having more time for other important police activities. Another plus of early warning in the contaminated area is a more effective remediation so that the territory can be back to his old self again. The treatment of small accumulations of waste requiring disposal and reclamation entails much smaller costs than those for the remediation of large volumes of waste and it's more safety for exposure to the risk of contamination from the people living around there. Early warning also prevents the contamination of wider areas due to the dispersion phenomena mediated by trophic chain and atmospheric agents. Government Bodies must ensure to citizens the healthy avoiding their exposure to contaminants.

2   IDES - Intelligent Data Extraction System

The IDES project [2] aims at implementing a software platform for data analysis within the domain of environmental criticalities. IDES provides an integrated repository of information extracted from heterogeneous, physically distributed, unstructured sources (satellite and airborne data, web pages, etc.) by means of a capture, extraction and analysis process. Based upon the integrated information stored in a Geographic Information System and elaborated with the aid of advanced data analysis techniques and tools, IDES will be able to extract the hidden information, that is information non immediately identifiable through a mere reading or a deeper analysis, even if performed by a domain expert; at this end, IDES will be able to uncover patterns, multi-disciplinary correlations not known a priori and it will be able to extract relevant information useful for Government Bodies. The project team focus on an innovative Environmental Monitoring System, that considers dumping and landfills data related to specific industrial installations, urban solid waste temporary deposits/facilities and statistical data about urban people. All above data, coming from different sources available in the project, are different for semantics (chemical, emissions, county people, installations address, etc.) and structure (tabular, vector, raster, structured, unstructured). In order to elaborate different types of data and to enable user analysis, the IDES software platform is based on the following components:

- *Semantic Search Module*: text analysis component with semantic analysis features; its objective is to analyze text document coming from intranet and web sources in order to automatically extract entities and relationships among them with which to build conceptual map useful for a primary illegal crime detecting;
- *Imagery Analysis Module*: image analysis component for analyzing multi-spectral and SAR images through advanced algorithmic features to mine pattern among data; this represents a powerful key to identify and geo-locate sites with potential illegal activity;
- *Environmental GIS Module*: Geographical information system and geostatistical analysis component for spatial data exploration and analysis with the capabilities to create statistically valid prediction information from a limited number of data measurements.
- *Epidemiological domain Module*: aimed at the implementation of a decision support system for epidemiological domain experts.

The applied methodology obtains information structured on which to perform innovative techniques of analysis and correlation of data to generate new knowledge and multidisciplinary of the environmental investigation, by using of natural Language Processing technologies and the semantic analysis of a large amount of documents written in natural language. This added scientific value correlates the data on the spatial distribution of productive activities, hydro-geographical pattern and road using geostatistical Kriging method. Results are structured into a geo-system reference, easily accessible by the end-user, highlighting the relationships between the geographical and non- geographical entities for mapping of risks of illegal spills. The illegal burning of waste is known to release toxic substances into the atmosphere. Even if such fires are easily hidden among legitimate incineration resulting from the more general waste disposal problem, an useful instrument of public complaint is the social network distribution of information able to highlight the common uneasiness and thoughts of the people.

Within the Campania Regional Operational Program FERS 2007-2013 the IDES Project responds to the specific objective 2.a - Enhancement System for Research and Innovation and Implementation of Technology in Production Systems and in particular the Operational objective 2.1 "Build and strengthen in the field of industrial research and experimental development of science, technology leadership that may lead to the placement of substantial shares of the productive fabric, including through joint development in the form of advanced services in industrial research and experimental development". The use of tools implemented in IDES opens a window onto the development of scientific research in a multidisciplinary arousing interest on the ability of the project to develop a comprehensive geo-information product to the user.

2.1   Search Method vs. Remote Sensing Technology

In recent years, many innovative and technological projects Silvestri et al. [4] have been developed in order to prove that the remote sensing images have an important role in the enforcement and prosecution of environmental crime, such as illegal waste management, illicit burning, abandonment, dumping or uncontrolled disposal of waste, etc. Also, the improvements to satellite technology is expanding by processing of the low-resolution imagery (like Moderate Resolution Imaging Spectroradiometer - MODIS), and high-resolution imagery (like IKONOS, GeoEye), and the use of this resource as a tool of environmental compliance and enforcement will increase. Remote sensing, developed in GIS domain (by Esri ArcGis software [7]), is used to detective many characteristics of landfill sites. If these characteristics indicate that the landfill have a negative impact to environmental, then these site could be potentially illegal. The remote sensing approach requests a tall budget for acquisition and processing of imaging. As stated, IDES Project conglobes also remote sensing analysis and data acquisition for the preparation of sample dataset, collected at different heights (with the help of aerial work platforms, DRONE, etc.). In this study IDES develops the Semantic Search module in order to highlight the advantages of this approach respect to monitoring by satellite technology. Note that the geographical area, in which this phenomena is developed, is often very wide; so the use of Airborne or Satellite platforms lead to costs and time too high.

Even if the localization of event is well determined tanks to high level of accuracy of images resolution, the temporal parameter cannot be continuously explicated because the research applications couldn't sustain a such cost of nonstop images acquisitions. In particular, the use of multispectral images can discriminate the different spectral responses of objects, but it is necessary to integrate high spatial resolution and radiometric images with data geo-archives for the constructing of investigations multitemporal not-always achievable. The Cogito approach tries to solve the problem of the geo-localization of data in a well-defined temporal space, proved by the human sensors (e.g. via social network).

2.2   IDES – Semantic Search Module

IDES Semantic Search module aims to demonstrate that the use of natural Language Processing technologies and the semantic analysis of the text allows you to extract structured or semi-structured information specific to the application domain of IDES from a large amount of documents written in natural language. The approach integrates information obtained from the analysis of the text with the data made available by the institutions participating in the "table" of the project available in GIS. Then the use of statistical and geostatistical analysis may provide support to the process of characterization of possible environmental crimes both from the point of view of scenario analysis both from the point of view of analysis of specific cases.

The main objective of the Semantic Search module is providing support to the identification of potential environmental wrongdoing related to "illegal disposal of waste". Illegal waste disposal can take many forms, including: burning of toxic substances, illegal dumping in hydro-geographical lattice, abandonment of waste, fly-tipping, etc.

The Semantic Search module rely on Expert System Cogito SEE Suite [6].

The first step then is to identify the documentary sources in which to execute semantic searches. For this purpose, in addition to the national and local press, were taken into account some groups on Facebook particularly active in reporting fires and neglect abuse. Persons resident in the province of Caserta, daily post in natural language on these groups, they report what they see and hear (fire, smoke, burning smell, etc.), the place where this happens (the road, the municipality, etc.) and often other information. The problem is that the descriptions of these events may be inaccurate or incomplete because written in natural language.

The Semantic Search module has been configured to extract from the post of the Facebook group and the national and local press the potential events of "illegal disposal of waste". The tool has been configured by expert linguists who have analyzed the documentary sources and in collaboration with the IDES project domain expert have contributed to the definition of a taxonomy specific domain and a list of events (named entities) to be extracted from documents. The extensions of Semantic Search tools focused mainly on the implementation of the taxonomy and the classification and extraction rules. There are five classes of events: *waste disposal, burning, discharge of waste, waste traffic, bad smell* and altogether 55 subclasses of events (named events). For example the class *burning* contains the events: *Burning of special waste, Burning of hazardous waste, Burning of discarded tires, The stake of asbestos, Burning of waste electrical and electronic equipment, The stake of hospital waste,* etc.

For each event retrieved the tool tries to locate even attribute values:

- *Author*: name and surname, if specified in the document, the offender (people, but also company names etc.).
- *Place*: proper name of the place where the event occurs.
- *Type of place*: the place where the offence occurs (e.g. marine waters, surface waters, soil, underground if you talk such as spills, but also places like railway stations, airports etc.).
- *Address*: address of the place or event venue type when specified.
- *Date*: the date of the event.
- *Type of vehicle*: vehicles, such as cars, motorcycles, trucks used for illegal trafficking, spills etc.
- *Vehicle*: The model of the vehicle. (Grande Punto, Classe A, etc.), if specified
- *Car manufacturer*: The manufacturer of the vehicle (Fiat, Alfa Romeo etc.), if specified
- *Plate number*: The number plate of the vehicle if specified

Of course it is possible that not all information appear in the text and information about an event are not organized into a rigid structure. For example, the address is an event attribute and it is not a *Place* attribute, as would be in a relational schema. This structure reflects the actual cases in which disclosures and complaints are incomplete.

It is preferred to get in the first instance this semi-structured organization, and perform at a later stage the appropriate processing events based on analysis to be carried out. The analysis on the events are both the quality and the quantity of extracted data.

The second extension of the search tool has been the design and the implementation of the domain taxonomy. The taxonomy is the hierarchical structure used to classify the documents. In this case, the classification is multidimensional, i.e. each document may be classified into zero, one, or more nodes. Nodes (or concepts) are linked together by IS-A relations. The taxonomy contains 79 concepts, at the first level there are 2 main concepts (*Waste Management* and *Waste Transport*) and the max depth of the taxonomy tree is 5. The taxonomy is designed to support information search tie abusive waste disposal in unstructured documents and is very dependent on the definition of events. The Semantic Search module indexes all documentary sources on a daily basis, although it is possible to define a different refresh rate for each document source if necessary. During the indexing process for each new document published shall be carried out the following steps:

- Semantic analysis: all the concepts present in the document are identified and disambiguated using the semantic network present in the module.
- Classification: the document is classified in none, one or more classes of domain taxonomy using the result of the previous analysis and classification rules.
- Extraction and meta-events: events and meta-events are extracted using the result of semantic analysis and extraction rules. Events and meta-events extracts at a certain date can be obtained in RDF format. In the RDF model in addition to the already described attributes of the event, there are also include: the source documents from which data were extracted (e.g. Facebook), the document (e.g. the post), the phrase, the date of acquisition, the unique id of the event, the subclass of the event, the event class and the event destination.

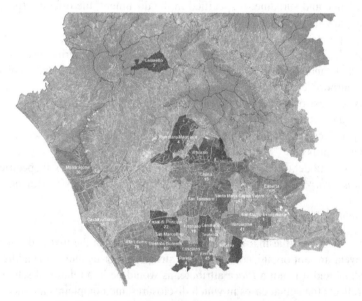

Fig. 1. Events distribution map on province of Caserta

3   Results

During the first six months of 2013 were indexed approximately 184,000 documents, Fig .3(a). The total number of 5 post Facebook groups analyzed is about 5,964 from which were extracted 2175 reports of events.

Only events that have at least one attribute between: address, place, town, type of place were processed. If there are multiple place for the same events, it is used the attribute with greater precision (i.e. address is more accurately and the type of place and so on). The result of this elaboration can be available in the GIS and therefore can be used for geostatistical and spatial analysis. For example, the Fig. 4 shows the Kriging model describing the distribution of the events in the province of Caserta.

4   Conclusion e Future Works

In this paper, the Semantic Search approach has been developed. In Table 1, the advantages and the limitations are shown for each approach. The results obtained by Semantic Search approach prove that the applied methodology provides the useful and less expensive instrument than satellite and airborne sensor system for environmental monitoring to support investigation of potential illicit crime.

Table 1. Advantages and limitations of different approaches

	Advantages	Limitations
Satellite approach (High Resolution Imaging)	High radiometric sensor resolution	High costs for acquisition database
	High spectral sensor resolution	High costs for data interpretation
	High spatial sensor resolution	Low temporal sensor resolution
	Georeferencing processing	
Airborne approach	High spatial sensor resolution	High costs database acquisition
	Detailed information on the composition and related physical properties of detected objects	
Semantic search approach	High temporal sensor resolution	Uncertainty in the event time/date
	Mid/low costs for database acquisition	Uncertainty in the event positioning

This approach strongly depends in turn on: the quality of the information provided by users and the correct extraction and classification of information from natural language texts. The biggest problem related to the quality of information is the possible presence of more posts that refer to the same event. In this case, the same event would be retrieved several times and this could have an effect on later analysis. In future work we intend to define a measure of similarity between events that allows us to identify potential duplicates (same event, same day, same place, etc.) with a degree of reliabilityand we plan the preparation of specific domain datasets for performance evaluation.

References

1. Persechino, G., Schiano, P., Lega, M., Napoli, R.M.A., Ferrara, C., Kosmatka, J.: Aerospace-based support systems and interoperability: the solution to fight illegal dumping. Waste Management (2010)
2. Persechino, G., Lega, M., Romano, G., Gargiulo, F., Cicala, L.: IDES project: an advanced tool to investigate illegal dumping. In: 6th International Conference on Waste Management and the Environment (2012)
3. Jones, H.K., Elgy, J.: Remote Sensing to Assess Landfill Gas Migration. Waste Management and Research 12, 327–337 (1994)
4. Silvestri, Omri, M.: A method for the remote sensing identification of uncontrolled landfills: formulation and validation. International Journal of Remote Sensing, 975–989 (2008)
5. Campbell, G., et al.: Il progetto Wastemon: la tecnologia satellitare per la gestione e il monitoraggio delle discariche. In: ASITA Conference (2009)
6. Expert System, http://www.expertsystem.net/
7. ArcGis, http://www.arcgis.com
8. NASA Earth Science Data Sources and Archives, http://www-v0ims.gsfc.nasa.gov/v0ims/RELSITES/other_source.html
9. U.S. Geological Survey USGS EarthExplorer, http://edcsns17.cr.usgs.gov/EarthExplorer/
10. EOLI Web client dell'Agenzia Spaziale Europea, http://eoli.esa.int/servlets/template/welcome/entryPage.vm
11. ITC Database, http://www.itc.nl/research/products/sensordb/searchsat.aspx
12. Amato, F., Mazzeo, A., Moscato, V., Picariello, A.: A system for semantic retrieval and long-term preservation of multimedia documents in the e-government domain. International Journal of Web and Grid Services 5(4), 323–338 (2009)
13. Amato, F., Mazzeo, A., Moscato, V., Picariello, A.: Exploiting Cloud Technologies and Context Information for Recommending Touristic Paths. In: Zavoral, F., Jung, J.J., Badica, C. (eds.) Intelligent Distributed Computing VII. SCI, vol. 511, pp. 281–287. Springer, Heidelberg (2013)
14. Amato, F., Mazzeo, A., Moscato, V., Picariello, A.: Semantic Management of Multimedia Documents for E-Government Activity. In: International Conference on Complex, Intelligent and Software Intensive Systems, CISIS 2009, pp. 1193–1198. IEEE (March 2009)

Impact of Biometric Data Quality
on Rank-Level Fusion Schemes

Emanuela Marasco[1], Ayman Abaza[2,3], Luca Lugini, and Bojan Cukic

[1] Lane Department of Computer Science and Electrical Engineering,
West Virginia University
P.O. Box 6109 Morgantown, WV, USA
emanuela.marasco,bojan.cukic@mail.wvu.edu, luligini@mix.wvu.edu
[2] West Virginia High Technology Consortium Foundation
Fairmont, WV 26554, USA
aabaza@wvhtf.org
[3] Biomedical Engineering and Systems,
Cairo University, Egypt

Abstract. Recent research has established benefits of rank-level fusion in identification systems; however, these studies have not compared the advantages, if any, of rank-level fusion schemes over classical score-level fusion schemes. In the presence of low quality biometric data, the genuine match score is claimed to be low and expected to be an unreliable individual output. Conversely, the rank assigned to that genuine identity is believed to remain stable even when using low quality biometric data. However, to the best of our knowledge, there is not a deepen investigation on the stability of ranks. In this paper, we analyze changes of the rank assigned to the genuine identity in multi-modal scenarios when using actual low quality data. The performance is evaluated on a subset of the database Face and Ocular Challenge Series (FOCS) collection (the Good, Bad and Ugly database), composed of three frontal faces per subject for 407 subjects. Results show that a variant of the highest rank fusion scheme, which is robust to ties, performs better than the other non-learning based rank-level fusion methods explored in this work. However, experiments demonstrate that score-level fusion results in better identification accuracy than existing rank-level fusion schemes.

1 Introduction

In a typical biometric identification system, the input probe (e.g., a fingerprint image) is compared to the labeled biometric data in the gallery database (e.g., fingerprint database) and a set of similarity scores is generated. Scores are sorted in decreasing order and based on this ordering a set of integer values or *ranks* is assigned to these retrieved identities. The lowest rank indicates the best match; Hence the corresponding identity is associated with that of the input probe. The identity of the gallery that corresponds to the true identity of the probe is known as the genuine identity; otherwise it is called imposter one.

J. Kołodziej et al. (Eds.): ICA3PP 2013, Part II, LNCS 8286, pp. 209–216, 2013.
© Springer International Publishing Switzerland 2013

The recognition accuracy of a biometric system generally decreases in the presence of low quality biometric data wherein the similarity between the probe and associated gallery image may be reduced [1] [2]. In such a scenario, the accuracy can be improved by incorporating multibiometric system that consolidates the evidence provided by multiple biometric sources [3] [4] [5]. This work focuses on fusion at the score-level and rank-level, which are described below:

Score-Level Fusion. Fusion can be applied at match score level, where match scores output by different biometric matchers are consolidated. This approach has been widely used since match scores are easy to access and combine. However, match scores output by different biometric matchers may not be homogeneous: each matcher can conform to different scales and they may not have the same interpretation across different matchers (they can be distances, confidences, etc.) [6]. Thus, before integration, each matcher may have to be transformed into a common domain via an effective normalization scheme [7]. *simple mean* fusion rule, which is commonly used in the literature, is employed in this work.

Rank-Level Fusion. Each matcher ranks the identities in the gallery based on the match scores between the input probe and these gallery identities. A sorted list of all the possible identities is generated with the topmost identity being the first choice [8] (see Fig. 1). Ranks are expected to offer a consistent comparable output across different matchers without requiring normalization. Let $\mathbf{R}=[r_{ij}]$ be the rank matrix in a multi-biometric system where r_{ij} is the rank assigned to the identity I_i by the jth matcher, i=1...N and j=1...K. A reordered statistic r_i is computed for each user I_i such that the highest consensus rank is assigned to the user with the lowest value of r.

In the presence of low quality biometric data, the genuine match score is claimed to be low. When combining multiple matchers, such a match score is expected to be an unreliable individual output, able to confuse a score level fusion algorithm and result in a potential identification error. Conversely, rank information is believed to be a relatively stable statistic. Further, the rank assigned to that genuine identity is expected to remain stable even when using low quality biometric data [9]. However, this statement has been argued but not experimentally demonstrated.

The contribution of this paper is to analyze the robustness of rank level and score level fusion schemes when using low quality data. This paper is organized as follows: Section 2 discusses benefits and drawbacks of ranks, and presents the approaches for fusion at rank level used to conduct this study. Section 3 reports results and Section 4 summarizes the conclusions of this work.

2 Exploiting Rank Information

Several works have focused on the problem of enhancing the performance of rank level fusion schemes in adverse operational environments (i.e., noise input data, etc.).

Monwar and Gavrilova presented a Markov chain approach for combining rank information in multimodal biometric systems comprising face, ear and iris [10].

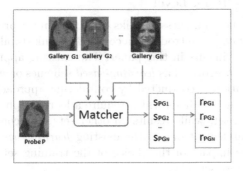

Fig. 1. For systems operating in identification mode, an input probe is compared against a set of galleries to determine the pertaining identity. A set of ranked scores pertaining to the different identities in the gallery database. The lowest rank indicates the best match and the identity corresponding to it is assigned to the input probe.

Their experiments showed the superiority in accuracy and reliability over other biometric rank aggregation methods.

Abaza and Ross proposed a quality-based Borda Count scheme that is able to increase the robustness of the traditional Borda Count in the presence of low quality images without requiring a training phase [11]. Marasco *et al.* proposed a predictor-based approach to perform a reliable fusion at rank level. In such a scheme, a predictor (classifier) was trained using both rank and match score information for each modality and designed to operate before fusion [12].

2.1 Benefits of Using Ranks

Ranks describe the relative order of the gallery identities, and they carry less information than the true values of match scores, as nothing is retained of the notion of distance (or similarity) between the probe and each gallery. Ranks can be referred to as *ordinal* variables since they only carry information about the relative ordering of the different identities. There are cases where the information about how the different identities are ranked can be useful. First, match scores may be not available for those systems that output only a list of candidate identities [13], [14]. Second, when conducting statistical parametric tests, distributions of match scores are assumed to be normal [15]. These tests may be heavily sensitive to the normality assumption and fail when the considered distributions are not normal. Using ranks instead of match scores, can lead to more robust results. Further, in cases where monotonous transformation are applied to match scores, the corresponding ranks are kept unchanged. Ranks do not change when the scale on which the corresponding numerical measurements changes [16]. Finally, as stated in the introduction, when combining multiple modalities, the fusion of ranks does not require a normalization phase as typically needed with heterogeneous match scores [17].

2.2   Fusion at the Rank Level

In order to evaluate the robustness of ranks and scores in the presence of low quality data, Marasco *et al.* [18] introduced a concept of rank stability. We will apply
this method for experiments in this paper. The existing approaches for fusion
at rank level can be categorized as *learning-based* schemes or *non learning-based*
schemes. The evaluation is conducted by considering approaches that combine
ranks with no learning. Methods which require a learning phase may be biased
to a specific training set; while results on other sets may change dramatically.
However, we also implement one of the existing *learning-based* fusion rules in
order to observe the impact of the choice of the training set on the matching
performance of the test set.

Let K be the number of modality matchers to be combined and N the number
of enrolled users. Let r_{ij} be the rank assigned to the jth identity in the gallery
by the ith matcher, $i = 1 \ldots K$, and $j = 1 \ldots N$.

Traditional Highest Rank. This method obtains consensus ranking by sorting
the identities according to their highest rank. The advantage of this method lies
in utilizing the best of the combined matchers. However, this method may lead
to one or multiple ties. This drawback can be effectively addressed by applying a
variant of the traditional highest rank fusion rule, referred to as *Modified Highest
Rank*, and formulated below [11]:

$$R_i = \min_{k=1}^{K} r_{ik} + \epsilon_i, \quad i = 1, 2, ...N \tag{1}$$

where $\epsilon_i = \sum_{k=1}^{K} r_{ik}$. The advantages of the lowest rank are maintained and the
epsilon factor is just used to break the ties.

Traditional Borda Count. In this method the consensus ranking is obtained
by summing the ranks assigned by the individual matchers, see Eqn. (2). This
approach is highly vulnerable to the effect of weak matchers since it assumes
that all the matchers present the same classification capability. This method
assumes that the ranks assigned to the identities in the gallery are statistically
independent and that the performance of all the matchers are uniform.

Quality-based Borda Count. This method is a redefinition of the traditional
Borda Count where the input data quality is incorporated in the fusion scheme
as follows:

$$R_i = \sum_{k=1}^{K} Q_{ik} r_{ik}, \quad i = 1, 2, ...N \tag{2}$$

Q_{ik} is defined as $Q_{ik} = min(Q_i, Q_k)$, where Q_i and Q_k are quality of the probe
and the gallery data, respectively [11]. Adding weights, to the matcher outputs,
leads to a reduction of the effect of poor quality biometric samples.

Logistic Regression. In this method, the fused rank is calculated as a weighted
sum of the individual ranks [19], and is defined in the following equation:

$$R_i = \sum_{k=1}^{K} w_{ik} r_{ik}, \quad i = 1, 2, ...N \tag{3}$$

In order to combine modality matchers with non-uniform performances, the ranks produced by each modality matcher should be appropriately weighted. The weights reflect the relative significance of the corresponding unimodal output [20]. The weight w assigned to the different matchers is determined in the training phase of Logistic Regression. This fusion rule is robust in the presence of matchers with significant differences in performance; however, its main drawback lies in requiring a learning phase to determine the weights. This negatively impacts the reliability of the final decision [21].

3   Experimental Results

This section starts by discussing the database, demonstrates various experiments to compare the performance of score and rank level fusion schemes using low quality input data, and discusses the results of these experiments.

3.1   Datasets

The performance of the proposed strategy was evaluated using a subset of the Face and Ocular Challenge Series (FOCS) collection (the Good, Bad and Ugly database). Images from the Face and Ocular Challenge Series (FOCS) database are of frontal faces taken under uncontrolled illumination, both indoors and outdoors. The partitions of interest are referred to as *Good* and *Ugly*, that have an average identification accuracy of 0.98 and 0.15 respectively [1].

The used dataset composed of 407 subjects, three frontal instances of faces:

- two high quality images (from the Good dataset)
- one actual low quality image (from the Ugly dataset)

Figure 2 shows examples of high and low quality face images. PittPatt[2] software was used for generating the face match scores. These results are generated from two different matching scenarios: both the gallery and probe are not degraded, referred to as *Good-Good* and the gallery is not degraded, but the probe is degraded, referred to as *Good-Ugly*.

3.2   Score and Rank Levels Fusion Comparison

Figures 3 show histograms of the match score value of the genuine identity for high and low quality face probes, compared to the rank value. Ranks (scores) are stable if the rank (score) assigned to the genuine identity when using high quality probes does not change when using low quality probes. A difference in ranks (scores) between high and low quality equal to zero indicates stability. Visually, the distributions of the differences of ranks (and match scores) suggest that ranks are more stable than match scores.

In this section, we report results obtained when integrating ranks in multimodal biometric systems, and compare them to the performance achieved using scores.

---

[1] http://www.nist.gov/itl/iad/ig/focs.cfm
[2] http://www.pittpatt.com/

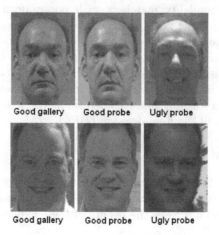

Fig. 2. Examples of a high quality (Good) and low quality (Ugly) face images

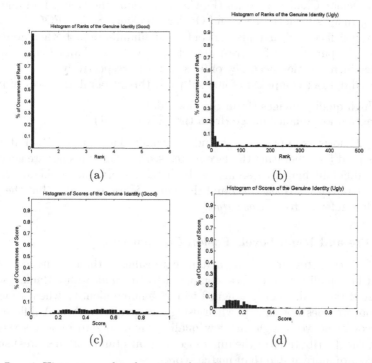

Fig. 3. Row 1. Histograms of ranks assigned to the genuine identity for the face modality taken from Good Ugly real database; a) High Quality (Good); b) Low Quality (Ugly). Row 2. Histograms of match scores of the genuine identity for the face modality taken from Good Ugly real database; c) High Quality (Good); d) Low Quality (Ugly).

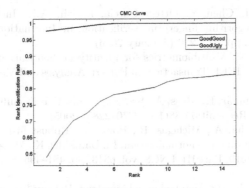

Fig. 4. Fusion of one face and two fingerprints: a) face is non-degraded, fingerprint is under degradation; b) both face and fingerprints are degraded. The face modality is taken from the GBU data set of the FOCS database and both fingerprints from WVU database.

4   Conclusion

This study carried out an investigation regarding the stability of the rank in the context of biometrics. Further, we analyzed different non learning-based rank level fusion schemes in the presence of both synthetically degraded fingerprint images and actual low quality face images. The experiments showed that rank is stable when the degradation level of the low quality image is not very significant. When the level of degradation is significant, both ranks and scores are not stable. Further, ranks are more stable than scores since they present a higher rank correlation coefficient value. (However, the performed study may be dependent upon the matcher used).

Acknowledgments. The authors are grateful to West Virginia University and, in particular, Dr. Arun Ross. This material is supported by ONR under Contract No. N00014-09-C-0388 awarded to West Virginia High Technology Consortium Foundation.

References

1. Monwar, M., Gavrilova, M.: Multimodal biometric system using rank-level fusion approach. IEEE Transactions on Systems, Man, and Cybernetics 39, 867–878 (2009)
2. Grother, P., Tabassi, E.: Performance of biometric quality measures. IEEE Transaction on Pattern Analysis and Machine Intelligence 29(4), 531–543 (2007)
3. Kittler, J., Li, Y.P., Matas, J., Sanchez, M.U.R.: Combining evidence in multimodal personal identity recognition systems. In: International Conference on Audio- and Video-based Biometric Person Authentication (1997)

4. Fierrez-Aguilar, J., Chen, Y., Ortega-Garcia, J., Jain, A.K.: Incorporating image quality in multi-algorithm fingerprint verification. In: International Conference on Biometrics (ICB), pp. 213–220 (January 2006)
5. Kittler, J., Poh, N.: Multibiometrics for identity authentication: Issues, benefits and challenges. In: IEEE Transaction on Pattern Analysis and Machine Intelligence (2009)
6. Jain, A., Nandakumar, K., Ross, A.: Score normalization in multimodal biometric systems. Pattern Recognition 38(12), 2270–2285 (2005)
7. Scheirer, W., Rocha, A., Micheals, R., Boult, T.: Robust fusion: Extreme value theory for recognition score normalization. In: Daniilidis, K., Maragos, P., Paragios, N. (eds.) ECCV 2010, Part III. LNCS, vol. 6313, pp. 481–495. Springer, Heidelberg (2010)
8. Ross, A., Jain, A.: Information fusion in biometrics. Pattern Recognition Letters 24, 2115–2125 (2003)
9. Tulyakov, S., Govindaraju, V.: Combining biometric scores in identification systems, pp. 1–34 (2006)
10. Monwar, M., Gavrilova, M.: Markov chain model for multimodal biometric rank fusion. In: Signal, Image and Video Processing, pp. 1863–1703 (2011)
11. Abaza, A., Ross, A.: Quality-based rank level fusion in biometrics. In: Third IEEE International Conference on Biometrics: Theory, Applications and Systems (September 2009)
12. Marasco, E., Ross, A., Sansone, C.: Predicting identification errors in a multibiometric system based on ranks and scores. In: Fourth IEEE International Conference on Biometrics: Theory, Applications and Systems (September 2010)
13. Labovitz, S.: The assignment of numbers to rank order categories. American Sociological Review 35(3), 515–524 (1970)
14. Bhat, D., Nayar, S.: Ordinal measures for image correspondence. IEEE Transactions on Pattern Analysis and Machine Intelligence 20(4), 415–423 (1998)
15. Friedman, M.: The use of ranks to avoid the assumption of normality implicit in the analysis of variance. Journal of the American Statistical Association 32(200), 675–701 (1937)
16. Wilcoxon, F.: Individual comparisons by ranking methods. Biometrics Bulletin 1(6), 80–83 (1945)
17. Nandakumar, K., Jain, A., Ross, A.: Score normalization in multimodal biometric systems. Pattern Recognition 38(12), 2270–2285 (2005)
18. Marasco, E., Abaza, A.: On the stability of ranks to low image quality in biometric identification systems. In: Petrosino, A. (ed.) ICIAP 2013, Part I. LNCS, vol. 8156, pp. 260–269. Springer, Heidelberg (2013)
19. Ross, A., Nandakumar, K., Jain, A.: Handbook of MultiBiometrics. Springer (2006)
20. Ho, T., Hull, J., Srihari, S.: Combination of decisions by multiple classifiers. In: Structured Document Image Analysis, pp. 188–202 (1992)
21. Moscato, F., Vittorini, V., Amato, F., Mazzeo, A., Mazzocca, N.: Solution workflows for model-based analysis of complex systems. IEEE Transactions on Automation Science and Engineering 9(1), 83–95 (2012)

A Secure OsiriX Plug-In for Detecting Suspicious Lesions in Breast DCE-MRI

Gabriele Piantadosi, Stefano Marrone, Mario Sansone, and Carlo Sansone

Dipartimento di Ingegneria Elettrica e delle Tecnologie dell'Informazione (DIETI)
University of Naples Federico II
{gabriele.piantadosi,ste.marrone.g}@gmail.com,
{mario.sansone,carlo.sansone}@unina.it

Abstract. Up-to-date medical image processing is currently based on very sophisticated algorithms that often require a large computational load not always available on conventional workstations. Moreover, algorithms are in continuous evolution and hence clinicians are typically required to update their workstation periodically. The main objective of this paper is to propose a secure and versatile client-server architecture for providing these services at a low cost. In particular, we developed a plug-in allowing OsiriX - a widespread medical image processing application dedicated to DICOM images coming from several equipments - to interact with a system for automatic detection of suspicious lesions in breast DCE-MRI. The large amount of data and the privacy of the information flowing through the network requires a flexible but comprehensive security approach. According to NIST guidelines, in our proposal data are transmitted over SSL/TLS channel after an authentication and authorization procedure based on X.509 standard digital certificate associated with a 3072bit RSA Key Pair. Authentication and authorization procedure is achieved through the services offered by Java JAAS classes.

Keywords: Big Data, Client-server, JAAS, TLS/SSL, DCE-MRI.

1   Introduction

Over last years the need of big-data computing is growing in many scientific disciplines. This also applies to medical research areas, with a closer and more direct impact on everyday life. Modern medical imaging technology (MRI, TAC, etc.) collects big amounts of patient's data that have to be suitably interpreted and analysed to produce a proper diagnosis in a reasonable (clinical) time. Accordingly, up-to-date processing of medical images is based on very sophisticated algorithms that often require a significant computational load, not always available on conventional workstations. Moreover, algorithms are in continuous evolution and hence clinicians are required to update their workstation periodically.

Some papers addressed so far this problem. Scheinine et al. [1] propose an Object-Oriented Client-Server System for Interactive Segmentation of Medical Images based on JAVA for the client and CORBA for the distributed system,

J. Kołodziej et al. (Eds.): ICA3PP 2013, Part II, LNCS 8286, pp. 217–224, 2013.
© Springer International Publishing Switzerland 2013

connected by a TCP/IP socket protocol. Mayer et al. [2] implemented a 'processing on demand' client-server architecture for 3D image processing in which the computation load is all on the server side, while the client requests the desired images one slice (2D) at a time. At last, Sherif et al. [3] present an evolution of the open standard DICOM to support communication between DICOM entities over a TCP/IP network.

The above cited papers were mostly designed for computing systems belonging to several generations ago, unable to handle even simple tasks like 3D visualization. Moreover, their focus is on the architecture, omitting an evaluation about the severe and complex security and privacy issues associated with the cloud computing [4].

This paper describes the design and the implementation of a secure client-server architecture able to provide advanced medical image processing operations (like automatic lesion detection, image registration, etc.) through the cloud.

The client takes care of simple tasks. When an operation with a high computational burden is required, the client side plug-in gathers protocol information (acquisition time, field of view, voxel spacing, TR/TE, thickness and acquisition time), produces an intensity file, compress it and submits the request to server. The server recognizes the requested operation, starts the most suitable procedure at hand and sends back results to the client. This operation is completely asynchronous: the client may require multiple tasks simultaneously and get back to usual operations waiting for server results. The server implementation is hidden to the client: operations are totally decoupled and the server can implement any architectural choice (cluster based system, GPU based, etc.) or upgrade itself at any time without client side modification. This gives rise to an highly general and versatile architecture. Underlying security polices complies with NIST recommendations [5]: privacy is guaranteed by data anonymization and 128bit TLS cryptography, while security is guaranteed by a symmetric 3072bit RSA certificates system.

As case-study, we have chosen cancer diagnosis for its worldwide diffusion [6]. To increase early detection, additional medical imaging techniques started to be used together with conventional screening procedures. This produces a big amount of information, giving rise to a big-data analysis problem. In particular, we focus on breast cancer and on Dynamic Contrast Enhanced Magnetic Resonance Imaging (DCE-MRI) that has demonstrated a great potential in screening of high-risk women, in staging newly diagnosed breast cancer patients and in assessing therapy effects [7] thanks to the possibility to visualize 3D high resolution dynamic (functional) information not available with conventional RX imaging.

On server-side we implement a system for automatic detection of suspicious lesions in breast DCE-MRI [8,9,10]; as client-side medical image tool we decided to support OsiriX [11], due to its powerful interface and since it has an open plug-in system. The paper is organized as follows: in Sec. 2 we present the design of the proposed architecture, together with system requirements and specifications. A case-study is presented in Sec. 3, while some preliminary testing results are reported in Sec. 4. Finally, we draw some conclusions in Sec. 5.

2 System Design and Implementation

2.1 System Requirements

The aim of the proposed work is to define a complete architecture for advanced medical images analysis in a secure and versatile client-server environment at a low cost. This means that the proposed system is not an image processing software by itself, but a remote support tool to constantly improve the local (i.e., client side) medical image processing software.

During the system design, some requirements and constraints have been considered. In particular, the system:

- must be secure and ensure patient privacy, making use of steady standards
- should be flexible and versatile (server side)
- should be independent of the particular network technology adopted to connect client and server
- should be compatible (or easy to extend) to common medical image processing software (client side)
- should have an user-friendly GUI (client-side)
- must be quite fast (to be used in a clinical environment) and let the end user continue his work (even on different patients) during server side operation.

2.2 System Overview

The client establishes a SSL/TLS channel over a TCP/IP connection. Security is improved by a symmetric authentication policy, issued during user registration as an authorized client. Certificates contain a Public Key and a Signature, both used to identify the user on server-side and to grant access to server features. The procedure for authentication and authorization through certificates is achieved by means of Java services. In particular we used Java Authentication and Authorization Service (JAAS) [12] classes: this choice guarantees compatibility over different networks architecture supporting the TCP/IP stack protocols and portability (all virtualization is made by the Java Virtual Machine).

The entire architecture is composed by three main modules (see Fig. 1):

- Client software: a client side medical images processing software with a plug-in system to interact with the described system
- jSecureSync: the Java synchronization system (composed by a client side and a server side application)
- Server software: any advanced medical image processing framework able to interact with JSecureSync

To interact with the proposed system, Server software has to track jSecureSync file system activity and, when data have been received, performs the requested procedure and provides results back to JSecureSync using file system. It similarly happens for the client side, where many medical images processing software can be supported.

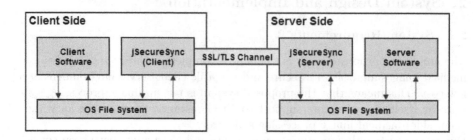

Fig. 1. The proposed architecture

The jSecureSync configuration files contain paths of data directories with relative read/write permissions, ensuring folders access with the required safety criteria. To reduce the transmission overhead, JSecureSync always performs a compression before starting a transmission.

2.3 System Specifications

Protocol Clients and server communicate through a very simple (with low overhead) protocol, whose commands are:

- $[C \rightarrow S]$ HELO: client has to open a synchronization process with the server
- $[S \rightarrow C]$ OK v1.0: the server acknowledges and, at the same time, it informs the client about the protocol version
- $[C \rightarrow S]$ C_SND_RQ: the client requests to synchronize a file
- $[S \rightarrow C]$ S_SND_ACK: the server allows the client to send over the channel
- $[S \rightarrow C]$ S_SND_RQ: the server requests to synchronize a file
- $[C \rightarrow S]$ C_SND_ACK: the client allows the server to send over the channel

Security Specifications. The client/server establishes a stateful SSL/TLS channel in a TCP/IP tunnel, over which command and data are transmitted. During the handshake, client and server define the connection security parameters according with the 2012 NIST recommendation [5]. After jSecureSync client installation, the user is asked to register. The system produces an unique X.509 standard digital certificate associated with a 3072bit RSA Key Pair, both stored on client side. The certificate is required to open the SSL/TLS channel and to authenticate the client on the server.

The channel uses TSL protocol with shared session key agreement based on the Elliptic curve Diffie-Hellman (ECDH) [13,14] algorithm; Cipher-Block Chaining (CBC) is adopeted and data is encrypted with a 128bit key AES algorithm [15]. NIST encoded string is "TLS_ECDHE_RSA_WITH_AES_128_CBC_SHA" [16].

3 Case-Study: Breast DCE-MRI Automatic Lesion Detection

Although the system architecture is versatile and also independent of the acquisition protocol, in order to show it in a real case, in this section we describe its application to the analysis of breast DCE-MRI T1-weighted FLASH 3D coronal images (TR/TE: 9,8/4,76 ms; flip angle: 25 degrees; field of view 330 x 247 mm x mm; matrix: 256 x 128; thickness:2 mm; gap: 0; acquisition time: 56s; 80 slices spanning entire breast volume). For each patient, 10 series were acquired: one series (t_0) was acquired before and 9 series (t_1-t_9) after intravenous injection of 0.1 mmol/kg of a positive paramagnetic contrast agent (Gd-DOTA, Dotarem, Guerbet, Roissy CdG Cedex, France). Data coming from a single patient occupies about 110 MB.

On server-side we implement a system for automatic detection of suspicious lesions in breast DCE-MRI [8,9,10]; as client-side medical image tool we decided to support OsiriX [11], due to its powerful interface and since it has an open plug-in system.

The plug-in window (see Fig. 2) allow the user to send patient's data (selecting the required operation), to check in-service operation (with an estimation of the remaining time) and to gather the results.

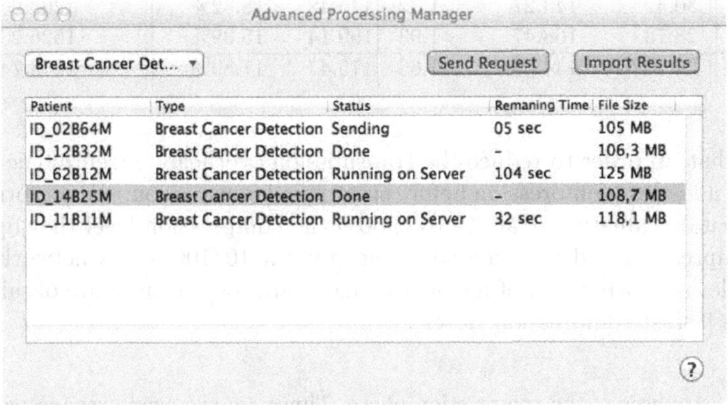

Fig. 2. The OsiriX plugin GUI

On the arrival of the results, jSecureSync alerts user by means of a pop-up. Clicking on the 'Import Results' button, the OsiriX 3D viewer interface is loaded and the automatically detected lesions are showed.

4 Testing

To verify the client-server architecture benefits in advanced medical images analysis, some preliminary testing was performed. Tab. 1 compares the total operation time, made up of both transmission time and server computational time, in the client-server architecture (a 2x Quad Core Xeon 3.0Ghz 32GB RAM has been used as server) with the time needed by the same operation when it is totally performed on a typical OsiriX workstation (Apple iMac with Intel Core 2 Duo 2.0 GHz with 3GB RAM).

Table 1. Performance comparation of remote computing time (including Client to Server transmission, image segmentation on the Server and Server to Client transmission) versus local computing time over ten patients

Patient ID	Remote Computing					Local Computing
	$C \to S$	Segmentation time	$S \to C$	Total time	Trasmission time	Segmentation time
p1	29.73	134.94	1.24	165.91	18.67%	1142.13
p2	28.34	158.48	2.04	188.85	16.09%	1322.21
p3	30.14	149.36	1.80	181.30	17.62%	1211.98
p4	30.27	115.48	1.55	147.30	21.60%	998.30
p5	31.32	148.99	1.65	181.96	18.11%	1223.94
p6	28.84	147.32	1.35	177.50	17.00%	1523.54
p7	29.71	152.82	1.81	184.35	17.10%	1342.35
p8	30.12	121.63	1.23	152.98	20.49%	1083.15
p9	30.42	143.27	1.72	175.42	18.32%	1263.65
p10	28.73	168.47	1.93	199.14	15.39%	1526.23
Average	29.76	144.08	1.63	175.47	17.89%	1263.74

Note that, in order to reduce the transmission overhead, JSecureSync always performs a lossless compression before starting a transmission. We performed an experimental evaluation (Tab. 2) to choose the compression level that optimize both compression and transmission time (over a 10/100 Mbps network). Due to the relevant correlation of medical images data, best results are obtained by using the fastest compression (level 1).

Table 2. Analysis of the compression phase. Times are averaged over ten patients.

Compression Level	Original Size (MB)	Compressed Size (MB)	Compression Ratio (%)	Compression Time (s)	Trasmission Time (s)
0 (Store)	111	111	0.00%	0.75	12.38
1 (Fastest)	111	34	69.36%	**3.47**	**3.82**
3 (Fast)	111	34	69.36%	3.55	3,76
5 (Normal)	111	32	70.85%	16.88	3.68
7 (Maximun)	111	31	71.66%	45.54	3.61
9 (Ultra)	111	31	72.12%	116.96	3.50

5 Discussion and Conclusions

In this work we have proposed a secure client-server architecture able to provide advanced medical images processing services at a low cost. In particular, we developed a plug-in for the OsiriX environment that can interact with a system for automatic detection of suspicious lesions in breast DCE-MRI.

In the proposed work the client only accomplishes simple tasks and asynchronously requests advanced medical images processing to the server. Server and client works are totally decoupled, allowing the server to upgrade or update hardware and/or algorithms, to add new functionalities, to improve results, and so on, without any alteration on the client. This results in a very versatile architecture.

The whole architecture is designed with a special focus on privacy and security, through a 128bit SSL/TLS cryptography system and unique X.509 standard digital certificate associated with a 3072bit RSA Key Pair, accordingly with the 2012 NIST recommendations.

Future works will focus on parameter optimizations (refresh time, symmetric/asymmetric compression), through real cases testing, and performance improvements (as distributed or GPU computing). A mobile version of the client will be also developed, to have an easy access and to smartly manage medical images. All operation could be requested from a mobile (phone, tablet) device and the results will be automatically synchronized with the workstation. We also would standardize the protocol of the presented architecture for modern medical image client-server applications, as a low-cost, secure, highly scalable and versatile architecture. Some improvements will be applied on the authentication phase, too. The adherence to the X.509 standard will allow certificates validation through a trusted third party Certification Authority. At last, a native auto-adaptive server-side architecture will be defined.

Acknowledgments. The authors are grateful to Dr. Antonella Petrillo, Head of Division of Radiology, Department of Diagnostic Imaging, Radiant and Metabolic Therapy, "Istituto Nazionale dei Tumori Fondazione G. Pascale"-IRCCS, Naples, Italy, for providing access to DCE-MRI data. Moreover, we would like to thank PhD Roberta Fusco, from the same institution, for useful discussions.

This work has been partially supported by the "SMART HEALTH – CLUSTER OSDH – SMART FSE – STAYWELL" project, funded by MIUR (Ministero dell'Istruzione, dell'Università e della Ricerca).

References

1. Scheinine, et al.: An Object-Oriented Client-Server System for Interactive Segmentation of Medical Images Using the Generalised Active Contours Model. In: VIII Mediterranean Conference on Medical and Biological Engineering and Computing, Medicon 1998 (1998)
2. Mayer, et al.: High performance medical image processing in client/server-environments. In: Comput. Methods Programs Biomed., pp. 207–217 (1999)

3. Sherif, et al.: The Development of a Client/Server Architecture for Standardized Medical Application Network Services. In: IEEE Symposium on Application-Specific Systems and Software Engineering and Technology (ASSET 1999), pp. 2–9 (1999)
4. Svantesson, D., Clarke, R.: Privacy and consumer risks in cloud computing. Computer Law and Security Review 26, 391–397 (2010)
5. Recommendation for KeyManagement Part 1: General (Revision 3). NIST Special Publication 800-57 (2012)
6. World Health Organization (WHO) Cancer, Fact Sheet N° 297 (retrieved January 2013)
7. Olsen, O., et al.: Cochrane review on screening for breast cancer with mammography. The Lancet 358(9290), 1340–1342 (2001)
8. Fusco, R., Sansone, M., Sansone, C., Petrillo, A.: Selection of Suspicious ROIs in Breast DCE-MRI. In: Maino, G., Foresti, G.L. (eds.) ICIAP 2011, Part I. LNCS, vol. 6978, pp. 48–57. Springer, Heidelberg (2011)
9. Fusco, R., Sansone, M., Sansone, C., Petrillo, A.: Segmentation and classification of breast lesions using dynamic and textural features in Dynamic Contrast Enhanced-Magnetic Resonance Imaging. In: Computer-Based Medical Systems, CBMS (2012)
10. Marrone, S., Piantadosi, G., Fusco, R., Petrillo, A., Sansone, M., Sansone, C.: Automatic lesion detection in breast DCE-MRI. In: Petrosino, A. (ed.) ICIAP 2013, Part II. LNCS, vol. 8157, pp. 359–368. Springer, Heidelberg (2013)
11. Rosset, A., et al.: OsiriX: An Open-Source Software for Navigating in Multidimensional DICOM Images. Journal of Digital Imaging 17(3), 205–216 (2004)
12. Java Authentication and Authorization Service (JAAS) Reference Guide.Oracle Corporation (retrieved May 22, 2012)
13. Recommendation for Pair-Wise Key Establishment Schemes Using Discrete Logarithm Cryptography. NIST, Special Publication 800-56A (2007)
14. Standards for efficient cryptography SEC 1: Elliptic Curve Cryptography, Certicom Research (2000)
15. RFC 3268 Advanced Encryption Standard (AES) Ciphersuites for Transport Layer Security (TLS), RFC 3268 (2002)
16. RFC 4492 Elliptic Curve Cryptography (ECC) Cipher Suites for Transport Layer Security (TLS), RFC 4492 (2006)

A Patient Centric Approach
for Modeling Access Control in EHR Systems

Angelo Esposito, Mario Sicuranza, and Mario Ciampi

National Research Council of Italy - Institute for High Performance
Computing and Networking (ICAR), Naples, Italy
{angelo.esposito,mario.sicuranza,mario.ciampi}@na.icar.cnr.it

Abstract. In EHR systems, most of the data are confidential concerning the
health of a patient. Therefore, it is necessary to provide a mechanism for access
control. This has not only to ensure the confidentiality and integrity of the data,
but also to allow the definition of security policies which reflect the need for
privacy of the patient who the documents refer to. In this paper we define a new
Access Control (AC) model for EHR systems, that allows the patient to define
access policies based on her/his need for privacy. Our model starts from the
RBAC model, and extends it by adding characteristics and components to manage the access policies in a simple and dynamic manner. It ensures patient privacy, and for this reason we refer to it as a patient-centric AC model.

Keywords: Access control model, privacy, EHR, patient consent, patient
centric.

1   Introduction

Electronic Health Record (EHR) systems enable the collection and sharing of electronic clinical maintained information about an individual's lifetime health status.

They provide a variety of high-level services that reduce medical errors and improve the quality of care. Iakovidis [2] defined an Electronic Health Record as "digi-
tally stored healthcare information about an individual's lifetime with the purpose of
supporting continuity of care, education and research, and ensuring confidentiality at
all times". The EHR system manages sensitive data, that should be protected from
unauthorized access. For this reason it is necessary to ensure the confidentiality of and
to guarantee the quality and integrity of the data. To meet the needs for integrity, confidentiality and quality of data a widely used mechanism is Access Control (AC). An
AC model for EHR systems should allow the definition of security policies that reflect the patients' needs for privacy. The European Data protection law [4] identifies
the needs of patients privacy, they must have the ability to know how to their documents are accessed by users who have access rights on them and also it specifying
that the management of access control must be more easily and quickly accessible in
cases of emergency, and confirming the property of purpose, whereby the data must
be used for the purposes indicated.

J. Kołodziej et al. (Eds.): ICA3PP 2013, Part II, LNCS 8286, pp. 225–232, 2013.
© Springer International Publishing Switzerland 2013

In literature, there are different access control models. Among these, the one most widely used for Health Information Systems [8, 9], is Role Based Access Control (RBAC) [1], which is based on the concept of the role to evaluate access to the objects on a system. Specifically, this model was standardized by NIST [5]. Unfortunately, the RBAC model does not fit well to the needs required by the EHR systems, because it is static and the association between roles, operations and objects being made upstream and being defined by the system. To have more flexibility Attribute-Based Access control (ABAC) has been introduced [6], a system that contemplates the use of additional attributes associated with the role. This model, however, does not offer privacy management to the patient either.

A model, which focuses on the need for definitions of policy related to the requirements of patient privacy, is the Privacy-Role Based Access Control Model (P-RBAC) [11]. This model is an extension of the RBAC model, in which not only the role and the permissions, that such a role has on the required object, are considered, but also the purpose of the access to the object and the defined privacy policies in compliance with the user's will. Each of these responds just partially to patients' needs for privacy, as most of them have limitations in the possibility of accurate and flexible management of the security policies. On the contrary the aim of our model is to obtain the maximum accordance between what the access policies allow us to define and what the patients want to define.

In this paper we define a new model to allow the patient to define access policies based on her/ his need for privacy. Our model starts from the RBAC model, and extends it by adding characteristics and components to manage the access policies in a simple and dynamic manner. It ensures patient privacy, and for this reason we refer to it as a patient-centric AC model. Another fundamental aspect taken into consideration in the definition of the model presented in this paper is the ability to manage access to clinical documents in emergency situations.

The paper is organized as follows. In Section 2 our model is presented. In Section 3 an AC flow chart using the proposed model is shown. Section 4 presents a possible scenario that highlights the features of the model. Section 5 concludes the paper and outlines some future work.

2   The Proposed Access Control Model

In this section we present our proposal, that extends the RBAC model to meet the needs of EHR systems for access control. In these systems, the patient plays a central role. Therefore, within the definition of the access control model, satisfying patient needs is of fundamental importance. Patients should be able to trust the system and should be able to specify the privacy associated to their documents.

An EHR system maintains a set of sensitive information related to a specific patient. Therefore, it is necessary that the data is accessible only to authorized subjects. In our solution, the patient-centric model, it is the patient who has full decision-making power in defining the security policy. The patients must be able to specify who can do what on their documents and must be able to change quickly and easily the rights of access. Furthermore, the patient must be able to hide her/his documents from specific healthcare practitioners previously granted the rights of access and to provide access to healthcare practitioners that had not been entitled to access the documents. Patients need to have the ability to know how their documents are accessed by users who have access rights on them, in accordance with the property of Disclosure, indicated by the related EU directive [4]. Our model extends the RBAC model with further components, in order to obtain a model attentive to the needs of the patients (privacy) and at the same time to allow emergency access, as with the BTG-RBAC [3]. The resulting model is an attribute-based solution, in the sense that it grants or denies access to certain operations depending not only on the role (as in the RBAC model) but also on other attributes. In our model, the attribute Purpose is particularly relevant, in that it indicates the intent of access to the document, and it allows us to satisfy patient privacy needs, as shown below. In Figure 1 the different model components and the relationships between them are shown: the components introduced in our model are colored in red; the others are taken from the RBAC standard model [16].

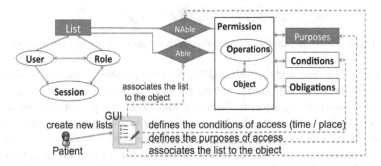

Fig. 1. - The proposed model. The components introduced in our model are colored. The figure shows how the patient interacts with the model.

The components introduced in our model are the **Purposes** Component, **List** Component, and *Able* and *NAble* relations. The first component that we propose is the **Purposes** component. The use of this element in the model allows a management in fine detail (compared to the RBAC model) of patient's privacy through the security policies. It allows also a faster handling in the case of access to the system in *Emergency* mode (when the access Purpose is "emergency"). It is possible with the use of the **Purposes** component, associated with a list of storing purposes, to ensure access to a document only for the purposes for which the document has been stored. Upon an access request to a document, the AC model checks if the access purpose is compatible with one of those for which the document is stored; otherwise, access is denied. In our model, the purpose management is hierarchical. An example of a purposes hierarchy in an EHR system is given in Figure 2. If the purpose associated with a document is *Medical Care*, this will automatically be associated with all the related leaf node purposes, for example *Specialist, Medical Check, Pathology* and *Dental Care*.

Finally, the **Purposes** component provides another important feature to the model, the possibility of preferential access in emergency situations. Indeed, in cases of emergency it is essential to ensure an "accelerated" access to documents. Our model implements the Break the Glass (BTG) function when the purpose of indicated access is "emergency". Break the Glass can be used in order to break or override the access controls in a controlled manner [3]. In fact, in the case of emergency access (the flow chart in Figure 4) some controls are bypassed. Auxiliary Functions are associated with the model which allow the patient to access the **Purposes** component in order to associate storage purposes to her/his documents or disassociate the purposes previously entered.

Fig. 2. Shows an example of a possible purposes hierarchy in an EHR system

The **List** component, and the *Able* and *NAble* relations give the patient the opportunity to manage the privacy of her/his documents in an accurate manner. In fact, through them (and through the appropriate Auxiliary Functions) the patient may associate to each of her/his documents a set of roles/users lists for which access is granted, and/or a set of roles/users lists for which access is denied. The patient can define her/his own lists, each containing a set of roles and/or users, and for a given document each list, defined by the patient, may be associated with the relations *Able* or *Nable*. The relation *Able* grants access to the document; instead, the relation *NAble* denies access.

The definition of our model includes several Auxiliary Functions Model, which are used, via interfaces or GUI, by the patient in order to use the various components of the model for a simple management of privacy. The patient through an interface can easily manage the privacy of her/his documents by:

- Creating a new list of users/roles
- Associating a list of authorized users/roles to a specific document
- Associating a list of users/roles that are not authorized for access to a specific document.
- Associating storage purposes to a specific document (see Figure 3)

Creating a New List of Users/Roles: With the auxiliary function model "creating a new list of users/roles", the patient is able to create a list of subjects in the system, identified by an ID or by the role. If the patient specifies a particular role in the list, this means that all the subjects that play that role in the system are part of the list. The auxiliary function uses the **List** component.

Associating a list of authorized users/roles to a specific document: With this aux-iliary function the patient is able to associate a previously created List to a specific document to provide the access right to subjects in that list. The function uses the relation *Able.*

Associating a list of not authorized users/roles to a specific document: With this auxiliary function the patient is able to associate a previously created List to a specific document with the relation *Nable.* In this way the set of subjects in the list will not have the right of access. The function uses the relation *NAble.*

Associating storage purposes to a specific document: With this auxiliary function, the patient can add storage purposes to the document. The function uses the compo-nent **Purposes.**

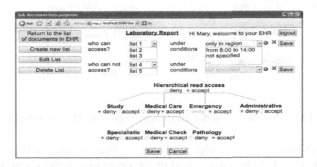

Fig. 3. Link document-lists-purposes

In Figure 1 the RBAC components and our model components are shown (our model components are colored). There are also interactions between the patient and the components, which occur via the auxiliary functionality presented above, in order to make privacy management simple for the patients.

3   A Flow Chart of the Model

In this section, we present a flow chart that regulates the management of an AC that uses our model. The AC allows or denies the access to an object on the basis of the inputs that it receives. The inputs are:

- **The Object identifier** which is the identifier of the clinical document in the EHR system, to which access is required;
- **The User identifier** is the identifier of the subject who requires access to the object;
- **The Role** which is the role associated with the user in the EHR system;
- **The Operation** is the action required on the object and
- **The Access purpose** is the purpose for which an object is accessed.

A description of the functions used in the flow chart is provided below and illustrated in Figure 4.

- *The checkinEmergency(object, role) function* first checks that the requested document is compatible with the emergency purpose (via **Purposes**); if so, it returns *true*, otherwise *false*. This function allows faster controls in the case of an emergency, providing a sort of Break the Glass AC model [3]. In fact, there is no cross checking of the object-list-operation, but the check occurs directly through **Purposes**. Furthermore, the constraint conditions are relaxed (these are expressed by **Condition**). Obviously, the operations in emergency mode are associated with **Obligations**, such as storage in logger, access information to the document and other obligations.

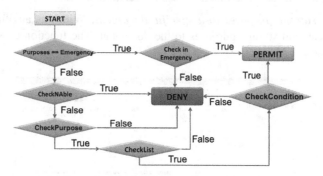

Fig. 4. - Flow Chart that regulates the management of an AC that uses our model

- *The checkNAble(user, role, object, operation) function* checks if the role/user is present in the *NAble* lists associated to the operation on the given document. If she/he/it is on these lists, the system returns deny.
- *The checkPurpose(Access Purpose, object, operation) function* checks if the specified access purpose is in compliance with the purposes associated to the document and the operation requested. If the check is successful, the function returns *true*.
- *The checklist(user, role, object, operation) function* checks whether the user or the user role is included in the lists associated to the object for the specified operation. If so, the function returns true.
- *The checkCondition(operation, object) function* retrieves the list of access conditions associated with the specific operation request. Next, it checks the compatibility of access in accordance with the conditions expressed in the **Conditions** component. For example, it is possible to specify additional access restrictions, related to temporal or geographical conditions.

The proposed model is extremely dynamic and simple for the handling of customized access policies. The patient can easily indicate who has access to a certain health document contained in the EHR system, when (via **Condition**) and for which purposes.

4   A Running Scenario

As previously argued in this paper, the model allows a simple and dynamic management of privacy through the **List** (*Able*, *NAble*) and **Purposes** components. For each document stored in the EHR the following information are associated:

(i) lists of users/roles authorized to access; (ii) lists of users/roles that are not authorized to access; (iii) list of hierarchical storage purposes (as in Figure 5).

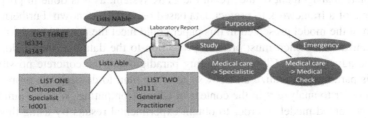

Fig. 5. Document and associated information in EHR System

Suppose that the document to which a user makes a request to access is "Laboratory Report" (Figure 5), characterized by the following properties:

- Lists *Able* associated: List One consisting of role Orthopedic Specialist, and user id001; List Two consisting of role General Practitioner and user id111.
- List *NAble* associated: List Three consisting of users id334 and id343.
- Set of *stored purposes*: Study, Specialist, Medical Check, Emergency.

Let us consider the following three scenarios where a "Laboratory Report" document is requested:

- *Scenario 1:* Supposing that an orthopedist with ID equal to Id005 requests the access the document for a medical check purpose (the access purposes is Medical Check), he/she will obtain a grant to access the document, since he/she is includes in the list one (*Able* users) and the access purpose is compatible with the stored purpose.
- *Scenario 2:* If the access request is performed by an orthopedist with id equal to Id334 with a scope of medical check, the AC model denies the access to the document since the user ID is contained in the *NAble* list.
- *Scenario 3*: Let us assume that an orthopedist with ID equal to Id334 tries to access to the document within the contest of an emergency (access purpose is emergency) then, the AC model returns the grant because the access purpose is Emergency, by behaving like the BTG-RBAC [3].

5   Discussion and Conclusions

In this paper we have introduced a new Access Control model for EHR systems. In fact, we have started from the RBAC model, and extended it by adding characteristics and components to enable the patient to manage in a simple and dynamic manner the access policies (via the **List** component). The AC patient-centric model introduced in this paper changes the role of the patient in the management of security policies in an EHR system. In this way, we have obtained a management of an EHR system similar to the one typically used for the Personal Health Record (PHR), where the patient plays a key role, as he/she is directly responsible for the management of health information. This model opens up possible scenarios of research of an AC model for EHR and PHR systems. A possible evolution of the work is to define a framework for complete management of the AC in the EHR system, as it is done in [10], where an example of a framework to protect data based on an AC is shown. Furthermore, an evolution of the model presented in this paper could meet the privacy needs of health-care organizations, which must provide protection to the data that they hold. Considering the advent of the Cloud Computing paradigm and the concrete possibility of using this paradigm to realize an EHR system, we plan to develop the proposed AC model in order to analyze it in the context of Cloud Computing. We also aim to validate the presented model in order to obtain experimental results by using this model for access control in the EHR system in an XACML architecture.

Acknowledgments. The work reported in this paper has been partially supported by the project "Evoluzione e interoperabilita' tecnologica del Fascicolo Sanitario Elettronico", Agreement DDI-CNR, 18 June 2012, Prot. AMMCNT-CNR N. 53060, 31/08/12.References

References

1. Ferraiolo, D.F., Cugini, J., Kuhn, D.R.: Role-Based Access Control (RBAC): Features and Motivations. In: Proceedings of the 11th Annual Computer Security Application Conference, New Orleans, LA, December 11-15, pp. 241–248 (1995)
2. Iakovidis, I.: Towards Personal Health Record: "Current Situation, Obstacles and Trends in Implementation of Electronic Healthcare Record in Europe". International Journal of Medical Informatics 52(1-3), 105–115 (1998)
3. Ferreira, A., Chadwick, D., Farinha, P., Correia, R., Zao, G., Chilro, R., Antunes, L.: How to Securely Break into RBAC: The BTG-RBAC Model. In: Annual Computer Security Applications Conference, ACSAC 2009, pp. 23–31, 7–11 (2009)
4. http://ec.europa.eu/justice/data-protection/document/review2012/com_2012_11_en.pdf
5. Sandhu, R., Ferraiolo, D.F., Kuhn, D.R.: The NIST Model for Role Based Access Control: Toward a Unified Standard. In: Postscript PDF Proceedings of the 5th ACM Workshop on Role Based Access Control, Berlin, July 26-27, pp. 47–63 (2000)
6. Kuhn, D.R., Coyne, E.J., Weil, T.R.: Adding Attributes to Role-Based Access Control. Computer 43(6), 79–81 (2010), doi:10.1109/MC.2010.155
7. Haux, R.: Health information systems - past, present, future. Int. J. Med. Inform. 75(3-4), 268–281 (2006)
8. Sicuranza, M., Ciampi, M., De Pietro, G., Esposito, C.: Secure Medical Data Sharing among Federated Health Information Systems. To be printed in the International Journal of Critical Computer-Based Systems (in press, 2013)
9. Ciampi, M., De Pietro, G., Esposito, C., Sicuranza, M., Donzelli, P.: On federating Health Information Systems. In: 2012 International Conference on Green and Ubiquitous Technology (GUT), July 7-8, pp. 139–143 (2012), doi:10.1109/GUT.2012.6344168
10. Amato, F., Casola, V., Mazzocca, N., Romano, S.: A semantic-based document processing framework: a security perspective. In: 2011 International Conference on Complex, Intelligent and Software Intensive Systems (CISIS), pp. 197–202. IEEE (2011)
11. Kim, Y., Song, E.: Privacy-Aware Role Based Access Control Model: Revisited for Multi-Policy Conflict Detection. In: ICISA 2010 International Conference, April 21-23, pp. 1–7 (2010)

A Privacy Preserving Matchmaking Scheme for Multiple Mobile Social Networks

Yong Wang, Hong-zong Li, Ting-Ting Zhang, and Jie Hou

School of Computer Science and Engineering
University of Electronic Science and Technology of China, 611731
Chengdu, China
cla@uestc.edu.cn

Abstract. Mobile social networks (MSNs) enable users to discover and interact with existing and potential friends in both the cyberspace and in the real world. Although mobile social network applications bring us much convenience, privacy concerns become the key security issue affecting their wide applications. In this paper, we propose a novel hybrid privacy preserving matchmaking scheme, which can help users to find their friends without disclosing their private information from multiple MSNs. Specifically, a user (called initiator) can find his best-matches among the candidates and exchange common attributes with them. However, other candidates only know the size of the common attributes with the initiator. The simulation results indicate that our scheme has a good performance and scalability.

Keywords: privacy preserving, matchmaking protocol, mobile social network, homomorphic encryption.

1 Introduction

With the popularity of personal hand-held mobile devices (e.g., smart phones and PDAs), mobile users can access plenty of Internet services, which brings convenience to users and improves social relationships. Mobile Social Networks (MSNs) provide ad-hoc networking functionality through the Internet, which enables mobile users to search and manage friends, build friendship connectivity, and further disseminate, query and share interesting data sources among them.

Matchmaking can help users to discover and make friends with others who share common attributes (e.g., interests). However, these applications raise a number of privacy concerns [1]. For example, if users' private attributes are directly exchanged with each other, the adversaries may easily collect users' personal information in either active or passive ways, which may be exploited for unauthorized purposes. To protect users' private information, it is essential to make sure that only the minimal personal information is disclosed during the matchmaking process and that the disclosure only goes to as few users as possible.

J. Kołodziej et al. (Eds.): ICA3PP 2013, Part II, LNCS 8286, pp. 233–240, 2013.
© Springer International Publishing Switzerland 2013

In this paper, we propose a novel privacy preserving matchmaking scheme for multiple mobile social networks, which adopts a hybrid architecture to reduce the burden of servers and satisfy certain security requirements. Our matchmaking protocol is based on the polynomial evaluation, which consists of two phases: (1) finding the best matches among numerous users; (2) exchanging the common attributes with them. Homomorphic encryption and (t, w)-Shamir Secret Sharing Scheme [2] are used to guarantee private computation of intersection set. The experimental results indicate the effectiveness of our matchmaking scheme.

2   Related Work

The core component of a matchmaking system is the matchmaking protocol. A matchmaking issue can be described as a private set intersection (PSI) problem or a private cardinality of set intersection (PCSI) problem [1]. A huge body of research have been done on PSI protocols and PCSI protocols, which can be classified into three categories:

In [3], Freedman et al. proposed a PSI protocol which is based on polynomial evaluation for the first time. The homomorphic encryption and balanced hashing are used to guarantee private computation of intersection set. However, the protocol is one way, that is, only the client knows the intersection set while the server knows nothing. So the protocol cannot be used in a distributed environment. Later, Kissner et al. [4] achieved a two-way privacy preserving intersection computation on multisets by employing the mathematic properties of polynomials. Ye et al. [5] extended the scheme proposed in [3] to a distributed private matching scheme by using a secret sharing scheme.

Agrawal et al. [6] proposed a protocol which takes the power function $f(x) = x^e \bmod n$ as communicative encryption and achieves linear complexity. However, it is a one-way protocol and doesn't take the defense to malicious attacks into consideration. Xie et al. [7] revised the protocol to defend against malicious attacks. A two-party PSI protocol in game-theoretic setting using crypto-graphic primitives is built in [8]. Commutative encryption is used as the underlying cryptographic primitive.

Freedman et al. [9] proposed the idea of constructing a set intersection protocol from the oblivious pseudo-random function(OPRF). Revisiting this idea, Hazay et al. [10] utilized specific properties of the Naor-Reingold PRF in order to achieve high efficiency in the presence of both semi-honest and malicious models. Recently, Jarecki et al. [11] presented a very efficient protocol for computing a pseudo random function with a committed key (informally, this means that the same key is used in all invocations), leading to an efficient PSI protocol.

Since most previous protocols are two-way, i.e., both two parties can obtained their intersection set at the end of protocol. Directly applying them to the matchmaking problem may lead to the leak of unnecessary attributes information. We propose a two-phase matchmaking protocol based on polynomial evaluation, which only allows the best-matched users exchange their common attributes with the initiator mutually.

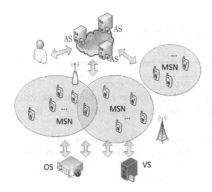 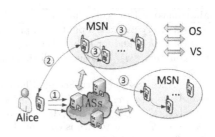

Fig. 1. System architecture

Fig. 2. Procedure of our matchmaking scheme

3 System Design

The system is designed to help a user (called initiator) find his best-matches among multi-parties(called candidates) from multiple MSNs, where the best-match means the user who shares at least ω (a threshold set by the initiator) attributes with the initiator.

3.1 System Architecture

Our matchmaking system consists of four components as shown in Fig. 1.

1) *Mobile users*: Including the initiator and a group of users from different MSNs, each of whom possesses a set of attributes.

2) *The Verification Server* (VS): Which is used to manage users' public keys and attributes information, deal with the deception cases. To initialize a user's identity and attributes, the VS assigns an identity certificate to him and signs his polynomial coefficients created by his attributes. In our matchmaking protocol, system distributes signed identity certificate (ID) to users (e.g., Alice). Each user sends his public key and encrypted polynomial coefficients (we compactly represent them as $\varepsilon_{pk}(P(y))$) to the VS. Then the VS signs $\varepsilon_{pk}(P(y))$ and returns $sign_{vs}(ID\|\varepsilon_{pk}(P(y)))$ to the user.

3) *The Online Server* (OS): Where mobile users can register their public attributes sets and friend lists.

4) *The Anchor Servers* (ASs): Which are semi-honest, having two basic functions: participating in the calculations to reduce the client-side computational burden and detecting malicious attacks.

3.2 Matchmaking Protocol

Fig. 2 shows the procedure of our matchmaking scheme.

Stage 1: Each user distributes his attribute set to w ASs using (t, w)-Shamir Secret Sharing Scheme, where the correctness of each share is publicly verifiable.

Table 1. Computation of $|A \cap B|$

Matchmaking Protocol: Phase 1

Setup: Every user has a public and private key pair (ε, D) for encryption. For Alice, it is (pk_A, sk_A) and for Bob, it is (pk_B, sk_B). Each AS_l also has a public and private key pair (pk_l, sk_l). Each user will do step a)-d). For future reference, we do it for Alice.

a).   Alice uses (t, w)-Secret Sharing scheme to distribute her attributes set $A = \{a_1, a_2, \ldots, a_n\}$ to w ASs verifiably, where the verification vector $\langle \{A_{0,i}\}_{i=0}^n, \{A_{1,i}\}_{i=0}^n, \ldots, \{A_{t-1,i}\}_{i=0}^n \rangle$ is broadcast in item c) and the share $(\beta_{\ell,0}, \cdots, \beta_{\ell,n})$ sent to AS_l is encrypted using pk_l. Note $(\beta_{\ell,0}, \cdots, \beta_{\ell,n})$ is the vector of coefficients of $F_l(y)$.

b). $\varepsilon_{pk_A}(P(y))$ has been registered at VS who returns a certificate $cert_A = sign_{vs}(Alice \| \varepsilon_{pk_A}(P(y)))$ to Alice.

c).   Alice authentically broadcasts the following to w ASs:
(I) $cert_A = sign_{vs}(Alice \| \varepsilon_{pk_A}(P(y)))$
(II) $\langle \{A_{0,i}\}_{i=0}^n, \{A_{1,i}\}_{i=0}^n, \ldots, \{A_{t-1,i}\}_{i=0}^n \rangle$
(III) $\{pk_A, \{\varepsilon_{pk_A}(a_1), \varepsilon_{pk_A}(a_1{}^2), \ldots, \varepsilon_{pk_A}(a_1{}^\tau)\}, \ldots, \{\varepsilon_{pk_A}(a_n), \varepsilon_{pk_A}(a_n{}^2), \ldots, \varepsilon_{pk_A}(a_n{}^\tau)\}\}$

(where τ is an upper bound of a user's attribute set size) together with a non-interactive zero-knowledge (NIZK)[1] σ that makes sure (II)(III) and $\varepsilon_{pk_A}(P(y))$ in (I) contain the same attribute set A.

d).   Alice takes $\gamma_i \xleftarrow{R} \mathbb{Z}_q^*$ and a random key ζ for a pseudorandom function Φ. She then uses authenticated broadcast encryption [12] to send $(\{\gamma_i\}_1^m, \zeta)$ to w ASs.

Assume Alice is an initiator who wishes to carry out matchmaking with Bob. Let $B = \{b_1, \cdots, b_m\}$ be Bob's attribute set. In the protocol below, symbols defined in Alice's setup are only w.r.t. her (if not exclusively defined, e.g., ζ). For Bob, only c(III) in his setup will be used in the protocol: $\{pk_B, \{\varepsilon_{pk_B}(b_1), \varepsilon_{pk_B}(b_1{}^2), \ldots, \varepsilon_{pk_B}(b_1{}^\tau)\}, \ldots, \{\varepsilon_{pk_B}(b_m), \varepsilon_{pk_B}(b_m{}^2), \ldots, \varepsilon_{pk_B}(b_m{}^\tau)\}\}$. So there is no conflict in symbols in the following for Alice and Bob.

Step 1: Alice requests Bob to compute the number of common attributes.

Step 2: Upon receiving Alice's request, Bob asks t selected ASs $AS_{l_1}, \ldots, AS_{l_t}$ to help.

Step 3: Let $\pi = \Phi_\zeta(Alice, Bob)$ be an encoding of a (pseudo) random permutation on $\{1, \cdots, m\}$. For $j = 1, \ldots, t$, AS_{l_j} uses Alice's setup and Bob's setup c(III) to do:
(a) for $i = 1, \ldots, m$, computes $\varepsilon_{pk_B}(F_{l_j}(b_i)) = \varepsilon_{pk_B}(1)^{\beta_{0,l_j}} \cdot \varepsilon_{pk_B}(b_i)^{\beta_{1,l_j}} \cdot \ldots \cdot \varepsilon_{pk_B}(b_i{}^n)^{\beta_{n,l_j}}$.
(b)   runs $\pi(\varepsilon_{pk_B}(\gamma_1 F_{l_j}(b_1)), \ldots, \varepsilon_{pk_B}(\gamma_m F_{l_j}(b_m)))$ to   get $(\varepsilon_{pk_B}(\gamma_{\pi(1)} F_{l_j}(b_{\pi(1)})), \ldots, \varepsilon_{pk_B}(\gamma_{\pi(m)} F_{l_j}(b_{\pi(m)})))$ and sends it to Bob.

Step 4: Let $S = 0$. For $i = 1, \ldots, m$, Bob:
(a) for $j = 1, \ldots, t$, computes $u_{\pi(i),j} \leftarrow D_{sk_B}(\varepsilon_{pk_B}(\gamma_{\pi(i)} F_{l_j}(b_{\pi(i)})))$.
(b) computes $g^{\gamma_{\pi(i)} F(0, b_{\pi(i)})} \leftarrow \prod_{j=1}^t (u_{\pi(i),j})^{c_j}$, where c_j is appropriate coefficient in
Lagrange interpolation for F.
(c) updates $S = S + 1$, if $g^{\gamma_{\pi(i)} F(0, b_{\pi(i)})} = 1$.
Finally, If $S \geq \omega$ (supposedly, $S = A \cap B$), ω is the threshold set by Alice, Bob sends S to Alice.

Stage 2: The initiator (e.g., Alice) broadcasts a matchmaking request to her friends, sets a TTL (Time To Live) on the request packet to determine the hops that the request can be forwarded in the MSNs.

Stage 3: When receiving Alice's request, a receiver will perform the matchmaking protocol (table 1 and 2, starting from step 2 and playing the role of Bob) with Alice. After this, he will randomly forward Alice's request to his friends. This stage will recursively repeat until TTL of the packet decreases to zero.

Table 2. Computation of $A \cap B$

Matchmaking Protocol: Phase 2 (only if $S \geq \omega$)
Step 5: Alice sends $cert_A = sign_{vs}(Alice \| \{\varepsilon_{pk_A}(\nu_0), \varepsilon_{pk_A}(\nu_1), ..., \varepsilon_{pk_A}(\nu_n)\})$ to Bob. $\{v_j\}_{j=0}^n$ is the polynomial coefficients that represent $P(y)$.
Step 6: For $i = 1, ..., m$, Bob computes
(a) $\varepsilon_{pk_A}(P(b_i)) = \varepsilon_{pk_A}(v_0) \cdot \varepsilon_{pk_A}(v_1)^{b_i} \cdot ... \cdot \varepsilon_{pk_A}(v_n)^{b_i^n}$.
(b) $\varepsilon_{pk_A}(\lambda_i' P(b_i) + b_i) = \varepsilon_{pk_A}(P(b_i))^{\lambda_i'} \cdot \varepsilon_{pk_A}(b_i)$ and sends $\varepsilon_{pk_A}(\lambda_i' P(b_i) + b_i)$ to Alice, where λ_i' is random in Z_q^*.
Step 7: Let $E = \emptyset$. For $i = 1, ..., m$, Alice computes $\rho_i \leftarrow D_{sk_A}(\varepsilon_{pk_A}(\lambda_i' P(b_i) + b_i))$. If $\rho_i \in A$, then adds b_i into E. Finally (supposedly, $E = A \cap B$), if $S = |E|$, Alice sends π to Bob, otherwise reject.
Step 8: (a) If Bob received π, he finds $\pi(i)$ such that $g^{\gamma_{\pi(i)} F(0, b_{\pi(i)})} = 1$. Set this collection of $b_{\pi(i)}$ as $A \cap B$.
(b) If Alice refuses to send π, Bob sends the following to $\{AS_{l_j}\}_{j=1}^t$:
(i) NIZK proof σ_1 that B used in Step 6 is identical to that encrypted in his setup c(III), where the witness is $\{b_i\}_1^m$, $\{\lambda_i'\}_{i=1}^m$ and randomness of ciphertexts at his setup c(III).
(ii) NIZK proof σ_2 that step 4 (b) is computed correctly, using witness sk_B.
Upon σ_1, σ_2, AS_{l_j} verifies their validity and checks if $S = \sharp$ of i's s.t. $\prod_{j=1}^t (u_{\pi(i),j})^{c_j} (= g^{\gamma_{\pi(i)} F(0, b_{\pi(i)})}) = 1$. If all checks pass, then AS_{l_j} sends his share $F_{l_j}(y)$ to Bob. Bob then computes $F(0, y)$ himself and evaluates $F(0, b_i)$ to obtain $A \cap B$.
Note, in step 8(b), if Bob is honest, Alice will leak more information (i.e., $F(0, y)$) than sending π to Bob; if Bob is dishonest, Lemma 4 shows that he can not pass step 8(i)(ii) and hence his disclaim is useless. So we can assume step 8(b) never occurs.

The matchmaking protocol proposed in our scheme contains two phases. Phase 1 is to find the best-matches among numerous candidates. Phase 2 is to exchange the shared attribute set with the best-matches. At the end of phase 1, each candidate can obtain the size of shared attribute set while the initiator knows nothing. Only if a candidate becomes a best match, he will send the shared attribute set size to the initiator. At the end of phase 2, the initiator and each best-match will learn their shared attribute set mutually. Phase 1 of our matchmaking protocol is shown in table 1 and phase 2 is shown in table 2. In both phase 1 and 2, we assume the authentication of each message is guaranteed with the signature from the sender.

3.3 Malicious Detection

Extremely, suppose a participant has only one attribute, then he can learn whether the only attribute is in the initiator's attributes set. To avoid this scan attack, ASs provide a malicious detection mechanism. In phase 1, ASs set a threshold value μ to filter out the users whose attributes are less than μ (e.g., μ can be set as the smallest attributes known by AS). Every user's records at ASs, VS can be updated every moderate long period. This prevents some malicious users to update frequently so as to localize a user's attribute set.

3.4 Computation Cost

The setup contains authenticated broadcast (encryption) and NIZK proof and hence is inefficient. However, this is executed once and will be updated after a long time. It does not affect the efficiency of the matchmaking procedure. Further, NIZK for Bob's disclaim procedure can be assumed to never occur as no one can gain from it. Following this, we can conclude that our matchmaking (steps 1-8) is efficient. If ε is ElGamal encryption [13], then in phase 1, it needs $2m(n+1)$ exps for each AS, $2tm$ exps for Bob; in phase 2, it needs $2(n+1)m$ exps for Bob (note the step 8 only can be obtained by de-permutated the result in step 4 and hence cost is negligible) and m exps for Alice. So we can see that our scheme is reasonably efficient.

4   Simulation and Evaluation

In this section, we evaluate the performance of our matchmaking scheme, the two evaluating metrics are:

1) *Hit rate (Hr)*: Hr is calculated as:

$$Hr = {\phi}/{\kappa},$$

where κ is the number of the users in the whole network, whose intersection size with the initiator reach the threshold value ω, ϕ is the actual number of the best-matches found by the initiator. Hr indicates the percentage of users can be successfully matched using our scheme.

2) *Message overhead (Mo)*: The messages in our scheme are classified into matchmaking messages and delivery messages. The matchmaking messages are those necessary for carrying out phase 1 and phase 2 protocols. The delivery messages are those responsible for forwarding requests in our scheme. Mo is defined as the ratio between the bits number for all delivery messages and that for the whole messages.

We implement our scheme in PeerSim simulator [14]. We select six samples (Sample-1–Sample-6) from Epinions social network datasets which have 574, 977, 1444, 2520, 3613, and 5341 nodes with the average degree 8.52, 11.9, 16.2, 21.1, 23.2, and 26.4 respectively [15]. We choose a prime p of length 1024 bits

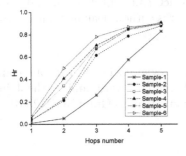 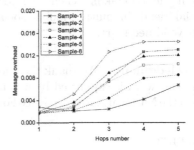

Fig. 3. *Hr* vs. message forwarding hops **Fig. 4.** Message overhead vs. hops number

and use the variant of ElGamal with a modulus length of 1024 bits. Each attribute is represented by 32 bits. We simulate the protocol on 4 PCs, with 1.5 GHz processor and 2G RAM. In order to get more accurate executing time, we repeated each experiments 20 times. The transmission delays are randomly set to be 50-100ms, and the delay of message processing is fixed to be 150ms. Each user has 20 attributes. The threshold value ω is 10. The number of ASs is 3.

The Fig. 3 results show that *Hr* rises to 0.80 averagely when hops number is 4, which indicate that the initiator can find about 80% of his best-matches in the network. Note that Sample-1 has lower *Hr* because of the network scale and connection density, which implies that our scheme may work well under the large-user-based environments. Generally, 3 hops would satisfy users' needs (more than 60% of best-matches can be found except the Sample-1).

The message overhead of our matchmaking scheme is shown in Fig. 4. The message overhead is less than 0.01, i.e., more than 99.9% message contents are used purely for attributes matchmaking. With the hops number increasing, because of the rises of forwarded requested messages, the message overhead also increases. On the other hand, Fig. 4 indicates that the network topological properties affect the message overhead dramatically, the experiments on the six samples show different message overhead variations. The larger and denser the network is, the more overhead messages are needed, which indicate that our scheme may spend more extra energy on large-user-based networks.

The experimental results show the efficiency and scalability of our matchmaking scheme. To find best-matches among a large number of users, the initiator doesn't need to be involved in phase 1. That is, when she sends her request to her friends, she only waits for the responses coming from the best-matches, which can improve user's experience.

5   Conclusion

Matchmaking helps users find their potential friends, but raises serious privacy issues. It is important to develop protocols and schemes to preserving users' privacy in such application scenarios. In this paper, we present a hybrid privacy preserving matchmaking scheme for MSNs, which can help users to find their potential friends in multiple mobile social networks without leaking their private data beyond necessary.

Acknowledgments. We thank the anonymous reviewers for their helpful comments. This work is supported by a SafeNet Research Award, and by the Joint Funds of the National Natural Science Foundation of China (Grant No.U1230106).

References

1. Li, M., Cao, N., Yu, S., Lou, W.: FindU: Privacy-Preserving Personal Profile Matching in Mobile Social Networks. In: Proc. of Infocom 2011 (2011)
2. Shamir, A.: How to Share a Secret. Communications of the ACM 22(11), 612–613 (1979)
3. Freedman, M.J., Nissim, K., Pinkas, B.: Efficient Private Matching and Set Intersection. In: Cachin, C., Camenisch, J.L. (eds.) EUROCRYPT 2004. LNCS, vol. 3027, pp. 1–19. Springer, Heidelberg (2004)
4. Kissner, L., Song, D.: Privacy-Preserving Set Operations. In: Shoup, V. (ed.) CRYPTO 2005. LNCS, vol. 3621, pp. 241–257. Springer, Heidelberg (2005)
5. Ye, Q., Wang, H., Pieprzyk, J.: Distributed Private Matching and Set Operations. In: Chen, L., Mu, Y., Susilo, W. (eds.) ISPEC 2008. LNCS, vol. 4991, pp. 347–360. Springer, Heidelberg (2008)
6. Agrawal, R., Evfimievski, A., Srikant, R.: Information Sharing Across Private Databases. In: Proc. of SIGMOD, pp. 86–97 (2003)
7. Xie, Q., Hengartner, U.: Privacy-Preserving Matchmaking for Mobile Social Networking Secure Against Malicious Users. In: Proc. 9th Int'l. Conf. on Privacy, Security, and Trust (PST 2011), pp. 252–259 (2011)
8. Rahman, M., Miyaji, A.: Private Two-Party Set Intersection Protocol in Rational Model. Journal of Internet Services and Information Security (JISIS) 2(1/2), 93–104 (2012)
9. Freedman, M., Ishai, Y., Pinkas, B., Reingold, O.: Keyword Search and Oblivious Pseudorandom Functions. In: Kilian, J. (ed.) TCC 2005. LNCS, vol. 3378, pp. 303–324. Springer, Heidelberg (2005)
10. Hazay, C., Lindell, Y.: Efficient Protocols for Set Intersection and Pattern Matching with Security Against Malicious and Covert Adversaries. In: Canetti, R. (ed.) TCC 2008. LNCS, vol. 4948, pp. 155–175. Springer, Heidelberg (2008)
11. Jarecki, S., Liu, X.: Efficient Oblivious Pseudorandom Function with Applications to Adaptive OT and Secure Computation of Set Intersection. In: Reingold, O. (ed.) TCC 2009. LNCS, vol. 5444, pp. 577–594. Springer, Heidelberg (2009)
12. Fiat, A., Naor, M.: Broadcast Encryption. In: Stinson, D.R. (ed.) CRYPTO 1993. LNCS, vol. 773, pp. 480–491. Springer, Heidelberg (1994)
13. Elgamal, T.: A Public Key Cryptosystem and a Signature Scheme Based on Discrete Logarithms. IEEE Transactions on Information Theory IT-31(4), 469–472 (1985)
14. PeerSim: A Peer-to-Peer Simulator (July 23, 2011), http://peersim.sourceforge.net/
15. Stanford Network Analysis Platform (July 23, 2011), http://snap.stanford.edu/data/soc-Epinions1.html

Measuring Trust in Big Data

Massimiliano Albanese

George Mason University, Fairfax, VA 22030, USA
malbanes@gmu.edu

Abstract. The huge technological progress we have witnessed in the last decade has enabled us to generate data at an unprecedented rate, leading to what has become the era of big data. However, big data is not just about generating, storing, and retrieving massive amounts of data. The focus should rather be on new analytical approaches that would enable us to extract actionable intelligence from this ocean of data. From a security standpoint, one of the main issues that need to be addressed is the trustworthiness of each source or piece of information. In this paper, we propose an approach to assess and quantify the trust level of both information sources and information items. Our approach leverages the vast literature on citation ranking, and we clearly show the benefits of adapting citation ranking mechanisms to this new domain, both in terms of scalability and in terms of quality of the results.

1 Introduction

The technological progress we have witnessed in the last decade, in areas such as consumer electronics and cloud computing, has enabled us to generate and store data at an unprecedented rate, leading to what has become the era of big data. Such massive amounts of data have created new challenges in the area of information retrieval and in several other related areas [1]. However, big data is not just about generating, storing, and retrieving massive amounts of data. The focus should rather be on new analytical approaches that would enable us to extract actionable intelligence from this ocean of data and make sense of it.

From a security standpoint, one of the main issues that need to be addressed is the trustworthiness of each source or piece of information. The approach presented in this paper aims at assessing the trust level of both information sources and information items in a large data collection by leveraging the collective intelligence latent in the data and computing a *global ranking* of all the data objects or information sources. Therefore, the objective is to evaluate trust on a relative, rather than absolute, scale. Our approach leverages the vast literature on citation ranking, which has the primary goal of aggregating the judgments of a multitude of agents in order to assess the reputation of each element of a given collection. We show the benefits of adapting citation ranking mechanisms to this new domain, both in terms of scalability and in terms of quality of the results.

The paper is organized as follows. Section 2 discusses related work, whereas Section 3 introduces some technical preliminaries. Then Section 4 discusses how

J. Kołodziej et al. (Eds.): ICA3PP 2013, Part II, LNCS 8286, pp. 241–248, 2013.
© Springer International Publishing Switzerland 2013

citation ranking can be adapted to asses the relative trustworthiness of elements in a large data collection. Finally, Section 5 gives some concluding remarks.

2   Related Work

The precursor of any citation ranking approach is the *theory of social choice* as formulated by Arrow [2]. Google's *PageRank algorithm* [6] is probably the best known and most successful application of citation ranking, and the *power method* for PageRank computation [4] makes it extremely efficient.

In the classical theory of social choice, as formulated by Arrow, a set of *voters* (or *agents*) are called to rank a set of alternatives. Given the voters' individual rankings, a social ranking of the alternatives is generated. The theory studies desired properties of the aggregation of individual rankings into a social ranking. Arrow's impossibility theorem shows that there is no aggregation rule that satisfies some minimal requirements, while, by relaxing any of these requirements, appropriate social aggregation rules can be defined.

The novel feature of ranking systems is that the set of agents and the set of alternatives coincide. Therefore, in such setting one may need to consider the transitive effects of voting. For instance, if agent a reports on the importance of (i.e., votes for) agent b, then this may influence the credibility of a report by b on the importance of agent c. These indirect effects should be considered when we wish to aggregate the information provided by the agents into a social ranking. The ranking of agents based on other agents' input is fundamental to multi-agent systems [7], and it has become a core element in a variety of applications, where perhaps the most famous examples are Google's PageRank algorithm [6] and *eBay*'s reputation system [8].

Google's PageRank algorithm is based on the link structure of the Web. Google describes PageRank as follows: *"PageRank reflects our view of the importance of Web pages by considering more than 500 million variables and 2 billion terms. Pages that we believe are important pages receive a higher PageRank and are more likely to appear at the top of the search results. PageRank also considers the importance of each page that casts a vote, as votes from some pages are considered to have greater value, thus giving the linked page greater value. We have always taken a pragmatic approach to help improve search quality and create useful products, and our technology uses the collective intelligence of the web to determine a page's importance"*. Therefore, PageRank is used to measure the quality of a web page, which in turn is directly related to the quality or trustworthiness of the information reported on it.

3   Technical Preliminaries

In this section, we examine the general process of designing a citation ranking mechanism, and specifically refer to Google's PageRank. To this aim, we consider a set O of web pages. Let all web pages in O be numbered from 1 to n, and let i denote a given web page. Then $O_i^l \subseteq O$ denotes the set of pages that i is linked

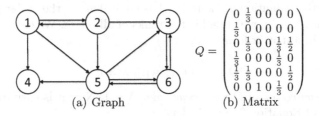

$$Q = \begin{pmatrix} 0 & \frac{1}{3} & 0 & 0 & 0 & 0 \\ \frac{1}{3} & 0 & 0 & 0 & 0 & 0 \\ 0 & \frac{1}{3} & 0 & 0 & \frac{1}{3} & \frac{1}{2} \\ \frac{1}{3} & 0 & 0 & 0 & \frac{1}{3} & 0 \\ \frac{1}{3} & \frac{1}{3} & 0 & 0 & 0 & \frac{1}{2} \\ 0 & 0 & 1 & 0 & \frac{1}{3} & 0 \end{pmatrix}$$

(a) Graph   (b) Matrix

Fig. 1. A graph with outlinks and inlinks and the corresponding matrix

to, the *outlinks*. The number of outlinks is denoted as $N_i = |O_i^l|$. The set of *inlinks*, denoted $I_i^l \subseteq O$, is the set of pages that have an outlink to i. Intuitively, the more inlinks a given page has, the more important that page is. However, a ranking system based only on the number of inlinks is easy to manipulate: when we design a web page i, we could simply create a large number of informationless and unimportant pages that have outlinks to i. To discourage this, one defines the rank of i so that if a highly ranked page j has an outlink to i, this adds to the importance of i more than multiple unimportant pages. The rank of page i is then defined as a weighted sum of the ranks of the pages that have outlinks to i. The weighting schema is such that the importance of a page j is divided evenly among its outlinks:

$$r_i = \sum_{j \in I_i^l} \frac{r_j}{N_j} \tag{1}$$

This preliminary definition is recursive, thus page ranks cannot be computed directly. Instead a fixed-point iteration might be used, starting from an initial ranking vector $r^{(0)}$.

$$r_i^{k+1} = \sum_{j \in I_i^l} \frac{r_j^k}{N_j}, \qquad k = 0, 1, ... \tag{2}$$

There are a few problems with this iterative process. For instance, if a page has no outlinks, then it *drains* importance from its inlinks without transferring importance to any ohter page. Equation 1 can be reformulated as an eigenvalue problem for a matrix Q representing the graph of the Internet, Q being a square matrix of dimension n such that:

$$Q_{i,j} = \begin{cases} \frac{1}{N_j} & \text{if there is a link from } j \text{ to } i, \\ 0 & \text{otherwise} \end{cases} \tag{3}$$

This means that row i has nonzero elements in the positions that correspond to inlinks of i. Similarly, column j has nonzero elements in the positions that correspond to the outlinks of j, and the sum of all the elements in column j is equal to one. Let us consider, for example, the web graph shown in Fig. 1(a), which represents a set of six web pages with several outlinks and inlinks. The corresponding matrix is shown in Fig. 1(b).

Note that the definition of Equation 1 is equivalent to the scalar product of row i and the vector r, which holds the ranks of all pages. We can then rewrite the equation in a matrix form:

$$\lambda \cdot r = Q \cdot r, \text{ with } \lambda = 1 \tag{4}$$

r being an *eigenvector* of Q with *eigenvalue* $\lambda = 1$. Now it is easy to note that the iteration of Equation 2 is equivalent to:

$$r^{k+1} = Q \cdot r^k, \qquad k = 0, 1, \ldots \tag{5}$$

which can be solved using the well-known *Power Method* for computing eigenvectors [4]. It can be demonstrated, using *Markov chain* theory, that the PageRank problem is well defined and the uniqueness of the largest eigenvalue of an irreducible, positive matrix is guaranteed by the *Perron-Frobenius* theorem [3].

4   Measuring Trust

In this section, we first discuss how citation ranking can be adapted to assess the trustworthiness of data items in a large collection. Then we show how the same approach can be used to assess the trustworthiness of relevant information sources. The result is a PageRank-like method to rank all data items, where the rank of an item denotes its relative trustworthiness. The idea behind our approach is to model trust assessment as a social choice problem, with the set of voters and the set of alternatives coinciding with the data collection. Given the volume of data involved in any big data application, we need highly scalable solutions, and citation ranking has proven to be extremely scalable. In 2008, Google declared that the size of their index of the web had reached an astonishing 1 trillion unique URLs [5]. Yet, the PageRank algorithm was able to scale to such volumes of data.

In order to apply citation ranking to this scenario, we first need to identify a directed graph structure within the data collection. To this aim, we assume that cross-references between data items correspond to directed edges in the graph. Specifically, we assume that a reference from a data item o_j to another data item o_i – denoted $o_j \rightarrow o_i$ – is equivalent to o_j *voting* for o_i. Note that the opposite may not be true, thus the the relationship between o_i and o_j is not symmetric.

In general, ranking systems – including PageRank – allow only two levels of preference over the alternatives (e.g., a page may either link or not link another page). Instead, we allow a voter (i.e., an object in the collection) to express different levels of preference for each of the linked objects. In other words, there may be different ways of referencing other data items, each one making a different type of statement about the trustworthiness of the referenced data.

Given a set $O = \{o_1, \ldots, o_n\}$ of data items, we use $G = (O, E, \hat{w})$ to denote a directed weighted graph where O is the set of items, $E = \{(o_j, o_i) \mid o_j \rightarrow o_i\}$ is the set of edges, and $\hat{w} : E \rightarrow R^+$ is a function that associates each edge (o_j, o_i) with a weight representing the strength of the reference from o_j to o_i. This reference transfers part of the importance of o_j to o_i, but not all objects referenced by o_j receive the same share of o_j's importance. Given a graph $G = (O, E, \hat{w})$, we can formulate the trust assessment problem more formally as follows.

Definition 1 (Relative Trust T). *Given an object $o_i \in O$, its relative trust $T(o_i)$ is defined as*

$$T(o_i) = \sum_{o_j \in P_G(o_i)} \hat{w}_{ij} \cdot T(o_j) \tag{6}$$

where $P_G(o_i) = \{o_j \in O \mid (o_j, o_i) \in E\}$ is the set of predecessors of o_i in G, and $\hat{w}_{ij} = \hat{w}(o_j, o_i)$ is the weight of the edge from o_j to o_i. For each $o_j \in O$, $\sum_{o_i \in S_G(o_j)} \hat{w}_{ij} = 1$ must hold, where $S_G(o_j) = \{o_i \in O \mid (o_j, o_i) \in E\}$ is the set of successors of o_j in G.

Differently from PageRank, which assumes that all the N_j links from o_j have the same weight $\frac{1}{N_j}$, we assume that links are weighted, therefore each object transfers a different portion of its importance to each of the linked objects. Given the iterative nature of Definition 1, it is easy to see that the vector $R = [T(o_1) \ldots T(o_n)]^T$ can be computed as the solution to the following equation:

$$R = C \cdot R \tag{7}$$

where $C = \{\hat{w}_{ij}\}$ is an ad-hoc matrix that defines how the importance of each object is transferred to other objects. Such matrix must satisfy certain conditions in order to guarantee that Equation 7 admits a solution and such solution is unique. These conditions are defined by the Perron-Frobenius theorem. Before discussing how to validate the properties of this matrix, we formally introduce the concept of ranking system.

Let $\mathcal{G}_O$ denote the set of all directed graphs G with vertex set $O = \{o_1 \ldots o_n\}$ and $\mathcal{L}(O)$ the set of total orderings on O[1]. We have the following definitions.

Definition 2 (Ranking System). *A ranking system ϱ is a function that, for every finite vertex set O, maps a graph $G \in \mathcal{G}_O$ to an ordering $\preceq_G^\varrho \in \mathcal{L}(O)$.*

Two examples of ranking systems are given in the following.

Definition 3 (Approval Voting Ranking System). *The approval voting ranking system is the ranking system defined by the following equation.*

$$\forall o_i, o_j \in O \quad o_i \preceq_G^\varrho o_j \Leftrightarrow |P_G(o_i)| \leq |P_G(o_j)| \tag{8}$$

where P_G is the predecessors' set.

---

[1] A relation $\preceq \ \subseteq O \times O$ is called a total ordering on O if it is **reflexive** (i.e., $T(o_i) \leq T(o_i)$), **antisymmetric** (i.e., $T(o_i) \leq T(o_j) \ \wedge \ T(o_j) \leq T(o_i) \Rightarrow T(o_i) = T(o_j)$), **transitive** (i.e., $T(o_i) \leq T(o_j) \ \wedge \ T(o_j) \leq T(o_k) \Rightarrow T(o_j) \leq T(o_k)$) and **complete** (i.e., $\forall o_i, o_j \in O, \ T(o_i) \leq T(o_j) \ \vee \ T(o_j) \leq T(o_i)$).

Definition 4 (PageRank-like Ranking System). *A PageRank-like ranking system is a ranking system defined by the following equation.*

$$\forall o_i, o_j \in O \quad o_i \preceq_G^\varrho o_j \Leftrightarrow T(o_i) \leq T(o_j) \tag{9}$$

where $R = [T(o_1) \dots T(o_n)]^T$ is the solution to Equation 7.

We now need to verify that the matrix $C = \{\hat{w}_{ij}\}$ guarantees the existence of a unique solution to Equation 7. To this aim, the matrix C must be a positive and irreducible column-stochastic matrix. Under these hypothesis, the Perron-Frobenius theorem establishes that the dominant eigenvalue is equal to 1.

First, we expect this matrix to be sparse, as only a relatively small fraction of all possible data objects are referenced by a given object. As discussed later, the sparseness property will be leveraged for computing ranks efficiently.

Second, we note that solving Equation 7 corresponds to finding the stationary vector of C, i.e., the eigenvector with eigenvalue 1. According to the Perron-Frobenius theorem, a real square matrix with positive elements has a unique largest real eigenvalue and the corresponding eigenvector has strictly positive components. Moreover the largest eigenvalue associated with a stochastic matrix is always 1. In other words, given an irreducible column-stochastic matrix, the dominant eigenvalue is equal to 1 and there is a unique corresponding eigenvector that is the only nonnegative one.

Note that the elements of each column of C (where each column represents a data item in the collection) either sum up to one or are all 0. The second case corresponds to the situation where an object o_j does not reference any other object, thus the elements of the j-th column of C are all 0. We can turn C into a stochastic-column matrix by introducing the following auxiliary matrices:

$$C' = C + S(C) \tag{10}$$

where S is a function that associates with each matrix $M = \{m_{ij}\}$ a matrix $S(M) = \{s_{ij}\}$ defined as follows:

$$s_{ij} = \begin{cases} 0, & \text{if } (\exists k \in [1, n])(m_{kj} \geq 0) \\ \frac{1}{n}, & \text{otherwise} \end{cases} \tag{11}$$

In other words, C' is obtained from C by replacing columns with all 0's with columns with all the elements equal to $\frac{1}{n}$, thus guaranteeing their stochasticity. However, matrix C' is not yet positive. In order to make it positive, we introduce a parameter $\sigma \in [0, 1]$ modeling the probability that agents will assign the same level of trust to all other agents. C' may be rewritten as follows:

$$C'' = (1 - \sigma) \cdot C' + \sigma \cdot \frac{1}{n} \cdot J_n \tag{12}$$

where J_n is an $n \times n$ matrix of 1's. This guarantees that C'' is also positive (and thus irreducible). Therefore, replacing C with C'' in Equation 7 we obtain:

$$R = C'' \cdot R \tag{13}$$

which is guaranteed to have a unique solution R.

In Equation 13, matrix C'' is a square matrix with one column for each object in the collection, which means that C'' might potentially have millions of columns and rows. We want to be able to solve this equation for very large matrices C'''. There are many ways to reach this goal, that means there are many methods to find the eigenvectors of a square matrix. Among the possible methods, we use the Power Method, an iterative algorithm which can be used for finding the stationary vector of a square matrix. This method consists in computing a sequence of vectors R^k, with $k \geq 1$, as follows:

$$R^1 = C'' \cdot R^0$$
$$\cdots$$
$$R^k = C'' \cdot R^{k-1}$$
(14)

where R^0 is an arbitrary initial vector whose elements sum up to one. This method iterates until convergence is reached or a given number of iterations has been performed. Specifically, the stopping criterion is the following:

$$|R^k - R^{k-1}| \leq tol \vee k \geq N \tag{15}$$

where tol is a relative tolerance and N is the maximum number of allowed iterations.

Note that it has been proved that, if the eigenvalues of C'' are $\lambda_1, \lambda_2, \ldots \lambda_n$ and $1 = \lambda_1 > |\lambda_2| \geq |\lambda_3| \geq \ldots \geq |\lambda_n|$ and a basis v_i of eigenvectors for C'' exists with the corresponding eigenvalues λ_i, *the solution of the Power Method is an eigenvector corresponding to the maximum eigenvalue which is equal to 1*. Moreover, it can be proved that convergence is faster for higher values of σ. However, there is a trade-off in the choice of σ, since higher values also imply a greater weight assigned to the baseline uniform trust, and this may not be desirable. Combining Equations 12 and 14, we obtain:

$$R^k = \left((1 - \sigma) \cdot C' + \frac{\sigma}{n} \cdot J_n \right) \cdot R^{k-1} \tag{16}$$

Combining Equations 10 and 16, R^k can be rewritten as follows:

$$R^k = (1 - \sigma) \cdot C \cdot R^{k-1} + (1 - \sigma) \cdot S(C) \cdot R^{k-1} + \frac{\sigma}{n} \cdot J_n \cdot R^{k-1} \tag{17}$$

Analyzing Equation 16, we can highlight the following facts, which clearly show that a ranking of all the data items can be computed efficiently.

- Because matrix C is sparse, the computation of the product $C \cdot R^{k-1}$ reduces to computing the product of a sparse matrix and a vector, which can be done efficiently.
- All the rows of matrix $S(C)$ are equal. Therefore, all the elements of the vector $(1 - \sigma) \cdot S(C) \cdot R^{k-1}$ are equal and can be computed by multiplying the first row of the matrix $S = (1 - \sigma) \cdot S(C)$, which is also sparse, and the vector R^{k-1}.

– The elements of matrix $\frac{g}{n} \cdot J_n$ are all equal, in fact it is a product between a scalar and a matrix of all ones, so all the elements of the vector $\frac{g}{n} \cdot J_n \cdot R^{k-1}$ are equal to $\frac{g}{n} \cdot \sum_{i=0}^{n} R^{k-1}(i)$, which needs to be computed only once.

So far, we have discussed how to adapt citation ranking to assess the relative trustworthiness of data items. Adapting this approach to assess the trustworthiness of information sources is straightforward, and there are at least two different ways of achieving this goal. The first solution consists in computing the trustworthiness of an information source as an aggregate of the trustworthiness of individual data items pertaining to that source. The second solution consists in considering a graph $G_s = (O_s, E_s, \hat{w}_s)$ where O_s is a set of sources, E_s is a set of edges representing cross references between sources, and $\hat{w}_s$ is a function that associate with edge a real number representing the strength of the corresponding reference. For instance, $\hat{w}_s(o_j, o_i)$ can take into account the number and type of references from data items in o_j to data items in o_i. The ranking of sources can then be computed using the same process described above.

5   Conclusions

Big data requires new analytical approaches to extract actionable intelligence from huge amounts of data. In this paper, we have proposed an approach to assess and quantify the trust level of information sources and data items in a large collection by leveraging the vast literature on citation ranking. We showed that the proposed approach is highly scalable, as proven by its successful application in the domain of web search. Our exploratory analysis demonstrates the potential benefits of a similar approach and encourages further research in this direction.

References

1. Amato, F., Mazzeo, A., Moscato, V., Picariello, A.: Semantic management of multimedia documents for e-government activity. In: International Conference on Complex, Intelligent and Software Intensive Systems (CISIS 2009), pp. 1193–1198 (2009)
2. Arrow, K.J.: Social Choice and Individual Values. John Wiley & Sons (1963)
3. Bapat, R.B., Raghavan, T.E.S.: Nonnegative Matrices and Applications. Encyclopedia of Mathematics and its Applications, vol. 64. Cambridge University Press (1997)
4. Eldén, L.: Matrix Methods in Data Mining and Pattern Recognition. Fundamentals of Algorithms, vol. 4. Society for Industrial and Applied Mathematics (2007)
5. Google Official Blog: We knew the web was big... (July 2008), http://googleblog.blogspot.com/2008/07/we-knew-web-was-big.html
6. Page, L., Brin, S., Motwani, R., Winograd, T.: The PageRank citation ranking: Bringing order to the web. Technical Report 1999-66, Stanford InfoLab (1999)
7. Resnick, P., Kuwabara, K., Zeckhauser, R., Friedman, E.: Reputation systems. Communications of the ACM 43(12), 45–48 (2000)
8. Resnick, P., Zeckhauser, R.: Trust Among Strangers in Internet Transactions: Empirical Analysis of eBay's Reputation System. In: The Economics of the Internet and E-commerce, Advances in Applied Microeconomics, vol. 11, pp. 127–157. Emerald Group Publishing (2002)

Part IV
Cloud-assisted Smart Cyber-Physical Systems (C-SmartCPS 2013)

Agent-Based Decision Support
for Smart Market Using Big Data

Alba Amato, Beniamino Di Martino, and Salvatore Venticinque

Department of Industrial and Information Engineering, Second University of Naples
{alba.amato,beniamino.dimartino,
salvatore.venticinque}@unina2.it

Abstract. In goal oriented problems, decision-making is a crucial aspect aiming at enhancing the user's ability to make decisions. The application of agent-based decision aid in the e-commerce field should help customers to make the right choice giving also to vendors the possibility to predict the purchasing behavior of consumers. The capability of extracting value from data is a relevant issue to evaluate decision criteria, and it is as difficult as volume and velocity of data increase. In this paper agents are enabled to make decisions accessing in the Cloud huge amount of data collected from pervasive devices.

1   Introduction

The history of computing to date has been marked by five important, and continuing, trends: ubiquity, interconnection, intelligence, delegation and human-orientation[15]. Intelligent software agents must be able to act autonomously and following the choice that best represents interests of their owners, during the interaction with a human being or another system [11]. In this kind of goal oriented problem, decision-making is a crucial aspect aiming at enhancing the user's ability to make decisions. The decision has to be made among possible alternatives taking into account all the certainty and uncertainty considerations and using a prescribed set of decision criteria. The reason for this intensive interest in decision-making [14] is that the metaphor of autonomous problem solving entities, which cooperate and coordinate each other in order to achieve their desired objectives, is an intuitive and natural way of the problem solving. Moreover, the conceptual apparatus of this technology provides a powerful and useful set of computational structures and processes for designing and building complex software applications. The multi-agent techniques combined with decision-making tools can help decision makers to deal with the problems of the information overload. In particular the application of agent-based decision aid in the e-commerce field should help customers to make the right choice giving also to vendors the possibility to predict the purchasing behavior of consumers. Such a *Smart Market* will ensure the vendors a competitive advantage given by the opportunities deriving from market prediction that improve the use of e-commerce in terms of customer satisfaction. In this paper a multi-criteria decision-aid has been used

J. Kołodziej et al. (Eds.): ICA3PP 2013, Part II, LNCS 8286, pp. 251–258, 2013.
© Springer International Publishing Switzerland 2013

to model a general solution for this kind of problems, and has been applied in an e-commerce scenarios. The specialized model has been implemented to allow agents to make decisions about the actions to be taken for achieving their own goals activated by requirements and preferences of their owners, accessing in the Cloud a huge amount of data collected from pervasive devices.

2 Related Work

Many research contributions discuss agent based decision aid systems. [17] presents the design and evaluation of a multi-agent based supply chain management system with reconfiguration ability based on decision aid. In [5] an agent based decision support system for companies is presented. [7] presents an agent based model management for decision support in a computing environment where enterprise data and models are distributed. In our previous works, a multi-agent decision support system is used in the Cloud market to broker the proposals that best fit user's needs [2], and into an e-commerce scenario for providing the most relevant recommendation to customers [1]. The present work, however, takes into account the huge volume of data and their velocity [4], which are produced by this kind of application when it reaches the dimension of a social network with well defined targets. In fact, in this case, it is necessary to reduce management and analysis time because in a very short time the data can become obsolete. Dealing effectively with Big Data requires to perform analytics against the volume and variety of data while it is still in motion, not just after [6]. According to IBM [6] Big Data solutions are ideal for analyzing not only raw structured data, but semistructured and unstructured data from a wide variety of sources. Big Data solutions should be chosen when all, or most, of the data needs to be analyzed versus a sample of the data; or a sampling of data is not nearly as effective as a larger set of data from which to derive analysis. Big Data solutions are suited for iterative and exploratory analysis when measures on data are not predetermined. Big data technologies can address the problems related to the collection of data streams of higher velocity and higher variety. They allow for building an infrastructure that delivers low, predictable latency in both capturing data and in executing short, simple queries; that is able to handle very high transaction volumes, often in a distributed environment; and supports flexible, dynamic data structures [8]. With such a high volume of information, it is relevant the possibility to organize data at its original storage location, thus saving both time and money by not moving around large volumes of data. The infrastructures required for organizing big data are able to process and manipulate data in the original storage location. This capability provides very high throughput (often in batch), which are necessary to deal with large data processing steps and to handle a large variety of data formats, from unstructured to structured [8]. The analysis may also be done in a distributed environment, where they are accessed for required analytics such as statistical analysis and data mining, on a wider variety of data types stored in diverse systems; scale to extreme data volumes; deliver faster response times driven by changes in behavior; and automate decisions based on analytical models. New insight comes not just from analyzing new data, but from analyzing it within the context of the old to provide new perspectives on old problems [8]. For these reasons context awareness in pervasive environments represent an interesting application field of big data technologies.

3 Pervasive Smart Market: Requirements and Problem Formulation

The proposed case study is an e-commerce service that profiles the customers and supports their purchases recommending products and shops. On the other side the service is used by vendors, who upload information about their offers, shops and sales. Let us imagine users of different ages and habits, and with different purposes, in a market. Each of them has a smartphone with a smart application that perceives the environment, provides simple facilities, and accesses the e-service. All the customers continuously update, by the smart application, their profile in the system. They can insert information about themselves such as name, sex, age, home country, e-mail address, languages spoken, level of education, lists of interests, etc. They also set a few preferences about what information the device can autonomously communicate, such as position, nearby objects, user's behaviour. Customers use a grocery list by their smartphone updating their shopping chart. Vendors add or remove their marketplaces and products, and update their description in the knowledge base. Just to simplify our requirements, we suppose that customers cannot add, describe and recommend products on their own. Using the autonomic behavior of the service, the objective of the system is to propose the best set of recommendations, which can help the user to improve his own utility, exploiting the available information about products, about the environment within which customers are moving and about the customers themselves.

Here we formulate the introduced problem as a BDI (Believes, Desires, Intentions) agent that aims at achieving those goals which are activated by the preferences of its owner. In particular it must take a decision about what products should be recommended to the user. The agent knowledge is represented as a set of *Believes* $B = \{b_1, \cdots, b_{ne}, \}$, described using a domain ontology. We suppose here that perceptions, coming from the field, enrich the user's profile with new concepts or individuals of the ontology. The domain ontology describes device technology and capability, environment and user's position, pervasive objects, time information, user's preferences, market goods. In particular, an appropriate classification of market goods allows to make better recommendations, since it is possible to identify the type of purchase made by the customer, the frequency he buys a certain product, and on the other hand it is possible to make more accurate cross-sell recommendation. A possible classification can be performed based on the buying habits of consumers. In [13], three product types are identified: *convenience, shopping,* and *speciality.* Convenience products are purchased frequently by the consumer, they do not require any major effort in the process of choice and any risk of making the wrong choice. Preference products are distinguished from the previous item primarily on the basis of a perceived greater risk in their purchase. The individual tends to address the problem of the choice of the brand, trying to find one that can better meet his needs. Shopping products are goods that the individual acquires after careful considerations, and after a prolonged comparison among different brands making the price the main driver of choice, or differentiated, making their attributes to play a key role in purchasing decisions. Speciality products are goods with special features, often characterized by prestigious brands and very high prices. Here we focus on shopping goods because in this case information discovery and decision making is more important than the others. The set of *Believes* is revised using the *perceptions* identified in the following list:

e_1 purchase of a product;
e_2 request for information relating to a product;
e_3 add/delete a product into the grocery list;
e_4 add/delete a product into the shopping cart;
e_5 detection of a product or a POI by a device;
e_6 detection of the user's position.

The first four events add/remove one or more individuals/concepts of the ontology, which describe the related product, into the user profile. The last two items update the user's position or update the set of nearby objects into the user profile.

A number of desires, some time conflicting, can drive the agent decision. In fact, in a market context the user would buy the best products at lower price. We could recommend user's preferred products, but also the one which are better ranked by the community. At the same time it is possible to optimize the costs by recommending the places where he can find a lower price, but also we can help him to save time and to shorten the distance to be covered for buying. In fact the utility of the user is improved if he receives effective recommendations, but also if it is able to save money, to spend less time and to find the shortest path for completing his shopping. So the set of *Goals* is:

g_1 Precision of the list of recommended products;
g_2 Recall of the the list of recommended products;
g_3 Time spent to buy;
g_4 Path length to the market;
g_5 Money saved.

The agent's rationality is defined as the preference about a future believes that satisfies the user, who activate some specific goals and set his/her priority. The occurrence of a new perception is used to update the user's profile and hence his/her preferences. It needs to evaluate for each active goals if there are some actions to be performed which increase the user utility as discussed in [2]. Here we focus on the decision about what products are more relevant to the user than others (g_1 and g_2). The set of recommendations is built in three steps. In the first all the products which have been annotated with at least one concept of the user profile are retrieved by a *semantic discovery* service. For each of this products the relevance of its semantic annotation to the user's profile is computed in the *evaluation* step. Finally the set of products that optimizes the relevance to the user profile and is compliant with a number of constraints is built in the *optimization* phase. For example we have to exclude from the set of recommendations those products that not exceed budget and time, but affect the affinity with a minimum penalty. We will limit the number of recommendations to not bore the user.

4   Decision Making on Big Data

Performance figures discussed in [3] demonstrate feasibility of the proposed solution implemented with a classical relational database. However a number of limitations have been assumed. First of all the amount of data are limited to the proprietary knowledge base with a limited number of marketplaces. The coverage of an increasing number of marketplaces, eventually wider, will affect the amount of geographical information and the number of connected mobile users. Data continuously received from thousands of devices scattered in the environment handling queries and providing perception will augment volume, velocity and variety of information. Finally the exploitation of the user's feedback could be used to improve the expertise of the system enriching the knowledge base with semantic annotation inferred by a social network of consumers who recommend themselves. The new vision of the smart market framework must be designed considering the Big Data requirements and solutions. Available Cloud technologies provide different NoSQL data models and technologies. However in our model products, users' profiles and ontology of the knowledge base are natively represented by RDF triples[9], which can dynamically change. They can be naturally represented using a labeled, directed, multi-graph. This graph view is the easiest possible mental model for RDF and is often used in easy-to-understand visual explanations. To enables inferences and as query language, is used SPARQL that is a subgraph pattern matching query language. Besides, we need to integrate multiple independent schemas that evolve separately depending on the different conditions correlated to the different marketplace. Graph databases [10] may overcome these limitation because they generally provide ACID transactions. Adoption of such solution will provide custom API's and Query Languages and many support the W3C's RDF standard, including a SPARQL engine. As shown in Figure 1 it allows for the collection, indexing and semantic retrieval of data. In fact the new knowledge base can be modeled as a unique ontology dynamically augmented and updated with new information. Besides it is possible to add spatial indexes to already located data, and perform spatial operations on the data like searching for data within specified regions or within a specified distance of a point of interest. In addition classes are provided to expose the data to geotools and thereby to geotools enabled applications like geoservers. Many Graph database implementations support the mapreduce programming model that allows for a distributed high performance execution of the *evaluation* and

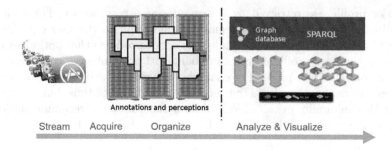

Stream   Acquire   Organize   Analyze & Visualize

Fig. 1. Graph Database utilization

the *optimization* steps. In fact for the evaluation, annotation and the user's profile are represented using the Vector Space Model (VSM). VSM is a model for semantic representations of contents as vectors of items created by G. Salton [12]. In our case a_j is the vector of concepts $c_{i,j}$ of the domain ontology.

$$a_j =< \{c_{1,j}, o_{1,j}\}, \{c_{2,j}, o_{2,j}\}, ..., \{c_{l,j}, o_{l,j}\} > \forall j = 1..N$$
$$p =< c_1, c_2, ..., c_m >$$

Sizes l and m are the number of different concepts that appear in the annotation a_j and in the profile p. If a term occurs in the annotation, $o_{k,j}$ is the number of occurrences of that term in the annotation. We defined a score $A(a_j, p)$ to measure the relevance of an annotation a_j to the profile p by the following formula 1

$$w_j = w(a_j, p) = \frac{1}{l} \sum_{k=1}^{l} r_k \text{ where } r_k = o_{k,j} * \frac{1}{m} \sum_{i=1}^{m} \frac{1}{d_{k,i} + 1} \tag{1}$$

where $d_{k,i}$ is the minimum number of edges that connect the node representing the concept $c_{k,j}$ of the annotation to c_i of the profile. In Equation 1, for each item $c_{k,j}$ of the vector a_j the relevance to the profile p is computed by adding the relevance of that concept to each concept of the profile, and by multiplying each contribution for the number of occurrences $o_{k,j}$. The relevance between two concepts is calculated by dividing 1 by the number of edges of the ontology that connect the node representing the concept c_k of the profile to $c_{k,j}$ plus 1. This kind of computation can be easily distributed mapping profiles to relevant annotations to profiles and reducing the computed score.

The *optimization* step can be reduced to a discrete optimization problem that consists in searching the optimal value (maximum or minimum) of a function $f : x \in \mathcal{Z}^n \to \mathcal{R}$, and the solution $x = \{x_1, ..., x_n\}$ in which the function's value is optimal. $f(x)$ is said *cost function*, and its domain is generally defined by means of a set of m constraints on the points of the definition space. Constraints are generally expressed by a set of inequalities:

$$\sum_{i=1}^{n} b_{i,j} x_i \leq a_j \qquad \forall j \in \{1, ..., m\} \tag{2}$$

and they define the set of feasible values for the x_i variables (the *solutions space* of the problem). In our case: $w_i \geq 0 \; \forall i = 1..N, W = \{b_1, .., b_m\}$ where w_i represents a score and B a set of constraints b_i, each one composed of $N + 1$ integer. We have to compute

$$max \sum_{k=1}^{N} w_i x_i \text{ so that } \sum_{k=1}^{N} b_{i,j} x_i \leq b_{j,N+1} \text{ with } x_i \in \{0,1\} \; \forall i = 1..N. \quad (3)$$

The goal is to maximize the value delivered. The vector x represents a possible solution: its components x_i are 1 or 0 depending on whether the recommendation is included or not in the best set. Mapreduce solution of this problem is described in [16].

5   Conclusion

In this paper we presented a general multi-criteria decision-aid and its utilization in an e-commerce service that profiles the customers and supports their purchases recommending products and shops and accessing in the Cloud a huge amount of data collected from pervasive devices. Future works will address the evaluation of the service implementation and the discussion of performance results.

Acknowledgements. This work has been supported by PRIST 2009, *Fruizione assistita e context aware di siti archelogici complessi mediante terminali mobile*, founded by Second University of Naples.

References

1. Amato, A., Di Martino, B., Venticinque, S.: A semantic framework for delivery of context-aware ubiquitous services in pervasive environments. In: Intelligent Networking and Collaborative Systems, INCoS 2012, pp. 412–419 (2012)
2. Amato, A., Venticinque, S.: Multi-objective decision support for brokering of cloud sla. In: Advanced Information Networking and Applications Workshops, WAINA 2013, pp. 1241–1246 (2013)
3. Amato, A., Di Martino, B., Scialdone, M., Venticinque, S.: Personalized Recommendation of Semantically Annotated Media Contents. In: Zavoral, F., Jung, J.J., Badica, C. (eds.) Intelligent Distributed Computing VII. SCI, vol. 511, pp. 261–270. Springer, Heidelberg (2014)
4. Gartner: Pattern-based strategy: Getting value from big data. Tech. rep. (2011)
5. Greco, L., Presti, L.L., Augello, A., Re, G.L., La Cascia, M., Gaglio, S.: A decisional multi-agent framework for automatic supply chain arrangement. In: Lai, C., Semeraro, G., Vargiu, E. (eds.) New Challenges in Distributed Inf. Filtering and Retrieval. SCI, vol. 439, pp. 215–232. Springer, Heidelberg (2013)
6. IBM, Zikopoulos, P., Eaton, C.: Understanding Big Data: Analytics for Enterprise Class Hadoop and Streaming Data, 1st edn. McGraw-Hill Osborne Media (2011)
7. Iyer, B., Shankaranarayanan, G., Lenard, M.L.: Model management decision environment: a web service prototype for spreadsheet models. Decision Support Systems 40(2), 283–304 (2005)

8. Oracle: Big data for the enterprise. Tech. rep. (2013)
9. RDF: Rdf (2012), http://www.w3.org/RDF/ (July 26, 2013)
10. Robinson, I., Webber, J., Eifrem, E.: Graph Databases. O'Reilly Media, Incorporated (2013)
11. Russell, S.J., Norvig, P.: Artificial intelligence: a modern approach. Prentice-Hall, Inc., Upper Saddle River (1995)
12. Salton, G., Lesk, M.E.: Computer evaluation of indexing and text processing. J. ACM 15(1), 8–36 (1968)
13. Sindhav, B., Balazs, A.L.: A model of factors affecting the growth of retailing on the internet. Journal of Market-Focused Management 4, 319–339 (1999)
14. Sperka, R., Slaninova, K.: The usability of agent-based simulation in decision support system of e-commerce architecture. I. J. Information Engineering and Electronic Business 4(1), 10–17 (2012)
15. Wooldridge, M.: An Introduction to MultiAgent Systems, 2nd edn. Wiley Publishing (2009)
16. Yu, L., Sebastian, F., Kento, E., Zhenjiang, H.: Implementing Generate-Test-and-Aggregate Algorithms on Hadoop. Japan Society for Software Science and Technology (2011)
17. Zhang, Z., Tao, L.: Multi-agent based supply chain management with dynamic reconfiguration capability. In: IEEE/WIC/ACM International Conference on Web Intelligence and Intelligent Agent Technology, vol. 2, pp. 92–95 (2008)

Congestion Control for Vehicular Environments by Adjusting IEEE 802.11 Contention Window Size

Ali Balador, Carlos T. Calafate, Juan-Carlos Cano, and Pietro Manzoni

Universitat Politecnica de Valencia
Camino de Vera, s/n, 46022 Valencia, Spain
alba6@upv.es, {calafate,jucano,pmanzoni}@disca.upv.es

Abstract. Medium access control protocols should manage the highly dynamic nature of Vehicular Ad Hoc Networks (VANETs) and the variety of application requirements. Therefore, achieving a well-designed MAC protocol in VANETs is a challenging issue. The contention window is a critical element for handling medium access collisions in IEEE 802.11, and it highly affects the communications performance. This paper proposes a new contention window control scheme, called DBM-ACW, for VANET environments. Analysis and simulation results using OMNeT++ in urban scenarios show that DBM-ACW provides better overall performance compared with previous proposals, even with high network densities.

1 Introduction

Medium Access Control (MAC) protocols play an important role since critical communications must rely on it. Unfortunately, research results [1] highlight that the topic of MAC support in VANETs has received less attention than in other research fields. Also, most of these relatively few research works are dedicated to V2I communications; therefore, MAC support for V2V communication needs more attention. MAC layer design challenges in VANET environments can be summarized as follows [2]: (a) achieving an effective channel access coordination in the presence of changing vehicle locations and variable channel characteristics; (b) supporting scalability in the presence of various traffic densities; and (c) supporting a diverse set of application requirements.

A lot of research has been done by the research community with the idea of supporting broadcast transmissions in mind (e.g., [3], [4]). In contrast to the most common research trend, this paper targets unicast applications including infotainment, P2P or VoIP.

The IEEE 802.11 has been selected by a wide range of research works for vehicular environments as the MAC layer standard because of its availability, maturity, and cost. However, it causes performance to be poor in VANETs compared to MANET environments. A well-known problem in IEEE 802.11 is scalability, which becomes more challenging in VANETs in the presence of high and

J. Kołodziej et al. (Eds.): ICA3PP 2013, Part II, LNCS 8286, pp. 259–266, 2013.
© Springer International Publishing Switzerland 2013

variable network densities. A lot of works have been proposed and carried out for MANET environments [5], [6], [7] to either solve or reduce this problem.

Among these studies, a dynamic and low-overhead method called HBCWC is proposed in [7]. This method estimates network density based on channel status observations without requiring complex calculations. This way, more than current network status, previous statuses are used in order to identify the channel traffic variations. As a consequence, the CW size is dynamically tuned based on the estimated network density.

To the best of our knowledge, very few studies address unicast communication in VANETs. A fuzzy logic based enhancement to 802.11p is proposed in [8] which adapts the CW size based on a non-linear control law, and relies on channel observation. Furthermore, [9] suggests a MAC mechanism which uses a modified version of RTS/CTS in order to estimate network density through message exchange. Therefore, in this paper we propose a new contention window control scheme, called DBM-ACW (Density Based Method for Adjusting the CW size), and prove that DBM-ACW not only outperforms the IEEE 802.11 DCF in different vehicular scenarios, but also previously proposed schemes.

The rest of this paper is organized as follows. In section 2, we describe the new proposed contention window control scheme in detail. Performance evaluation of DBM-ACW, including simulation results in urban scenarios, is presented in section 3. Finally, section 4 concludes this paper.

2   The Proposed Algorithm

In order to adequately adjust the CW size for vehicular environments, we propose DBM-ACW, a new method to select the CW size based on the network traffic density. In this method, the channel condition is estimated based on the packet transmission status, and the result is stored into a Channel State (CS) vector. A significant part of the protocol relies on how the channel conditions are captured by the CS vector, and how this vector is used to update the CW size in order to improve throughput, which it is the key contribution of this paper. These two issues will be further explained in the following sections.

2.1   Initialization

Similarly to the IEEE 802.11, the CW value is initially set to CW_{min}, and it is updated during the execution. The CS vector that is used for keeping track of channel conditions is set to one in order to assume a collision free status before starting the simulation. Parameters A and B which are used in Algorithm 2 are set to 1.7 and 0.8, respectively. Basically, parameters A and B try to optimally adapt the CW size to network density. A more detailed discussion on how these parameters were obtained is presented in the section 2.3.

2.2   The Channel State Vector

In legacy 802.11 DCF, and after each data frame transmission, each node sets its timer and waits for an acknowledgement. In DBM-ACW, upon each timer expiration or upon receiving a packet, Algorithm 1 is called. If the transmitter receives an ACK frame from the receiver, a value of 1 is inserted into the channel state vector (Operation 5). Otherwise, if a collided/faulty frame is received, or if the transmitter waiting timer expires before receiving the acknowledgement, a value of 0 is inserted into the channel vector (Operation 3).

The CS vector is updated by shifting after setting the CS_0 value (Operation 1). The vehicle then calls Adapt (Algorithm 2) through which the CW is adapted. Based on extensive simulations, we chose a three-element array for DBM-ACW in order to achieve a trade-off between overhead and performance. If we choose a smaller array, it will not be able to reflect the real network conditions, while larger array values do not lead to a significant performance improvement.

Algorithm 1. Time-out expiration or ACK reception

1: Shift the CS array to right by one
2: **if** receiving a time-out or a corrupted ACK packet **then**
3:     $CS_0 = 0$
4: **else**
5:     $CS_0 = 1$
6: **end if**
7: Adapt

2.3   Changing the Contention Window Size

As explained before, upon each timer expiration or packet reception, Adapt (Algorithm 2) is called, in order to update the value of the CW. The CW size is doubled (similarly to the IEEE 802.11 DCF) in order to obtain the highest PDR, except for the case in which the CS array contains two consecutive ones before the new state; in that case the CW is multiplied by parameter A (Operation 3). Furthermore, the CW size is set to the minimum CW, CW_{min}, upon each acknowledgement reception, except for the case in which the CS array contains two consecutive zeros before the new state; in that case the CW is multiplied by parameter B (Operation 9).

The value of parameters A and B in Algorithm 2 was achieved based on extensive simulations in which different combinations of values were used to obtain the best performance. According to the severity of channel congestion, the current CW size is multiplied by a value in the range from 0.2 to 2 or set to CW_{min}. The upper bound is selected as in the IEEE 802.11 DCF, so that the CW size is multiplied by 2 when the channel is detected as busy or a collision has occurred. When the channel is very congested, the current CW size is multiplied by a value in the upper part of this range in order to decrease the probability of selecting the same backoff number. Otherwise, when the channel density is low, the current CW size is multiplied by a value in the lower range or set to CW_{min} in order to avoid waiting for a long time when the channel occupation is low. In our study, the optimal value for parameters A and B was found to be equal to 1.7 and 0.8, respectively.

Algorithm 2. Adapt

1: **if** $CS_0 = 0$ **then**
2:     **if** $CS_1 = 1$, $CS_2 = 1$ **then**
3:         CW $= CW \times A$
4:     **else**
5:         CW $= CW \times 2$
6:     **end if**
7: **else**
8:     **if** $CS_1 = 0$, $CS_2 = 0$ **then**
9:         CW $= CW \times B$
10:    **else**
11:        CW $= CW_{min}$
12:    **end if**
13: **end if**

---

3   Simulation

In this section, we study the performance of DBM-ACW in comparison with the IEEE 802.11 DCF and HBCWC in vehicular environments by using OMNeT++ (version 4.2.2) [10]. Therefore, we use this simulator coupled with the INET-MANET framework [11] and SUMO [12] in order to provide a realistic vehicular scenario. Also, the VACaMobil [13] tool is used in order to maintain the same number of vehicles throughout the simulation time.

3.1   Simulation Parameters

Each vehicle generates constant bitrate traffic. The size of the data payload is 512 bytes, and each node generates data packets at a rate of 4 packets per second. Each vehicle starts a new connection after joining the network, and sends its

Table 1. The simulation parameters

Simulation Parameter	Value
Traffic type	CBR
CBR packet size	512 byte
CBR data rate	4 packet/s
MAC protocol	802.11a
Max. and Min. of CW	7, 1023
Max. number of retransmissions	7
Max. transmission range	250 m
Propagation model	Nakagami
Nakagami-m	0.7
Simulation time	300 seconds
Number of repetitions	10

packets to a randomly selected destination among the current vehicles in the network.

Considering the routing protocol, we assessed different routing protocols (i.e., AODV, OLSR, DYMO, DSR) and, despite of the different overall performance levels obtained by these protocols, we found that they experience the same impact when combined with the different MAC protocols evaluated in this paper. As a consequence, we chose the AODV routing protocol, which is a simple routing protocol that can be easily implemented when attempting to test it in practical scenarios. The radio propagation range for each node is set to 250 m. We used the Nakagami radio propagation model, commonly used by the VANET community, in order to present a more realistic vehicular environment [14]. Parameter m for this propagation model is set to 0.7. Moreover, each point in the figures that follow represents the average of 10 independent simulation experiments in which the simulation time is 300 seconds. Table 1 summarizes the simulation parameters.

The urban scenario represents an area of $1,500 \times 1,500 \ m^2$ that is obtained by using digital maps freely available in OpenStreetMap [15] from the downtown area of Valencia (Spain) with real obstacles.

3.2   Result and Analysis

Figure 1 shows a clear packet delivery ratio improvement for DBM-ACW in comparison to the IEEE 802.11. This improvement was achieved by adapting the CW size based on the channel history. As a consequence, it reduces CW size variations since increasing the CW size starting from CW_{min} is no longer required to find the optimal CW size. This mechanism allows decreasing the number of retransmissions and, consequently, the number of dropped packets. Furthermore, DBM-ACW outperforms HBCWC by not resetting the CW size to the minimum CW size when the CS array contains two consecutive zeros before a successful transmission (Algorithm 2-Operation 9). The average number of MAC collisions, shown in Figure 2, offers a hint on how to achieve improvements in terms of PDR. As can be observed, the optimal CW size for DBM-ACW was chosen so that it decreases the probability of picking the same backoff value, and, consequently, the number of collisions is also reduced.

Our approach achieves a lower end-to-end delay compared to the IEEE 802.11, as depicted in Figure 3. Although IEEE 802.11 cannot guarantee a delay boundary, DBM-ACW does not show a delay increase when the number of nodes is larger than 175, which can help to mitigate the unbounded delay problem in the IEEE 802.11 standard. DBM-ACW gradually decreases the CW, and it does not reset the CW to CW_{min} (Algorithm 2-Operation 9), as occurs with IEEE 802.11, thereby increasing the MAC layer delay. However, as a result of decreasing the number of collisions, this increase in terms of MAC layer delay does

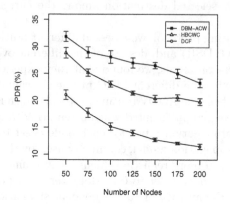

Fig. 1. PDR for the urban scenario

Table 2. Standard Deviation of delays for the urban scenario

	50	75	100	125	150	175	200
DBM-ACW	0.42	0.45	0.46	0.47	0.49	0.52	0.53
HBCWC	0.44	0.44	0.48	0.50	0.55	0.54	0.53

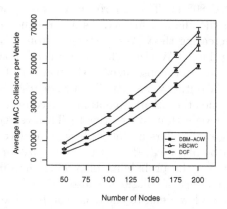

Fig. 2. Average number of collisions for the urban scenario

not have a negative impact in terms of end-to-end delay. Figure 3 evidences the differences between our approach and HBCWC, which are further clarified in Table 2. DBM-ACW is able to achieve improvements in terms of end-to-end delay, as well as improved standard deviation values for delay when comparing DBM-ACW to HBCWC, as shown in Table 2.

Overall, our approach improves the PDR by 47%, and the end-to-end delay by 16% when compared with the IEEE 802.11 DCF, and the PDR improves by 16% in comparison with HBCWC.

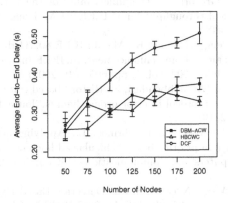

Fig. 3. Average end-to-end delay for the urban scenario

4   Conclusion

This paper presents DBM-ACW, a new IEEE 802.11-based MAC protocol, which controls the CW size based on a network density estimation. In each vehicle, transmission trials are stored as an array which is used to determine the optimal contention window value. Extensive simulations using OMNeT++ in urban scenarios prove that our scheme has better overall performance compared with the IEEE 802.11 DCF and HBCWC in terms of PDR, end-to-end delay and average number of collisions in both scenarios.

As future work, we will study the effect of deploying RSUs on the performance of our scheme. Also, we will dynamically adapt the algorithm's parameters for each specific network scenario.

Acknowledgment. This work was partially supported by the *Ministerio de Ciencia e Innovación*, Spain, under Grant TIN2011-27543-C03-01.

References

1. Booysen, M.J., Zeadally, S., van Rooyen, G.-J.: Survey of media access control protocols for vehicular ad hoc networks. IET Communications 5(11), 1619–1631 (2011)
2. Kenney, J.: Standards and regulations. In: Hartenstein, H., Laberteaux, K.P. (eds.) VANET: Vehicular Applications and Inter-networking Technologies, ch. 10, pp. 365–428. Wiley (2010)
3. Stanica, R., Chaput, E., Beylot, A.-L.: Enhancements of IEEE 802.11p Protocol for Access Control on a VANET Control Channel. In: 2011 IEEE International Conference on Communications (ICC), June 5-9, pp. 1–5 (2011)
4. Calafate, C.T., Fortino, G., Fritsch, S., Monteiro, J., Cano, J., Manzoni, P.: An efficient and robust content delivery solution for IEEE 802.11p vehicular environments. Journal of Network and Computer Applications 35(2), 753–762 (2012)

5. Cali, F., Conti, M., Gregori, E.: Dynamic tuning of the IEEE 802.11 protocol to achieve a theoretical throughput limit. IEEE/ACM Transactions on Networking 8(6), 785–799 (2000)

6. Wu, H., Cheng, S., Peng, Y., Long, K., Ma, J.: IEEE 802.11 distributed coordination function (DCF): analysis and enhancement. In: IEEE International Conference on Communications, ICC 2002, vol. 1, pp. 605–609 (2002)

7. Balador, A., Movaghar, A., Jabbehdari, S.: History based contention window control in ieee 802.11 mac protocol in error prone channel. Journal of Computer Science 6(2), 205–209 (2010)

8. Chrysostomou, C., Djouvas, C., Lambrinos, L.: Applying adaptive QoS-aware medium access control in priority-based vehicular ad hoc networks. In: 2011 IEEE Symposium on Computers and Communications (ISCC), June 28-July 1, pp. 741–747 (2011)

9. Jang, H.-C., Feng, W.-C.: Network Status Detection-Based Dynamic Adaptation of Contention Window in IEEE 802.11p. In: 2010 IEEE 71st Vehicular Technology Conference (VTC 2010-Spring), May 16-19, pp. 1–5 (2010)

10. http://www.omnetpp.org/

11. http://inet.omnetpp.org/

12. Behrisch, M., Bieker, L., Erdmann, J., Krajzewicz, D.: SUMO - Simulation of Urban MObility: An Overview. In: The Third International Conference on Advances in System Simulation, SIMUL 2011 (2011)

13. Baguena, M., Tornell, S., Torres, A., Calafate, C.T., Cano, J.C., Manzoni, P.: VACaMobil: VANET Car Mobility Manager for OMNeT++. In: IEEE International Conference on Communications 2013 - 3rd IEEE International Workshop on Smart Communication Protocols and Algorithms (SCPA 2013), Budapest, Hungary (June 2013)

14. Baguena, M., Calafate, C.T., Cano, J., Manzoni, P.: Towards realistic vehicular network simulation models. In: 2012 IFIP Wireless Days (WD), November 21-23, pp. 1–3 (2012)

15. http://www.openstreetmap.org/

QL-MAC: A Q-Learning Based MAC
for Wireless Sensor Networks

Stefano Galzarano[1,2], Antonio Liotta[1], and Giancarlo Fortino[2]

[1] Department of Electrical Engineering,
Eindhoven University of Technology (TU/e), Eindhoven, The Netherlands
{s.galzarano,a.liotta}@tue.nl
[2] Department of Informatics, Modelling, Electronics and Systems (DIMES),
University of Calabria (UNICAL), Rende, Italy
g.fortino@unical.it

Abstract. WSNs are becoming an increasingly attractive technology thanks to the significant benefits they can offer to a wide range of application domains. Extending the system lifetime while preserving good network performance is one of the main challenges in WSNs. In this paper, a novel MAC protocol (QL-MAC) based on Q-Learning is proposed. Thanks to a distributed learning approach, the radio sleep-wakeup schedule is able to adapt to the network traffic load. The simulation results show that QL-MAC provides significant improvements in terms of network lifetime and packet delivery ratio with respect to standard MAC protocols. Moreover, the proposed protocol has a moderate computational complexity so to be suitable for practical deployments in currently available WSNs.

1 Introduction

Wireless Sensor Networks (WSNs) have grown in popularity in the last years and have proved to be beneficial in a wide range of applications in military, industry, and environmental monitoring domains [1]. A WSN is usually composed of small, low-cost, and low-power devices (sensor nodes) providing data acquisition, processing and wireless communication capabilities. Since sensor nodes can be deployed in unreachable areas, where charging or replacing batteries may be a very difficult task (sometimes impossible), the lifetime of the network is one of the most important characteristics of a WSN.

The medium access control (MAC) protocol is responsible for the access to the shared communication channel and, since energy is mostly consumed by the radio, it should guarantee an energy-efficiency radio management. This can be done by preventing the sources of energy waste such as overhearing, idle listening, excessive retransmissions, and packet collisions, by means of an adaptive behaviour that takes into account the actual network conditions.

The need for adaptive behaviours motivates the adoption of computational intelligence methods in sensor networks [2], also supported by the fact that machine learning approaches can be viable solutions even in the context of lightweight

J. Kołodziej et al. (Eds.): ICA3PP 2013, Part II, LNCS 8286, pp. 267–275, 2013.
© Springer International Publishing Switzerland 2013

sensor system [3,4]. In the area of machine learning, Q-Learning is a simple yet powerful reinforcement learning technique widely used in application contexts where an on-line optimal action-selection policy is required [5].

In this paper, a novel contention-based MAC protocol for WSNs, named QL-MAC and based on a Q-learning approach, is proposed. The protocol aims to find an efficient wake-up strategy to reduce energy consumption on the basis of the actual network load of the neighbourhood. Moreover, it benefits from a cross-layer interaction with the network layer, so to better understand the communication patterns and then to significantly reduce the energy consumption due to both idle listening and overhearing. Moreover, since it is well known that, along with network-level protocols [6,7], the MAC layer also contributes to the packet-delivery performance, QL-MAC has been designed to guarantee a high packet delivery ratio. Finally, the proposed protocol is inherently distributed and has the benefits of simplicity, low computation and overheads.

The rest of this paper is organised as follows. In Sect. 2, we report some of the most representative MAC approaches proposed for WSNs. Some basics on Q-Learning and a detailed description of QL-MAC are provided in Sect. 3. Section 4 discusses the simulation results. Finally, conclusions are drawn.

2   Related Work

Some of the simplest MAC protocols for wireless networks rely on the time division multiple access (TDMA) [8], which is a "contention-free" approach, where a pre-defined time slot is reserved for each node in each frame. Although such a fixed duty cycling does not suffer from packet collisions, it needs an extremely exact timing in order to avoid critical behaviours.

S-MAC [9] is a contention-based MAC protocol aiming at reducing energy consumption and collisions. It divides time into large frames, and each frame into two time portions (a sleeping phase and an active phase). Compared to the TDMA approach, S-MAC requires much looser synchronization among neighbouring nodes. However, due to a fixed duty cycle it is not capable of adapting to network traffic condition.

The Timeout-MAC (TMAC) protocol [10] is an improvement of S-MAC as it uses an adaptive duty cycle. In particular, by means of a time-out mechanism it detects possible activities in its vicinity. If no activity is detected during the time-out interval, the node goes to sleep for a certain period of time. Such a mechanism occurs every time a communication between two nodes is over. Although T-MAC outperforms S-MAC, its performance degrades under high traffic loads.

In the P-MAC [11] protocol the sleep-wakeup schedules of the sensor nodes are adaptively determined on the basis of a node's own traffic and that of its neighbours. The idle listening periods, which are source of energy wastage, are minimized by means of some kind of matching algorithm among patterns of schedules in the neighbouring.

Other adaptive MAC protocols have been proposed in the literature and few of them employ online machine learning approaches such as reinforcement learning [12,13] and Q-learning [14].

3   QL-MAC Protocol

The aim of the proposed protocol is to allow nodes to infer each other's behaviours in order to adopt a good sleep/active scheduling policy that dynamically learn over the time to better adapts to the network traffic conditions. Specifically, each node, not only takes into consideration its own packet traffic due to the application layer, but also considers its neighbourhood's state.

The basic underlying behaviour of the QL-MAC is similar to most of other MAC protocols: a simple asynchronous CSMA-CA approach is employed over a frame-based structure. It basically divides the time into discrete time units, the *frames*, which are further divided into smaller time units, the *slots*. Both frame length and slot number are parameters of the algorithm and remain unchanged at execution time.

By means of a Q-Learning based algorithm, each node independently determines an efficient wake-up schedule in order to limit as much as possible the number of slots in which the radio is turned on. Such a non-fixed and adaptive duty-cycle reduces the energy consumption over the time without affecting the other network performances, as shown by the simulations results discussed in Sect. 4.

3.1   Reinforcement Learning and Q-Learning

Reinforcement Learning (RL) [5] is a sub-area of machine learning concerned with how an agent take actions so as to maximize some kind of long-term reward. In particular, the agent explores its environment by selecting at each step a specific action and receiving a corresponding reward from the environment. Since the best action is never known a-priori, the agent has to learn from its experience, by means of the execution of a sequence of different actions and deducing what should be the best behaviour from the obtained corresponding rewards.

One of the most popular and powerful algorithm based on RL is Q-Learning, which does not need the environment to be modelled and whose actions depend on a so called *Q-function*, which indicates the quality of a specific action at a specific agent's state. Specifically, the Q-values are updated as follows:

$$Q(s_{t+1}, a_t) = Q(s_t, a_t) + \lambda[r_{t+1} + \phi \max_a Q(s_{t+1}, a) - Q(s_t, a_t)] \qquad (1)$$

where $Q(s_t, a_t)$ is the current value at state s_t, when action a_t is selected.

At some state s_t, the agent selects an action a_t. It finds the maximum possible Q-value in the next state s_{t+1}, given that a_t is taken, and updates the current Q-value. The discounting factor $0 < \phi < 1$ gives preference either to immediate rewards (if $\phi << 1$) or to rewards in the future (if $\phi >> 0$), whereas the learning rate $0 < \lambda < 1$ is used to tune the speed of learning.

3.2 Protocol Details

The actions available to each agent/node consist in deciding whether it should stay in active or in sleep mode during each single time slot. Thus, the action space of a node is determined by the number of slots within a frame. Setting the optimal length of the frames or the amount of time slots within a frame will not be discussed in this paper due to space restrictions.

Every node stores a set of Q-value, each of which is coupled to a specific slot within the frame. The Q-value represents an indication of the benefits that a node has when is awake during the related time slot. The Q-value is updated over the time on the basis of some specific events occurring during the same slot at each frame. Moreover, it is also dependent on some state information coming from the node's neighbours.

Specifically, every Q-value related to a specific node i is updated as follows:

$$Q_s^i(f+1) = (1-\lambda)Q_s^i(f) + \lambda R_s^i(f) \tag{2}$$

where $Q_s^i(f) \in [0,1]$ is the current Q-value associated to the slot s on the frame f, $Q_s^i(f+1)$ is the updated Q-value, which will be associated to the same slot s but on the next frame, λ is the learning rate and R_s^i is the earned reward. Differently from the update rule shown in (1), the future reward is not considered and the discount factor ϕ is set to 0.

In such a decentralized approach, it is important to define a suitable reward function that consider both the condition of the node and the one of its neighbourhood. Specifically, the events that the protocol takes into considerations are related to the packet traffic load, so that the reward function calculated on node i and related to a specific slot s is modelled as follow:

$$R_s^i = \alpha \left(\frac{RP - OH}{RP} \right) + \beta S_i + \gamma \left(\frac{\sum_{j=1}^{|N_i|} P_j}{|N_i|} \right) \tag{3}$$

where:

- OH is the number of over-heard packets, i.e. the packets received but actually not intended for node i;
- RP is the total amount of packets received by node i during the slot s of frame f. It includes also over-heard packets;
- S_i has a value of $+1$ if node i has at least one packet to broadcast during slot s, 0 otherwise;
- P_j has a value of $+1$ if the neighbouring node j has sent at least one packet to node i during slot s, 0 otherwise;
- N_i is the set of neighbours of node i;
- the constants α, β, and γ weigh the different terms of the function accordingly.

It is worth noting that, at the beginning, all the Q-values on every node are set to 1, meaning that all nodes have their radio transceiver ON on every slot (i.e. for the entire frame). During the learning process, the Q-values changes over the time accordingly to the variation of the reward function. In order to properly set the state for the radio transceiver on the basis of the Q-values, we employ a further parameter T_{ON}, which represents a threshold value:

$$Radio_{[slot\ s]} = \begin{cases} On & \text{if } Q_s^i(f) \geq T_{ON} \\ Off & \text{otherwise} \end{cases}$$

In case the MAC packet exchange takes place always in broadcast mode, so that a node is not able to figure out whether each single received packet is actually destined for itself or not, it is necessary to get some extra information from the upper layers. In particular, our MAC protocol employs a simple cross-layer communication: every received packet are decapsulated and delivered to the network layer, which in turns checks whether the packet is intended for the node. In case the packet is discarded, the network layer signals the MAC protocol about the reception of a overheard packet, and the reward function is updated accordingly to (3).

If the radio is turned off at a specific slot but at some point, during the same time window, the node needs to send a packet, we prefer to buffer it and postpone its transmission on the next available slot (i.e. the first one with the radio "on").

The last term of (3) is an aggregated information about the state of the node neighbourhood and, in particular, it represents the packet traffic activity during a specific time slot. This is the only information exchanged by the protocol and is fundamental when the node is in sleep mode at a specific slot so to figure out that it should be better to turn on the radio because of the presence of packets destined for it.

4 Simulations and Evaluation

QL-MAC is simulated and evaluated in Castalia[1], a plugin for OMNET++ specifically for simulating WSNs. In the following, the simulation scenarios are first described and then the obtained results are discussed. In particular, the performance evaluation considers two metrics: the average energy consumption of nodes and the Packet Delivery Ratio (PDR). Under these metrics, QL-MAC is compared to two well known MAC protocols for WSNs, SMAC and TMAC, as well as to a simple asynchronous CSMA-CA.

4.1 Scenario and Traffic Model

The protocol has been tested on two different scenarios, one with a regular grid topology (nodes have been uniformly placed) and the other with a random one. For both scenarios, the parameters setting summarized in Tab. 1 have been adopted. All nodes have been set with the same radio transceiver, the CC2420 with a transmission power level of 0dBm (which allows roughly 46 meters transmission range).

---

[1] http://castalia.research.nicta.com.au

Table 1. Parameters used in the simulations

Scenario Parameter	Value	QL-MAC Parameter	Value
# of nodes:	16	Frame length	1 sec
Sim. Area [mxm]:	100x100	Slot number	4
Radio device:	CC2420	λ	0.05
Transmission power:	0dBm	$alpha$	0.33
Collision model:	real	β	0.33
Packet rate:	$\approx$ 1 pkt/sec	γ	0.33
Data packet payload:	32 bytes	T_{ON}	0.40
Routing protocol	Multipath Rings Routing		
Initial energy	10000 J		

In the following, the communication pattern is detailed. The application we consider in our simulations employ a nodes-to-sink communication pattern, since data-collection applications are one of the most typical use cases of a WSN in real contexts. The sensor data acquired by all the nodes are sent to a sink node centered in the middle of the simulation area. Since the sink is not in the transmission range of every node, a simple multipaths ring routing has been used as a network layer protocol. During an initial setup phase, the sink broadcasts a specific packet with a counter set to 0. Once the packet is received by a node, it sets its own level/ring number to 0, increments the counter and rebroadcasts the packet. This process goes further on until all nodes get their ring level.

After this initial setup phase, every node has a ring number representing the hop distance to the sink. When a node has data to send, it broadcasts a data packet by attaching its ring number. Only the neighbours with a smaller ring number process the packet (i.e. attach its own ring number) and rebroadcast it. This process goes further on until the data packet gets to the sink.

4.2   Results

In order to understand the impact of the dynamic radio schedule adopted by QL-MAC on the network performance, the PDR has been first analysed, as shown in Fig. 1. As it can be seen, both on grid and random topology, QL-MAC outperforms all other MAC protocols with the exception of the CDMA-CA with a 100% duty cycle. In this case, both protocols have almost the same performance because of the underlying QL-MAC channel access, which is essentially the same.

Although both QL-MAC and CSMA-CA (with a 100% duty cycle) share the same PDR performance, their comparison result changes if we consider the node energy expenditure. In fact, as shown in Fig. 2, QL-MAC allows nodes to spend much less energy, as a result of the sleep/wake-up radio schedule. Moreover, it performs better even if compared to a CSMA-CA having a duty cycle of 60%. Both S-MAC and T-MAC show lesser energy consumption but, because of their limited capabilities, they are not able to adapt well to the network traffic pattern.

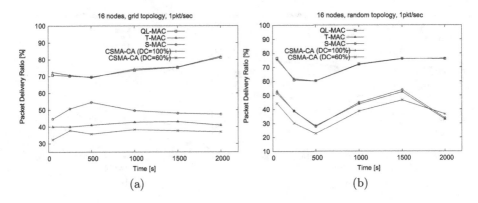

Fig. 1. Packet Delivery Ratio on grid (a) and random (b) topologies

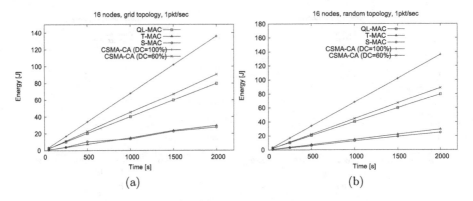

Fig. 2. The average energy consumption per node on grid (a) and random (b) topologies

QL-MAC has been also evaluated by varying the number of slots constituting the frame. In Fig. 3, the simulation results of both PDR and average energy consumption per node are depicted. In general, as the number of slots decreases, QL-MAC shows better performance with respect to the PDR but, as a consequence, the energy spent by node tends to increase. Actually, with the use of 8 slots, the protocol exhibits the better trade-off, i.e. the PDR is similar to the case with 4 slots, but the energy spent is less.

The results shown in Fig. 4 are obtained by varying the packet rate of the application layer, from 2 pkt/sec to 8 pkt/sec. As it can be seen, the PDR plots are similar over the time, demonstrating that QL-MAC behaves well under different traffic loads. But, since different amount of packets per time unit are transmitted and delivered, the energy expenditure increases with the increase of the packet rate.

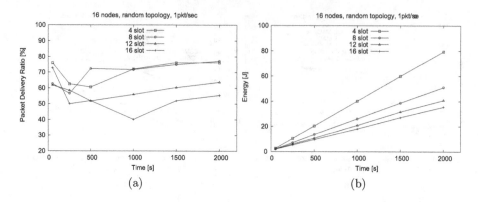

Fig. 3. QL-MAC: Packet Delivery Ratio and average energy consumption per node by varying the slot number

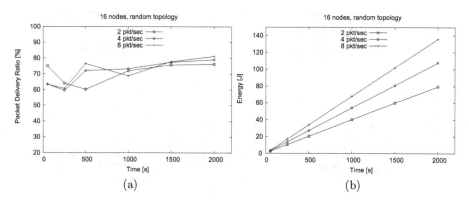

Fig. 4. QL-MAC: Packet Delivery Ratio and average energy consumption per node by varying the application packet rate

5   Conclusion

In this paper, a Q-Learning based MAC protocol is proposed. The learning algorithm is employed to find an efficient radio schedule on the basis of the node packet traffic and the traffic load of its neighbours. The simulation results show that, compared to other standard MAC protocols for WSNs, the adaptive behaviour of QL-MAC guarantees better network performances with respect to both the packet delivery ratio and the average energy consumption. Moreover, the learning approach requires minimal overhead and very low computational complexity.

References

1. Yick, J., Mukherjee, B., Ghosal, D.: Wireless sensor network survey. Computer Networks 52, 2292–2330 (2008)
2. Liotta, A.: The Cognitive Net is Coming. IEEE Spectrum 50, 26–31 (2013)
3. Bosman, H., Liotta, A., Iacca, G., Woertche, H.: Online extreme learning on fixed-point sensor networks. In: Proceedings of IEEE ICDM 2013 Workshop on Data Mining in Networks (DaMNet), Dallas, USA (2013)
4. Bosman, H., Liotta, A., Iacca, G., Woertche, H.: Anomaly detection in sensor systems using lightweight machine learning. In: Proceedings of IEEE International Conference on Systems, Man, and Cybernetics (SMC), Manchester, UK (2013)
5. Kaelbling, L.P., Littman, M.L., Moore, A.P.: Reinforcement learning: A survey. Journal of Artificial Intelligence Research 4, 237–285 (1996)
6. Liotta, A., Exarchakos, G.: Networks for Pervasive Services: Six Ways to Upgrade the Internet. Springer (2011)
7. Galzarano, S., Savaglio, C., Liotta, A., Fortino, G.: Gossiping-based AODV for Wireless Sensor Networks. In: Proceedings of IEEE International Conference on Systems, Man, and Cybernetics (SMC), Manchester, UK (2013)
8. Havinga, P.J., Smit, G.J.: Energy-efficient tdma medium access control protocol scheduling. In: Asian International Mobile Computing Conf., AMOC, pp. 1–10 (2000)
9. Ye, W., Heidemann, J., Estrin, D.: An energy-efficient mac protocol for wireless sensor networks. In: Proc. 21st International Annual Joint Conference of the IEEE Computer and Communications Societies, New York, USA (2002)
10. van Dam, T., Langendoen, K.: An adaptive energy-efficient mac protocol for wireless sensor networks. In: Proceedings of the 1st International Conference on Embedded Networked Sensor Systems, SenSys 2003 (2003)
11. Zheng, T., Radhakrishnan, S., Sarangan, V.: Pmac: an adaptive energy-efficient mac protocol for wireless sensor networks. In: Proceedings of the 19th IEEE International Parallel and Distributed Processing Symposium, 8 p. (2005)
12. Liu, Z., Elhanany, I.: RL-MAC: a reinforcement learning based MAC protocol for wireless sensor networks. Int. J. Sen. Netw. 1, 117–124 (2006)
13. Mihaylov, M., Tuyls, K., Nowé, A.: Decentralized learning in wireless sensor networks. In: Taylor, M.E., Tuyls, K. (eds.) ALA 2009. LNCS, vol. 5924, pp. 60–73. Springer, Heidelberg (2010)
14. Chu, Y., Mitchell, P., Grace, D.: ALOHA and q-learning based medium access control for wireless sensor networks. In: 2012 International Symposium on Wireless Communication Systems (ISWCS), pp. 511–515 (2012)

Predicting Battery Depletion
of Neighboring Wireless Sensor Nodes

Roshan Kotian, Georgios Exarchakos,
Decebal Constantin Mocanu, and Antonio Liotta

Eindhoven University of Technology, Den Dolech 2, 5612 AZ Eindhoven
{r.kotian,g.exarchakos,d.c.mocanu,a.liotta}@tue.nl

Abstract. With a view to prolong the duration of the wireless sensor
network, many battery lifetime prediction algorithms run on individual nodes. If not properly designed, this approach may be detrimental
and even accelerate battery depletion. Herein, we provide a comparative
analysis of various machine-learning algorithms to offload the energy-
inference task to the most energy-rich nodes, to alleviate the nodes that
are entering the critical state. Taken to its extreme, our approach may
be used to divert the energy-intensive tasks to a monitoring station,
enabling a cloud-based approach to sensor network management. Experiments conducted in a controlled environment with real hardware have
shown that RSSI can be used to infer the state of a remote wireless
node once it is approaching the cutoff point. The ADWIN algorithm was
used for smoothing the input data and for helping a variety of machine
learning algorithms particularly to speed up and improve their prediction
accuracy.

1 Introduction

When sensor nodes operate in harsh environments, there are many points of
failures. They need to have enough computational intelligence to cope with failures [8]. One of the main causes of failure could be fast, unpredictable battery
depletion of the nodes. Failure of strategic nodes can bring down the entire network and is not favorable for the end users who depend on it for their day-to-day
operation. Besides the support of critical applications, battery level prediction is
important for self-organization of wireless sensor networks (WSN). An important
action for topology control in a WSN is the power scaling of the transmitters.
The aim of such action is to improve the connectivity of the transmitter and
reduce the interference in a highly dense wireless network. However, a node is
not aware of how the transmission power should be scaled in order to avoid shad-
owing the neighbors. Symmetrically, in self-organized networks, nodes may react
on behalf of their neighbors to report a critical state to a monitoring system.

Within that context, this paper analyses the possibilities of using machine
learning algorithms to infer the critical state of the battery of a neighboring
node. Inference of that state can be used in both transmitter power scaling
or collaborative cloud-based monitoring. Failing nodes which lack the power to

J. Kołodziej et al. (Eds.): ICA3PP 2013, Part II, LNCS 8286, pp. 276–284, 2013.
© Springer International Publishing Switzerland 2013

transmit their state can be reported by neighboring nodes to a cloud service with a global overview of the network status. The cloud aggregates multiple data about the failing node from neighbors. It is, hence, more safely inferred whether that node is a strategic node and whether it can easily be assumed that the reported node is reaching the cutoff point.

The approach presented is a two-step processing of Received Signal Strength Indicator (RSSI) values. RSSI was chosen as it is an already available indicator in every sensor node and provides some indirect information about the remote transmitting node. The RSSI values are filtered at the node level with a fast inexpensive data smoothing algorithm. Then, the smoothened values are submitted to prediction algorithms running in the cloud for estimating the voltage level those values correspond to.

The contribution of this work lies on the comparative analysis of various well-established machine learning algorithms for predicting the voltage level of a remote node using exclusively RSSI values. Although our experimentations show that, the nature of RSSI values does not allow for an early and accurate inference of the nodes current voltage level, we found that the cutoff point is very quickly detectable by many algorithms. However it is essential that the chosen data smoothing algorithm (ADWIN) [3] does not only prune the outliers but also significantly reduces the amount of necessary data points for training the learning algorithms.

The remaining parts of this study are as follows. Section 2 provides a focused criticism on similar efforts to estimate the battery depletion rate. Section 3 is a description of the envisioned cloud-based system; and section 4 describes our experimental setup. Section 5 analyses the conducted experiments; and section 6 concludes and provides suggestions for further research steps on this topic.

2   Related Work

In the literature, we find two broad categories of techniques to maximize the lifetime of a sensor network based, respectively on 1) the prediction of the energy consumption in the WSN and 2) the prediction of the battery depletion of the sensor network. The latter one is an indirect way in the sense that knowing how fast the energy is depleting can help the network engineer replace the dying batteries of the node and thereby extend the operation time of the network. Further, the battery depletion techniques can be further classified into: a) battery life modeling and b) estimating techniques.

[7] points out that both the Received Signal Strength Indicator (RSSI) and the Link Quality Indicator (LQI) become unstable shortly before the depletion of the nodes battery. Based on the fact that as RSSI values deteriorate, Inacio et al [12] used six mathematical models such as Simple Average, linear regression, Auto regressive, etc. They found that auto regression could adequately represent the charge depletion process thereby permitting to predict the node behavior and to detect the moment to replace its batteries.

However, our experimental results point out that RSSI values are so unpredictable that the accuracy of most of the classification algorithms are not

plausible to claim that battery depletion can be predicted by the RSSI parameter alone.

3 System Overview

Figure 1 represents the system overview.

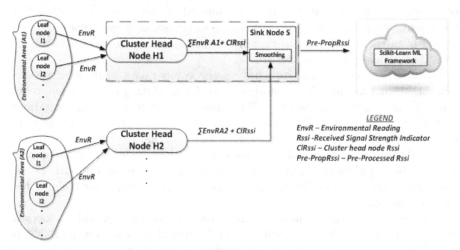

Fig. 1. System Overview

$\sum_{i=1}^{n} l_i$ represents the end nodes that are responsible for collecting the domain specific readings such as temperature, humidity, etc.

$\sum_{i=1}^{n} C_i$ represents the cluster head nodes that aggregates the data at local level. Once the head nodes collect aggregated data, it transmits it to the sink node S. The sink node S contains the ADWIN algorithm that does the pre-processing of the data and sends the pre-processed data to the cloud, which runs the popular scikit-Learn Machine Learning framework [10].

Due to environmental conditions such as interference or temperature, the RSSI values are non-linear in nature. Providing the Machine Learning algorithms with data having sharp variations can give less accurate predictions. In order to increase the prediction accuracy of the machine learning algorithms and to reduce the number of outliers, we need to smooth the data. Due to sharp variations in the RSSI values, it is not possible to classify whether the battery level is good, average, or bad with single RSSI value. Hence, we need to maintain a window that keeps the most recently read RSSI values. Furthermore, since machine learning is a time consuming process it should be triggered only when the average of the sequence of RSSI values in the window crosses the sensitivity threshold set by the network engineer. To meet the above-mentioned requirements, the algorithm of choice for our experiments is ADWIN as it uses the concept of sliding window allows for the engineers to set the sensitivity threshold an a priori parameter.

We used the scikit-Learn Machine learning framework to check how feasible it is to predict the battery depletion level classes (good, average, and bad), based on various popular classification algorithms.

4   Experimental Setup

Since RSSI is the sum of the pure received signal and the noise floor [1], it is important to reduce the noise floor to get accurate received signal strength readings. Therefore, the experimentation was conducted inside an anechoic chamber that is an interference free room.

The noise in the sensor node communication is introduced due to co-location of 802.11b network [11]. In addition to this, the presence of Bluetooth network and domestic appliances can significantly affect the transmission in the IEEE 802.15.4 network [1,13].

Since the concurrent transmission from other nodes in the network can introduce the noise in the communication channel [9] and for the sake of simplicity, only the communication between one cluster head node (transmitting) and sink node (receiving) was performed.

We conducted two sets of experiments using CrossBows TelosB motes. In the first setup, the distance between the transmission node and the receiving node was set to 2 meters. In the second setup, the distance was increased by 5 meters. The battery depletion of the transmitting cluster head node was emulated using Benchmark power supply.

The following settings were kept constant for the entire experiment.

1. The transmitting node was configured to send the data to the receiving node every 250 ms.
2. The receiving node connected to the laptop was our sink node.
3. The position of the transmitting and the receiving node was not changed during the entire experimentation process.
4. The amps were set at 0.25mA.
5. For every voltage ranging from 3V to 1.5V, 1000 RSSI reading were taken.

5   System Evaluation

This section presents the experimental results from conducting the aforementioned experiments. The section is split in two parts: data smoothing and battery level prediction. Data smoothing is executed at the sensor node level and aims at reducing either the processing or the communication or both. Moreover, it contributes on the efficiency of the prediction algorithm by reducing the outlier data points and, hence, the overlap of the classes used at classifiers or reducing the bias in the regression models. Smoothened data are the input to the prediction algorithms which are running in the cloud. The algorithms are evaluated based on their accuracy and speed.

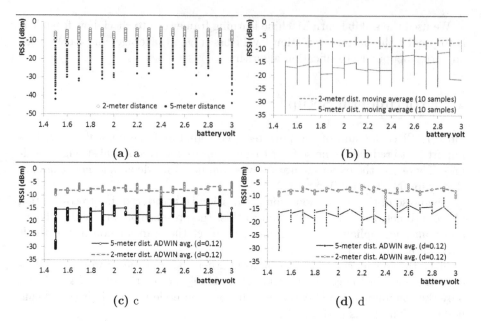

Fig. 2. Raw and pre-processed input data from the two monitored network conditions (two datasets for 2-meter and 5-meter distance between two sensors). Fig. 2a illustrates all raw datapoints, Fig. 2b presents the moving average of those datasets with a sliding window of 10 samples, Fig. 2c depicts the output of ADWIN algorithm in verbose mode and Fig. 2d illustrates the ADWIN output when the window size changes. you need to add the labels a to d to the actual plots.

Fig. 2 presents the raw input RSSI data in the two datasets as well as the smoothing of that data using a naive moving average (Fig. 2b) and the ADWIN (Fig. 2c and Fig. 2d) algorithms. The moving average algorithm outputs the average value of a window of the 10 latest samples for every new RSSI value received. The ADWIN algorithm is used in two modes:

- *Verbose*: for every RSSI value received, ADWIN outputs the average value of the current window (Fig. 2c).
- *Change-detection*: ADWIN provides the average value of the last window just on moments of a change at the window size (Fig. 2d).

As shown in Fig. 2a, the two RSSI raw datasets are overlapping. On the one hand, the moving average algorithm filters out many outliers that were causing that overlap. On the other hand, ADWIN has reduced significantly the variance of the two datasets and has increased the gap in between. As expected, the data-points generated by ADWIN in Fig. 2d are significantly fewer than those in Fig. 2c as data are submitted to the prediction algorithms in the cloud solely upon a considerable change to the ADWIN window size.

An ADWIN window changes upon a shift of the estimated voltage level, i.e. concept, based on the received RSSI values. Had such concept shift not been

Table 1. Legends for Table 2, 3, 4, and 5

SVM-RBK: Support Vector Machine with Radial Basis Kernel[6]
SVM-PK: Support Vector Machine with Polynomial Kernel[6]
GMM: Gaussian Mixture Model[4]
RFT: Random Forest Trees[5]
KNN: K Nearest Neighbors[4]
LogR+RBM: Logistic Regression[4] built on a top of a
Restricted Boltzmann Machine[2]
LogR: Logistic Regression[4]
LR: Linear Regression[4]
RC: Random Classifier
Not available(NA): Algorithm was halted if being executed for more
than 1 minute.

Table 2. Prediction algorithms evaluation. Input data come from the output of AD-WIN in verbose mode. RSSI values are classified to one of the 16 voltage levels i.e. classes.

Classification Algorithms	2-meter distance dataset		5-meter distance dataset	
	Accuracy (%)	Time (sec)	Accuracy (%)	Time (sec)
SVM-RBK	10.76%	3.7464	10.51%	3.7499
SVM-PK	NA	> 1 minute	NA	> 1 minute
GMM	5.51%	2.3817	7.27%	3.2728
RFT	10.23%	0.3366	9.76%	0.3472
KNN	10.19%	0.0108	9.89%	0.0107
LogR+RBM	12.86%	4.1106	13.99%	4.0429
LogR	12.71%	0.1648	12.36%	0.1727
LR	5.62%	0.0277	10.56%	0.0221
RC	6.25%		6.25%	

present, there would also be no need for triggering the battery voltage level prediction algorithm. Therefore, ADWIN on change-detection mode reduces the communication overhead for the sensor nodes and the processing overhead for the prediction algorithms.

The input data shown in Fig. 2 are the training data for the prediction algorithms. Every training data-point in those datasets is classified to one of the 16 voltage levels (1.5v-3v). Therefore, any RSSI value from the testing datasets has to be fed into the prediction algorithm and classified to one of those levels i.e. classes. The output of ADWIN algorithm in both modes was used for the classification process. Tables 2 and 3 (please see Table 1 for the acronyms description) present the evaluation of various algorithms with regards to their accuracy (percentage of input data-points classified in the correct class) and execution time (seconds spent during training phase). From Table 2, it becomes clear that all tested algorithms perform at most twice as good as a random classifier. On the other hand, Table 3 demonstrates a slightly improved situation when the

Table 3. Prediction algorithms evaluation. Input data come from the output of AD-WIN in change-detection mode. RSSI values are classified to one of 16 voltage levels i.e. classes.

Classification Algorithms	2-meter distance dataset		5-meter distance dataset	
	Accuracy (%)	Time (sec)	Accuracy (%)	Time (sec)
SVM-RBK	7.86%	0.0010	12.10%	0.00309
SVM-PK	17.97%	0.4803	NA	> 1 minute
GMM	8.98%	0.0523	8.28%	0.0630
RFT	17.97%	0.0050	15.92%	0.0050
KNN	12.35%	0.0007	12.10%	0.0005
LogR+RBM	12.35%	0.0492	14.01%	0.0799
LogR	11.23%	0.0492	13.37%	0.0034
LR	7.86%	0.0019	12.74%	0.0003
RC	6.25%		6.25%	

Table 4. Prediction algorithms evaluation. Input data come from the output of AD-WIN in verbose mode. RSSI values are classified to one of two classes (1.5-1.6V or 1.7-3V).

Classification Algorithms	2-meter distance dataset		5-meter distance dataset	
	Accuracy (%)	Time (sec)	Accuracy (%)	Time (sec)
SVM-RBK	89.11%	1.5670	86.08%	2.1382
SVM-PK	NA	> 1 minute	NA	> 1 minute
GMM	67.08%	0.4543	64.14%	0.4907
RFT	83.19%	0.1664	79.19%	0.2405
KNN	81.10%	0.0109	76.95%	0.0110
LogR+RBM	87.44%	2.8912	87.41%	4.8276
LogR	92.44%	0.1741	84.65%	0.1659
LR	24.75%	0.0218	26.03%	0.0220
RC	50.00%		50.00%	

classifiers use ADWIN output exclusively when the window adapts to the concept drifting. However, even in that case (ADWIN in change-detection mode) their performance is limited. Therefore, the results in tables 2 and 3 are inconclusive with regards to the inference of the battery level of a neighboring sensor node using only received RSSI values.

There are various reasons behind this inaccuracy. The input raw RSSI values have very high variance for each voltage level. This variance, in a well-controlled environment like the anechoic chamber, might be caused by the inaccuracy of RSSI register at the receiver, which, in TelosB nodes, varies for 6dBm. Moreover, the average RSSI value of any voltage level differs maximum 3dBm from any other level. These two issues create a very wide overlapping among the voltage classes that all the tested classifiers cannot easily detect. However, during the experiments above we noticed that two voltage levels were more accurately

Table 5. Prediction algorithms evaluation. Input data come from the output of AD-WIN in change-detection mode. RSSI values are classified to one of two classes (1.5-1.6V or 1.7-3V).

Classification Algorithms	2-meter distance dataset		5-meter distance dataset	
	Accuracy (%)	Time (sec)	Accuracy (%)	Time (sec)
SVM-RBK	86.51%	0.0004	85.35%	0.0009
SVM-PK	92.13%	0.3010	78.34%	10.8300
GMM	68.53%	0.0137	73.88%	0.0206
RFT	88.76%	0.0040	85.35%	0.0040
KNN	88.76%	0.0006	84.71%	0.0005
LogR+RBM	91.01%	0.0387	85.98%	0.0629
LogR	89.88%	0.0019	85.98%	0.0032
LR	29.21%	0.0003	31.84%	0.0003
RC	50.00%		50.00%	

inferred than others. As shown in Table 4 and Table 5, the classifiers can perform much better when just two classes are considered. Instead of 16 classes, the classifiers were trained with the same input data to classify data-points into either the 1.5V-1.6V class or the 1.7V-3.0V class. That classification can practically infer if the battery of the remote sensor has maximum 0.2V before it is drained. Table 4 presents an accuracy of tested classifiers up to 92.4% for the 2-meter distance dataset and up to 87.4% for the 5-meter distance dataset. The benefit of using ADWIN in change-detection mode is shown in Table 5 as the accuracy or execution time of many algorithms is considerably improved compared to Table 4.

6   Conclusions and Future Work

We found through our experimentation that the nature of the RSSI values does not allow for an early and accurate prediction of the stationary node's current voltage level. On the contrary, the cut-off point (1.6V and 1.5V), most of the time detectable by majority of the classification algorithms.

In the course of the experiment, we discovered that providing the classification algorithm with raw RSSI values reduces the accuracy of the prediction of the algorithms. The reason for this being large of number of outliers.

Furthermore, we found that it is not possible to classify whether the battery level is good, average, or bad with single RSSI value. Therefore, we needed to maintain a window that buffers the most recent RSSI values.

In addition to this, since classification algorithms are computational intensive process it should be triggered only when the average sequence of RSSI values in the windows exceeds the sensitivity set by the users.

To cater these demanding needs, we found ADWIN algorithm to be best suited to reduce the time and computing cost of the machine learning algorithms.

References

1. Baccour, N., Koubaa, A., Mottola, L., Zuniga, M.A., Youssef, H., Boano, C.A., Alves, M.: Radio link quality estimation in wireless sensor networks. ACM Transactions on Sensor Networks 8(4), 1–33 (2012)
2. Bengio, Y.: Learning deep architectures for ai. Found. Trends Mach. Learn. 2(1), 1–127 (2009)
3. Bifet, A., Holmes, G., Kirkby, R., Pfahringer, B.: Data stream mining (May 2011)
4. Bishop, C.M.: Pattern Recognition and Machine Learning. Information Science and Statistics. Springer-Verlag New York, Inc., Secaucus (2006)
5. Breiman, L.: Random forests. Mach. Learn. 45(1), 5–32 (2001)
6. Cortes, C., Vapnik, V.: Support-vector networks. Mach. Learn. 20(3), 273–297 (1995)
7. Forster, A., Puccinelli, D., Giordano, S.: Sensor node lifetime: An experimental study. In: 2011 IEEE International Conference on Pervasive Computing and Communications Workshops (PERCOM Workshops), pp. 202–207. IEEE (March 2011)
8. Liotta, A.: The cognitive NET is coming. IEEE Spectrum 50(8), 26–31 (2013)
9. Mottola, L., Picco, G.P., Ceriotti, M., Guna, S., Murphy, A.L.: Not all wireless sensor networks are created equal. ACM Transactions on Sensor Networks 7(2), 1–33 (2010)
10. Pedregosa, F., Varoquaux, G., Gramfort, A., Michel, V., Thirion, B., Grisel, O., Blondel, M., Prettenhofer, P., Weiss, R., Dubourg, V., Vanderplas, J., Passos, A., Cournapeau, D., Brucher, M., Perrot, M., Duchesnay, E.: Scikit-learn: Machine learning in Python. Journal of Machine Learning Research 12, 2825–2830 (2011)
11. Srinivasan, K., Dutta, P., Tavakoli, A., Levis, P.: An empirical study of low-power wireless. ACM Transactions on Sensor Networks 6(2), 1–49 (2010)
12. Yano, I.H., Oliveira, V.C., Alberto, E., Fagotto, D.M., Mota, A.D.A., Toledo, L., Mota, M.: Predicting battery charge depliton in Wireless Sensor Networks using received signal strength indicator. Journal of Computer Science 9(7), 821–826 (2013)
13. Zhou, G., He, T., Krishnamurthy, S., Stankovic, J.A.: Models and solutions for radio irregularity in wireless sensor networks. ACM Transactions on Sensor Networks 2(2), 221–262 (2006)

TuCSoN on Cloud:
An Event-Driven Architecture
for Embodied / Disembodied Coordination

Stefano Mariani and Andrea Omicini

DISI, Alma Mater Studiorum–Università di Bologna
via Sacchi 3, 47521 Cesena, Italy
{s.mariani,andrea.omicini}@unibo.it

Abstract. The next generation of computational systems is going to mix up pervasive scenarios with cloud computing, with both intelligent and non-intelligent agents working as the reference component abstractions. A uniform set of MAS abstractions expressive enough to deal with both *embodied* and *disembodied* computation is required, in particular when dealing with the complexity of interaction. Along this line, in this paper we define an *event-driven coordination architecture*, along with a coherent *event model*, and test it upon the TuCSoN model and technology for MAS coordination.

1 Embodied / Disembodied Coordination in MAS

MAS (multi-agent systems) have proven to be quite an effective technology to deal with complex systems [1] in a plethora of different application scenarios: sensor networks [2], biological systems simulation [3, 4], robotics [5] are just a few to mention. In turn, coordination models, languages and infrastructures have been deeply influenced by the evolution of MAS application scenarios [6], mostly due to their very nature: that is, being conceived and designed to manage the *interaction space* of MAS [7], typically working as their foremost source of complexity [8].

Such heterogeneity is reflected by the diversity of MAS (and coordination) abstractions, models, and architectures adopted to deal with different MAS deployment scenarios. In particular, one fundamental issue is raised by the increasing popularity of two apparently antithetical technological paradigms: *pervasive systems* on the one hand, *cloud computing* on the other. Whereas pervasive systems strongly rely on the situated, *embodied* nature of their software and hardware components to provide the features of context-awareness, (self-)adaptation, and self-organisation required to cope with an ever-changing environment [9], cloud computing has its strength in its *disembodiment* of the computation, that is, in its being essentially independent of its physical nature [10]. Nonetheless, we believe *embodied* systems – as pervasive ones – and *disembodied* systems – as cloud-based ones – should be viewed and dealt with as complementary technologies, to be exploited in synergy so as to better tackle real-world problems with the right *"degree of situatedness"*.

J. Kołodziej et al. (Eds.): ICA3PP 2013, Part II, LNCS 8286, pp. 285–294, 2013.
© Springer International Publishing Switzerland 2013

Accordingly, in this paper we first propose an *event-driven architecture*, along with a coherent *event model*, promoting the integration of embodied and disembodied coordinated systems, then test it so as to bring the TuCSoN coordination technology [11] to the cloud.

2   Embodied *vs.* Disembodied: Event-Driven Architecture

Integrating coordination of embodied and disembodied systems in a coherent conceptual framework requires a number of issues to be addressed:

- how to characterise both embodied and disembodied entities within a system, and how to refer them—essentially, an *identification & reference* problem
- which abstractions should be used to reconcile embodied computations with disembodied ones—a *modelling* problem
- which architectural design should be used to support embodied computations as well as disembodied ones—an *architectural* problem

2.1   Embodied / Disembodied Identification and Reference

In order to seamlessly integrate embodied and disembodied coordinated systems, two things are required first of all: *(i)* a single, coherent notion of *identity*; *(ii)* some means to *refer* entities based on their properties. A reference may be as complex as needed not only by the application at hand, but also by the technological paradigm adopted: e.g., whereas pervasive systems may exploit some spatio-temporal properties of coordinated entities to denote them – e.g., "the 1-hop neighbourhood of entity X" –, cloud computing typically relies on system-generated global identifiers, mostly because the cloud system itself should not expose its awareness of the spatio-temporal fabric it lives in.

In any sort of distributed systems, a computational entity, either a disembodied or an embodied one, is first of all identified by means of a *global, univocal* identifier, and accessed through white-pages services. Also, components – as in the case of heterogeneous *environment resources* – could be referred through their properties, typically represented in the form of key-value pairs (as in attribute-based naming), and accessed through yellow-pages services.

In addition, in the case of situated entities, an entity can be referred also according to its spatio-temporal properties:

spatial reference — it could be any spatial characterisation identifying a set of nodes whose chosen spatial property has the same value—e.g., "all the nodes within range (X, Y, Z) from node n", but also "all nodes at latitude X, longitude Y, altitude Z"

time reference — it can be any temporal characterisation identifying a set of nodes whose chosen temporal property has the same value—e.g., "all the nodes in range δ from instant t", but also "all nodes at instant t"

Thus, an integrated reference & identification model for embodied / disembodied computational systems should account for both *disembodied references* (white and yellow pages) and *embodied references* (time and spatial references).

Table 1. Event model integrating embodied / disembodied coordination

⟨*Event*⟩ ::= ⟨*Start*⟩ , ⟨*Cause*⟩ , ⟨*Evaluation*⟩
⟨*Start*⟩ , ⟨*Cause*⟩ ::= ⟨*Activity*⟩ , ⟨*Source*⟩ , ⟨*Target*⟩ , ⟨*Time*⟩ , ⟨*Space : Place*⟩
⟨*Source*⟩ , ⟨*Target*⟩ ::= ⟨*AgentId*⟩ | ⟨*CoordMediumId*⟩ | ⟨*EnvResId*⟩ | ⊥
⟨*Activity*⟩ ::= ⟨*Operation*⟩ | ⟨*Situation*⟩

2.2 Embodied Event Model

Once complex computational systems are conceptualised as coordinated MAS, the core entity which all revolves around is the one of *event* [12, 13]. Everything occurring in a coordinated MAS generates an event, be it a coordination operation request issued by an agent, a change in environmental properties, as well as a change in the space-time fabric. Events should be handled so as to keep track of all the related information, such as the *cause* of the event, and its *context*—what "action" caused the event, who did it, toward whom it has been done, when and where, what its outcome is.

The generic reference model for embodied / disembodied events is sketched by the grammar rules in Table 1, which are based on the formal syntax of the ReSpecT language event model [14–17], here extended to cope with both embodied and disembodied coordination. There, ⟨*AgentId*⟩, ⟨*CoordMediumId*⟩, and ⟨*EnvResId*⟩ represent global identification terms for agents, coordination media, and environment resources, respectively. Furthermore:

⟨**Event**⟩ is the complete event descriptor
⟨**Start**⟩ is the primary cause of the event—either an agent or the environment
⟨**Cause**⟩ is the direct cause of the event—an agent, a medium, the environment
⟨**Evaluation**⟩ represents the effect of the event on the MAS
⟨**Activity**⟩ is the "stimulus" that actually produced the event—such as a coordination operation or an environmental property change
⟨**Operation**⟩ represents any coordination operation
⟨**Situation**⟩ represents any change, either spatio-temporal or environmental
⟨**Time**⟩ is any expression of time—e.g, absolute time, relative time
⟨**Space**⟩ is the sort of the spatial characterisation—e.g., physical, organisational, network space
⟨**Place**⟩ is any expression of location in space—e.g., physical location, organisational place, network node, etc.

The need for a distinction from direct cause and original, "starting" cause comes from the need of recording *chains* of events, where an initial event starts a sequence of events—as in the case of *linking* of coordination media [18].

It is easy to see how the proposed event model suits both embodied and disembodied coordination. In an embodied coordinated MAS, all the expressive power of the the event model is required to deal with environmental as well as spatio-temporal situatedness. In a disembodied coordinated MAS, instead, some of the available properties could be simply ignored. However, when integrating embodied and disembodied coordinated systems, disembodied computation could usefully handle situation aspects—e.g., for recording situated properties of events in the cloud. The main point here is that we need a language able to represent any potentially-useful aspect of an event, including situation properties. The event model just described is a fundamental part of such a language.

2.3   Embodied / Disembodied Architecture

Roughly speaking, once both a reference system and an event model are defined, components can be named and interact with each other. How they do actually interact with each other can be described by defining the architecture for embodied / disembodied coordinated systems.

The core abstraction of our coordination architecture is the (coordination) *node*, that is, the entity responsible for the management of the *interaction space* where all entities – such as agents and other nodes – interact with each other according to a disciplined set of coordination policies. In order to preserve and support situatedness for embodied coordination, and transparency for disembodied coordination, the node is given both an embodied and a disembodied nature. As a disembodied abstraction, a node is identified by using a universal identifier. As an embodied abstraction, a node is denoted by its spatio-temporal properties—typically depending on the computational device hosting the node itself.

Other abstractions and architectural components, depicted in Fig. 1 and Fig. 2, are referred and identified with respect to the node and its properties. Fig. 1 shows the three fundamental abstractions exploited by the proposed architecture, along with the relationships with their classification according to the A&A meta-model [19, 20]:

ACC — The *Agent Coordination Context* (ACC) [21] is the abstraction governing agents interaction with the coordination media within a node. It *enables* and *constraints* the space of interaction by providing agents with the coordination operations available according to the agent's role in the MAS. Since every ACC associates a node with a single agent, the ACC is an *individual, boundary* artefact according to [19, 20].

tuple centre — The *tuple centre* is a programmable coordination medium, ruling and decoupling (in control, reference, space and time) agents' interactions [22]. Since it manages the overall agent interaction space, the tuple centre is a *social, coordination* artefact according to [19, 20].

transducer — The *transducer* is the abstraction modelling arbitrary environmental resources that a MAS interacts with [16]. Analogously to ACC for agents, transducers enable and constraint environmental resource interaction capabilities, by translating resource-generated events into the event model suitable to be handled by the coordination medium. Being aimed at modelling an environmental resource, the transducer is a *resource, boundary* artefact.

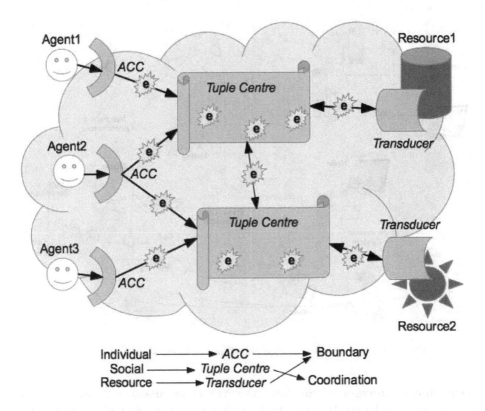

Fig. 1. Embodied/disembodied abstractions in a coordination node

As highlighted by Fig. 1, communication between these abstractions is entirely *event-driven*, by adopting the event model proposed in Subsection 2.2. Furthermore, each abstraction communicate *asynchronously* with any other. This, coupled with the persistent and autonomous nature of tuple centres, allows for a complete *decoupling in control*, which is a mandatory feature if are willing to deal with open, distributed MAS.

Fig. 2 further details our reference architecture by specifying the role of the node, and introducing new architectural elements:

node — The *node* collects all tuple centres running locally on the same device and reachable at the same "address"—be it the IP:port pair or any other notion of identity. It is responsible for tuple centres lifecycle, ACC negotiation, transducers (de)registration, events dispatching.

ACC manager — The *ACC manager* is delegated by the node to handle ACC requests by MAS agents. As such, it must take care of the negotiation process as well as of the mediation process, that is, allowing admissible interactions while forbidding others. Furthermore, it keeps track of all the ACC-agent mappings for the node it belongs to.

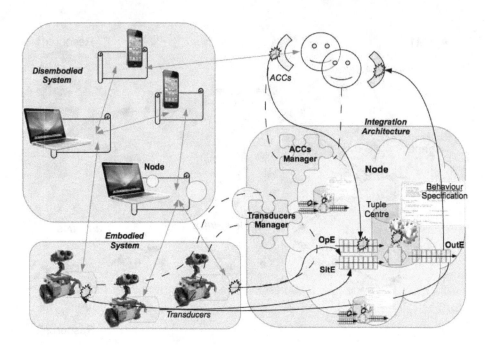

Fig. 2. Embodied/disembodied coordination integration architecture

transducer manager — Similarly, the *transducer manager* is delegated by the node to handle transducers dynamic registration. As such, it is responsible to act as an interface between the resource communication paradigm and working cycle and the tuple centre own. Obviously, it keeps track of Transducer-resource mappings on behalf of the Node.

OpE — The *Operation Event multiset* is the data structure in which incoming operation events – that is, whose source is an agent or a tuple centre – are stored, waiting to be processed. Whenever an agent issues a coordination operation request, its ACC maps such request to an operation event, which is then sent to the OpE. This happens asynchronously, thus preserving both agents and nodes autonomy.

SitE — Similarly, the *Situation Event multiset* stores situation events – that is, transducers-generated ones or those belonging to the space-time fabric – waiting to be processed. Whenever a space, time, or environmental property changes, this is mapped onto a situation event – by the resource transducer, in the case of an environmental property, or by the coordination medium itself in the case of the space-time fabric –, which is then sent to SitE. Again, all of this happens asynchronously, thus preserving also resources autonomy.

OutE — Finally, the *Output Event multiset* should store outgoing events of any kind—e.g., changing a "switched on" property of a motion actuator via a resource transducer. This multiset is filled as soon as the tuple centre generates outgoing events in response to incoming events processing. As usual, this data structure is managed asynchronously—that is, insertion of an event and its dispatching happen in two distinct computational steps.

3   Case Study: TuCSoN on Cloud

The TuCSoN coordination technology[1] [11] is a Java-based middleware supporting tuple-based coordination of autonomous agents in an open environment. Featuring tuProlog [23] first-order logic tuples, and ReSpecT [14] tuple centres – that is, programmable tuple spaces –, TuCSoN supports coordination of intelligent agents – e.g., BDI-based – according to custom-defined coordination policies, dependent on the application at hand. The TuCSoN middleware adopts the embodied / disembodied integration architecture introduced in Section 2, in particular:

- TuCSoN *nodes* host the coordination media (tuple centres), and are univocally identified by a Java UUID[2]
- the ReSpecT *language* [22], used to program TuCSoN tuple centres, features the event model sketched in Subsection 2.2, thus supporting recording and inspection of all the properties described in Table 1
- the TuCSoN middleware itself is built according to the logical architecture depicted in Subsection 2.3, therefore featuring ACC as well as transducers

Recently, TuCSoN has been successfully wrapped into a *Cloudify*[3] service, so as to be run as a disembodied coordination service—in particular, a private cloud. Nevertheless, the *on-Cloud* distribution can seamlessly integrate with the *out-Cloud* one, indeed, thanks to the adopted event model and architecture. Fig. 3 depicts a typical embodied / disembodied coordination integration scenario: on the left, a TuCSoN-coordinated WSN (thus, embodied) [2]; on the right, a cloud computing infrastructure (disembodied).

Between the two coordinated subsystems, a new architectural component is added to the TuCSoN middleware: the *node manager*. In fact, the core of the integrated embodied / disembodied architecture as depicted in Subsection 2.3 is the notion of node, as a twofold abstraction: an embodied and a disembodied notion, at the same time, as described above. Since coordination media are hosted by nodes, ACC are associated to nodes, agents and resources interact with nodes, this seamlessly allows all coordination entities to participate to both embodied and disembodied coordination, without affecting their coordination behaviour.

Node managers have a twofold duty: *(i)* handle cloud-related issues, such as user accounting, nodes startup/shutdown, relocation, load-balancing and the like; *(ii)* translate events back and forth the embodied / disembodied systems (if needed). In fact, whereas embodied events can be effortlessly handled by in-Cloud TuCSoN – it can either ignore situated event properties or consider them,

---

[1] http://tucson.unibo.it, LGPL-available

[2] http://docs.oracle.com/javase/7/docs/api/java/util/UUID.html

[3] http://www.cloudifysource.org

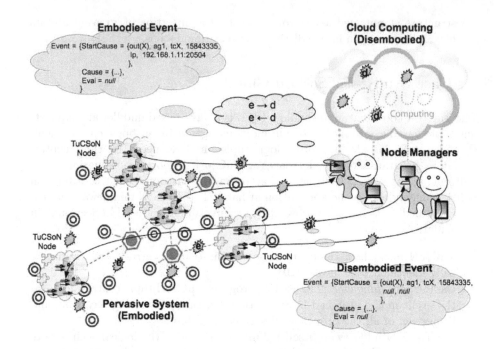

Fig. 3. TuCSoN on Cloud typical deployment scenario

thanks to ReSpecT –, disembodied events *can* be filled-in with situated data to be effectively handled by out-Cloud TuCSoN—e.g., ⟨*Space : Place*⟩ attribute could be either left blank or filled with internal information from the cloud infrastructure.

4   Conclusions

In this paper we faced the problem of integrating embodied and disembodied systems, when computational systems are modelled as coordinated MAS. Accordingly, we proposed an event-driven coordination architecture exploiting a coherent event model and a uniform reference system promoting the seamless integration of embodied and disembodied coordination. Then, we briefly described how the TuCSoN middleware for tuple-based coordination of autonomous agents can work as an effective technology upon which such architecture and event model can be straightforwardly implemented.

Acknowledgments. We would like to thank Richiard Casadei and Luca Guerra for their early work on TuCSoN on Cloud.

This work has been partially supported by the EU-FP7-FET Proactive project SAPERE – Self-aware Pervasive Service Ecosystems, under contract no. 256874.

References

1. Omicini, A., Mariani, S.: Agents & multiagent systems: En route towards complex intelligent systems. Intelligenza Artificiale 7(2) (November 2013); Special Issue for the 25th Anniversary of AI*IA
2. Aiello, F., Bellifemine, F.L., Fortino, G., Galzarano, S., Gravina, R.: An agent-based signal processing in-node environment for real-time human activity monitoring based on wireless body sensor networks. Engineering Applications of Artificial Intelligence 24(7), 1147–1161 (2011)
3. González Pérez, P.P., Omicini, A., Sbaraglia, M.: A biochemically-inspired coordination-based model for simulating intracellular signalling pathways. Journal of Simulation 7(3), 216–226 (2013); Special Issue: Agent-based Modeling and Simulation
4. Pianini, D., Montagna, S., Viroli, M.: Chemical-oriented simulation of computational systems with Alchemist. Journal of Simulation 7(3), 202–215 (2013); Special Issue: Agent-based Modeling and Simulation
5. Cossentino, M., Sabatucci, L., Chella, A.: A possible approach to the development of robotic multi-agent systems. In: IEEE/WIC International Conference on Intelligent Agent Technology, IAT 2003, pp. 539–544 (2003)
6. Omicini, A.: Nature-inspired coordination for complex distributed systems. In: Fortino, G., Badica, C., Malgeri, M., Unland, R. (eds.) Intelligent Distributed Computing VI. SCI, vol. 446, pp. 1–6. Springer, Heidelberg (2012)
7. Omicini, A., Viroli, M.: Coordination models and languages: From parallel computing to self-organisation. The Knowledge Engineering Review 26(1), 53–59 (2011)
8. Wegner, P.: Why interaction is more powerful than algorithms. Communications of the ACM 40(5), 80–91 (1997)
9. Zambonelli, F., Castelli, G., Ferrari, L., Mamei, M., Rosi, A., Di Marzo Serugendo, G., Risoldi, M., Tchao, A.E., Dobson, S., Stevenson, G., Ye, Y., Nardini, E., Omicini, A., Montagna, S., Viroli, M., Ferscha, A., Maschek, S., Wally, B.: Self-aware pervasive service ecosystems. Procedia Computer Science 7, 197–199 (2011)
10. Hill, R., Hirsch, L., Lake, P., Moshiri, S.: Guide to Cloud Computing. Principles and Practice Computer Communications and Networks. Springer, London (2013)
11. Omicini, A., Zambonelli, F.: Coordination for Internet application development. Autonomous Agents and Multi-Agent Systems 2(3), 251–269 (1999)
12. Mariani, S., Omicini, A.: Event-driven programming for situated MAS with ReSpecT tuple centres. In: Klusch, M., Thimm, M., Paprzycki, M. (eds.) MATES 2013. LNCS, vol. 8076, pp. 306–319. Springer, Heidelberg (2013)
13. Fortino, G., Garro, A., Mascillaro, S., Russo, W.: Using event-driven lightweight DSC-based agents for MAS modelling. International Journal of Agent-Oriented Software Engineering 4(2), 113–140 (2010)
14. Omicini, A.: Formal ReSpecT in the A&A perspective. Electronic Notes in Theoretical Computer Science 175(2), 97–117 (2007)
15. Omicini, A., Ricci, A., Viroli, M.: Time-aware coordination in ReSpecT. In: Jacquet, J.-M., Picco, G.P. (eds.) COORDINATION 2005. LNCS, vol. 3454, pp. 268–282. Springer, Heidelberg (2005)
16. Casadei, M., Omicini, A.: Situated tuple centres in ReSpecT. In: Shin, S.Y., Ossowski, S., Menezes, R., Viroli, M. (eds.) 24th Annual ACM Symposium on Applied Computing, SAC 2009, Honolulu, Hawai'i, USA, vol. III, pp. 1361–1368. ACM (March 8-12 2009)

17. Mariani, S., Omicini, A.: Promoting space-aware coordination: ReSpecT as a spatial-computing virtual machine. In: Spatial Computing Workshop (SCW 2013), AAMAS 2013, Saint Paul, Minnesota, USA (May 2013)

18. Omicini, A., Ricci, A., Zaghini, N.: Distributed workflow upon linkable coordination artifacts. In: Ciancarini, P., Wiklicky, H. (eds.) COORDINATION 2006. LNCS, vol. 4038, pp. 228–246. Springer, Heidelberg (2006)

19. Ricci, A., Viroli, M., Omicini, A.: The A&A programming model and technology for developing agent environments in MAS. In: Dastani, M., El Fallah Seghrouchni, A., Ricci, A., Winikoff, M. (eds.) ProMAS 2007. LNCS (LNAI), vol. 4908, pp. 89–106. Springer, Heidelberg (2008)

20. Omicini, A., Mariani, S.: Coordination for situated MAS: Towards an event-driven architecture. In: Moldt, D., Rölke, H. (eds.) International Workshop on Petri Nets and Software Engineering (PNSE 2013), Milano, Italy, June 24-25. CEUR Workshop Proceedings, vol. 989, pp. 17–22. Sun SITE Central Europe, RWTH Aachen University (2013) (invited paper)

21. Omicini, A.: Towards a notion of agent coordination context. In: Marinescu, D.C., Lee, C. (eds.) Process Coordination and Ubiquitous Computing, pp. 187–200. CRC Press, Boca Raton (2002)

22. Omicini, A., Denti, E.: From tuple spaces to tuple centres. Science of Computer Programming 41(3), 277–294 (2001)

23. Denti, E., Omicini, A., Ricci, A.: tuProlog: A light-weight Prolog for Internet applications and infrastructures. In: Ramakrishnan, I.V. (ed.) PADL 2001. LNCS, vol. 1990, pp. 184–198. Springer, Heidelberg (2001)

Integrating Cloud Services in Behaviour Programming for Autonomous Robots

Fabrizio Messina, Giuseppe Pappalardo, and Corrado Santoro

University of Catania – Dept. of Mathematics and Computer Science
Viale Andrea Doria, 6 — 95125 - Catania, Italy
{messina,pappalardo,santoro}@dmi.unict.it

Abstract. This paper introduces CLEPTA, an extension to the PROFETA robotic programming framework for the integration of *cloud services* in developing the software for *autonomous robots*. CLEPTA provides a set of basic classes, together with a software architecture, which helps the programmer in specifying the invocation of cloud services in the programs handling robot's behaviour; such a feature allows designers *(i)* to execute computation-intensive algorithms and *(ii)* to include, in robot's behaviour, additional features made available in the Cloud.

1 Introduction

Cyber-physical systems like *autonomous robots* are expected to pervade our lives in the near future [1–3]. Robots will become more and more technologically advanced, in terms of both the hardware needed to perform actions and to sense the environment, and the complexity of the software driving the autonomous behaviour. Features like speech-to-text, text-to-speech, voice/speaker recognition, face recognition [4], object tracking [5], which will be present in future home robots, need not only fast platforms onto which to execute their algorithms, but also large databases containing datasets useful to perform matching. However, home robots are expected to be equipped with embedded systems, which could not be able to offer the said features.

Conversely, the Cloud [6] is a facility which is now present everywhere and everytime and supports both social [7, 8] and scientific activities (e.g. simulations of complex systems [9–11]). Accordingly, above all in home environments, features which cannot be implemented inside a robot can be provided by exploiting *cloud computing services* [12]. This happens, for example, for the speech-to-text feature provided by many smartphones today [13]. In a similar way, artificial vision [14] can be performed by acquiring an image and sending it to a cloud service which executes the requested analysis and sends back extracted data.

In taking into account such a model, the software executing on the robot, which drives its autonomous behaviour, must be designed to support cloud services through a suitable software architecture.

Given the above premises, this paper introduces *CLEPTA* (*CLoud Extension for ProfeTA*), a software library able to integrate cloud services into the robot

J. Kołodziej et al. (Eds.): ICA3PP 2013, Part II, LNCS 8286, pp. 295–302, 2013.
© Springer International Publishing Switzerland 2013

programming tool PROFETA [15–17]; the latter is Python-based software platform, written by some of the authors, for the implementation of the behaviour of an autonomous robot. PROFETA is based on a declarative language which a dialect of AgentSpeak(L) [18, 19].

CLEPTA provides a software architecture, together with a set of classes, for modelling cloud services as basic entities of the declarative language. This is performed by abstracting cloud services as proper *sensors* or *actuators* on the basis of the specific relationship of the service itself with respect to the *sensing-reasoning-acting* model. In this sense, since a PROFETA program handles *beliefs* and *actions*, CLEPTA includes the proper mechanisms for interfacing such a kind of concepts with the pieces of code invoking the required cloud services.

The paper is structured as follows. Section 2 provides a basic overview of PROFETA. Section 3 describes the software architecture of CLEPTA. Section 4 concludes the paper.

2   Overview of PROFETA

PROFETA (*Python RObotic Framework for dEsigning sTrAtegies*) [15, 16] is a Python framework for programming autonomous systems, like agents or robots, using a declarative approach. As a derivation from AgentSpeak(L) [19], PROFETA is based on the *Belief-Desire-Intention (BDI)* theory [18], which models the behaviour of an autonomous system using some concepts and mechanisms proper of the human reasoning. To this aim, PROFETA provides four basic entities: *beliefs*, *sensors*, *actions* and *goals*.

Beliefs are used to represent the *knowledge*; they can be *asserted*, if they represent a true situation, or *retracted* when such a situation no longer holds. A *knowledge base (KB)*, managed by the PROFETA Engine, stores all asserted beliefs. Beliefs, declared by subclassing the `profeta.attitude.Belief` framework class, are used in behaviour specification as logic atomic formulae with ground terms or free variables. Syntax is Prolog-like, therefore expressions like `my_position(1230,450)`, `object_got()` are valid beliefs.

A belief can be asserted either by following a certain reasoning process or as generated from a physical sensor. In the latter case, a piece of code has to be involved, which perform data sampling, asserting the proper beliefs when it is necessary. PROFETA provides the class `profeta.lib.Sensor` which can be extended by overriding the `sense()` method and implementing there the specific code to poll the sensor and generate the belief(s).

Actions represent computations triggered to "perform something", generally physical actions performed onto the environment, like activating an arm to pick an object, etc. Actions are declared by defining a sub-class of `Action` and overriding the `execute()` method, which must include the Python code to concretely perform the action. In behaviour specification, an action is represented with an atomic formula, thus expressions like `move_to(1500,1000)` or `activate_arm("X")` are valid action representations.

Goals represent states in which a certain specific objective has been fulfilled by the agent, and can be reached by performing a certain sequence of actions.

Goals are also represented by means of atomic formulae with zero or more parameters. A goal is defined as a sub-class of `Goal`.

A PROFETA program specifies the behaviour of an autonomous system by means of a set of *reactive rules* written according to the following syntax:

event ["/" *condition*] ">>" "[" *body* "]"

where

event := (("+" | "-")*belief* | "+"reactor | "~" *goal*)
condition := *belief* ["," ...]
body := (("+" | "-")*belief* | "~"*goal* | *action*) ["," ...]

Each rule is triggered by the occurrence of a certain event, specified in the rule's *header*, given that a certain *condition* is true, which is in general expressed as a specific state of the knowledge base; the rule *body* specifies a (set of) action(s) to execute whenever the rule is fired.

The first operation of a PROFETA program must be a call to `PROFETA.start()`, by which the *PROFETA Engine*, whose main task is to interpret and executes the rules, is instantiated and initialised. After this operation, the specification of the rules can appear in the program, hence the proper structures to represent the defined rules can be created inside PROFETA Engine.

Before starting the execution of the PROFETA program, the Engine must know the user code for environment sensing, which, as stated above, is performed by means of proper `Sensor` classes. The `PROFETA.add_sensor()` primitive is provided to allow a programmer to setup the user-defined classes for sensor data acquisition.

Rule execution is finally started by a call to the method `PROFETA.run()` and managed by the PROFETA Engine. During the execution an *event queue* is managed to hold and treat all the generated *events* which need to be consumed. The basic behaviour of the PROFETA Engine, whose architecture is shown in Figure 1, can be expressed by a loop which runs the following tasks:

1. The `sense()` method of each sensor class is called; if such a method returns a belief, it is asserted in the *KB* and an *add belief* event is placed in the PROFETA event queue.
2. The first event of the queue is picked, and the rules matching that event are selected; for each rule, the condition is analysed and, if met, the body part is executed.
3. During rule execution, if other events are generated (according to PROFETA rule syntax) they are properly placed in the event queue[1].

---

[1] Add or remove belief events are always placed in the tail of the queue; instead, goal achievement events are placed at the head of the queue.

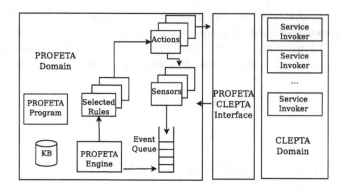

Fig. 1. Basic Architecture of PROFETA and CLEPTA

3   The Cloud Extension for PROFETA

As stated in the previous section, the execution model of a PROFETA program
is based on a loop performing *(i)* sensor polling (with belief generation), *(ii)* rule
selection, and *(iii)* action execution.

Sensor polling is related to the interaction with the environment, and performed by calling the `sense()` method of all `Sensor` objects registered in the
PROFETA Engine. Accordingly, only during this method call what it is happening in the environment can be detected: if an event is "too fast", and such that
its duration is less than the time between two consecutive calls to the `sense()`
method of the related `Sensor` object, the event could not be detected.

In other words, the time interval between two consecutive instances of the
main PROFETA loop is an important parameter which affects the way in which
the (evolution of the) environment can be properly sensed. This interval is influenced by the time required for sensor polling and by the duration of the
execution of action(s) related to a selected rule; the higher this time the higher
the probability, for the robot, to be "blind" with respect to certain events.

This problem is much more stressed when the robot needs to invoke cloud
services to perform certain computations, due to network and service latencies,
which are in general *unpredictable*.

In our vision reducing the *strict synchrony* among the various activities involved in the execution of a PROFETA program will offer better results than
trying to shorten latencies and improve predictability. We made CLEPTA design
according to this vision, and will provide details in the following.

3.1   CLEPTA Architecture

The main role of CLEPTA is to provide a bridge between the *PROFETA world*
and the invocation of *cloud services* exploited to perform remote computations.
The overall architecture is sketched in Figure 1. Basically, two execution domains
are present, the *PROFETA Domain* and the *Cloud/CLEPTA Domain*.

The former, *PROFETA domain* (left part of Figure 1), is composed of the PROFETA Engine, which has its own thread of control and behaves according to what it has been explained above. The *CLEPTA domain* (right part of Figure 1) includes several *Service Invokers*, i.e components entailed with the task of performing the invocation of a specific cloud service. In the center of Figure 1, the *PROFETA/CLEPTA Interface* performs the adaptation between the two domains, handling the required asynchrony and the proper connection between *sensor* and *action* objects and the components performing service invocation.

In CLEPTA, invokers are instances of the `Service` class, which can be extended in order to implement the code for a specific service[2]. The invokers are then connected to a PROFETA program by means of some classes which perform the proper adaptation between the two domains.

3.2   Sensors in the CLEPTA Domain

Sensors are used to get data and events from the environment. Cloud services could be exploited here to perform computation-intensive processing of sampled data in order to extract proper features.

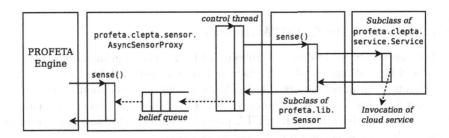

Fig. 2. Sensor interaction between PROFETA and CLEPTA

Interaction between the two domains is performed by means of an object of class `AsyncSensorProxy` (see Figure 2), which is able to transform the semantics of a PROFETA sensor from *synchronous* to *asynchronous*.

The proxy is a subclass of `Sensor` and is viewed by PROFETA as a classical sensor. The *real sensor* is implemented as a classical PROFETA sensor, and its connection with the Engine is decoupled by exploiting the `AsyncSensorProxy`. Indeed the code (i.e. the `sense()` method) of the real sensor is executed in its own thread of control, created and managed by the proxy itself. The proxy also embeds a *belief queue* which is used to transfer data between the sensor thread and the PROFETA Domain.

With reference to the Figure 2, the proxy executes the following activities:

---

[2] CLEPTA also provides the (sub)class `HttpService`, specifically designed for HTTP-based cloud service clients.

– It starts a new thread which performs a loop invoking the `sense()` method of the real sensor; if such a method returns a belief, it is then placed in the queue of the proxy.
– Its `sense()` method, which is called by the PROFETA Engine during sensor polling, extracts a belief (if present) from the queue using a non-blocking call and returns it to the PROFETA Engine[3].

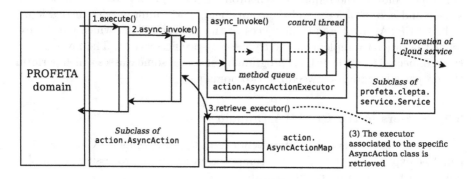

Fig. 3. Action interaction between PROFETA and CLEPTA

3.3 Actions in the CLEPTA Domain

Actions appear in the body of the rules of a PROFETA program as syntactically expressed by writings like *ACT* (), where `ACT` is an identifier defined as a subclass of `Action`. Such a writing actually implies not only the execution of an action, but also the creation of an instance of class `ACT`. Since the same action can be invoked several times in a PROFETA program, multiple instances of the class representing the same action may exist at run-time.

Such a policy described above has the drawback of impeding the use of object's attributes to store state information, but it has a precise reason: actions in PROFETA must not be intended to be used as *objects* but as *procedures*, such that a rule is intended as a direct call to the `execute()` method of the `action`.

In CLEPTA, due to the said feature, for a certain action tied to a cloud service, not only the decoupling needed to introduce asynchrony has to be taken into account, but also the fact that, as it has been state above, a 1-to-1 direct reference to the relevant *service invoker*, from an action object, cannot be done, otherwise multiple service invokers (for the same service) could be created. Such an issue is handled in CLEPTA by means of some components which are described below and whose interaction is represented in Figure 3.

From the CLEPTA side, cloud service invocation is handled in a subclass of `profeta.clepta.services.Service` (like in sensor management). An instance of each subclass is intended to be created at run-time (and therefore an instance for each cloud service to be invoked).

---

[3] When the proxy `sense()` method returns *null* it means that nothing has been detected by the sensor.

From the PROFETA side, the action triggering the invocation of the service must be implemented as a subclass of `profeta.clepta.action.AsyncAction`[4]. This base class has the role of performing the *asynchronous invocation* of the specific method of the service object concretely invoking the cloud service; this asynchrony is reached through the presence of an instance of class `profeta.clepta.action.AsyncActionExecutor`, such an instance is associated to a specific service to be invoked. The `AsyncActionExecutor` manages a *queue of identifiers of methods* to be invoked: on the PROFETA side, the specific `AsyncAction` has the responsibility of putting the identifier in this queue, through the `async_invoke()` method; on the CLEPTA side, instead, such identifiers are extracted by a *control thread* which, in turn, has the responsibility of performing concrete method invocation on the target service class.

For each service, an instance of `Service` class exists as well as a single instance of the relevant `AsyncActionExecutor`; however, as stated before, multiple instances of the same `AsyncAction` class could exist. To handle the connection between the executor and an `AsyncAction`, CLEPTA provides the class `profeta.clepta.action.AsyncActionMap`, a singleton which handles a map storing the association between the *name of the specific `AsyncAction` class* and the relevant executor. On this basis, the `AsyncAction.async_invoke()` method performs the following operations: *(i)* it retrieves the name of its own class; *(ii)* it uses this name to retrieve the associated executor, via the `AsyncActionMap`; and *(iii)* it calls, in turn, the `async_invoke()` method of the said executor in order to put, in the queue, the identifier of the method to be called asynchronously.

4   Conclusions

This paper has introduced CLEPTA, an extension for the PROFETA robotic framework which adds cloud-computing support in robot behaviour specification. By means of a proper software architecture, CLEPTA allows a programmer to use remote cloud service to perform computation-intensive tasks or include features, such as speech-to-text, text-to-speech or high-performance image processing, which are now made available in the cloud.

As a proof of concepts, the framework has been used in various robotic projects developed at the laboratories of the authors. The PROFETA framework, including the CLEPTA extension, is freely usable with BSD license, and downloadable at the address `https://github.com/corradosantoro/profeta`.

Acknowledgements. This work is a part of the research project **PRISMA**, code **PON04a2_A/F**, funded by the Italian Ministry of University within the **PON 2007-2013** framework program.

---

[4] Which, in turn, is a subclass of `profeta.lib.Action`.

References

1. Forlizzi, J., DiSalvo, C.: Service robots in the domestic environment: a study of the roomba vacuum in the home. In: ACM SIGCHI/SIGART, pp. 258–265. ACM (2006)
2. Gouaillier, D., et al.: The nao humanoid: a combination of performance and affordability. CoRR abs/0807.3223 (2008)
3. Ha, I., et al.: Development of open humanoid platform darwin-op. In: 2011 Proceedings of SICE Annual Conference (SICE), pp. 2178–2181. IEEE (2011)
4. Li, S.Z., Jain, A.K.: Handbook of face recognition. Springer (2011)
5. Babenko, et al.: Robust object tracking with online multiple instance learning. IEEE Trans. on Pattern Analysis and Machine Intelligence 33, 1619–1632 (2011)
6. Armbrust, et al.: A view of cloud computing. Comm. of the ACM 53, 50–58 (2010)
7. Messina, F., Pappalardo, G., Rosaci, D., Santoro, C., Sarné, G.M.L.: HySoN: A distributed agent-based protocol for group formation in online social networks. In: Klusch, M., Thimm, M., Paprzycki, M. (eds.) MATES 2013. LNCS, vol. 8076, pp. 320–333. Springer, Heidelberg (2013)
8. Messina, F., Pappalardo, G., Rosaci, D., Santoro, C., Sarné, G.M.L.: A distributed agent-based approach for supporting group formation in P2P e-learning. In: Baldoni, M., Baroglio, C., Boella, G., Micalizio, R. (eds.) AI*IA 2013. LNCS (LNAI), vol. 8249, pp. 312–323. Springer, Heidelberg (2013)
9. Messina, F., Pappalardo, G., Santoro, C.: Exploiting gpus to simulate complex systems. In: CISIS, pp. 535–540. IEEE (2013)
10. Messina, F., Pappalardo, G., Santoro, C.: Complexsim: An smp-aware complex network simulation framework. In: CISIS, pp. 861–866. IEEE (2012)
11. Messina, F., Pappalardo, G., Santoro, C.: Complexsim: a flexible simulation platform for complex systems. International Journal of Simulation and Process Modelling (2013)
12. Fortino, G., Pathan, M., Di Fatta, G.: Bodycloud: Integration of cloud computing and body sensor networks, pp. 851–856 (2012)
13. Gandhewar, N., Sheikh, R.: Google android: An emerging software platform for mobile devices. IJCSE Journal 1, 12–17 (2010)
14. Ayache, N.: Artificial vision for mobile robots: stereo vision and multisensory perception. The MIT Press (1991)
15. Fichera, L., Marletta, D., Santoro, C., Nicosia, V.: A Methodology to Extend Imperative Languages with AgentSpeak Declarative Constructs. In: WOA 2010, Rimini, Italy. CEUR-WS Publisher (2010) ISSN 1613-0073
16. Fichera, L., Marletta, D., Nicosia, V., Santoro, C.: Flexible Robot Strategy Design using Belief-Desire-Intention Model. In: Obdržálek, D., Gottscheber, A. (eds.) EUROBOT 2010. CCIS, vol. 156, pp. 57–71. Springer, Heidelberg (2011)
17. Fortino, G., Russo, W., Santoro, C.: Translating statecharts-based into BDI agents: The DSC/PROFETA case. In: Klusch, M., Thimm, M., Paprzycki, M. (eds.) MATES 2013. LNCS, vol. 8076, pp. 264–277. Springer, Heidelberg (2013)
18. Bratman, M.E.: Intentions, Plans and Practical Reason. HUP (1987)
19. Rao, A.: AgentSpeak (L): BDI agents speak out in a logical computable language. In: Perram, J., Van de Velde, W. (eds.) MAAMAW 1996. LNCS, vol. 1038, pp. 42–55. Springer, Heidelberg (1996)

RFID Based Real-Time Manufacturing Information Perception and Processing

Wei Song, Wenfeng Li, Xiuwen Fu, Yulian Cao, and Lin Yang

School of Logistics Engineering, Wuhan University of Technology, Wuhan, P.R. China
songwei28@163.com, {liwf,XiuwenFu}@whut.edu.cn,
yulian@uw.edu, gnwd@msn.com

Abstract. Timeliness, accuracy and effectiveness of manufacturing information in manufacturing and business process management have become important factors of constraint to business growth. Single RFID (Radio Frequency Identification) technology with uncertainty will cause great difficulties for application systems. This paper mainly focuses on the process of manufacturing information, real-time information perception and processing problems. It achieves real-time manufacturing information acquisition and processing by combining RFID and sensor technology, which uses Complex Event Processing (CEP) mechanism to realize sensor and RFID data fusion. First of all, the event processing framework which is from the perspective of the integration of sensors and RFID is given. Then, real-time acquisition and intelligent information processing models were introduced, including primitive event handling and complex event processing method. Finally, the practicality of our method was verified through applying it to a mold manufacturing enterprise management field.

Keywords: Manufacturing information, real-time data processing, RFID, CEP, Internet of Things.

1 Introduction

With the rapid development of information technology, sensor technology and communication technology, timeliness, accuracy and validity of manufacturing information in manufacturing and business process management have become important factors of constraint to business growth, which have caught much closer attention. In recent years, the flow characterization, storage and optimized control to production process of real time material flow, process flow and control flow has gradually become a central feature of intelligent manufacturing [1]. Manufacturing company's existing information system has greatly improved the operational efficiency of enterprises, but there is a certain lack of automated, real-time and accuracy.

RFID as an advanced automatic identification technology has received widespread concern from industry field, which is widely used in all aspects of manufacturing in recent years. The characteristics of real-time identification, accurate and long distance reading from RFID make it possible to collect real-time manufacturing information

J. Kołodziej et al. (Eds.): ICA3PP 2013, Part II, LNCS 8286, pp. 303–310, 2013.
© Springer International Publishing Switzerland 2013

accurately [2]. Because of RFID wireless communication features and manufacturing complexity of the system environment, the single RFID technology with uncertainty will cause great difficulties to the application system. The uncertainty of RFID data is mainly reflected in the following points.

1) Rereading: In order to cover a certain reading area, RFID reader antenna's reading power is set to be larger, making the object affixed with RFID tags repeatedly been recognized when pass by a reader coverage area, resulting in a large number of redundant, ineffective RFID data.

2) Data missing: When a tagged object go through the reader reading range, due to interference between objects blocking or other reasons, the reader does not read the label. Such information is lost so that the target cannot be correctly identified.

3) Over reading: When a tagged object has not gone through a RFID reader, due to reflection or reader antenna power's large setting, the object might be recognized by reader and will record this event which actually did not occur.

4) Misreading: RFID data read need several electromagnetic conversions and need to transfer out the acquired data through communication interface. Error exists in both the process of decoding and transmission, making the reader collected data with the label sent back data inconsistencies, causing data errors, or garbled.

In order to solve above problems, this paper will combine sensors with RFID and use CEP mechanism on the sensor and RFID data fusion to reduce uncertainty in the data, which can help realizing real-time collection and processing of manufacturing information. Firstly, framework for event processing is given from the perspective of the sensor and RFID integration. Then, the introduction of intelligent real-time information collection and processing models were given followed, including primitive event processing and complex event processing method. Finally, the practicality of this method was verified by applying it to the mold management of a manufacturing enterprise.

2   Related Works

Currently, in the manufacturing enterprise production information management and real-time data process, domestic and foreign scholars have done a lot of research and gained a relatively abundant research results. Patrik Spiess[3], Sun Zhengwu[4] and Shen Bin [5] have studied application framework and service model of Internet of Things(IoT) technology applied in industry, which provide a reference for IoT application. However, they haven't investigated the use of real-time data acquisition and processing. Francesco Aiello[6] present the MAPS to realize the real-time human activity monitoring, provide a reference for real-time information processing in manufacturing environment.The method of extracting useful data from large amounts of data and analyze correlation between data is top priority of IoT applications in manufacturing, which is able to help enterprise make respond to these key information critical and timely.

Complex event processing is performed by David Luckham at Stanford University [7]. CEP matches events sequence that meet event definition based on event attributes from the event stream according. The basic idea of complex event processing is as follows. 1) Abstracting original event from large amount of data. These events can be changes in the state, the implementation of activities, etc., can also be a user or the system concerned information. 2) Through a certain event operator to correlate different events form a composite event, which means a new meaning and reveals hidden information between data. 3) It obtains causal relationship and hierarchical relationships between events through the event handling. Causality can help users analyze the nature causes of the system macroscopic phenomena, and hierarchical relationships can provide users of different areas and different levels with personalized event information, improving enterprises' response ability.

CEP mechanism is effective means to deal with the uncertainty of RFID data, which has received widespread concern from research scholars. Wang Fusheng [8] used directed graph in the RFID event flow for complex event processing. Zang Chuanzhen [9] proposed real-time enterprise architecture based on intelligent objects, giving the event's basic concepts, time model, and hierarchical model. Jin Xingyi [10] used timed Petri nets (TPN) in RFID complex event to detect data stream, which provided a theoretical support and reference for this study. With further research, there are some CEP prototype system for RFID applications, such as SASE [11], Cayuga [12] and ZStream [13] and so on. These systems are mainly for complex event processing systems on real-time data streams RFID applications, which provide the basic functions of complex event processing, but did not consider the uncertainty of the input RFID data stream, also did not consider the environmental complexity of the manufacturing site and process correlation of applied aspects.

3 Real-Time Data Collect and Process Model

An event can be defined as a record of an activity in a system for the purpose of computer processing [7], or an occurrence of interest in time [8].

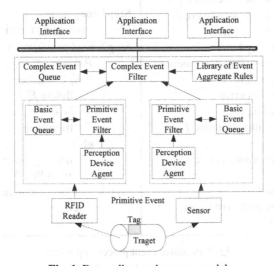

Fig. 1. Data collect and process model

In general, events can be categorized into primitive event and complex event. A primitive event occurs at a point in time, while a complex event is a pattern of primitive events and happens over a period of time. Considering multi-tag, multi-reader, multi-sensor manufacturing information environment, we propose a hierarchical data acquisition and processing model, shown in Figure 1.

First, perception device Agent collect data from reader or sensor and generate primitive event, then upload it to primitive event filter. Primitive event filter clean the redundant event based on primitive event filter rules, and put the filtered event into basic event queue. Complex event filter aggregates basic events into complex based on complex event aggregation rules, then put it into the complex event queue. The application system can easily get an appropriate complex event from the application interface.

3.1   Primitive Event Process

When the physical objects installed with RFID tags crosses through the RFID reader, the phenomenon such as tag *re-reading* and *misreading* will create a huge amount of redundant data. The layer of Primitive event process will clean the redundant data created by tag re-reading and misreading according to the content of tag and tag objects. Given the circumstance of multi-tags reading, the algorithm of primitive events process is designed. The algorithm can be divided into 2 steps, the first step is to acquire the primitive events from agent of equipment resources, filter the redundant or error data and then store the post-filter data into queue of basic events. The task of step 2 is to filter the timeout data from queue of basic events.

Algorithm 1: Primitive Event Filter	**Algorithm 2:** Primitive Event Queue Filter
Step1: read a primitive event *Ep1*	
Step2: **if** the *Ep1* is not exist in *Primitive Event Queue* **turn** Step4	**Step1**:**for**(i=queue_min; i<queue_max; i++)
Step3: **if** *Ep1.TimeStamp* is timeout **turn** Step6	**Step2**: read primitive event *Epi* from *Primitive Event Queue* **if** *Epi.TimeStamp* is timeout **delete** *Epi*
Step4: **if** the *Es1* is error **turn** Step6	i++ **turn** Step2
Step5: put *Ep1* into *Primitive Event Queue* **end** this primitive event process	**else** *queue_min = i* **turn** Step3
Step6: abandon *Ep1* **end** this primitive event process	**Step3**: end this primitive event queue filter

Fig. 2. Primitive event process algorithm

The algorithm 1 can only be triggered. When perception device Agent finishes the reading of one primitive event, the algorithm 1 is triggered. If the event has already listed in the queue of basic event, the time stamp of the event will be acquired. If the difference between newly time stamp and already-existed stamp is lower than the pre-configured threshold, here we can consider the newly coming event as the false redundant event and delete it correspondingly. If the events don't exist in the queue of basic events, we can take the event as the newly coming event. Next, the procedure comes into the stage of fault tolerance.

The sensing equipment should be fault-tolerant among when collecting and delivering data. Before judgment, the error data should be filtered. Due to the variety of sensor data, the fault tolerance should be determined according to the variety of situation. In the scene of manufacturing, each tag has its own physical meaning. According to the corresponding relationship between tag and objects, we can find out whether the physical meaning of the tag is listed in the mapping list. If the physical meaning of the tag fails to find, we can consider the data is error data. If the relation is established, the data is listed in the queue of the basic events and the primitive event process is completed.

The manufacturing scene has strict request for real-time data sampling and processing. Aiming to guarantee the timeliness, we need to establish the filter mechanism to filter the timeout redundant data from the queue of the basic events. The algorithm 2 is based on this idea.

3.2   Complex Event Process

Although the layer of primitive events process is able to filter the redundant or error events and guarantee the real-time of perception device, the *misreading* and *over reading* fail to disposed. According to the various request of different steps in manufacturing scene, we need to fuse the events from different equipment to meet the disposal request of the above layer. The complex events reflect the group of the events following certain rules.

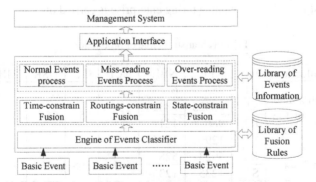

Fig. 3. Architecture of the complex events disposal

According to the fusion methods of the events, the events includes: complex events fusion based on time-constrain, complex events fusion based on routings-constrain and complex events fusion based on states-constrain.

The complex events fusion based on time-constrain: the events are closely time-related. The events always happen at the same time or not happen in certain period.

The complex event fusion based on routings-constrain: the sensing object is closely related to its location. According to the information of the location, the order of the events happening can be determined.

Complex event fusion based on states-constrain: the event happening is closely related to the state of the objects. Only in the certain states, the sensing events are able to happen.

Based on the proposed rules, architecture of the complex events disposal is designed in this section (figure 3).The goal of library of fusion rules are to store the relevant fusion rules and conditions in terms of the application requirement; the library of events information is to store the complex events and related process consequences; the engine of events classifier is to access the simple events from the layer of primitive event process and classify the uploaded basic events according to the fusion rules. The responsibility of processor of abnormal event is to detect the abnormal event and then deal with the abnormal events. The processor of abnormal events makes reasonable judgments based on the library of fusion rules. When detect the over-reading events, the redundant events will be deleted and this behavior will be stored into the library of events information. When detect the miss-reading events, the redundant events will be complemented and this behavior will be stored into the library of events information. When deal with the normal events, the record of normal events will be added into the library of events information. The application interface is to provide query interface and call interface for the backstage management system.

4   Case Study

To testify the proposed method of the real-time sensing and information processing, the related test in a discrete manufacturing enterprise is carried on.

Table 1. Statistics table of production

Collection point		NPE	NBE	NCE	CT	NSR	RRE
Entry and exit of the workshop	R1	753	62	55	55	55	0
	S1	68325	68325				
	R2	986	121				
	S2	12961	12961				
No.3 door	R3	5923	528	401	368	368	9%
	S3	1235	1235				
No.4 door	R4	652	48	30	27	27	11%
	S4	2358	2358				

The statistics of a certain month in the workshop is shown in table 1. R1 is the fixed RFID reader located in the NO.1 door. S1 is the infra sensor installed nearby the NO.1 door. In table 1, the NPE represent the number of primitive events, the NBE represent the number of basic events. The number of complicated events (NCE) is the amount of the complicated events fused by data flow. The circulation times (CT) is the real circulation times of the molds. The number of the system recognition (NSR) indicates the circulation time of the molds though judgments by complicated events. The rate of the redundant event recognition (RRE) is the proportion of the non-effective events in the complex events auto-recognized by the system.

From table 1, we can conclude:

1) Through filtering the primitive events, amount of the redundant data is able to decrease significantly. Take entry R3 as an example, the simple events accessed in the mouth is 5923. After filtering, the number decreased to 528. The data amount has been decreased by 90%.

2) The introduction of the sensors also contributes to the accuracy of the event disposal. Take door 3 as an example, the subsequent events has been decreased by 32% ;

3) Deployment of promising mounts of sampling sites and making reasonable fusion rules are able to enhance the recognition rate of the effective events. The entry and exit of the workshop both deployed 4 sampling sites respectively. The redundant rate is zero. For No.3 and 4 doors, as the sampling sites are only 2, the redundant rate is 10%.

4) Through combining the actual production procedures, the recognition of the system rate can be improved effectively. Through data matching between recognized events and mold usage plan, the redundant events can be filtered.

Form the application results we can conclude that, the proposed method, combined with sensor and RFID can effectively improve the efficiency of complex event processing in manufacturing environment, combined with production process and complex event process mechanism can effectively eliminate redundancy event and increase system recognition rate. It also demonstrated that the proposed method is practical and feasible.

5   Conclusion

In this paper, through application of RFID and sensing technologies and building disposal mechanism of complex events, the uncertainty of the data can be lowered and the timeliness and accuracy of the data processing can be achieved. Firstly, our work is to give an architecture of the real-time information processing. And then, the disposal methods are analyzed in details about primitive event process and complex event process. Finally, the practical application in manufacturing testifies the availability and practicability of the proposed method.

The application of the disposal method of the complex events is able to enhance the accuracy of the system. The making of cohesion rules is closely related to manufacturing procedures. In the future work, we will continue the research on the process of the event cohesion, enhance the cohesion efficiency and further enhance the information level of the manufacturing industry.

Acknowledgment. This research is partly supported by National Key Technology R&D program (2012BAJ05B07), Key Project of Natural Science Foundation of Hubei Province (2010CDA022), Science and Technology Project of Guangdong Province (2010A080408011) and the modern information service special funds competitive distribution project in Dongguan City (DG201007).

References

1. Vlad, M.S., Valentin, S.: A RFID system designed for intelligent manufacturing process. WSEAS Transactions on Information Science and Applications, 36–41 (2007)
2. Atzori, L., Iera, A., Morabito, G.: The Internet of Things: A survey. Computer Networks 15, 2787–2805 (2010)
3. Spiess, P., Karnouskos, S., Guinard, D., et al.: SOA-based integration of the internet of things in enterprise services. In: Proceedings of IEEE ICWS 2009, Los Angeles, CA, USA, pp. 968–975 (2009)
4. Sun, Z.W., Li, W.F., Song, W., et al.: Research on manufacturing supply chain information platform architecture based on Internet of Things. Advanced Materials Research, 314-316, 2344-2347 (2011)
5. Shen, B., Zhang, G.Q., Wang, S.L., et al.: The Development of Management System for Building Equipment Internet of Things. In: 2011 IEEE 3rd International Conference on Communication Software and Networks, pp. 423–427 (2011)
6. Aiello, F., Fortino, G., Gravina, R., et al.: A java-based agent platform for programming wireless sensor networks. The Computer Journal 54(3), 439–454 (2011)
7. Luckham, D.C.: The power of events: an introduction to complex event processing in distributed enterprise systems. Addison-Wesley (2002)
8. Wang, F.S., Liu, S.R., Liu, P.Y.: Complex RFID event processing. The International Journal on Very Large Data Bases 18(4), 913–931 (2009)
9. Zang, C.Z., Fan, Y.: Complex event processing in enterprise information systems based on RFID. Enterprise Information Systems 1, 13–23 (2007)
10. Jin, X.Y., Kong, N.: Efficient complex event processing over RFID data stream. In: The 7th IEEE International Conference on Computer and Information Science in Conjunction with 2nd IEEE International Workshop on e-Activity, Portland, pp. 75–81 (2008)
11. Wu, E., Diao, Y., Rizvi, S.: High-performance complex event processing over streams. In: Proceedings of the 2006 ACM SIGMOD International Conference on Management of Data, Chicago, USA, pp. 407–418 (2006)
12. Mei, Y., Madden, S.: ZStream: A cost-based query process or for adaptively detecting composite events. In: Proceedings of the 35th SIGMOD International Conference on Management of Data, Providence, USA, pp. 193–206 (2009)
13. Brenna, L., Alan, D., Johannes, G., et al.: A high-performance event processing engine. In: Proceedings of the 2007 ACM SIGMOD International Conference on Management of Data, Beijing, China, pp. 1100–1102 (2007)
14. Yao, W., Chu, C.H., Li, Z.: Leveraging complex event processing for smart hospitals using RFID. Journal of Network and Computer Applications, 799–810 (2011)

Author Index

Abaza, Ayman II-209
Abbes, Heithem I-143
Abdullah, Azizol II-51
Achour, Fehima I-166
Albanese, Massimiliano II-241
Amano, Hideharu II-77
Amato, Alba II-251
Amato, Flora II-125, II-133
Anjo, Ivo I-153
Aumage, Olivier II-59

Balador, Ali II-259
Balzanella, Antonio I-1
Ban, Yunmeng I-446
Barbareschi, Mario II-125, II-141
Batouche, Mohamed I-176
Belalem, Ghalem II-22
Benmounah, Zakaria I-176
Benner, Peter II-3
Ben Salem, Malek I-166
Bochicchio, Mario A. II-149
Boku, Taisuke II-59
Bossard, Antoine II-11
Bouaziz, Rafik I-166
Bouazizi, Emna I-166
Bouvry, Pascal I-380
Brook, Matthew I-115
Bücker, H. Martin I-226, II-30
Bui, Thach V. II-167

Cachopo, João I-15, I-153
Calafate, Carlos T. II-259
Cano, Juan-Carlos II-259
Cantiello, Pasquale I-186
Cao, Yulian II-303
Carvalho, Fernando Miguel I-15
Casola, Valentina II-125
Castro, Harold I-380
Chen, Guoliang I-324
Chen, Haopeng I-446, II-112
Chen, Heng I-196
Chen, Miao I-206
Chen, Quan I-196
Ciampi, Mario II-225

Cilardo, Alessandro II-177
Corporaal, Henk I-346
Cristea, Valentin I-416, II-94
Cukic, Bojan II-209

Dai, Dong I-267
Dai, Ziqing I-312
Dawson, Laurence I-216
De Pasquale, Davide II-185
Diaz, Cesar O. I-380
Di Martino, Beniamino I-186, II-251
Djebbar, Esma Insaf II-22
Dong, Fang I-206
Dümmler, Jörg I-30
Duvallet, Claude I-166

Echizen, Isao II-167
Elia, Annibale II-193
Errico, A. II-201
Esposito, Angelo II-225
Exarchakos, Georgios II-276
Ezzatti, Pablo II-3

Feuerriegel, Stefan I-226, II-30
Fortino, Giancarlo II-267
França, Felipe M.G. I-346
Franz, Wayne I-236
Fryza, Tomas I-336
Fu, Cuijiao I-436
Fu, Xiuwen II-303

Galzarano, Stefano II-267
Gao, Yanyan I-87
Gargiulo, Francesco II-133, II-201
Gąsior, Jakub I-247
Ghafarian, Toktam I-44
Ghosal, Amrita I-58
Gonzalez-Mesa, Miguel A. I-257
Guglielmo, Daniela II-193
Guo, Minyi I-196
Gutierrez, Eladio I-257

Halder, Subir I-58
Hanawa, Toshihiro II-59
Hao, Qinfen I-72

He, Liang   II-102
Hiragushi, Takaaki   II-40
Hou, Jie   II-233
Hussin, Masnida   II-51

Javadi, Bahman   I-44
Jia, Gangyong   I-267
Jiang, Congfeng   I-267
Joe, Kazuki   I-402
Jozwiak, Lech   I-346
Jrad, Foued   I-101

Kadowaki, Hiroshi   II-157
Kaneko, Keiichi   II-11
Karas, Pavel   I-279
Karimi, Siamak Najjar   I-468
Kim, Jongman   I-291
Kirner, Raimund   I-357
Kodama, Yuetsu   II-59
Koibuchi, Michihiro   II-77
Kołodziej, Joanna   I-101
Kotian, Roshan   II-276
Kuderjavý, Michal   I-279

Lee, Junghee   I-291
Lee, Sang-Won   I-291
Lega, M.   II-201
Li, Deguo   I-301
Li, Hong-zong   II-233
Li, Wenfeng   II-303
Li, Xi   I-267
Li, Yanhua   I-458
Li, Yongnan   I-301
Liotta, Antonio   II-267, II-276
Liu, Feng   I-87
Liu, Xunyun   I-312
Longo, Antonella   II-149
Louati, Thouraya   I-143
Lu, Zhaoming   II-86
Luan, Zhongzhi   I-129, I-426, I-436
Lugini, Luca   II-209
Luo, Junzhou   I-206
Luo, Tao   I-324

Maisto, Alessandro   II-193
Manzoni, Pietro   II-259
Marasco, Emanuela   II-209
Marchetta, Pietro   II-185
Mariani, Stefano   II-285
Marrone, Stefano   II-217

Marsalek, Roman   I-336
Matsutani, Hiroki   II-77
Mazzeo, Antonino   II-125, II-141
Messina, Fabrizio   II-295
Mhedheb, Yousri   I-101
Mocanu, Decebal Constantin   II-276
Morgan, Graham   I-115
Moscato, Vincenzo   II-133

Namyst, Raymond   II-59
Natale, Eduard   II-185
Nedjah, Nadia   I-346
Nery, Alexandre S.   I-346
Nguyen, Binh Q.   II-167
Nguyen, Thuc D.   II-167
Nguyen, Vu Thien Nga   I-357
Nicopoulos, Chrysostomos   I-291

Odajima, Tetsuya   II-59
Oh, Gi Hwan   I-291
Omicini, Andrea   II-285
Ouyang, Yiming   I-87

Pan, Wen   I-87
Pappalardo, Giuseppe   II-295
Park, Sangsoo   II-69
Pecero, Johnatan E.   I-380
Pelosi, Serena   II-193
Persechino, G.   II-201
Persia, Fabio   II-133
Piantadosi, Gabriele   II-217
Picariello, Antonio   II-133
Piccolo, Francesco   I-186
Plata, Oscar   I-257
Pop, Florin   I-416, II-94
Pospisil, Martin   I-336

Qian, Depei   I-129, I-426, I-436
Qu, Peng   I-458
Quintana-Ortí, Enrique   II-3
Quislant, Ricardo   I-257

Ramazzina, Sergio   II-149
Remón, Alfredo   II-3
Ren, Xiaoguang   I-312
Romano, Sara   II-125
Ruan, Li   I-72, I-301
Rünger, Gudula   I-30

Saha, Ranjan   I-370
Salvi, Alessandro   II-185
Sansone, Carlo   II-217

Sansone, Mario   II-217
Santoro, Corrado   II-295
Sasaki, Daisuke   II-77
Sato, Mitsuhisa   II-59
Seredyński, Franciszek   I-247
Sharma, Bhanu   I-370
Shen, Yao   I-196
Sicuranza, Mario   II-225
Simandl, Martin   I-336
Solamain, Kamal   I-115
Sonehara, Noboru   II-167
Song, Wei   II-303
Sotelo, German A.   I-380
Stewart, Iain A.   I-216
Streit, Achim   I-101
Subramaniam, Shamala K.   II-51
Suda, Akihiro   I-390
Svoboda, David   I-279

Takagi, Kazuyoshi   I-390
Takagi, Naofumi   I-390
Takahashi, Daisuke   II-40
Takase, Hideki   I-390
Takata, Masami   I-402
Tanabe, Noboru   I-402
Tang, Yuhua   I-312
Tao, Jie   I-101
Thibault, Samuel   II-59
Thulasiram, Ruppa K.   I-236, I-370
Thulasiraman, Parimala   I-236, I-370
Tirri, Antonio   II-185
Tomimori, Sonoko   I-402
Tong, Yi   II-86
Tufo, Manuela   II-185
Tutueanu, Radu-Ioan   I-416, II-94

Ushaw, Gary   I-115

Vaira, Lucia   II-149
Vasile, Mihaela-Andreea   I-416, II-94

Venticinque, Salvatore   II-251
Verde, Rosanna   I-1
Vespoli, Antonino   II-141
Villamizar, Mario   I-380

Wagner, Dorothea   II-157
Wan, Jian   I-267
Wang, Chao   I-267
Wang, Gang   II-86
Wang, Hongwei   I-458
Wang, Kun   I-426
Wang, Lin   I-436
Wang, Rui   I-426, I-436
Wang, Yong   II-233
Wang, Zhenhua   I-446
Wen, Xiangming   II-86
Wu, Benbin   II-102

Xiao, Limin   I-72, I-301
Xie, Tao   I-87
Xu, Xinhai   I-312

Yang, Hailong   I-129
Yang, Jing   II-102
Yang, Lin   II-303

Zhang, Gang   II-112
Zhang, Haijun   II-86
Zhang, Hao   II-77
Zhang, Ting-Ting   II-233
Zhang, Youhui   I-458
Zhang, Yunquan   I-324
Zhang, Zhenzhong   I-72, I-301
Zhao, Jiaqi   I-101
Zhao, Liang   II-157
Zhao, Qi   I-129
Zhao, Zhenmin   II-86
Zheng, Weimin   I-458
Zhong, Qianqian   I-72